INTERCULTURAL COMMUNICATION THEORY

INTERNATIONAL AND INTERCULTURAL
COMMUNICATION ANNUAL

VOLUME XIX 1995

Editor

Richard L. Wiseman
California State University, Fullerton

Editorial Assistant

Tasha Van Horn
California State University, Fullerton

Consulting Editors for Volume XIX

Charles A. Braithwaite
Arizona State University West

Benjamin J. Broome
George Mason University

Mary Jane Collier
Oregon State University

Kristine Fitch
University of Colorado

Gao Ge
San Jose State University

Howard Giles
University of California, Santa Barbara

William B. Gudykunst
California State University, Fullerton

Mitchell Hammer
American University

Jolene Koester
California State University, Sacramento

Myron Lustig
San Diego State University

William J. Starosta
Howard University

Thomas M. Steinfatt
University of Miami

Stella Ting-Toomey
California State University, Fullerton

INTERNATIONAL AND INTERCULTURAL COMMUNICATION ANNUAL
VOLUME XIX   1995

INTERCULTURAL COMMUNICATION THEORY

edited by
Richard L. WISEMAN

SAGE Publications
International Educational and Professional Publisher
Thousand Oaks London New Delhi

For information address:

SAGE Publications, Inc.
2455 Teller Road
Thousand Oaks, California 91320

SAGE Publications Ltd.
6 Bonhill Street
London EC2A 4PU
United Kingdom

SAGE Publications India Pvt. Ltd.
M-32 Market
Greater Kailash I
New Delhi 110 048 India

Printed in the United States of America

Library of Congress Cataloging-in-Publication Data

ISBN 0-8039-7242-3

ISBN 0-8039-7243-1 (pbk.)

ISSN 0270-6075

This book is printed on acid-free paper.

95 96 97 98 99 10 9 8 7 6 5 4 3 2 1

Sage Production Editor: Astrid Virding
Sage Typesetter: Andrea D. Swanson

Contents

Preface

This is the nineteenth volume of the **International and Intercultural Communication Annual**, which is sponsored by the Speech Communication Association's International and Intercultural Communication Division. The series of theme-based publications aims at promoting better understanding of communication processes in international and intercultural contexts. The guiding principle in preparing this volume was to bring together current theories on intercultural communication. Two earlier volumes (VII in 1983 and XII in 1988) in the series had a similar goal. The present volume advances some of the work reflected in those earlier volumes and introduces new theoretical developments. It is hoped that this new volume will generate as much thought and research as have Volumes VII and XII on intercultural communication theory.

The chapters in this volume cover a wide range of approaches. At the same time, they share a focus on face-to-face communication among members of different cultures and subcultures. Taken together, they represent most of the major current approaches to the study of intercultural communication. Unfortunately, despite the attempts of the editor, some theoretical approaches are not represented in this volume. Additional theories that would be of interest to the scholar of intercultural communication include constructivism, the coordinated management of meaning, and face negotiation theory.

The volume is developed in three parts. Part I presents an overview of the role of theory in intercultural communication research and a summary of the chapters. Part II includes theories on intercultural communication competence and adaptation. The foci of the chapters in this section are more general and should transcend many contexts in which intercultural communication occurs. Part III presents chapters that focus on specific contexts for intercultural communication, that is, health delivery, small group decision making, and tourism. The whole volume should be of great assistance to scholars, students, and practitioners involved in intercultural communication.

Many people were involved in the completion of the volume. First, I would like to extend my appreciation to all the authors who dedicated their time and energy to this endeavor. Without their creative thinking, articulate expression, and long hours of work, this project would not have come to fruition. Second, I want to thank Tasha Van Horn, the editorial assistant, for her keen eye for composition, logic, and coherence, as well as all the editorial board members for generously offering their time and expertise in reviewing manuscripts. Last, but not least, I extend my appreciation to my special children—Michael, Michele, and Nicole—for continually reminding me of the joys of life and for the "semiuninterrupted" time they gave this single parent to work on this volume.

Richard L. Wiseman
California State University, Fullerton

I

THE ROLE OF THEORY
IN INTERCULTURAL
COMMUNICATION RESEARCH

1

Theorizing in Intercultural Communication

RICHARD L. WISEMAN • *California State University,*
Fullerton
TASHA VAN HORN • *California State University, Fullerton*

Theory construction should be a central concern in intercultural communication research. Without theories to guide our research in this complex and diverse area, we are at a loss in determining what we should observe, how we should measure it, how our findings should be interpreted, and how the findings of various studies can be compared and integrated. One of the problems that exists within our field is that there are few well-developed guides for our efforts at theory construction. Typically, studies are variable analytic in nature; that is, they examine a few concepts across particular cultures or contexts and hope that a theory will emerge to account for the findings. Theory emergence has not often occurred. Frequently, researchers investigating the same variables conceptualize them differently, implement them differently, and use diverse measuring techniques. This often precludes the comparison and integration of theories and the studies they guide.

Fortunately, a growing number of scholars (e.g., Gudykunst & Nishida, 1989; Kim, 1988b) have expressed the need to move from disparate variable-analytic studies to more consistent theoretical frameworks for the analysis of communication between people from different cultures. This volume of the **International and Intercultural Communication Annual** represents another attempt to advocate the development of theoretical frameworks in the study of intercultural communication. Some of the theories presented in this volume have been extensively researched (e.g., Gudykunst's anxiety/uncertainty management theory in Chapter 2, Burgoon's expectancy violations theory in Chapter 8, and Gallois, Giles, Jones, Cargile, and Ota's communication accommodation theory in Chapter 5), and some of the theories are relatively new innovations (e.g., Ady's differential demand model in Chapter 4 and Baldwin and Hecht's layered perspective of cultural intolerance in Chapter 3). All of the theories presented, in our opinion, perform valuable functions in the pursuit of our understanding of the dynamics involved in intercultural communication.

FUNCTIONS OF THEORY

To assess a theory's contribution to our understanding of social phenomena, we need to examine the functions theory performs in human inquiry. Frey, Botan, Friedman, and Kreps (1991) discuss several functions performed by theory and thus ways of evaluating theory: "A theory is . . . a useful explanation to the extent that it excites us about inquiry, organizes our knowledge, leads us to expect certain outcomes to occur, and focuses research efforts" (p. 11). Frey et al. are more specific in their articulation of these functions and, by extrapolation, we can apply this functional analysis to the theories in this volume.

First, a theory should provide an *explanation*. As Frey et al. suggest: "Theories clarify, make sense of, and account for a subject matter. Theories help us understand what something involves by organizing and summarizing knowledge into a system. To the extent that a theory explains something, it is considered to have explanatory power" (p. 12). The theories presented in this text each contribute in their own way to our explanation of intercultural communication. Explanations of intercultural adjustment and adaptation are the foci of Gallois et al.'s accommodation theory (Chapter 5), Ady's differential demand model (Chapter 4), Burgoon's expectancy violations theory (Chapter 8), and Young Kim's integrative theory of cross-cultural adaptation (Chapter 7), and the explanations of intercultural effectiveness in its various contexts are the foci of Gudykunst's anxiety/uncertainty management theory (Chapter 2), Min-Sun Kim's theory of conversational constraints (Chapter 6), Witte and Morrison's analysis of cross-cultural health communication (Chapter 9), and Oetzel's decision-making theory for intercultural small groups (Chapter 10). Finally, Baldwin and Hecht attempt to elaborate on our conceptualization of cultural intolerance (e.g., racism, sexism) in Chapter 3, and Katriel advocates the greater inspection of contexts in which intercultural communication occurs (Chapter 11). While several of these theories share similar explanatory foci, they often differ in the manner or metatheory they use (e.g., Oetzel, Gallois et al., and Y. Kim use systems theory; Burgoon, M. Kim, and Ady rely on causal process theory; Katriel, and Witte and Morrison tend more toward ethnographic analysis; Gudykunst uses axiomatic theory; and Baldwin and Hecht provide a taxonomic approach). These diverse metatheoretic approaches advance our understanding of the phenomena under study as well as our knowledge of the epistemological approaches in our inquiry into the phenomena.

Second, a theory should provide a *prediction* for the social phenomenon. As Frey et al. (1991) explain: "Theories offer a way of foretelling what will happen beforehand. They provide informed guesses about what will occur and when. To the extent that a theory provides testable predictions about something, it is considered precise" (p. 12). To predict the occurrence of some social phenomenon, we need to know the antecedent causal variables for that phenomenon. The theories in this volume rely on a number of variables to account for the phenomena they are trying to explain. Generally, cultural and psychological orientations are used to explain intercultural phenomena in the theories provided by Gallois et al. (Chapter 5), Gudykunst (Chapter 2), M. Kim (Chapter 6), Burgoon (Chapter 8), Witte and Morrison (Chapter 9), and Baldwin and Hecht (Chapter 3); environmental and contextual factors are incorporated as causal agents in the theories by Ady (Chapter 4) and Katriel (Chapter 11); and intra- and intercultural communication are the generative mechanisms in the theories of Y. Kim (Chapter 7) and Oetzel (Chapter 10).

Third, a theory should help us *control* social behavior. As Frey et al. (1991) explain:

> To the extent that a theory explains and predicts the occurrence of a process, we can gain some measure of control over that process. Such control allows us to produce the object of inquiry and direct it in meaningful ways, by setting up the necessary conditions for causing or inhibiting its occurrence. (p. 12)

This notion of control in the social sciences involves a number of factors. As Frey et al. recognize, control involves both explanation and prediction; that is, to the extent that we understand the phenomenon and its causes, we should be able to control its occurrence. However, control also involves the necessary and sufficient conditions or qualifications that must exist before the social process (i.e., the causal relationships) are compelled or inhibited. Finding these necessary and sufficient conditions is an arduous task. It involves considerable research, theoretical refinement, and testing. This is a rigorous standard, and close approximations would be those theories that have had the greatest testing and history, such as Gudykunst's anxiety/uncertainty management theory (Chapter 2), Burgoon's expectancy violations theory (Chapter 8), and Gallois et al.'s communication accommodation theory (Chapter 5). One other nuance of control should be mentioned, namely, the temporal ordering of variables. Given that all communication is processual in nature, it is important that the researcher examine communication as such, that is, as a dynamic and evolving interrelationship among variables over time. It is encouraging to note that several of the theories presented in this volume recognize this critical characteristic of intercultural communication (e.g., Ady's differential demand model in Chapter 4, Oetzel's decision-making model in Chapter 10, and Y. Kim's integrative theory of cross-cultural adaptation in Chapter 7).

Fourth, a theory should be *heuristic*. Frey et al. (1991) describe this function of a theory when they state: "A theory should generate scholarly research. Theory serves as an impetus for testing its concepts and predictions. Scholars usually devote their energies to testing the most promising theories. Thus theories that have been examined widely are usually deemed most worthwhile" (p. 12). Based upon extant research, the theories that currently have the greatest heuristic impact would be the ones by Gudykunst (Chapter 2), Gallois et al. (Chapter 5), Burgoon (Chapter 8), and Y. Kim (Chapter 7). However, the remaining theories have the potential of generating research of their own. Empirical and testable propositions—the gist of research questions and hypotheses— are provided in each of the chapters. Only time and the research of scholars of intercultural communication will determine the ultimate heuristic value of these theories.

Fifth, a theory should be an *inspiration*. Frey et al. (1991) elaborate on this function: "A theory ought to be exciting, catch our imagination, and teach us something. It ought to solve important puzzles and intriguing mysteries and should address important and meaningful concerns" (p. 12). Given the complexity and importance of intercultural communication, theories in this field are at an advantage in examining a topic that is intriguing, meaningful, and often mysterious. Whether the theory *itself* satisfies this function of inspiration is another matter. As with the heuristic function, the final assessment of the theory's performance of the function of inspiration is found in the history of human inquiry. However, it should be noted that all theories are created and creative. Dubin (1978) elaborates on this point:

> The idea of order, and the tools utilized to create the sense of order, are in the mind of the theorist. . . . The locus of theory is the human mind. The mind is where the "need" for theory (order) exists. . . . In short, theories serve human purposes; their creation is motivated and their logic organized by the skills

and limitations of human capabilities. . . . Theories, then, serve to satisfy a very human "need" to order the experienced world. The only instrument in the ordering process is the human mind and the "magic" of human perception and thought. (pp. 5-7)

Theories are the creations of useful explanations so that we can understand the world around us. They structure and provide meaning to an otherwise chaotic world.

THEORETICAL REFINEMENT

The theories provided in this volume provide a unique way of conceptualizing and understanding intercultural communication. These varied theories are not necessarily incompatible or inconsistent. Rather, like the cultures we study, they are different ways of viewing the world. Furthermore, as Polkinghorne (1983) pointed out, there is no one theory that is *the* correct theory for guiding human inquiry. The diverse explanatory approaches, instead, offer guides for investigating the complex phenomena of intercultural communication. Each approach makes its own contribution in furthering our understanding of that phenomenon. The field of intercultural communication should benefit from the continued development of different theoretical approaches. Each of these approaches will need to be further refined in terms of the criteria for theory construction, that is, parsimony, heuristics, internal coherence, and aesthetics (Littlejohn, 1983). This refinement must occur in the context of empirical testing, verification, and replication. Over time, we will create theories that are more useful, elegant, and appropriate than even the ones presented in this volume.

The process of theoretical refinement will be facilitated through scholarly dialogue. These dialogues among differing theoretical representatives offer opportunities to make explicit some of the obscure assumptions and metatheories that direct our scholarly pursuits. In a sense, theories are masks of scholarly culture that hide many basic aspects of inquiry from one's own perception even though these aspects are apparent to outsiders. Opportunities to explore another's theory increase tolerance and understanding for that theory and, more important, provide insight into one's own theory, such as its assumptions, beliefs, goals, outcomes, data, methodology, and values. It is hoped that this volume stimulates such dialogues.

II

THEORIES ON INTERCULTURAL COMMUNICATION COMPETENCE AND ADAPTATION

2

Anxiety/Uncertainty Management (AUM) Theory
Current Status

WILLIAM B. GUDYKUNST • *California State University, Fullerton*

> Theories . . . are nets cast to catch what we call "the world": to rationalize, to explain. . . . We endeavor to make the mesh ever finer and finer.
>
> —*Karl Popper*

Over the last 10 years, I have been working on developing a theory of effective interpersonal and intergroup communication. Initially, I (e.g., Gudykunst, 1985a) extended a theory of interpersonal communication, uncertainty reduction theory (URT; e.g., Berger & Calabrese, 1975), to intercultural contexts. While it is not an explicit scope condition of URT, it is designed to explain communication between people from the same culture and ethnic group.[1] I selected URT as a starting point for

AUTHOR'S NOTE: I want to thank Harry Triandis, Gao Ge, Michael Bond, Stella Ting-Toomey, and Hiroshi Ota for their comments on a draft of this chapter. Tsukasa Nishida, Gao Ge, Karen Schmidt, Elizabeth Chua, and Mitch Hammer collaborated on much of the research leading to the theories presented. Stella Ting-Toomey has provided comments and suggestions on the theory in its various stages of development. Georg Simmel's writing on the stranger provided the hook I needed to integrate interpersonal and intergroup processes. Chuck Berger and G. R. Miller influenced the way I view interpersonal processes, while Henri Tajfel influenced the way I view intergroup processes. Walter Stephan and Cookie Stephan have affected the way I see intergroup anxiety. Harry Triandis and Michael Bond influenced how I view cross-cultural variability, and both have provided valuable comments on my work over the years. Finally, Kurt Lewin's writing convinced me that theories must be practical.

my work for several reasons. First, the theory intuitively made sense to me.[2] Second, URT includes concepts (e.g., similarity) that allow a relatively straightforward extension from interpersonal to intergroup contexts. Third, the focus on predictability in URT was consistent with my conceptualization of culture (i.e., our culture provides us with implicit theories that allow us to predict others' behavior). Fourth, I thought that predictability of behavior (e.g., reducing uncertainty) was an important issue in communication across cultures.[3] Fifth, I could see direct applications of URT to improving the quality of communication.

To extend URT to intergroup relationships, modifications are necessary (e.g., intergroup factors such as social identity must be incorporated). A straightforward extension of URT is limited because it focuses only on cognitive processes. Affective processes are critical in understanding intergroup communication. One of the major factors influencing intergroup communication, for example, is the amount of anxiety that we experience. Anxiety, however, also is present any time people communicate (May, 1977). I (Gudykunst, 1988, 1993), therefore, incorporated anxiety as the affective equivalent of cognitive uncertainty. To clearly distinguish the theory I am developing from URT, I refer to the present theory as anxiety/uncertainty management (AUM) theory.[4]

I have developed AUM theory in several stages. Initially, I extended URT to intergroup communication (Gudykunst, 1985a). Next, I incorporated anxiety into an abstract theory of effective communication and intercultural adaptation (Gudykunst, 1988). At about the same time, Mitch Hammer and I (Gudykunst & Hammer, 1988b) developed a special version of the theory that was designed to explain intercultural adaptation. Neither of these theories was labeled AUM. In 1993 I modified the 1988 version of the theory by expanding the number of axioms and making them more practical. This was the first version of the theory to be labeled AUM. In this chapter, I will outline and update the theory.[5] To put the theory in context, I begin with the theoretical foundations.

THEORETICAL FOUNDATIONS

To explain interpersonal and intergroup communication in the same theory, linking concepts are needed. I use the concept of the stranger to accomplish this and it provides the starting point for the discussion of the foundations of the theory. The other concepts that provide the foundation for the theory are uncertainty, anxiety, effective communication, and mindfulness.

The Concept of the Stranger

To explain communication between people from the same group and communication between people from different groups at the same time, linking concepts are needed. The major linking concept that I use is that of the "stranger."[6] Simmel (1908/1950) views strangers as possessing the contradictory qualities of being both near and far at the same time:

> The unity of nearness and remoteness in every human relation is organized, in the phenomenon of the stranger, in a way which may be most briefly formulated by saying that in the relationship to him [or her], distance means that he [or she], who is also far, is actually near. (p. 402)

In other words, strangers represent both the idea of nearness in that they are physically close and the idea of remoteness in that they have different values and ways of doing things. Strangers are physically present and participate in a situation and, at the same time, are outside the situation because they are members of different groups.

Strangers, as I conceive of them, are people who are different because they are members of other groups. Because we do not share all of our group memberships with anyone else, everyone we meet is a potential stranger. Because everyone is a potential stranger, both interpersonal and intergroup processes must operate in our interactions with them. Interacting with strangers is characterized by anxiety and uncertainty. Herman and Schield (1961) point out that "the immediate psychological result of being in a new situation is lack of security. Ignorance of the potentialities inherent in the situation, of the means to reach a goal, and of the probable outcomes of an intended action causes insecurity" (p. 165). Attempts to deal with the ambiguity of new situations involve a pattern of information-seeking (uncertainty reduction) and tension (anxiety) reduction (Ball-Rokeach, 1973). Managing uncertainty and anxiety, therefore, is a central process affecting our communication with strangers.

Uncertainty

Uncertainty is a cognitive phenomenon; it affects the way we think about strangers. Berger and Calabrese (1975) isolate two distinct types of uncertainty present in initial interactions with strangers. Predictive uncertainty is the uncertainty we have about predicting strangers' attitudes, feelings, beliefs, values, and behavior. We need to be able, for example, to predict which of several alternative behavior patterns strangers will choose to employ. Explanatory uncertainty involves the uncertainty we have about explaining strangers' attitudes, feelings, and thoughts.

Whenever we try to figure out why strangers behave the way they do, we are engaging in explanatory uncertainty reduction.

Berger (1979) also differentiates between cognitive uncertainty and behavioral uncertainty. Cognitive uncertainty involves our knowledge about strangers, while behavioral uncertainty involves the degree to which we are relatively certain that strangers will behave in a predictable way. In interacting with others for the first time, we have cognitive uncertainty about their thoughts, feelings, and values, but we may have sufficient behavioral certainty to interact effectively because of the cultural scripts that tell us how to behave in initial interactions. Scripts are "a coherent sequence of events expected by the individual involving him [or her] either as a participant or observer" (Abelson, 1976, p. 33).

Some degree of uncertainty exists in all relationships, but there tends to be more uncertainty when we communicate with members of different groups than when we communicate with members of our own groups (Gudykunst, 1985a; Lee & Boster, 1991). While uncertainty tends to be higher when we interact with members of different groups, this does not mean that we are motivated to actively try to reduce our uncertainty. We try to reduce uncertainty when others act in a deviant fashion, when they provide us with rewards, and when we anticipate seeing them again in the future (Berger, 1979). Because we do not necessarily see strangers as providing rewards, we may not be motivated to reduce our uncertainty about them.

We can never totally predict or explain others' behavior. We all have maximum and minimum thresholds for uncertainty (Gudykunst, 1993).[7] Our maximum threshold is the highest amount of uncertainty we can have and think we can predict strangers' behavior sufficiently to feel comfortable interacting with them. Our minimum threshold is the lowest amount of uncertainty we can have and not feel bored or overconfident about our interactions with others. If our uncertainty is above the maximum threshold or below the minimum threshold, we will have difficulty communicating effectively. If our uncertainty is above our maximum threshold, we do not think we have enough information to predict or explain strangers' behavior.[8] When uncertainty is above our maximum threshold, strangers' behavior is seen as unpredictable and/or we do not have confidence in our predictions and explanations of their behavior. When we do not have confidence in our ability to predict strangers' behavior, we may choose to end the interactions as soon as possible or we may try to gather the information we need to bring our uncertainty below our maximum thresholds.

If our uncertainty is below our minimum threshold, we think others' behavior is highly predictable; we have a high level of confidence in our ability to predict their behavior. High levels of predictability, however, often are associated with boredom. When this occurs, there may not be sufficient novelty in our relationships for us to sustain interest in interacting with other people. As Kruglanski (1989) points out, we have a need to avoid closure to allow for some "mystery." It also is important to remember that confidence in our predictions does not mean that our predictions are accurate. When we see others' behavior as highly predictable, we also are likely to misinterpret their messages because we do not consider the possibility that our interpretations of their messages are wrong. In other words, overconfidence can breed misinterpretations.

Communicating effectively requires that our uncertainty be between our minimum and maximum thresholds (Gudykunst, 1993). When our cognitive and behavioral uncertainty is between the two thresholds, we have sufficient confidence in our ability to predict others' thoughts, feelings, and behavior that we feel comfortable but our confidence is not sufficiently high that we become overconfident. Because we are not overconfident, we may recognize cues indicating potential misunderstandings when they occur. If our uncertainty is above our maximum thresholds or below our minimum thresholds, we need to consciously manage our uncertainty to improve the effectiveness of our communication.

Uncertainty fluctuates over time and within specific interactions.[9] One way to view this fluctuation is as a dialectic between predictability and novelty (Baxter, 1988). We need both predictability *and* novelty to maintain our relationships. Predictability is necessary to know how to expect other people to behave, but novelty is needed to keep our relationships interesting. When we communicate on automatic pilot, however, we may focus exclusively on our need for predictability and ignore our need for novelty.

Anxiety

Anxiety is the affective (emotional) equivalent of uncertainty. We experience some degree of anxiety any time we communicate with others.[10] Anxiety is a "generalized or unspecified sense of disequilibrium" (imbalance; J. H. Turner, 1988, p. 61). It stems from feeling uneasy, tense, worried, or apprehensive about what might happen. Anxiety is an emotional (affective) response to situations based on the anticipation of negative consequences (Stephan & Stephan, 1985). Anxiety is one of the fundamental problems with which all humans must cope (Lazarus, 1991; May, 1977), but it tends to be higher in intergroup than interpersonal encounters (Ickes, 1984; Word, Zanna, & Cooper, 1974).

We have maximum and minimum thresholds for anxiety (Gudykunst, 1993). Our maximum thresholds are the highest amount of anxiety we can have and feel comfortable interacting with strangers. Our minimum thresholds are the lowest amount of anxiety we can have and care about our interactions with others. If our anxiety is above our maximum threshold, we are so uneasy that we do not want to communicate with strangers. When our anxiety is above our maximum thresholds, our anxiety may be "vague—but it is more powerful for its vagueness. As there is no definite threat or danger upon which we could act, it paralyzes action" (Riezler, 1960, p. 147). Of course, there also may be a specific source that brings our anxiety above our maximum thresholds. No matter how our anxiety gets above our maximum thresholds, when it is too high our attention focuses exclusively on the anxiety and not on our communication with others. When anxiety is above our maximum thresholds, we tend to process information in a simplistic fashion. To illustrate, when our anxiety is too high, we only use our stereotypes to predict other people's behavior. Because stereotypes are never accurate when applied to an individual, our predictions are inaccurate and our communication, therefore, is likely to be ineffective.

If our anxiety is below our minimum thresholds, there is not enough adrenaline running through our system to motivate us to communicate with strangers. Tuan (1979), for example, points out our curiosity is primed by our anxiety. When our anxiety is below our minimum thresholds, we do not care what happens. In some respects, we feel too safe and secure to pay attention to what is happening when we are communicating with others. Not paying attention, however, leads us to miss important cues about potential misunderstandings.

To be motivated to communicate with strangers, our anxiety has to be below our maximum thresholds and above our minimum thresholds. Some anxiety, but not too much, can be "transformed into a type of useful highly adaptive social response, which leaves the self protected from the impact of its own emotions and its own imperatives while it promotes the highest vigilance, albeit uncritical, toward the behavior of others" (Schneiderman, 1960, pp. 161-162). The role of anxiety in communication is similar to its role in our performance on tests. If we are too anxious, we do not perform well on tests. Similarly, if we are not at all anxious, we do not perform well. This argument is consistent with Janis's (1958, 1971, 1985) theory of anticipatory fear. He argues that moderate levels of fear lead to adaptive processes, while low and high levels do not. My position also is compatible with Csikszentmihalyi's (1990) argument that there is an optimal level of anxiety that facilitates our experiencing "flow," or having optimal experiences.

Managing anxiety over time is associated closely with developing trust. Trust is "confidence that one will find what is desired from another, rather than what is feared" (Deutsch, 1973, p. 149). When we trust others, we expect positive outcomes from our interactions with them; when we have anxiety about interacting with others, we fear negative outcomes from our interactions with them. When we first meet someone, "trust is often little more than a naive expression of hope" (Holmes & Rempel, 1989, p. 192). For us to have hope about the relationship, our anxiety must be below our maximum threshold. For relationships to become close, some minimal degree of trust is necessary. Anxiety is a dialectic involving fear and trust.

There is a relationship between uncertainty and whether we experience fear or trust when we communicate with strangers. Demerath (1993), for example, points out that

> if the perception of an object [or person] leads to greater certainty—either by adding to the old knowledge or by replacing lesser knowledge with better knowledge—positive affect will result [e.g., trust]. If it leads to less certainty and undermines predictive capacity, negative affect will result [e.g., fear]. (p. 136)

The anxiety we experience when we communicate with strangers usually is based on negative expectations. Stephan and Stephan (1985) argue that we fear four types of negative consequences when interacting with members of other groups: We may fear negative consequences for our self-concepts, we may fear negative behavioral consequences, we may fear negative evaluations by strangers, and we may fear negative evaluations by members of our ingroups.

One of the behavioral consequences of anxiety is avoidance (Stephan & Stephan, 1985). We avoid strangers because it allows us to manage our anxiety.[11] When we are experiencing anxiety and cannot avoid strangers, we often terminate the interaction as soon as we can. Cognitively, anxiety leads to biases in how we process information. The more anxious we are, the more likely we will focus on the behaviors we expect to see, such as those based on our stereotypes, and the more likely we are to confirm these expectations and not recognize behavior that is inconsistent with our expectations (Stephan & Stephan, 1985).

Turner's (1988) theory of motivation suggests that lack of predictability leads to anxiety and lack of trust. Demarath's (1993) knowledge-based affect theory, in contrast, suggests that decreases in uncertainty lead to positive affect (e.g., trust) and increases in uncertainty lead to negative affect (e.g., fear). Combining these two frameworks suggests that there is a reciprocal relationship between uncertainty and anxiety.[12]

When our anxiety or uncertainty is too high or too low, we cannot communicate effectively. Before discussing the process that allows us to manage our uncertainty and anxiety, that is, being mindful, it is necessary to take a brief detour to define effective communication.

Effective Communication

To say we communicated does not imply an outcome. Communication is a process involving the exchange of messages and the creation of meaning. When we communicate, we attach meaning to messages we construct and transmit to others, and we interpret the messages we receive from others. We are not always aware of this process, but we do it nevertheless. One reason we are not highly aware of the process is that much of our everyday communication is based on the implicit personal theories of communication we learned as children.

Our implicit personal theories of communication are our unconscious, taken-for-granted assumptions about how communication takes place. Because we are not aware that we are using implicit theories to guide our behavior, we do not question our theories. Not questioning our implicit theories leads us to assume that the predictions we make about strangers' behavior (based on our implicit theories) are accurate. The predictions we make based on our implicit theories, nevertheless, are not always accurate. One of the major consequences of assuming that our implicit theories are accurate is that we tend to assume that other people are interpreting our messages the same way we intended them. This is not the case. No two people ever interpret a message in the same way.

Communication is effective to the extent that the person interpreting the message attaches a meaning to the message that is relatively similar to what was intended by the person transmitting it. Stated differently, communication is effective to the extent that we are able to minimize misunderstandings. Misunderstandings, however, often occur when we communicate with strangers. The vast majority of the time, we interpret strangers' messages using our own frame of reference and they interpret our messages from their frame of reference. When we interact with strangers, we may or may not recognize that communication is ineffective. It is possible that our interpretations of strangers' messages are different than they intended or that their interpretations of our messages are different than we intended and neither of us recognizes the difference. When this happens, the interaction is not disrupted. Alternatively, we may recognize that there are differences in meaning or strangers may perceive that there are differences in meaning. Although the differences in meaning are recognized, we may or may not attempt to repair the problem. Whether or not we recognize the differences in meaning, they involve misinterpretations. Correcting misinterpretations requires that we be mindful.

Being Mindful

As indicated earlier, most of the time when we communicate we are not highly aware of our behavior. In other words, we communicate mindlessly or automatically. Bargh (1989) argues that automatic information processing can involve various combinations of attention, awareness, intention, and control. Automatic information processing also can take place in conjunction with conscious information processing. When we communicate based on our implicit theories, we generally are not highly aware of our information processing and we do not pay much attention to it. We may or may not have intentions in the situation, but even if we do have intentions, we may not be highly aware of them. Our ability to control our automatic processing also varies. Much of the time when we communicate using our implicit theories, we can control our automatic processing. That is, we can consciously decide to stop automatically processing information and start to consciously process information. At other times, we may not be able to control our automatic processing.

When we are aware of our communication behavior, we become mindful to some extent. Mindfulness involves "(a) creation of new categories; (b) openness to new information; and (c) awareness of more than one perspective" (Langer, 1989, p. 62). Langer (1989) argues that "categorizing is a fundamental and natural human activity. . . . Any attempt to eliminate bias by attempting to eliminate the perception of differences is doomed to failure" (p. 154). Being mindful involves making more, not fewer, distinctions. To illustrate, when we are mindless, we tend to use broad categories to predict strangers' behavior, such as their culture, ethnicity, sex, or the role they are playing. When we are mindful, we can create new categories that are more specific. The more subcategories we use, the more personalized the information we use to make predictions.

Mindfulness also involves being open to new information (Langer, 1989). When we are mindless, we tend to see the same thing occurring in the situation that we saw the previous time we were in the same situation, even when strangers behave differently. If we are consciously open to new information, we see the subtle differences in our own and strangers' behavior that may take place. Being open to new information involves focusing on the process of communication that is taking place, *not* the outcome of our interactions. When we focus on the outcome, we miss subtle cues in our interactions and this often leads to misunderstandings. To be mindful, we must also recognize that there are different perspectives that can be used to understand or explain our interaction with strangers (Langer, 1989). When we are mindful, we recognize that strangers interpret our messages differently than we do. When we are mindless, in contrast, we tend to assume strangers interpret our messages the same way we intended. Being mindless limits our ability to see the choices we actually have about how to behave in most situations (Langer, 1989).

AUM THEORY

In presenting the theory, I begin with the theoretical assumptions I make (the metatheoretical assumptions are summarized in Gudykunst, 1993). I then present the axioms of the theory. I subdivide the presentation of the axioms into seven categories: self and self-concept; motivation; reactions to strangers; social categorization; situational processes; connections with strangers; and anxiety, uncertainty, mindfulness, and effective communication.

Theoretical Assumptions

I see the management of uncertainty and anxiety as mediating processes between other variables and effective communication. Lieberson (1985) suggests that theorists need to isolate the "basic causes" of the phenomenon under investigation. In generating the theory, I assume that the management of anxiety and uncertainty is the basic cause influencing effective communication. Other variables (e.g., identity, positive expectations, similarity), therefore, are treated as "superficial causes" of effective communication (i.e., they influence uncertainty and anxiety but are not directly related to the outcomes). Stated differently, the influence of these superficial causes on effective communication and adaptation is mediated through uncertainty and anxiety. Gudykunst and Shapiro's (in press) research supports this assumption for quality of communication. Gao and Gudykunst's (1990) and Hammer, Wiseman, Rasmussen, and Bruschke's (1992) research also supports this assumption with respect to adaptation processes.

Given that I view anxiety and uncertainty as the direct causes of effective communication, I focus on isolating the superficial causes that affect our ability to manage the anxiety and uncertainty we experience.[13] Obviously, the superficial causes are interrelated. These interrelationships, however, are beyond the scope of the present discussion of the theory (see the discussion of the theorems below).

In constructing AUM theory, I was concerned with presenting the theory in a form so that it has direct application to improving the effectiveness of communication.[14] This requires that the theoretical statements be written at a concrete level. The more concrete the statements included in the theory, the larger the number of statements that are needed to explain the phenomenon under study. Reynolds (1971) points out that

> in dealing with logical systems that are completely abstract . . . a common criteria is to select the smallest number of axioms from which all other statements can be derived, reflecting a preference for simplicity and elegance. There is reason to think that this is inappropriate for a substantive theory, particularly when it makes it more difficult to understand the theory. (p. 95)

In addition to making the axioms as concrete as possible, I also state the axioms informally to make applications easier.[15]

I make several theoretical assumptions regarding communication. First, as indicated earlier, both interpersonal and intergroup factors influence all of our communication. Theories designed to explain communication between people must include both interpersonal and intergroup factors. Second, the identities we use in different situations influence the nature of the encounters we have with strangers. When our social identities predominantly generate our behavior, our encounters tend to be mainly intergroup in nature; when our personal identities predominantly generate our behavior, our encounters tend to be mainly interpersonal in nature. Third, at least one person in any encounter is a stranger in some way.[16] Most group differences have an effect on our communication, and any group difference can be a basis for misunderstandings. Fourth, most of the time that we communicate, we are not highly aware of our communication behavior. When we communicate with strangers, we tend to become aware of our behavior, but we focus on the outcome, not the process of communication. Fifth, we do not have sufficient intersubjective understanding to avoid misunderstandings when we communicate with strangers when we are mindless, or when we are mindful and focus on the outcome. We can communicate effectively with strangers when we make a conscious decision to do so and are mindful of the process of communication.[17] Sixth, cognitive uncertainty and affective anxiety directly influence our ability to communicate effectively and other variables influence our anxiety and uncertainty. To communicate effectively, our anxiety and uncertainty must be between our minimum and maximum thresholds. Seventh, uncertainty involves a dialectic between novelty and predictability, and anxiety involves a dialectic between trust and fear.

I have several biases in terms of how to construct theories. First, following Blalock (1969), I see axioms as "propositions that involve variables that are taken to be directly linked causally" (p. 18). When combined, the axioms form a causal process theory (Reynolds, 1971) that explains effective communication. Second, theories should include clear statements of boundary conditions that specify the conditions under which axioms hold. Third, all levels of analysis (i.e., individual, interpersonal, intergroup, and cultural) must be taken into consideration to explain effective communication. Fourth, culture can be treated as a theoretical variable to explain cross-cultural variability in the processes involved (the role of culture in the theory is discussed in the final section). Fifth, theories should be able to be used to improve the quality of our communication.

Given the assumptions and biases, the scope of the theory can be specified. Although I use the term *stranger* in the axioms, the theory is *not* limited to initial interactions between people who are meeting for the first time (i.e., the everyday usage of the term *stranger*). As indicated earlier, I conceive of strangers as members of different groups. Anyone who is a member of a different group is a potential stranger. The theory, therefore, is meant to explain effective communication in any encounter in which some form of group difference is manifested. I believe this is virtually all of our encounters with other humans. The theory, however, is not designed to explain how relationships begin and develop over time. Some variables involved in defining the nature of our relationships with strangers, nevertheless, are included (e.g., interdependence, intimacy of relationship).

Given the overview of the theoretical assumptions, let's turn to the axioms of the theory. I'll begin with the self and self-concept.

Self and Self-Concept

Our self-concept is our view of ourselves. How we define ourselves has a tremendous influence on how we communicate. J. C. Turner (1987a) defines the self-concept as "the set of cognitive representations of self available to a person" (p. 44). He argues that we place ourselves in categories with others that we see as similar to ourselves on some dimension and different than others on that dimension. This leads to our defining ourselves in terms of our human, social, and personal identities. Social identity is the major generative mechanism for intergroup behavior, while personal identity is the major generative mechanism for interpersonal behavior.[18] Both forms of identity, however, influence behavior in virtually all interactions.[19]

Smith and Bond (1993) point out that some social categories appear to be salient in most situations (e.g., ethnicity, gender). Some categories, in contrast, are important when they are distinctive (e.g., when there are only a few members of the category present). The degree to which we perceive strangers to be typical members of their groups affects whether we use the category in interacting with strangers. The social relations among the groups in society also affect whether we emphasize the category in our interactions with strangers.

Our social identities tend to be activated when we communicate with strangers because we have defined strangers as being different than us in terms of some group membership. In any particular situation, one social identity will be activated (R. Turner, 1987). The social identity activated depends on how we categorize ourselves and the strangers with whom we are interacting. If we categorize them based on ethnicity, for example, the social identity activated will be ethnic identity.

Feeling secure in the social identities we use to guide our behavior when we communicate with strangers facilitates our ability to manage our anxiety and uncertainty.[20] This claim, however, has to be qualified. Gudykunst and Hammer (1988a) point out that strength of social identity reduces uncertainty only when we recognize that the strangers are from another group and when the strangers with whom we are communicating are perceived to be typical members of their group. When we perceive strangers to be atypical members of their group, we do not treat them based on their group membership (i.e., we see them as "an exception to the rule"). In this case, our communication is influenced by our personal identities, not by our social identities. When communication is based on our personal identities, we use information about individual strangers with whom we are communicating to reduce uncertainty.

Closely related to our identities are our self construals. Markus and Kitayama (1991) argue that there are two different ways that we conceive of ourselves: We can see ourselves as independent of others and we can see ourselves as interdependent with others. When an independent construal of the self predominates, we view ourselves as unique individuals with clear boundaries that separate us from others. When an interdependent construal of self predominates, we view ourselves as part of a social relationship. Our view of our self is not totally separate from others, but interlinked with others.

Our independent and interdependent self construal are individual-level processes that reflect individualism and collectivism at the cultural level, respectively (Gudykunst et al., 1994). People in individualistic cultures tend to use person-based information to reduce uncertainty about others, while people in collectivistic cultures tend to use group-based information to reduce uncertainty about others (Gudykunst & Nishida, 1986a). By extension, it can be argued that we tend to focus on person-based information in reducing uncertainty when our independent self construals are activated, and we tend to focus on group-based information when our interdependent self construals are activated.

Our identities and our self construals are not the only components of the self-concept that affect our communication with strangers. Our self-esteem, the positive or negative feelings we have about ourselves, also influences our communication. Our self-esteem affects the way we process information and the amount of anxiety we experience. Burns (1985), for example, argues that low self-esteem leads us to distort our cognitive processing of information about ourselves and others. When our self-esteem is high, in contrast, we are able to look for objective information about ourselves and others, even in stressful situations. Low self-esteem also leads us to be anxious about interacting with others. The greater our self-esteem, the better able we are to manage our anxiety (e.g., Becker, 1971; Epstein, 1976).

Closely related to self-esteem is shame. Scheff (1990) argues that shame emerges from the constant monitoring of the self. When we feel shame, our ability to process information about strangers is hindered because we focus on the shame rather than gathering information (e.g., we focus on the outcome). The greater our shame, the less accurately we are able to predict strangers' behavior and the more anxiety we experience.

How we define ourselves affects the way we communicate as well as the way we manage the anxiety and uncertainty we experience when we communicate with strangers. Six axioms regarding the self and self-concept, therefore, are included in the theory:

Axiom 1: An increase in the degree to which our social identities influence our interactions with strangers will produce an increase in our ability to manage our anxiety and an increase in our confidence in predicting their behavior. Boundary Condition: This axiom holds only if strangers are perceived to be members of another group and they are perceived to be typical group members.

Axiom 2: An increase in the degree to which our personal identities influence our interactions with strangers will produce an increase in our ability to manage our anxiety and an increase in our ability to accurately predict their behavior. Boundary Condition: This axiom only holds in individualistic cultures.

Axiom 3: An increase in our use of our independent self construals to guide our interactions with strangers will produce a reliance on person-based information to reduce uncertainty about their behavior; an increase in our use of our interdependent self construals to guide our interactions with strangers will produce a reliance on group-based information to reduce uncertainty about their behavior.

Axiom 4: An increase in our dependence on our ingroups for our self-esteem when interacting with strangers will produce an increase in our anxiety and a decrease in our ability to accurately predict their behavior.

Axiom 5: An increase in our self-esteem (pride) when we interact with strangers will produce an increase in our ability to manage our anxiety.

Axiom 6: An increase in our shame when we interact with strangers will produce a decrease in our ability to manage our anxiety and a decrease in our ability to accurately predict their behavior.

How we think about ourselves in isolation cannot fully explain how we manage our anxiety and uncertainty when we communicate with strangers. The identities we activate in a particular encounter affect whether we are motivated to communicate with strangers. If we are not motivated to communicate with strangers, we tend to avoid interactions rather than try to manage our anxiety and uncertainty. If we are motivated to communicate with strangers, in contrast, we will try to manage our anxiety and uncertainty so we can interact with strangers comfortably.

Motivation

J. H. Turner (1988) suggests that certain basic needs motivate us to interact with others. Needs are "fundamental states of being in humans which, if unsatisfied, generate feelings of deprivation" (p. 23). Four needs are critical to AUM: (a) our need for a sense of predictability (or trust), (b) our need for a sense of group inclusion, (c) our need to avoid or diffuse anxiety, and (d) our need to sustain our self-conception.

We "need to 'trust' others in the sense that, for the purposes of a given interaction, others are 'reliable' and their responses 'predictable' " (Turner, 1988, p. 56). If we see strangers' behavior as reliable and predictable, it helps confirm our self-concepts and helps us to feel included. Our cultural, ethnic, and gender identities provide us with implicit predictions about strangers' behavior. The categories in which we place strangers also provide us with implicit predictions of their behaviors. When we categorize strangers, our stereotypes of the groups in which we categorize them are activated. Our stereotypes provide predictions of strangers' behavior and our interactions will appear to have rhythm if strangers conform to our stereotypes. If strangers do not follow our stereotypes, our interaction with them will seem to lack rhythm.

Our need for group inclusion results from *not* feeling involved in or part of social relationships with strangers (Turner, 1988). When we do not feel included, we experience anxiety and uncertainty. The need for inclusion is related directly to how we see our social identities. Our social identities are derived from a tension between our need to be seen as similar to and fit in with others and our need to be seen as unique people (Brewer, 1991). The need to be seen as similar allows us to identify with different groups and involves the general process of inclusion, or making ourselves fit in with others. The need to be seen as unique is expressed in the general process of differentiation, making ourselves stand out from others. We need to be seen as similar to and different than others.

Closely related to our need for inclusion is our need for self-concept confirmation. Our need for self-concept support directly influences our communication. When our self-conceptions are confirmed, we feel secure in our identities. When we feel secure in our identities, we feel confident in our interactions with strangers. The more secure we are in our identities, the better able we are to manage our anxiety and the more confident we are in predicting strangers' behaviors. While avoiding anxiety is an important motivating factor in our communication with people who are similar, it is critical in our communication with strangers. Intergroup anxiety is largely a function of our fear of negative consequences when we interact with people who are different (Stephan & Stephan, 1985). As our anxiety becomes high, our need for group inclusion and our need to sustain our self-conception become central (J. H. Turner, 1988).

Most of us spend the vast majority of our time interacting with people who are relatively similar to us. Our actual contact with people who are different is limited; it is a novel form of interaction. If our attempts to communicate with strangers are not successful and we cannot easily get out of the situations in which we find ourselves, then our unconscious need for group inclusion becomes unsatisfied. This leads to anxiety about ourselves and our standing in a group context (J. H. Turner, 1988). The net result is that we retreat into known territory and limit our interactions to people who are similar.[21]

If our needs are not met, we are not motivated to communicate with strangers. If our needs are met, in contrast, we tend to be motivated to manage our anxiety and uncertainty. Five axioms regarding our motivation to communicate with strangers, therefore, are included in the theory:

Axiom 7: An increase in our need for a sense of group inclusion when we interact with strangers will produce an increase in our anxiety.

Axiom 8: An increase in our need to sustain our self-conceptions when we interact with strangers will produce an increase in our anxiety.

Axiom 9: An increase in the degree to which strangers confirm our self-conceptions when we interact with them will produce a decrease in our anxiety.

Axiom 10: An increase in the predictability of strangers' behavior will produce a decrease in our anxiety. Boundary Condition: This axiom only applies to increases in predictability that bring uncertainty below our maximum thresholds.

Axiom 11: An increase in our sense of security in our personal and social identities when we interact with strangers will produce a decrease in our anxiety and an increase in our confidence in predicting their behavior.

When our needs are met, we are motivated to interact with strangers. When we interact with strangers, how we react to them cognitively, affectively, and behaviorally influences our ability to manage our anxiety and uncertainty.

Reactions to Strangers

The way we react to strangers affects the amount of anxiety and uncertainty we experience. Cognitively, our ability to complexly process information, the rigidity of our attitudes, and the degree to which we monitor our behavior affect our anxiety and uncertainty. Affectively, our ability to tolerate ambiguity and our empathy influence whether we experience anxiety and can make accurate predictions about strangers' behavior. Behaviorally, the degree to which strangers accommodate to us and our ability to adapt our behavior affect the amount of anxiety and uncertainty we experience. Let's begin by looking at our ability to complexly process information.

Cognitively complex people form impressions of others that are more extensive and differentiated, and better represent the behavioral variability of others, than cognitively simple people (O'Keefe & Sypher, 1981). Downey, Hellriegel, and Slocum (1977) point out that there is a negative association between cognitive complexity and perceived uncertainty. Our ability to complexly process information affects mainly our uncertainty regarding strangers' behavior. The better able we are to complexly process information, the better able we are to search for alternative explanations of strangers' behavior. Being able to isolate alternative explanations for behavior facilitates accurately predicting strangers' behavior.

Our attitudes toward strangers affect how we interpret their behavior. When our attitudes are rigid, we tend to be intolerant of other viewpoints, we tend to be resistant to change, and we try to ward off threatening aspects of our social environments. The more rigid our attitudes, the more difficulty we have differentiating the types of information we gather; we mix information about the world with the source of the information and we are not able to discriminate between the two (Rokeach, 1960). Holding rigid attitudes leads us to need nonspecific closure when we are interacting with strangers (Kruglanski, 1989). If we hold rigid attitudes, we prefer any form of closure to ambiguity because closure provides "assured knowledge that affords predictability and a base for action" (Kruglanski, 1989, p. 14). The rigid attitudes that affect our communication with strangers include ethnocentrism, prejudice, racism, authoritarianism, sexism, ageism, dogmatism, and other closely related attitudes.

Holding rigid attitudes creates negative expectations for our interactions with strangers. Stephan and Stephan (1985, 1989, 1992) point out that the more ethnocentric and prejudiced we are, the more anxiety we experience interacting with strangers. When we hold rigid attitudes and have negative expectations, we also do not look for new information about the strangers with whom we interact. Holding rigid attitudes, therefore, decreases our ability to accurately predict strangers' behavior.

Our attitudes are not the only factors that affect how we seek out information about strangers. The degree to which we monitor our behavior (e.g., Snyder's, 1974, self-monitoring construct)[22] also influences the nature of information we seek out about strangers. In comparison with low self-monitors, high self-monitors are better able to discover appropriate behavior in new situations, have more control over emotional reactions, and create the impressions they wish (Snyder, 1974), modify their behavior to changes in situations more (Snyder & Monson, 1975), make more confident and extreme attributions (Berscheid, Graziano, Monson, & Dermer, 1976), and seek more information about others with whom they anticipate interacting (Elliott, 1979). High self-monitors use the information they gather about others when they decide how to respond to them more than low self-monitors (Douglas, 1983). High self-monitors also appear to communicate in a way that facilitates friendly communication with others more than low self-monitors (Douglas, 1984).

Lennox and Wolfe (1984) argue that self-monitoring involves the ability to modify self-presentations and sensitivity to others' expressive behavior. Concern for social appropriateness, in contrast, involves cross-situational variability in behavior and paying attention to social comparison information. Wolfe, Lennox, and Cutler (1986) point out that a concern for social appropriateness is based on a protective self-presentation style (Arkin, 1981). Arkin contends that the protective self-presentation style is directed at avoiding disapproval and it is associated with reticence, conformity, and social anxiety. Wolfe et al. observe that concern for social appropriateness is related positively to social anxiety.

Monitoring our behavior and being able to modify our self-presentations make us confident in our abilities to interact with strangers. Specifically, they allow us to manage our anxiety because we know we can adjust to fit into the situation. When we are confident in our own behavior, we also tend to be confident in our ability to predict strangers' behavior. When we are concerned with behaving in a socially appropriately manner with strangers, we experience anxiety.

Our ability to monitor our behavior is not the only factor that facilitates our adjustment in new situations. We also can better adjust in new situations if we are able to tolerate ambiguity. Budner (1962) argues that lack of tolerance for ambiguity involves perceiving ambiguous situations as threatening and undesirable. Ambiguous situations are situations where we do not have sufficient cues to know how to behave. Our tolerance for ambiguity affects the type of information we gather about others. If we have a low tolerance for ambiguity, we tend to base our judgments of strangers on first impressions, which are prematurely formed before all information is available (Smock, 1955). Also, if we have a low tolerance for ambiguity, we tend to seek out information that is supportive of our belief systems when we are in ambiguous situations (McPherson, 1983). If we have a high tolerance for ambiguity, in contrast, we tend to seek out "objective" information about the situation and the people in it. If we are high in tolerance for ambiguity, we also tend to be open to new information about ourselves and others (Pilisuk, 1963). The greater our tolerance for ambiguity, the more comfortable we feel in situations where we do not have all of the information we would like. Our tolerance for ambiguity, therefore, helps us to manage the anxiety we experience interacting with strangers.

Once we can tolerate the ambiguity in our interactions with strangers, we need to be able to look at the interaction from their perspective. This is facilitated if we are empathic. Bell (1987) points out that "cognitively, the empathic person takes the perspective of another person, and in so doing strives to see the world from the other's point of view. Affectively, the empathic person experiences the emotion of another; he or she *feels* the others' experiences" (p. 204). Stephan and Stephan (1992) argue that increases in empathy are associated with decreases in anxiety about interacting with strangers.[23] Empathy also should influence our ability to accurately predict strangers' behaviors. Because we are trying to understand strangers' perspectives when we empathize, the greater our empathy, the more accurate our predictions should be. The use of sympathy in our interactions with strangers invariably leads to misunderstanding rather than understanding. The use of empathy, in contrast, increases the likelihood that understanding occurs. The reason for this is that empathy involves using strangers' frames of reference for interpreting their behavior. In other words, we are adjusting our affective perspective toward strangers.

We also adjust our behavior when we communicate with strangers and strangers adjust their behavior toward us. We have a tendency to react favorably to strangers who linguistically converge toward us (Giles & Smith, 1979). Convergence, however, is not always viewed favorably. Giles and Byrne (1982) point out that, as strangers begin to learn our speech styles, we may diverge in some way to maintain linguistic distinctiveness. Our reaction to strangers' speech convergence also depends on the intent ingroup members attribute to strangers (Simard, Taylor, & Giles, 1976). When we perceive strangers' intent to be positive, we evaluate the convergence positively.

Although our accommodation to strangers and strangers' accommodation to us both affect the communication that takes place, it is strangers' accommodation to us that influences our anxiety and uncertainty. If strangers diverge from us, their behavior appears to be unpredictable and we, therefore, will have anxiety and uncertainty about communicating with them. If strangers accommodate to our communication style and we perceive their intent to be positive, in contrast, it will lead to reductions in our uncertainty and anxiety about communicating with them.

To communicate effectively with strangers requires that we be able to adapt our communication. Duran (1983) argues that communication adaptability involves the following:

1. The requirement of both cognitive (ability to perceive) and behavioral (ability to adapt) skills;
2. Adaptation not only of behaviors but also interaction goals;
3. The ability to adapt to the requirements posed by different communication contexts; and
4. The assumption that perceptions of communicative competence reside in the dyad. (p. 320)

The more we are able to adapt our communication, the more confident we are in our ability to deal with new situations. The more we are able to adapt our communication, the more we are able to adapt the way we think about strangers. Increases in adaptability, therefore, lead to lower levels of anxiety and increases in our confidence in predicting strangers' behavior. The way we think about strangers, our affective responses to strangers, and the ways we behave toward them affect our ability to manage our anxiety and uncertainty. Seven axioms regarding how we react to strangers, therefore, are included in the theory:

Axiom 12: An increase in our ability to complexly process information about strangers will produce an increase in our ability to accurately predict their behavior.

Axiom 13: An increase in the rigidity of our attitudes toward strangers will produce an increase in our anxiety and a decrease in our ability to accurately predict their behavior.

Axiom 14: An increase in our self-monitoring when we interact with strangers will produce an increase in our confidence in predicting their behavior; an increase in our concern for social appropriateness will produce an increase in anxiety.

Axiom 15: An increase in our ability to tolerate ambiguity when we interact with strangers will produce an increase in our ability to manage our anxiety and an increase in our ability to accurately predict strangers' behavior.

Axiom 16: An increase in our ability to empathize with strangers will produce an increase in our ability to accurately predict their behavior.

Axiom 17: An increase in the degree to which strangers accommodate to our behavior will produce a decrease in our anxiety and an increase in our confidence in predicting their behavior.

Axiom 18: An increase in our ability to adapt our communication to strangers will produce an increase in our ability to manage our anxiety and an increase in our confidence in predicting their behavior.

The way we react to strangers affects our ability to manage our anxiety and uncertainty when we interact with them. There are, however, many different ways we can react to strangers. Our reactions are dependent, in part, on how we categorize strangers.

Social Categorizations

Social categorizations refers to the way we order our social environment by grouping people into categories that make sense to us (Tajfel, 1978b).[24] In categorizing ourselves and others, we become aware of being members of social groups. When we categorize others, our stereotypes of the groups in which we categorize them become activated. This leads us to focus on differences between ourselves and strangers.

To communicate effectively with strangers, we must understand both our differences from and our similarities to them. When we interact with strangers mindlessly, we gather information regarding dissimilarities between ourselves and strangers (Wilder & Allen, 1978). If strangers identify with their groups strongly, we must recognize their group memberships so as to support their self-concept. If we ignore strangers' group memberships when they identify strongly with their groups, they perceive our behavior as disconfirming. Knowledge of the similarities and differences between our group and strangers' groups when the strangers strongly identify with the group, therefore, is critical to effective communication. Group differences, in contrast, are not as critical when strangers do not strongly identify with their groups as when they do identify strongly with their group. Similarities, nevertheless, are still important.

To communicate effectively with strangers, we must seek out similarities between ourselves and them. Bellah, Madsen, Sullivan, Swidler, and Tipton (1985), for example, point out that we need to seek out commonalities because "with a more explicit understanding of what we have in common and the goals we seek to attain together, the differences between us that remain would be less threatening" (p. 287). Finding commonalities requires that we be mindful of our prejudices.

Group similarities are not the only similarities that are important to effective communication with strangers. Perceived personal similarities are major factors we use in deciding who to approach and the people with whom we form relationships (see Berscheid, 1985, for a review of this research). When we perceive ourselves to be similar to others, we tend to be attracted to them, we tend to form social networks with them, and we tend to be persuaded by them. Perceived similarity is related to reducing uncertainty (e.g., Gudykunst, Chua, & Gray, 1987) and anxiety (e.g., Stephan & Stephan, 1985). If we initially perceive similarities between ourselves and others and later discover dissimilarities in the areas in which we perceived similarities, the perceived dissimilarities will lead to increases in our anxiety and uncertainty. The greater the perceived differences between our group and strangers' groups, the more intense the negative affect (e.g., anxiety) we have about interacting with them (Dijker, 1987).

When we search for similarities and differences between our groups and strangers' groups, we recognize that not all members of strangers' groups are alike. Linville, Fischer, and Salovey (1989) point out that we tend to view our ingroups as more differentiated than outgroups (e.g., strangers' groups). When we are not familiar with strangers' groups, we tend to assume that all members are alike when we communicate on automatic pilot. Linville et al. point out that the more familiar we are with outgroups, the greater our perceived differentiation of the group. As we become familiar with outgroups, we recognize that all members are not alike and we begin to create new subcategories within the group and/or recognize some members as exceptions to the rule. Johnston and Hewstone (1990) argue that the more variability we perceive in outgroups, the less our tendency to treat all members in a similar negative fashion. When we recognize variability in outgroups and do not treat all members alike, we begin to look for person-based information about the members of the group. Increases in the variability we perceive in outgroups, therefore, provide additional information about the strangers with whom we are communicating and decrease our uncertainty and anxiety.

When we categorize strangers, or think about strangers and their groups either consciously or unconsciously, we form expectations for strangers' behavior. Expectations involve our anticipations and predictions about how others will communicate with us.[25] Our expectations are derived from social norms, communication rules, scripts, and strangers' personal characteristics of which we are aware. Intergroup cognitions create expectations and influence our preconscious or automatic thoughts regarding our affective reactions to strangers. Negative cognitive expectations (e.g., ethnocentrism, negative stereotypes, prejudice) lead to uncertainty and intergroup anxiety. Positive expectations (e.g., positive stereotypes), in contrast, help us reduce uncertainty and anxiety (Gudykunst, 1988). Positive expectations lead us to behave in a positive manner toward strangers (see Hamilton, Sherman, & Ruvolo, 1990, for a discussion of expectancy confirming processes). Positive expectations for strangers' behavior lead to decreases in the anxiety we experience about interacting with them and in our ability to accurately predict their behavior (Gudykunst & Shapiro, in press). Positive expectations alone, however, do not necessarily increase our explanatory certainty. To reduce our explanatory uncertainty, we need to have accurate information regarding the stranger's culture, group memberships, and the individual stranger with whom we are communicating.

Strangers' violations of our expectations influence our ability to reduce our uncertainty and anxiety. If one person violates another's expectations to a sufficient degree that the violation is recognized, the person recognizing the violation becomes aroused and has to assess the situation (Burgoon & Hale, 1988). In other words, the violation of expectations leads to some degree of mindfulness. Violations of expectations by communicators with low reward valence tend to lead to negative outcomes. Because strangers are not perceived to provide rewards and have low reward valence, the more strangers violate our positive expectations and we are aware of the violations, the greater our uncertainty and anxiety. Stephan (1985) points out that strangers' disconfirmations of positive expectations and their confirmations of negative expectations lead to negative affect (e.g., anxiety). When we are aware of strangers violating our positive expectations or confirming our negative expectations, we will experience increases in our anxiety and decreases in our confidence in predicting their behavior.

When we communicate mindlessly, our predictions and explanations for strangers' behavior are based on our stereotypes, attitudes, and previous experiences with the strangers involved. We may be highly confident of our predictions and explanations, but it is important to recognize that our predictions and explanations may *not* be accurate. If our predictions are based only on our stereotypes of strangers' groups, for example, our predictions will not be accurate if our stereotypes are inaccurate or the strangers are not typical members of their groups. Accurate predictions or explanations of strangers' behavior require that we use cultural, social, *and* personal information (Gudykunst, 1994). Accurate predictions also require that we be able to mindfully stop our tendency to behave in a prejudicial fashion toward strangers when our negative expectations are activated (Devine, 1989).

To make accurate predictions and explanations, we must be able to gather accurate information about strangers. When our anxiety is too high, we are not able to gather accurate information about strangers (Wilder & Shapiro, 1989). Also, when our anxiety is high, we do not perceive variability in outgroups (Islam & Hewstone, 1993). If our anxiety is too low, we also will have problems gathering accurate information about strangers. To gather accurate information, we must mindfully manage our anxiety so that it is below our maximum threshold and above our minimum threshold.

The way we deal with our stereotypes also affects the accuracy of our predictions. When we place strangers in a category, our stereotype of people in that category helps us predict their behavior if we perceive them as typical of their groups.[26] We are able to reduce our uncertainty because we assume that our stereotypes tell us how typical group members communicate (Krauss & Fussell, 1991). If strangers have informed us of their category memberships, our predictions may be accurate. It is rare, however, for others to tell us their group memberships directly (Kellermann, 1993).

Rather than using strangers' self-categorizations (the group memberships they announce), we tend to base our categorizations on their skin color, dress, accents, the car they drive, and so forth (Clark & Marshall, 1981). The cues we use, however, are not always accurate ways to categorize strangers (i.e., an inaccurate categorization occurs when we put strangers in a category in which they would not place themselves in the interaction). This is true for all social categories, including ethnicity. To illustrate, strangers vary in the degree to which they identify with their ethnic groups and cultures. If we categorize strangers who do *not* identify strongly with an ethnic group based on ethnicity and make predictions based on this categorization, our predictions will be inaccurate. Predictions based on ethnicity will only be accurate for strangers who identify strongly with their ethnic group and do not identify strongly with their culture.

Another source of inaccuracy in our predictions based on our stereotypes is that the boundaries between many social groups are fuzzy (Clark & Marshall, 1981). Skin color, for example, may not be a good predictor of category membership. To illustrate, there are light-colored African Americans who look like European Americans. These individuals may be categorized as European American based only on skin color. They may, however, identify strongly with being African Americans. Obviously, predictions about their behavior based on skin color will be inaccurate.

Even if strangers are typical members of the groups in which we categorize them, the inferences we make about them based on their group memberships still may not be accurate. Our predictions may not be accurate because the group membership we use to categorize strangers may not be affecting their behavior in the situation. We are all members of many social groups that influence our behavior and provide us with different social identities. We might categorize strangers based on one group membership (e.g., ethnicity) and assume that the social identity based on this category is influencing their behavior. Strangers, however, may be basing their behavior on a different social identity (e.g., social class, gender, role). To increase our accuracy in making predictions, we must try to understand which social identity is guiding strangers' behavior in a particular situation.

The way we categorize strangers affects the amount of anxiety and uncertainty we experience when interacting with them. The way we categorize strangers also influences the accuracy of our predictions about strangers' behavior. Seven axioms regarding social categorizations, therefore, are included in the theory:

Axiom 19: An increase in our understanding of similarities and differences between our groups and strangers' groups will produce an increase in our ability to manage our anxiety and our ability to accurately predict their behavior.

Axiom 20: An increase in the personal similarities we perceive between ourselves and strangers will produce an increase in our ability to manage our anxiety and our ability to accurately predict their behavior. Boundary Condition: Understanding group differences is critical only when strangers strongly identify with the group.

Axiom 21: An increase in our ability to categorize strangers in the same categories in which they categorize themselves will produce an increase in our ability to accurately predict their behavior.

Axiom 22: An increase in the degree to which we attribute strangers' behaviors to their group memberships will produce a decrease in our ability to manage our anxiety and a decease in our ability to accurately predict their behavior.

Axiom 23: An increase in the variability we perceive in strangers' groups will produce an increase in our ability to manage our anxiety and an increase in our ability to accurately predict their behavior.

Axiom 24: An increase in our positive expectations regarding strangers' behavior will produce a decrease in our anxiety and an increase in our confidence in predicting their behavior.

Axiom 25: An increase in our awareness of strangers' violations of our positive expectations and/or their confirming our negative expectations will produce an increase in our anxiety and a decrease in our confidence in predicting their behavior.

The way we categorize strangers affects the amount of anxiety and uncertainty we experience interacting with them. The amount of anxiety and uncertainty we experience, however, is mediated by the situation in which we are interacting with strangers.

Situational Processes

The situation in which we interact with strangers affects our communication with them. One of the major ways that situations influence our behavior is in the scripts situations activate. The situations also affect whether our interactions with strangers will lead to favorable or unfavorable outcomes.

One important aspect of our perceptions of the contexts in which we come into contact with strangers is the complexity of our scripts for communication in particular situations. A script is "a coherent sequence of events expected by the individual, involving him [or her] either as a participant or an observer" (Abelson, 1976, p. 33). Scripts are cognitive structures that help us to understand the situations in which we find ourselves. The more we engage in particular activities, the more likely we are to learn scripts for the activity. We learn scripts by participating in the situation or by observing others participate (Abelson, 1976). Scripts provide guides for the conversations we have in different situations, and help us reduce the uncertainty we have about various situations (Berger & Bradac, 1982). Scripts allow us to coordinate our behavior with others in different situations without paying attention to what we are doing.

Although we have thousands of scripts, most of us do not have complex scripts for communicating with strangers. If we interact with strangers following our usual scripts, misunderstandings may occur because we assume strangers use the same perspective we do when we communicate on automatic pilot. Some scripts, however, are useful in interacting with strangers. Activating an information-seeking script, for example, reduces our anxiety about interacting with people we do not know (Leary, Kowalski, & Bergen, 1988). We may, nevertheless, have problems gathering useful information if our information-seeking script does not include gathering information about strangers' group memberships. The more we interact with strangers, the more likely we are to develop complex scripts for communicating with them. The complexity of our scripts influences our ability to manage our anxiety and uncertainty.

Scripts are not the only situational factors affecting our interaction with strangers. The conditions under which we have contact also are important. The most critical conditions that affect our anxiety and uncertainty when we interact with strangers appear to be informal interaction, working on cooperative goals, and institutional/normative support for contact with strangers. When we interact with strangers in informal situations, for example, we cannot rely on their roles to predict their behavior. We, therefore, are likely to focus on strangers' individual behavior when we gather information about them.

Cooperation is critical to establishing positive relationships with strangers. Argyle (1991) defines *cooperation* as "acting together, in a coordinated way at work, leisure, or in social relationships, in the pursuit of shared goals, the enjoyment of the joint activity, or simply furthering the relationship" (p. 4). He argues that cooperation leads to positive feelings toward the people with whom we cooperate, and we receive emotional rewards from cooperative interaction. We also are attracted to people who cooperate with us. Cooperation between members of different groups is facilitated when there is institutional or normative support for cooperation. When we work with cooperative goals with strangers, and when there is institutional and normative support for contact with strangers, we do not experience high levels of anxiety and we have confidence in our ability to predict their behavior.

The situation in which we interact with strangers affects the amount of anxiety and uncertainty we experience interacting with them. Five axioms regarding situational influences on communication, therefore, are included in the theory:

> *Axiom 26*: An increase in the complexity of our scripts for communicating with strangers will produce a decrease in our anxiety and an increase in our confidence in predicting their behavior.
>
> *Axiom 27*: An increase in the informality of the situation in which we are communicating with strangers will produce a decrease in our anxiety and an increase in our confidence in predicting their behavior.
>
> *Axiom 28*: An increase in the cooperative structure of the goals on which we work with strangers will produce a decrease in our anxiety and an increase in our confidence in predicting their behavior.
>
> *Axiom 29*: An increase in the normative and institutional support for communicating with strangers will produce a decrease in our anxiety and an increase in our confidence in predicting their behavior.
>
> *Axiom 30*: An increase in the percentage of our ingroup members present in a situation when we interact with strangers will produce a decrease in our anxiety.

The situations in which we interact with strangers affect the nature of the contact we have with strangers. The nature of the contact we have with strangers, in turn, affects whether we form connections with them. The nature of the connections we form with strangers affects the amount of anxiety and uncertainty we experience when we interact with them.

Connections to Strangers

The types of connections we form with strangers affect the amount of anxiety and uncertainty we experience communicating with them. The type of connection we form with strangers is based on our attraction toward them, how we treat them, our respect for them, the nature of the contact we have, whether we are interdependent with them, the intimacy of our relationship, and whether we share networks with them.

Attraction, or liking for others, is one of the major factors contributing to the development of relationships with others. If we are not attracted to others in some way, we do not want to form connections with them. If we are attracted to others, in contrast, we want to get to know them better. We tend to be attracted to people we perceive to be similar to us. This is especially true before we interact with others (Sunnafrank & Miller, 1981). When we have a chance to interact with people we perceive to be dissimilar to us, however, we often become attracted to them. Sunnafrank and Miller argue that this is because we recognize similarities when we interact with people we initially perceive to be dissimilar. Sunnafrank (1983) suggests that recognizing that we can predict others' behavior is an important factor contributing to our attraction to them. The degree to which we are attracted to others and want to establish an interpersonal relationship with the specific strangers also contributes to the reduction of uncertainty (Gudykunst, 1988). If we are physically or socially attracted to the strangers with whom we are communicating, our predictive uncertainty is reduced (Berger & Calabrese, 1975; Gudykunst, Chua, & Gray, 1987). Stephan and Stephan (1985) also suggest that attraction should reduce anxiety.

When we are attracted to others, treating them in a moral fashion is important to us. When we are not attracted to others, however, we might unconsciously treat them in a morally exclusive fashion. We are morally exclusive when we see individuals or groups "as *outside the boundary in which moral values, rules, and considerations of fairness apply.* Those who are morally excluded are perceived as nonentities, expendable, or undeserving; consequently, harming them appears acceptable, appropriate, or just" (Opotow, 1990, p. 1). Because moral exclusion emerges from blaming strangers and distancing ourselves psychologically from them, it leads to high levels of anxiety about interacting with strangers.[27] We have high anxiety because we do not expect those we treat in a morally exclusive fashion to apply the rules of fair play to us. When we are morally inclusive toward strangers, however, we expect strangers to apply the rules of fair play to us; we do not experience high levels of anxiety about interacting with them.

Before proceeding, I want to point out that we can affect others' moral inclusion. Blanchard, Lilly, and Vaughn (1991), for example, point out that, when we express antiprejudice sentiments, others are not likely to express prejudice when we are present. Similarly, Staub (1989) claims that "bystanders can exert a powerful influence. They can define the meaning of events and move others toward empathy and indifference. They can promote values and norms of caring, or by passivity or participation in the system they can affirm the perpetrators" (p. 87).

Treating strangers in a morally inclusive fashion is not sufficient for developing connections with them. Developing connections with strangers also requires some minimal level of respect (e.g., Taylor, 1992). The more we respect strangers, the better able we are to manage our anxiety and uncertainty. When we do not respect strangers, we are likely to avoid contact with them. When we respect strangers, in contrast, we are open to the possibility of having frequent, positive contact with them.[28]

The quantity and quality of contact we have with strangers affects our anxiety and uncertainty.[29] Stephan and Stephan (1985, 1989, 1992) argue that the quality of contact with members of different groups affects the amount of anxiety individuals experience interacting with each other. Islam and Hewstone (1993) contend that the quantity of contact we have with strangers also affects the amount of anxiety we experience.

The quantity and quality of contact we have with strangers also affects the amount of uncertainty we experience (Gudykunst, in press). Berger and Calabrese's (1975) URT, for example, posits that the more verbal communication in which we engage with others, the less uncertainty we have about their behavior. URT also suggests that the greater the intimacy of our communication with others (e.g., nonsuperficial contact), the less uncertainty we have about them. Extending URT implies that the more contact we have with strangers and the greater the quality of the contact (e.g., it meets the conditions for favorable contact outlined earlier), the more information we are able to collect about strangers and their groups, and the less uncertainty we will have. One reason for this is that the more contact we have with strangers, the more variability we perceive in their groups (Islam & Hewstone, 1993). Seeing variability in strangers' groups helps us reduce our uncertainty about individual strangers.

When we interact with strangers, we open the possibility of developing some form of ongoing relationship with them. One important aspect of ongoing relationships that affects the amount of anxiety and uncertainty we experience is the amount of interdependence between us and the other person. Our interdependence with strangers affects our communication with them. When we are interdependent with strangers, for example, we do not experience high levels of anxiety about interacting with them. When we are interdependent, we also tend to have some degree of confidence in our ability to predict their behavior. High levels of interdependence, however, may lead to overconfidence in predicting strangers' behavior. Interdependence, therefore, does not necessarily lead to accuracy in predicting strangers' behavior.

Becoming interdependent with strangers implies an ongoing relationship. Interdependence alone, however, does not explain the amount of anxiety and uncertainty we experience in ongoing relationships. The amount of intimacy present in our relationship with strangers also affects how we communicate with them. As relationships between people from different groups become more intimate (i.e., move from initial interactions to close friend), communication becomes more personalized, more synchronized, and there is less difficulty (Gudykunst, Nishida, & Chua, 1987). Group similarities appear to have a major influence on our communication in the early stages of relationship development (i.e., initial interactions and acquaintance relationships) but not in later stages of relationship development (e.g., close friend; Gudykunst, Chua, & Gray, 1987).[30]

Our interdependence with strangers and the intimacy of our relationships with them affect the amount of anxiety and uncertainty we experience. It is important to remember, however, that our relationships with strangers do not exist in isolation. Rather, they are embedded in shared social networks. Parks and Adelman (1983) point out that the relationships of individuals "do not spring from a social void. They are embedded in the ongoing social context created by partners' communication networks" (p. 56). They go on to argue that communication with partners' communication networks (i.e., their family and friends) helps us reduce uncertainty about partners because the networks provide third-party information about the partner. The amount of uncertainty we experience when we communicate with strangers also is influenced by the degree to which we share communication networks with the strangers (e.g., Gudykunst, Chua, & Gray, 1987). Shared networks also help us reduce anxiety about strangers (e.g., Dyal & Dyal, 1981). The more we know the same people that the strangers with whom we are communicating know, the more we can reduce uncertainty and anxiety.

The nature of the connections we have with strangers affects the amount of anxiety and uncertainty we experience interacting with them. Seven axioms dealing with the nature of our connections with strangers, therefore, are included in the theory:

Axiom 31: An increase in our attraction to strangers will produce a decrease in our anxiety and an increase in our confidence in predicting their behavior.

Axiom 32: An increase in our moral inclusiveness toward strangers will produce an increase in our ability to manage our anxiety.

Axiom 33: An increase in our respect for strangers will produce an increase in our ability to manage our anxiety and an increase in our ability to accurately predict their behavior.

Axiom 34: An increase in the quantity and quality of our contact with strangers and members of their groups will produce a decrease in our anxiety and an increase in our ability to accurately predict their behavior.

Axiom 35: An increase in our interdependence with strangers will produce a decrease in our anxiety and an increase in our confidence in predicting their behavior.

Axiom 36: An increase in the intimacy of our relationships with strangers will produce a decrease in our anxiety and an increase in our confidence in predicting their behavior. Boundary Condition: This axiom only applies to broad trends across stages of relationship development. Within any stage of relationship development or within specific conversations, anxiety and uncertainty will fluctuate (i.e., act as dialectics).

Axiom 37: An increase in the networks we share with strangers will produce a decrease in our anxiety and an increase in our confidence in predicting their behavior.

As indicated in the discussion of interdependence, the nature of our connections with strangers does not directly affect our ability to accurately predict their behavior. Our ability to manage our anxiety and accurately predict strangers' behavior is dependent on our ability to be mindful of our communication when we interact with them. Our ability to be mindful moderates the influence of managing anxiety and uncertainty on effective communication.

Anxiety, Uncertainty, Mindfulness, and Effective Communication

To communicate effectively with strangers, we must be able to gather the appropriate information to manage our anxiety and uncertainty. By "appropriate information" I mean information that helps us understand how strangers are interpreting what is happening when we communicate with them. To accomplish this, we must be mindful. Mindfulness involves creating new categories,[31] being open to new information, and recognizing alternative perspectives.

To accurately predict strangers' behavior, we must try to understand how they interpret the information we gather about them (i.e., recognize alternative perspectives). If we interpret information we gather about strangers from our own perspective, as we do when we communicate mindlessly, we will make inaccurate predictions. If strangers are present when we recognize that a misunderstanding might be occurring, we can ask them how they are interpreting the messages being exchanged or the behavior taking place. To do this, we must describe the message or behavior to the strangers and ask how they interpret what happened.

To make accurate predictions of and explanations for strangers' behavior, we must understand the "stocks of knowledge" (Scheff, 1990) strangers use to interpret messages.[32] Stated differently, we need knowledge of strangers' cultures and group memberships. In addition to understanding of strangers' stocks of knowledge, knowledge of their language, dialect, slang, and/or jargon facilitates the management of our anxiety and uncertainty. Second-language competence, for example, increases our ability to cope with uncertainty in cultures where the language is spoken (Naiman, Frohlich, Stern, & Todesco, 1978). Knowledge of strangers' language, dialect, or jargon also helps us manage our anxiety in communicating with strangers (Stephan & Stephan, 1985). When we have negative expectations (e.g., rigid negative attitudes or stereotypes) for strangers' behavior, we tend to look for information that confirms our expectations when we interact with them (Hamilton et al., 1990). If we have negative stereotypes of strangers' groups, for example, we expect strangers to act consistently with our stereotypes when we communicate mindlessly. We also tend to be more accurate in interpreting strangers' intentions when they are negative than when they are positive (Bodenhausen, Gaelick, & Wyer, 1987). Our negative expectations for strangers' behavior, therefore, often lead us to behave in a prejudicial fashion toward them.

Devine (1989) argues that conscious control of our reactions when our negative stereotypes are activated is necessary to control our prejudiced response to strangers. She points out that

> nonprejudiced responses are . . . a function of intentional controlled processes and require a conscious decision to behave in a nonprejudiced fashion. In addition, new responses must be learned and well practiced before they can serve as competitive responses to the automatically activated stereotype-congruent response. (p. 15)

When we are mindful of our negative expectations being violated, we can cognitively manage our reactions. Being mindful of negative expectations, therefore, allows us to manage our anxiety and increase our ability to accurately predict others' behavior.

The amount of anxiety we experience when we interact with strangers affects the quality of the information we gather. Wilder and Shapiro (1989) point out that, when anxiety is high (e.g., above our maximum thresholds), we tend to process information in a simplistic fashion. Wilder (1993) points out that high levels of anxiety generate arousal, which leads to self-focused attention that distracts us and decreases our ability to make differentiations regarding others. The distraction also leads us to process information in a superficial fashion. When we are distracted, we tend to rely on existing stereotypes (Bodenhausen, 1993, draws a similar conclusion from a different perspective). Pennebraker (1989) also points out that when our anxiety is high, we use a narrow perspective in looking at the world, we tend not to think about the causes or effects of our behavior, and we tend not to be aware of our emotions. This line of reasoning suggests that we are not able to gather new or accurate information about strangers when our anxiety is high and, therefore, we are not able to make accurate predictions or explanations of strangers' behavior. If our anxiety is high, we must first manage our anxiety (e.g., bring it below our maximum threshold) before we try to gather information to predict strangers' behavior.

We cannot communicate effectively if our anxiety and uncertainty levels are too high or too low. Effective communication requires that our anxiety and uncertainty be between our minimum and maximum thresholds. The optimal levels of anxiety and uncertainty that facilitate effective communication with strangers are somewhere between our minimum and maximum thresholds.[33] For uncertainty, our optimal level is the point at which we think that strangers' behavior is predictable, but we also recognize that we may not be able to accurately explain their behavior. For anxiety, the optimal level is the point where we feel comfortable interacting with strangers, but we still have sufficient anxiety that we are not complacent in our interactions with them.

Our ability to mindfully manage our anxiety and uncertainty is critical to effectively communicating with strangers. We cannot communicate effectively if our anxiety or uncertainty is too high or too low. When our anxiety and our uncertainty are between our minimum and maximum thresholds, we can communicate effectively with strangers when we are mindful. Ten axioms summarize the relationships among anxiety, uncertainty, mindfulness, and effective communication:

Axiom 38: An increase in our ability to gather appropriate information about strangers will produce an increase in our ability to accurately predict their behavior.

Axiom 39: An increase in our ability to describe strangers' behavior will produce an increase in our ability to accurately predict their behavior. Boundary Condition: This is only possible if we are mindful of the process of communication, and our anxiety and uncertainty are between our minimum and maximum thresholds.

Axiom 40: An increase in our understanding of the stocks of knowledge of the groups of which strangers are members will produce an increase in our ability to manage our anxiety and our ability to accurately predict their behavior. Boundary Condition: This axiom only holds when we are mindful.

Axiom 41: An increase in our knowledge of strangers' language (dialect, jargon, slang) will produce an increase in our ability to manage our anxiety and an increase in our ability to accurately predict their behavior.

Axiom 42: An increase in our openness to new information about strangers and our interactions with them will produce an increase in our ability to accurately predict their behavior. Boundary Condition: This axiom holds only when our anxiety and uncertainty are between our minimum and maximum thresholds.

Axiom 43: An increase in our ability to place strangers in new categories (or recognize how strangers are different than other members of their groups) will produce an increase in our ability to accurately predict their behavior. Boundary Condition: This axiom only holds when our anxiety and uncertainty are between our minimum and maximum thresholds.

Axiom 44: An increase in our awareness of the perspectives strangers use to interpret our messages (and the perspectives strangers use to transmit their messages to us) will produce an increase in our ability to accurately predict their behavior. Boundary Condition: This axiom only holds when our anxiety and uncertainty are between our minimum and maximum thresholds.

Axiom 45: An increase in our anxiety above our maximum thresholds or a decrease below our minimum thresholds when we interact with strangers will produce a decrease in our ability to accurately predict their behavior.

Axiom 46: An increase in our ability to be mindful when our negative expectations for strangers' behavior are activated will produce an increase in our ability to manage our anxiety and an increase in our ability to accurately predict their behavior.

Axiom 47: An increase in our ability to manage our anxiety about interacting with strangers *and* an increase in the accuracy of our predictions and explanations regarding their behavior will produce an increase in the effectiveness of our communication. Boundary Condition: This axiom only holds when we are mindful. Anxiety and uncertainty below our minimum thresholds will not produce increases in our effectiveness; anxiety and uncertainty above our maximum threshold will produce decreases in effectiveness.

While these 10 axioms are the most critical for effective communication, the preceding 37 axioms provide ways that we can successfully manage our anxiety and uncertainty when we communicate with strangers.

Theorems

Theorems can be generated by logically combining the axioms. To illustrate, if Axioms 7 and 8 are combined, the theorem that there is a positive association between our need for group inclusion and sustaining our self-conceptions can be generated. This theorem is consistent with J. H. Turner's (1988) theory of motivation. Some theorems generated will be consistent with previous research and some will form hypotheses for future research. To illustrate, combination of Axioms 20 and 31 yields the similarity-attraction hypothesis, which has received extensive empirical support (e.g., Byrne, 1971). Combination of Axioms 12 and 13 yields the theorem that the rigidity of our attitudes is related negatively to our ability to process information complexly. Not all axioms should be combined to form theorems. Some combinations of axioms will involve the fallacy of the excluded middle and should not be generated. To illustrate, if A → C and B → C, it can be deduced that A and B are related. The fallacy of the excluded middle involves not recognizing that there may be another variable mediating the relationships between the two variables (e.g., A → D → B).

VARIABILITY IN ANXIETY/UNCERTAINTY MANAGEMENT

Some might argue that the theory presented to this point is complete. The version of the theory presented in the preceding sections, however, would have to be limited to the United States. For the theory to apply in other cultures, culture must be incorporated. I assume that the processes involved in AUM generalize across cultures. Anxiety and uncertainty exist in all cultures. How people in the cultures define them, however, varies.[34] Incorporating culture in the theory requires a way to treat it as a theoretical variable. Foschi and Hales (1979), for example, point out that when culture is treated as a theoretical variable "culture x and culture y serve to operationally define a characteristic *a*, which the two cultures exhibit to different degrees" (p. 246). In generating the axioms regarding cross-cultural variability, I use the four dimensions of cultural variability Hofstede (1980) isolated: individualism-collectivism (IC), uncertainty avoidance (UA), power distance (PD), and masculinity-femininity (MF).[35]

Dimensions of Cultural Variability

Individualism-collectivism (IC) is the major dimension of cultural variability used to explain cross-cultural differences in behavior.[36] Individuals' goals take precedence over the group's goals in individualistic cultures, while the group's goals take precedence over individuals' goals in collectivistic cultures. In individualistic cultures, "people are supposed to look after themselves and their immediate family only," while in collectivistic cultures, "people belong to ingroups or collectivities which are supposed to look after them in exchange for loyalty" (Hofstede & Bond, 1984, p. 419). People in individualistic cultures tend to be universalistic and apply the same value standards to all. People in collectivistic cultures, in contrast, tend to be particularistic and, therefore, apply different value standards for members of their ingroups and outgroups.

Triandis (1988) argues that the relative importance of ingroups is one of the major factors that differentiates individualistic and collectivistic cultures. Ingroups are "groups of people about whose welfare one is concerned, with whom one is willing to cooperate without demanding equitable returns, and separation from whom leads to discomfort or even pain" (Triandis, 1988, p. 75). People in individualistic cultures are members of many specific ingroups (e.g., family, religion, social clubs, profession) that might influence their behavior in any particular social situation. Because they are members of many ingroups, specific ingroups exert relatively little influence on individuals' behavior. People in collectivistic cultures are members of a few general ingroups (e.g., work group, university, family) that have a strong influence on their behavior across situations. While the ingroup may be the same in individualistic and collectivistic cultures, the sphere of its influence is different. The sphere of influence in an individualistic culture is very specific (e.g., the ingroup affects behavior in very specific circumstances), while the sphere of influence in a collectivistic culture is very general (e.g., the ingroup affects behavior in many different aspects of a person's life).

The way people in individualistic and collectivistic cultures view themselves (i.e., their self-concepts) also differs. Markus and Kitayama (1991) call the different self-conceptions independent construal of self and an interdependent construal of self. Independent self-construals tend to predominate in individualistic cultures and interdependent self-construals tend to predominate in collectivistic cultures (Gudykunst et al., 1994).

In comparison with members of cultures low in uncertainty avoidance (UA), members of cultures high in UA have a lower tolerance "for uncertainty and ambiguity, which expresses itself in higher levels of anxiety and energy release, greater need for formal rules and absolute truth, and less tolerance for people or groups with deviant ideas or behavior" (Hofstede, 1979, p. 395). There is a strong desire for consensus in high UA cultures, therefore, deviant behavior is not acceptable. People in high UA cultures tend to display emotions more than people in low UA cultures. People in low UA cultures have lower stress levels and weaker superegos and accept dissent and taking risks more than people in high UA cultures.

Hofstede (1991) points out that UA should not be equated with risk avoidance. People in "uncertainty avoiding cultures shun ambiguous situations. People in such cultures look for a structure in their . . .

relationships which makes events clearly interpretable and predictable" (p. 116). Hofstede summarizes the view of people in high UA cultures as "what is different, is dangerous" (p. 119), and the credo of people in low UA cultures as "what is different, is curious" (p. 119). Different degrees of UA exist in every culture, but one tends to predominate.

Power distance (PD) is "the extent to which the less powerful members of institutions and organizations accept that power is distributed unequally" (Hofstede & Bond, 1984, p. 419). Individuals from high PD cultures accept power as part of society. Hofstede (1991) points out that "in small power distance countries there is limited dependence of subordinates on bosses, and a preference for consultation, that is, *interdependence* between boss and subordinate. . . . In large power distance countries there is considerable dependence of subordinates on bosses" (p. 27). Low and high PD tendencies exist in all cultures, but one tends to predominate.

People in highly masculine cultures value things, power, and assertiveness, while people in cultures low on masculinity or high on femininity value quality of life and nurturance (Hofstede, 1980). Members of highly masculine cultures emphasize differentiated sex roles, performance, ambition, decisiveness, and independence. Members of cultures low on masculinity, in contrast, value fluid sex roles, quality of life, service, intuition, and interdependence. Both masculinity and femininity exist in all cultures, but one pattern tends to predominate.

I take the position that both ends of each of the dimensions of cultural variability can exist in all cultures. To illustrate, individualism and collectivism exist in all cultures, but one tends to predominate. Because there is variability within cultures, each of these dimensions of cultural variability also operates at the individual level.[37] There are three individual-level equivalents of cultural IC (Gudykunst et al., 1994); personality equivalents of IC are idiocentrism-allocentrism (Triandis, Leung, Villareal, & Clack, 1985), IC values (Schwartz & Bilsky, 1990), or independent and interdependent self construals (Markus & Kitayama, 1991). The individual-level equivalent of cultural UA is uncertainty orientation, while psychological sex roles are the individual equivalent of cultural MF, and egalitarianism is the individual-level equivalent of cultural PD (Gudykunst, 1993).

The axioms regarding variability are stated differently than the axioms in the main part of the theory. Kashima (1989) argues that it is not possible to test causal effects attributed to culture. In generating predictions regarding variability in AUM processes, I therefore have not worded the axioms as causal statements. Rather, the axioms are worded as statements of association. This wording has several advantages. First, the wording recognizes that cultures vary in the degree to which they demonstrate the various dimensions of cultural variability, and it does not treat the dimensions as simple dichotomies. The wording used, however, can easily be translated into "mean difference" hypotheses. Second, the wording used allows the axioms to be tested at the cultural level of analysis (i.e., correlating country scores on the various dimensions of cultural variability with cultural mean scores on the variables involved in the axioms). Third, the wording used allows individual-level equivalents for the dimensions of cultural variability to be substituted in testing the axioms within cultures. Let's begin with the self and self-concept.

Self and Self-Concept

The self and self-concept processes operating in AUM are affected by IC. Members of individualistic cultures tend to emphasize the use of independent self construals. Members of collectivistic cultures, in contrast, emphasize the use of interdependent self construals. Members of collectivistic cultures emphasize their ingroups and fitting in as sources of collective self-esteem, and members of individualistic cultures emphasize their uniqueness and separateness as sources of personal self-esteem (Markus & Kitayama, 1991). Because of the importance placed on fitting in, avoiding shame is more important in collectivistic cultures than in individualistic cultures (Creighton, 1990). Because of the emphasis on standing out and achieving, feeling pride is more important for members of individualistic cultures than for members of collectivistic cultures.

Six axioms in the theory deal with variability in the self and self-concept (the corresponding axiom numbers from the main theory are presented in parentheses):

> *Axiom 48* (1): An increase in collectivism will be associated with an increase in the degree social identities influence behavior when interacting with strangers.
>
> *Axiom 49* (2): An increase in individualism will be associated with an increase in the degree personal identities influence behavior when interacting with strangers.
>
> *Axiom 50* (3): An increase in individualism will be associated with an increase in the use of independent self construals to guide behavior when interacting with strangers; an increase in collectivism will be associated with an increase in the use of interdependent self construals to guide behavior when interacting with strangers.

Axiom 51 (4): An increase in collectivism will be associated with an increase in dependence on ingroups for self-esteem when interacting with strangers.

Axiom 52 (5): An increase in individualism will be associated with an increase in the effect of our self-esteem (pride) on behavior when interacting with strangers.

Axiom 53 (6): An increase in collectivism will be associated with an increase in the shame experienced when interacting with strangers.

The self and self-concept are not the only AUM processes that vary. Our motivation to communicate with strangers also varies systematically across and within cultures.

Motivation

Meeting the need for group inclusion is more important for members of collectivistic cultures than for members of individualistic cultures. Given the emphasis on the group, members of collectivistic cultures are most concerned with sustaining their interdependent self construals and feeling secure in their social identities. Members of individualistic cultures, in contrast, are most concerned with sustaining their independent self construals and feeling secure in their personal identities.

Members of individualistic cultures tend to use person-based information to predict others' behavior (Gudykunst & Nishida, 1986a). Members of collectivistic cultures, on the other hand, tend to use group-based information to predict others' behavior. Because members of collectivistic cultures draw a strong distinction between the ingroup and the outgroup, they tend not to support the self-conceptions of members of outgroups (including strangers' self-conceptions).

Five axioms in the theory deal with the role of variability in motivation:

Axiom 54 (7): An increase in collectivism will be associated with an increase in the need for a sense of group inclusion when interacting with strangers.

Axiom 55 (8): An increase in collectivism will be associated with an increase in the need to sustain interdependent self-conceptions when interacting with strangers; an increase in individualism will be associated with an increase in the need to sustain independent self-conceptions when interacting with strangers.

Axiom 56 (9): An increase in individualism will be associated with an increase in the degree to which strangers confirm self-conceptions.

Axiom 57 (10): An increase in individualism will be associated with an increase in the use of person-based information to predict strangers' behavior; an increase in collectivism will be associated with an increase in the use of group-based information to predict strangers' behavior.

Axiom 58 (11): An increase in individualism will be associated with an increase in the sense of security in personal identities when interacting with strangers; an increase in collectivism will be associated with an increase in the sense of security in social identities when interacting with strangers.

Motivation to communicate with strangers is closely related to reactions to strangers. Reactions to strangers vary systematically within and across cultures.

Reactions to Strangers

PD appears to be related to individuals' ability to process information complexly. The ability to process information complexly is associated with the degree of differentiation in individuals' cognitive systems. The greater the differentiation in cognitive systems, the greater the field independence. Witkin and Berry (1975) argue that field dependence is associated with "social settings characterized by insistence on adherence to authority" (p. 46). These settings are more likely to occur in high PD cultures than in low PD cultures.

Rigidity of attitudes toward strangers and tolerance for ambiguity are affected by the UA dimension of cultural variability. In high UA cultures, people want consensus and deviant behavior is viewed as unacceptable (Hofstede, 1980). Also, in high UA cultures, people have a low tolerance for ambiguity.

Members of individualistic cultures monitor their self-presentations more than members of collectivistic cultures, while members of collectivistic cultures are more concerned with social appropriateness than members of individualistic cultures (Gudykunst, Gao, Nishida, Nadamitsu, & Sakai, 1992). Because members of collectivistic cultures draw a strong distinction between the ingroup and outgroup, they tend not to empathize with members of outgroups (e.g., strangers). For strangers to be accepted in collectivistic cultures, they must accommodate their behavior to members of the ingroup. Some degree of accommodation also is necessary in individualistic cultures, but the expectation for accommodation is not as high as in collectivistic cultures because there is not a strong distinction between ingroup and outgroup.[38]

Seven axioms in the theory focus on variability in reactions to strangers:

Axiom 59 (12): An increase in power distance will be associated with a decrease in the ability to complexly process information about strangers.

Axiom 60 (13): An increase in uncertainty avoidance will be associated with an increase in the rigidity of attitudes toward strangers.

Axiom 61 (14): An increase in individualism will be associated with an increase in self-monitoring when interacting with strangers; an increase in collectivism is associated with an increase in concern for social appropriateness when interacting with strangers.

Axiom 62 (15): An increase in cultural uncertainty avoidance will be associated with a decrease in the ability to tolerate ambiguity when interacting with strangers.

Axiom 63 (16): An increase in collectivism will be associated with a decrease in the ability to empathize with strangers.

Axiom 64 (17): An increase in collectivism will be associated with an increase in the degree to which strangers accommodate their behavior.

Axiom 65 (18): An increase in collectivism will be associated with an increase in the ability to adapt communication when interacting with strangers.

Reactions to strangers influence the way they are categorized. Social categorizations of strangers also vary systematically across and within cultures.

Social Categorization

Members of collectivistic cultures draw a greater distinction between members of ingroups and outgroups than members of individualistic cultures (Triandis, 1988). This leads to a differentiation in how members of collectivistic cultures communicate with strangers and members of their ingroups (Gudykunst, Gao, Schmidt, et al., 1992). Because members of individualistic cultures identify with numerous ingroups, there is little differentiation in how they communicate with strangers and members of their ingroups.[39] The emphasis on group memberships and the relatively few ingroups in collectivistic cultures lead to collectivists being better able to categorize strangers in the same categories (groups) in which they place themselves than individualists are.

Because members of collectivistic cultures focus on group-based information, it is easier for them to isolate similarities and differences between their groups and strangers' groups than for members of individualistic cultures. Members of individualistic cultures, in contrast, can more easily recognize personal similarities and differences between themselves and strangers than members of collectivistic cultures because they focus on person-based information. The focus on group-based information leads members of collectivistic cultures to attribute strangers' behavior to their group memberships more than it does members of individualistic cultures. Members of collectivistic cultures, however, are likely to see more variability in strangers' groups than are members of individualistic cultures (Triandis, McCusker, & Hui, 1990).

If people from high UA cultures interact with strangers in a situation where there are not clear rules, they may ignore the strangers—treat them as though they do not exist. Because strangers may deviate from expectations, members of high UA cultures tend to have less positive expectations for interacting with strangers than members of low UA cultures. Members of high UA cultures, however, tend to be more aware of when strangers violate their expectations than members of low UA cultures.

Seven axioms in the theory deal with variability in categorization of strangers:

> *Axiom 66* (19): An increase in collectivism will be associated with an increase in understanding of similarities and differences between ingroups and strangers' groups.
>
> *Axiom 67* (20): An increase in individualism will be associated with an increase in perceiving personal similarities with strangers.
>
> *Axiom 68* (21): An increase in collectivism will be associated with an increase in the ability to categorize strangers in the same categories as they categorize themselves.
>
> *Axiom 69* (22): An increase in collectivism will be associated with an increase in the degree to which strangers' behaviors are attributed to their group memberships.
>
> *Axiom 70* (23): An increase in individualism will be associated with a decrease in the variability perceived in strangers' groups.
>
> *Axiom 71* (24): An increase in uncertainty avoidance will be associated with a decrease in positive expectations regarding strangers' behavior.
>
> *Axiom 72* (25): An increase in uncertainty avoidance will be associated with an increase in awareness of strangers' violations of positive expectations and/or their confirming negative expectations.

The way strangers are categorized is affected by the situations in which the interaction takes place. The way individuals respond in situations also varies systematically.

Situational Processes

People in high UA cultures try to avoid ambiguity and, therefore, develop rules and rituals for virtually every possible situation in which they might find themselves, including interacting with strangers. Interaction with strangers in cultures high in UA may be highly ritualistic and/or very polite.[40] Interaction with strangers may be avoided in informal situations that do not have clear norms to guide behavior in high UA cultures. The rituals that are developed in high UA cultures provide clear scripts for interaction and allow individuals to attune their behavior with strangers.[41] The scripts for interacting with strangers are much more complex in high UA cultures than in low UA cultures. Because strangers may deviate from expectations, there is little normative or institutional support for interacting with strangers in high UA cultures.

The degree to which individuals cooperate with strangers should be a function of PD. Power differences are expected in high PD cultures. People with less power are expected to do what people with more power tell them to do. This leads to low levels of cooperation between people with different amounts of power. Because strangers are outsiders, they have less power than insiders. It is expected, therefore, that there is less cooperation with strangers in high PD cultures than in low PD cultures.

Five axioms in the theory deal with variability in situational processes:

Axiom 73 (26): An increase in uncertainty avoidance will be associated with an increase in the complexity of scripts for communicating with strangers.

Axiom 74 (27): An increase in uncertainty avoidance will be associated with a decrease in the informality of the situation in which interaction with strangers occurs.

Axiom 75 (28): An increase in power distance will be associated with a decrease in the cooperative structure of the goals on which work occurs with strangers.

Axiom 76 (29): An increase in uncertainty avoidance will be associated with a decrease in the normative and institutional support for interacting with strangers.

Axiom 77 (30): An increase in collectivism will be associated with an increase in the percentage of ingroup members present in situations when interacting with strangers.

The situations in which individuals interact with strangers affect whether they form connections with them. The way individuals form connections varies across and within cultures.

Connections to Strangers

Interacting with strangers often is avoided in high UA cultures because strangers' behavior is viewed as unpredictable. This leads to low levels of attraction toward strangers. Members of low UA cultures, therefore, should be more attracted to and respect strangers more than members of high UA cultures.

The distinction between the ingroup and outgroup drawn by members of collectivistic cultures leads to members of collectivistic cultures having less contact and fewer shared networks with strangers than do members of individualistic cultures. It also leads to members of collectivistic cultures seeing relationships with strangers as less intimate than do members of individualistic cultures. Because outgroup members are viewed as different than ingroup members, there is more moral exclusiveness toward outgroup members in collectivistic cultures than in individualistic cultures.

MF should have the most direct effect on the interdependence individuals perceive with strangers. Given that members of high MF cultures value independence and members of low MF cultures value interdependence, there should be greater interdependence between individuals and strangers in low MF cultures than in high MF cultures.

Seven axioms in the theory deal with variability in connections to strangers:

> *Axiom 78* (31): An increase in uncertainty avoidance will be associated with a decrease in attraction to strangers.
>
> *Axiom 79* (32): An increase in individualism will be associated with an increase in moral inclusiveness toward strangers.
>
> *Axiom 80* (33): An increase in uncertainty avoidance will be associated with a decrease in respect for strangers.
>
> *Axiom 81* (34): An increase in individualism will be associated with an increase in the quantity or quality of contact with strangers.
>
> *Axiom 82* (35): An increase in femininity will be associated with an increase in interdependence with strangers.
>
> *Axiom 83* (36): An increase in individualism will be associated with an increase in the perceived intimacy of relationships with strangers.
>
> *Axiom 84* (37): An increase in individualism will be associated with an increase in the networks shared with strangers.

The connections individuals form with strangers affect how they manage their anxiety and uncertainty. The way people manage anxiety and uncertainty varies across and within cultures.

Anxiety, Uncertainty, Mindfulness, and Effective Communication

Members of individualistic cultures seek out person-based information to reduce uncertainty about strangers, and members of collectivistic cultures seek out group-based information to reduce uncertainty (Gudykunst & Nishida, 1986a). The focus on person-based information leads members of individualistic cultures to search for personal similarities when communicating with strangers. The focus on group-based information, in contrast, leads members of collectivistic cultures to search for group similarities when communicating with strangers. Members of collectivistic cultures, however, are likely to see more variability in strangers' groups (outgroups) than are members of individualistic cultures (Triandis, McCusker, & Hui, 1990).

Members of collectivistic cultures emphasize the importance of context in explaining others' behavior more than do members of individualistic cultures (e.g., Miller, 1984). The emphasis on context in collectivistic cultures affects other aspects of their communication as well. To illustrate, adapting and accommodating to the context in which they are communicating is an important part of the high-context communication patterns used in collectivistic cultures (Hall, 1976). Further, because cognitions are context independent in individualistic cultures (Markus & Kitayama, 1991), members of individualistic cultures should be more aware of strangers' perspectives and be better able to understand the stocks of knowledge used by strangers.

Ten axioms in the theory deal with variability in anxiety, uncertainty, and mindfulness:

Axiom 85 (38): An increase in collectivism will be associated with an increase in the ability to gather appropriate information about strangers.

Axiom 86 (39): An increase in individualism will be associated with an increase in the ability to describe strangers' behavior.

Axiom 87 (40): An increase in individualism will be associated with an increase in understanding the stocks of knowledge of strangers' groups. Boundary Condition: This axiom holds when individuals are mindful.

Axiom 88 (41): An increase in collectivism will be associated with an increase in our knowledge of strangers' language (dialect, jargon, slang).

Axiom 89 (42): An increase in individualism will be associated with an increase in openness to new information about strangers' behavior.

Axiom 90 (43): An increase in individualism will be associated with an increase in the ability to place strangers in new categories (or recognize how strangers are different than other members of their groups).

Axiom 91 (44): An increase in individualism will be associated with an increase in awareness of the perspectives strangers use to interpret others' messages.

Axiom 92 (45): An increase in uncertainty avoidance will be associated with an increase in anxiety about interacting with strangers.[42]

Axiom 93 (46): An increase in individualism will be associated with an increase in the ability to be mindful when negative expectations for strangers' behavior are activated.

Axiom 94 (47): An increase in uncertainty avoidance will be associated with a decrease in the ability to manage anxiety about interacting with strangers; an increase in individualism will be associated with an increase in the accuracy of predictions and explanations regarding strangers' behavior. Boundary Condition: This axiom holds when individuals are mindful.

These 10 axioms conclude the statements explaining variability in AUM processes.

Conclusion

Some may argue that the theory is overcomplicated with 47 axioms in the main theory and 47 axioms on variability in AUM processes. It is, nevertheless, important to keep in mind that the goals of a theory must be balanced with the number of theoretical statements when theories are constructed. Because one of the goals of the theory is to apply the theory, the axioms cannot be highly abstract. While increasing the abstractness of the axioms could increase parsimony, it would decrease applicability. The present form of the theory allows direct application in many practical areas including, but not limited to, improving the effectiveness of communication, managing diversity, managing conflict, and adapting to new cultural environments.

When I specified the scope conditions of the theory, I did not include intercultural adaptation. The theory can be extended, however, so that its scope includes intercultural adaptation. The original version of the theory (Gudykunst, 1988) explicitly focused on effective communication and adaptation, and the special version of the theory (Gudykunst & Hammer, 1988b) specifically addresses adaptation. To extend the current version to adaptation, minor modifications are necessary. First, because the people adapting to the new cultural environments are the strangers, Axioms 1-46 need to be reworded. To illustrate, Axiom 19 would be reworded as follows: An increase in strangers' understanding of the similarities and differences between their culture and the host culture will produce an increase in their ability to manage their anxiety and their ability to accurately predict host nationals' behavior. Second, ability to "adapt to the host culture" needs to be substituted for "effectiveness of communication" in Axiom 47. Third, two additional axioms that focus on issues specific to adaptation need to be added: (95) An increase in the pluralistic tendencies in the host culture will produce a decrease in the anxiety strangers experience when entering the host culture (Axiom 13 in the special version). (96) An increase in the permanence of strangers' stay in the host culture will produce an increase in the anxiety they experience entering the host culture (Axiom 22 of the special version).

Because AUM theory is a theory in the process of being developed, refinements are still necessary. One area where refinements are needed is in incorporating the dialectical aspects of uncertainty and anxiety into the theory. As indicated earlier, the uncertainty dialectic involves predictability-novelty (similar to Baxter's, 1988, dialectic). The anxiety dialectic involves fear-trust. Fully incorporating dialectics into the theory requires developing a way to write theoretical statements that include causal relationships and dialectical relationships. At the present time I have not been able to develop a satisfactory way of doing this, so dialectics are incorporated as boundary statements in the axioms.

Another area where the theory needs elaboration involves the scope of the theory. While two axioms dealing with the interdependence and the intimacy of relationships are included, the theory is not designed to explain how or why we form relationships with members of other groups. Many factors dealing with the formation of relationships are included in the theory (e.g., self-concept support, attraction), but additional concepts need to be incorporated for AUM to be considered a theory of relationship development (including outcome variables).

A final area where additional specification is needed is in the relationship between the management of anxiety and uncertainty and effective communication. To illustrate, how can individuals recognize their optimal levels of uncertainty and anxiety and manage their anxiety and uncertainty so that they are at optimal levels to increase the effectiveness of their communication? Similarly, the role of mindfulness in moderating this process needs to be more fully explicated. When, for example, do we want to be mindful? One issue that needs to be addressed to increase the practicality of the theory is to isolate the cues individuals can use to trigger mindfulness when they perceive that misunderstandings are occurring.[43] We all make choices, whether conscious or not, of when we want to communicate effectively. In those situations where we want to communicate effectively, we need to know when and how to, that is, become mindful of our communication. Including these issues in the theory will increase its practical applicability.

To summarize, I have outlined the development of the theory and updated the axioms. The current version of the theory is not a finished product. Rather, the theory is in a constant state of revision. The current version, nevertheless, does accomplish its purpose in that it makes the net finer than in the 1993 version.

NOTES

1. The original version of the theory only focused on initial interactions. It has been extended, however, to other relationships as well (see Berger & Gudykunst, 1991).

2. This criterion for selecting a theory to guide research often is overlooked, but it is critical.

3. This assumption is supported, in part, by the emergence of the uncertainty avoidance in Hofstede's (1980) study of the dimensions of cultural variability. There also is extensive writing on uncertainty in ethnographic descriptions of communication in cultures around the world. Some writers have questioned this assumption. Ting-Toomey (1989a), for example, suggests that uncertainty may be a Western-biased concept. I disagree. Most writing on Eastern cultures that draws on Confucianism and its emphasis on interrelatedness of people suggests that people place a great emphasis on others' reactions to their behavior when deciding how to behave (e.g., Yang, 1981). This is clearly a predictive uncertainty process. What is being predicted, however, differs from that emphasized in Western cultures. It also is possible that explanatory uncertainty may not be emphasized in Eastern cultures. Chang and Holt (1991) point out that Chinese do not search for causal explanations for others' behavior; rather, they attribute it to *yuan*. Concepts such as yuan must be incorporated when the theory is extended to deal with issues of relationship development, but they are not necessary when the focus is on effective communication.

4. A name may seem like a small thing when it comes to theory, but this is *not* the case. Until I named the theory, many people assumed that it was still totally consistent with URT and they referred to the theory as URT. While AUM is derived from URT, it is clearly a different theory.

5. Obviously my presentation of the rationale for the theory must be limited because of space considerations.

6. There are different types of relationships we can form with strangers (see Gudykunst, 1985b).

7. I see thresholds for uncertainty and anxiety as catastrophe points. When uncertainty or anxiety goes above our maximum thresholds or below our minimum thresholds, there is not a linear change in the effectiveness of communication. Rather, effectiveness drops dramatically. It is important to recognize that individuals' thresholds will differ. Individuals can learn to recognize their thresholds and this can help them improve the effectiveness of their communication. Witte (1993) supports the argument for thresholds from a different theoretical position.

8. When uncertainty is above the maximum thresholds, people in different cultures will respond differently. European Americans, for example, gather person-based information and Japanese gather group-based information (Gudykunst & Nishida, 1986a), while Native Americans will be silent (Basso, 1970). Wright and Phillips (1980) argue there are cultural differences in probabilistic thinking about uncertainty. These are linked to individualism-collectivism; people in individualistic cultures tend to think probabilistically, while people in collectivistic cultures tend to think nonprobabilistically (Gudykunst, 1988).

9. Uncertainty can increase or decrease in relationships. See Planalp, Rutherford, and Honeycutt (1988) for a discussion of uncertainty increases. The fluctuations of uncertainty over time will be similar to those that Van Lear (1991) describes for openness. One reason uncertainty may increase is because of others' equivocal messages (Bavelas, Black, Chovil, & Mullett, 1990).

10. My focus on anxiety is broader than what typically is discussed as communication apprehension. Much of the research on communication apprehension (e.g., McCroskey, 1984), however, can be integrated with the argument presented here.

11. Avoidance was the most widely used strategy in unobtrusive studies of interracial interaction (Crosby, Bromley, & Saxe, 1980).

12. This relationship probably only holds when uncertainty and anxiety are between the minimum and maximum thresholds.

13. Because my concern is with explaining effective communication and I see the management of anxiety and uncertainty as the mediating processes, I focus on explaining these processes. It is important to recognize, however, that the outcome of one interaction, the effectiveness of communication, affects the amount of anxiety and uncertainty we experience in the next interaction. Similarly, the amount of anxiety and uncertainty we experience in one interaction also affects the superficial causes in the next interaction. While the relationships are reciprocal across interactions, I focus on the unidirectional aspects of the processes that we can use to improve the quality of our communication.

14. The theory has been used to design and implement general cultural awareness training programs, cultural adjustment training programs, and training programs designed to help participants manage conflict between members of different groups. It also has been applied to diplomacy (Gudykunst, 1990) and interpersonal communication effectiveness (Gudykunst, Ting-Toomey, Sudweeks, & Stewart, 1995).

15. One reason people often do not see theories as "practical" (to use Kurt Lewin's term) is that the theoretical statements are highly abstract with no connection to everyday life. I have stated the theorems at a lower level to make them easier to apply. This, however, necessitates an increase in the number of statements needed.

16. Simmel uses *stranger* as a figure-ground phenomenon; the person approaching the new group is a stranger. I am using the term more broadly. It is important to recognize that both people are potential strangers, but the person approaching the new group will be expected to adapt the most. The two people form a communication system.

17. The theory can be used to help us improve the effectiveness of our communication when we want to do so. Obviously, we should not "hit our head against a brick wall." If strangers do not try to communicate effectively with us, we must make a decision on whether to continue our efforts at some point.

18. See Brewer (1991) and Deaux (1991) for recent discussions of social identity.

19. All encounters involve both interpersonal and intergroup components. For a more complete discussion of this issue, see Gudykunst and Kim (1992). One identity, however, tends to predominate in any encounter (R. H. Turner, 1987).

20. This axiom is slightly different than presented in the 1988 version of the theory. I have modified the axiom to suggest the same relationship between social identity and uncertainty and anxiety. There probably is an "optimal" strength of social identity for facilitating the management of uncertainty and anxiety. This, however, is beyond the scope of this chapter.

21. Confronting the anxiety we experience strengthens the self (e.g., May, 1977).

22. Snyder's conceptualization of self-monitoring is biased toward individualistic cultures. Gudykunst, Gao, Nishida, et al. (1992) present a derived etic conceptualization and measurement.

23. Their research did not yield a statistically significant association. The relationship was in the predicted direction.

24. See Zerubavel (1991) for a discussion of categorization in everyday life.

25. I believe that Sunnafrank's (1986) notion of predicted outcome value is part of our expectations and can easily be incorporated into the current theory.

26. Many of the ideas presented in this section were first brought to my attention in Kellermann (1993).

27. See Staub (1989) for an extensive discussion of these issues.

28. See Sampson (1993), Selznick (1992), Smiley (1992), and Wilson (1993) for recent discussion of the importance of respect.

29. Knowledge-based affect theory (Demarath, 1993) also postulates that the significance of our experiences is a function of their frequency, stability, and effect.

30. See Gudykunst (1989b) for an elaboration of the argument being made here.

31. If you disagree with Langer's assumption that we cannot stop categorizing, you can think of creating new categories as recognizing how strangers are different than members of their ingroups. I think these are two ways of describing the same processes and they lead to the same outcomes.

32. This use is consistent with Keesing's (1974) definition of culture, which I have used in most recent writings (see Gudykunst, 1991; Gudykunst & Kim, 1992).

33. Witte (1993) discusses critical points rather than optimal levels. She argues that the critical point is where anxiety exceeds confidence in predictions.

34. This argument is compatible with Hamill's (1990) contention that humans are endowed with innate logical structures, but cultures create unique meanings out of the innate knowledge.

35. There are other dimensions of cultural variability that could be used, such as Confucian work dynamism (Chinese Culture Connection, 1987) and cultural tightness (Pelto, 1968). See Smith and Bond (1993) and Triandis (1994) for recent discussions of alternative dimensions. My focus is on how culture influences communication. Our communication also influences our culture, but this process occurs over long periods of time and does not occur within any particular interaction (the focus of the theory). Not discussing the effect of communication on culture does not mean that I am giving this idea "lip service" as B. J. Hall (1992) suggests; it means that it is outside the scope of the theory.

36. See Hofstede (1980, 1991), Kim, Triandis, Kagitcibasi, and Yoon (1994), Kluckhohn and Strodtbeck (1961), and Triandis (1988, 1990, in press) for extended discussions of this dimension of cultural variability. It should be noted that this dimension not only is isolated by theorists in "Western" cultures but is also isolated by theorists from "Eastern" cultures (see Chinese Culture Connection, 1987, for an example). Triandis (in press) draws a distinction between horizontal and vertical individualism, and horizontal and vertical collectivism.

37. An alternative way of approaching this is to focus on Fiske's (1991) universal forms of social behavior.

38. The exception to this is when the stranger comes from a different ethnic group. In interethnic interactions, there is a relatively strong distinction between ingroup and outgroup in individualistic cultures.

39. The major exception is when the other person comes from a different ethnic group.

40. It might be argued that this phenomenon also is related to cultural tightness (Pelto, 1968). This dimension could be integrated with many axioms presented because behavior is more predictable in tight than in loose cultures. At the individual level, cultural tightness is related to narrow categorization.

41. The attunement that occurs may be only at the superficial level, however.

42. In the 1993 version of the theory, I wrote this axiom backward.

43. Some of these issues are addressed in Gudykunst (1994) for general intergroup communication. Gudykunst and Nishida (1994) address some of these issues for Japanese-North American communication.

3

The Layered Perspective of Cultural (In)Tolerance(s)
The Roots of a Multidisciplinary Approach

JOHN R. BALDWIN • *Illinois State University*
MICHAEL L. HECHT • *Arizona State University*

> In the nearly five decades since the war, the quantum leap in global communications, the liberation struggles of Third World peoples and the defeat of the United States in Vietnam, the mass migration of Third World peoples into First World cities, the resurgence of Islam, and, now, the emergence of Japan as the driving force in the world economy have made it clear that we are living in a multipolar world.
>
> *Boggs* (1990, pp. 13-14)

We seem to be at a juncture in world history. Just as this world becomes increasingly multipolar with a greater need to respect other peoples' perspectives (Boggs, 1990), conflicts attributed to group belonging arise at every pole: intolerance against the Japanese in America, against immigrants in various European countries, and against people of different religions in various corners of the world. At the same time many believe that racism and other such forms of intolerance are decreasing in significance (Wilson, 1978), the number of hate crimes in Los Angeles County has increased 31% between 1991 and 1992 (Nakagawa, 1993). The problem of hate crimes is not unique to the United States, of course. In Germany, the number of hate crimes approached 2,000 in 1992 (compared with the 4,558 reported hate crimes in the larger United States; "FBI: Racism," 1993), and daily news reports

AUTHORS' NOTE: We would like to thank Thomas Nakayama, David Goldberg, and the **International and Intercultural Communication Annual** *readers for comments on drafts of this chapter, as well as Steve Duck and Brian Spitzberg for theoretical insights.*

convey crimes of intergroup intolerance of various kinds from the former Yugoslavia (Wiesel, 1992), Ireland, Israel, and Ethiopia. Gordon Allport (1979) defines prejudice as a "generalized attitude" (p. 68). That is, Allport claims that intolerances are related to one another: One who is prejudiced against the communists may be similarly prejudiced toward Catholics. This, Allport suggests, is because

> prejudice is ultimately a problem of personality formation and development; no two cases of prejudice are precisely the same. No individual would mirror his [or her] group's attitude unless he [or she] had a personal need, or personal habit, that leads him [or her] to do so. (p. 41)

While Allport readily admits the influences of social structures and group-based needs and habits that today would be called cultural, these are important only as they affect the individual psyche. Allport argues that the same psychological structure that supports intolerance toward someone because of "race" would also support intolerance based on biological sex, religion, and so on. At the same time, recent scholars suggest that such things as "race," gender, and class are articulated differently within a society and between societies, and that while these articulations frequently overlap (e.g., intolerance toward both blackness and femaleness; Collins, 1990; Gilman, 1990; Wallace, 1992), they are, at the same time separate.[1]

In view of the complex nature of intolerance, this chapter proposes a modified perspective of prejudice, or "(in)tolerance."[2] We feel that the understanding of intolerance should allow for the comparison of different (in)tolerances. At the same time, the current perspective of tolerance needs to be broadened to include a more positive outlook (appreciation). Further, we feel communication theory about expression of (in)tolerance needs to consider diverse perspectives. This chapter presents a framework that, we hope, will facilitate understanding of the complex nature of intolerance. The focus of this chapter is to show the interrelation of certain broader components of the intolerance puzzle, making our perspective more useful as one from which to develop theory or research agendas than as a theory proper.

THE LAYERED PERSPECTIVE OF (IN)TOLERANCE(S)

This chapter introduces the notion of *layering* (Hecht, 1993; Hecht, Collier, & Ribeau, 1993) to represent our ontological and epistemological assumptions. Layering is a metaphor used to describe people's experiences and their understandings of those experiences. "Layering implies that there are alternative ways of knowing that are continually juxtaposed and played off each other and/or blended together" (Hecht, 1993, p. 76).

Layering is first of all a metatheoretical concept. The metaphor of layering suggests that there are alternative ways of experiencing the world. For example, some authors argue that behavior is determined by prior actions (caused); others, that we behave with intention or purpose, following rules. In fact, the rules people follow may be layered upon the stimuli they receive, and many stimuli are, in fact, the results of their intentional behavior. In the same sense, there are some "realities" out there that are objective and generalizable. At the same time, each individual experiences these realities differently, sometimes to the point that consideration of the reality itself is not as important as understanding people's interpretations of it. Rather than opposing one another, different ontologies or epistemologies can actually complement one another. The focus of one's research depends on the layer one wants to examine. "Theories and [experiential] realms may present competing assumptions about the world" (Hecht, 1993, p. 77), but this is a strength, and not a weakness, of the perspective: The divergent theories can be combined in creative and enlightening ways.

As an example, one could look at Brazilian "race" relations objectively by analyzing historical documents for traces of racism (Mitchell, 1984), measuring stereotypes among various ethnic groups (Pacheco, 1976), or counting and categorizing representations of people of color in advertisements (Hasenbalg, 1982; Leslie, 1992). A critical approach might look at the social structures maintained in power by national ideology and how those marginalize certain groups (Ortiz, 1985) or at the characters in folk stories to see what they reveal about social structures (da Matta, 1979). A subjectivist or interpretivist might instead ask people how they construct or experience color or conduct an ethnography in a racially divided sector of the country.[3] Rather than seeing the various views of reality and epistemologies as mutually exclusive, this chapter focuses on how they can inform one another.

Second, layering can be a descriptive concept in which the layers of meaning at different levels of analysis are discussed. For an individual, the perception of a certain group begins at a young age, when people around the individual speak of group members in terms of their distinctness from the person's own group. Images and messages from parents, media, friends, textbooks, teachers, as well as personal experiences with members of the "other" group layer upon each other and interplay with one another to form the person's own, often inconsistent view of the "others." A layered perspective at the individual level would look at the conflicting desires within the individual and society (Billig et al.'s, 1988, dialectic or dilemma discussed below). However, one must also look at how events, ideologies (e.g., the Enlightenment), social movements, and other aspects also affect and are affected by individual behavior and how they maintain and create the contradictions at work with (in)tolerance. Thus layering can also be used to describe what happens at societal or communal levels.

To continue the Brazil example, one might ask how intergroup perceptions and relations represented in media and cultural representations are layered upon a foundation of legislative action (Levine, 1984; Ortiz, 1985). How are legislative actions layered upon philosophical and scientific history (Meira-Penna, 1980; Stepan, 1991)? How are cultural representations (such as folktales and *Carnaval* parades) layered together with public and private social structure to exclude those of color (da Matta, 1979)? How are personal actions of exclusion layered upon socially shared biases and economic practices (Paim, 1988)? How do literary authors of color negotiate their own ethnic identity (Haberly, 1983), and what is the effect of the institutionalized inclusion or exclusion of these authors in the literary canon taught to Brazilian students (Nascimento, 1978)? Individual cognitions of "race" in Brazil thus are layered through historical articulations and ongoing images, institutions, and cultural practices. At the same time, these latter expressions are interpenetrated, or interrelated (Hecht, 1993), with the personal cognitions of those who produce them.

Third, layering is a methodological concept. The above example shows that many layers of social action may be at work at a given time. Most scholars acknowledge that individual behavior is influenced by cultural norms, shared meanings, and social influences. But cultures and relationships are processes, with new layers added on by new actors. Community rituals, literature, politics, popular culture, personal experience, and relationships all interact with each other, with different layers being important at different times. Different methodologies may work better for certain layers or connections between layers. But even at a single layer, methodologies can be layered one upon another to gain better understanding, a concept Denzin (1978) calls "triangulation." Thus Hecht, Ribeau, and Alberts (1989) used a combination of open-ended questionnaires and interpretive interviews; Hecht, Ribeau, and Sedano (1990) compared the results of interpretive interviews with rhetorical analysis of Chicano poetry. Triangulation can also be through cross-validation via multiple samples, as demonstrated in Hecht's (1984) analysis of relational frames. In each of these cases, the methods were layered, either through comparison of samples or through comparison

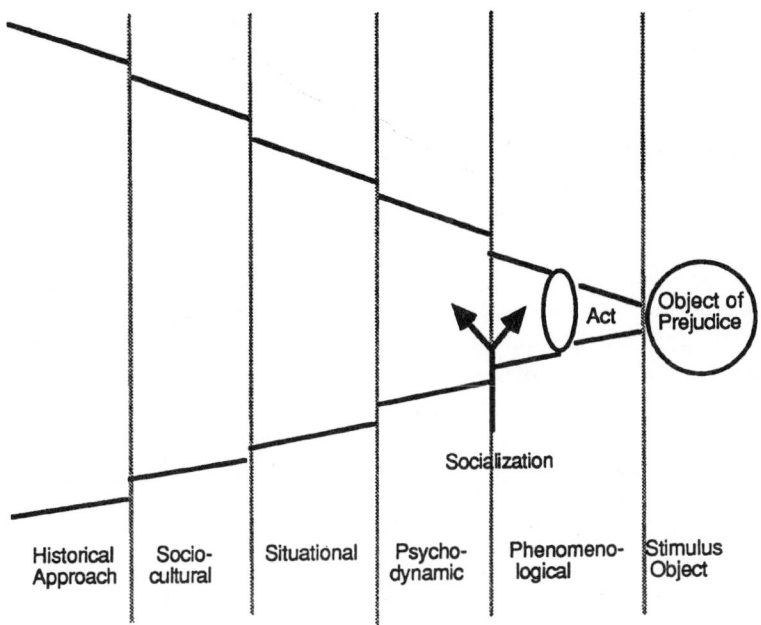

Figure 3.1: Allport's Model of Psychological and Social Causation
SOURCE: Allport (1950). Used by permission from the Society for the Psychological Study of Social Issues

of methods. To understand "race" in Brazil, one might use an experimental treatment, in-depth interviews, and rhetorical analyses.

This chapter proposes the layering perspective not so much as a theory to replace other theories but as a perspective allowing new theories that show the interrelationships between different aspects of intolerance. Allport (1950) presents a sort of telescoping "diagrammatic view" of approaches to prejudice (Figure 3.1). In this, Allport attempts to show the interrelationships between various lines of theories of prejudice. This figure seems to indicate that the historical affects the sociocultural, which in turn affects the psychological, which finally affects the cognitive. We agree with Allport in that "we do not wish to slight any one of [the theories], for none alone gives a complete picture. Quarrels among them are unprofitable" (1979, p. 207). Each adds insight to a different piece of the puzzle, looking at a different layer of human experience. Unlike research by Allport, more complex interrelationships between the layers of experience are seen. The complexity of intolerance leads us to reexamine Allport's six approaches to prejudice, as well as some of Allport's other assumptions.

In brief, this chapter's perspective includes four main components. First, we approach the delineation by Allport (1979) and others between the prejudiced and tolerant personalities, analyzing the different *stances* one can have toward perceived group-based differences (e.g., intolerant, tolerant, appreciative). Second, these stances can occur within different *spheres* or types of intolerance (for example, intolerance based on "race," age, religion). Third, there can be different *levels of analysis*. That is, one can look at intolerance at an individual level, in an interaction, in a relationship, or in a community. Fourth, there are different *ways of understanding*—different sorts of analysis, both in methodology (e.g., critical, empirical, phenomenological) and in "disciplinary" point of view (e.g., psychology, sociology, communication).

These four aspects of the perspective will now be explained in more detail, listing our underlying assumptions. Sample research questions will be provided that might appear as part of a theory or research agenda of either (in)tolerance or intergroup behavior. These questions will highlight the utility of this perspective.

Stances

A person's stance can be defined as *her or his level of acceptance of an outgroup or a person of that outgroup based on group membership.* Various levels of acceptance or nonacceptance are possible. These levels are important because they are closely related to behavior. If people are to make the world a more livable place for the groups that exist together in it, it is worth our while to locate intolerant behaviors and do what we can to reduce them. This discussion raises several key questions, however: What are the possible stances one can have? How "stable" are they? What is the relationship between stances and behavior? Isn't the reduction of intolerance a "value-driven" project? Each of these questions and the assumptions to which it leads will be shown.

The possible stances and their stability. The initial focus of our Western minds leads us to suggest that there are primarily two stances— *tolerant* and *intolerant* (Allport, 1979)—and that for much of intolerance there is a base level, so that one is either intolerant or not (Adorno, Frenkel-Brunswick, Levinson, & Sanford, 1982). Byrd (1993), in the same line, discusses *tolerance for human diversity*. Bennett (1986a, 1986b) expands this view to suggest that there are at least six stances (three negative, which indicate *ethnocentrism*, and three positive, which refer to *ethnorelativism*). One of the strengths of Bennett's conceptualization is the inclusion of something beyond *tolerance*—a word that, regardless of the intention of the authors who use it, conjures up images of "putting up with" or "being able to live together with" people of other groups.

The higher levels of Bennett's (1986a, 1986b) continuum show stances where people *not only allow or even adapt some behaviors of people from other cultures, they integrate some of them into their being.* For this level of acceptance, the term *appreciation* is preferred. Those who are appreciative will see differences from a point of view of synergy (Harris & Moran, 1987), where people are not merely trying to manage diversity and conform it to corporate or individual goals; instead, they are attempting to incorporate valuable aspects of the different groups (ethnic, religious, political, and so on) to enhance themselves and the organizations to which they belong. This is similar to Kim's (1994) proposal that people take the best perspectives of the Eastern and Western worldviews and communication styles to become better intercultural persons. People who appreciate diversity welcome difference into their lives and see it as a positive experience.

Initially, we felt that there should be at least three stances. Appreciation, as we have just defined, would be at one end. *Intolerance*, at the other end, could be defined much as Allport (1979) defined negative prejudice: *"an avertive or hostile attitude toward a person who belongs to a group, simply because he [or she] belongs to that group, and is therefore presumed to have the objectionable qualities ascribed to the group"* (p. 7). Somewhere in the middle is *tolerance*, which one might define as *the application of the same moral principles and rules, caring and empathy, and feeling of connections to human beings of other perceived groups* (based on Staub, 1990). This, as earlier noted, falls short of appreciation, leading to the first assumption:

1. Attitudes toward diversity can have at least three positions: intolerance, tolerance, and appreciation.

The expansion of *tolerance/intolerance* to include *appreciation* is useful but still may oversimplify the nature of (in)tolerance. For example, a white English person might, on Bennett's (1986a, 1986b) continuum, be ethnocentric toward Pakistani customs and values but more accepting of Anglo-Australian or Anglo-American values. Further, the same person might be more ethnocentric toward Pakistani customs at some times than at others. This admits that (in)tolerance may better be understood as a continuum than as three categories. Further, it suggests that there may be some base levels of intolerance (e.g., generalized prejudice; Allport, 1979) but that many feelings and attitudes toward a group may depend on the circumstance. For example, Clément and Noels (1992) have suggested that ethnic identity is situated and changeable—perhaps one's intolerance of a given group is based largely on the identity or identities salient at the moment. Part of the salience of the identities could be the situational norms, such as peer pressure, defined by Byrd (1993) as situational intolerance.

Some have opposed the idea that one has a set authoritarian or prejudiced personality, suggesting that there are multiple forces at work—such as both the desire to be rational and at the same time the perceived need to exclude others. Billig et al. (1988) speak of the dilemma or dialectic of prejudice. That is, "prejudice" is used in discourse to "express the very same ideas as it ostensibly appears to contradict": The discourse "simultaneously contains its own dominant explicit meanings as well as its counter-meanings or negation" (p. 24) combining its own thesis and antithesis. Everyday life is full of contradictions (Baxter, 1990; Hecht, 1993), and these include the desire to be reasonable combined with expressions that exclude others. If a person is to accept Gudykunst and Kim's (1992) argument that people "may be prejudiced and tolerant at the same time" (p. 103), a person may not have one stance at a given time but have opposing stances—perhaps conceptualized as opposing continua—that may not even be reconciled within an individual. Layering explains these stances well, allowing a society or an individual to have competing layers, the relationships between which can be investigated. This leads to the next assumptions:

2. Attitudes toward diversity might be better understood as either a continuum or as competing continua or forces within individuals and society (a dialectic).
3. One's stance, or expression of a stance, can have both situational (state) and stable (trait) components.

Stances and behavior. How circumstances and competing identities might affect feelings and attitudes has already been discussed. This, however, assumes that stances are internal. There are at least two possible views of the relationship between stances and behavior. The first collapses Allport's (1979) distinction between prejudice (which Allport sees as having a belief component and an attitude component, the former being more affective) and its effects (e.g., antilocution, discrimination, physical attack) into one concept: Stances would contain components that are *cognitive, emotional,* and *behavioral.* In this view, for example, "racism" could be defined in terms of internal dispositions *or* effects: If someone's actions exclude others, they are racist (an intolerant stance in the sphere of "race"). Thus some writers focus on the effects of racism, looking at voting behavior (Sears, 1988) or attitudes (McConahay, 1986) or personal stories (Essed, 1990, 1991) and discourse (van Dijk, 1984, 1987) to locate racism, assigning intent or motivation to the actors based on the actions. Some focus exclusively on effects. Hoetink (1974) notes that "prejudice . . . was viewed by quite a few as a final cause, rather than as a symptom of group conflicts, latent or active" (p. 29).

While in the above example there seem to be "racist" people and/or "racist" actions, a different view sees stances as internal, but potentially leading to behaviors. Following Allport (1979), this view suggests that there is a strong connection between the internal processes and behavior. Given that intolerance is prevalent and people live daily with the effects of it, this justifies study of both internal dispositions and actions. However, Brislin (1991) and Merton (1957) note the imperfect relationship between intolerance and expression. One can express tolerance but either hold intolerant views (Brislin, 1991) or support the continuation of unfair distribution of resources (Jackman & Crane, 1986). On the other hand, one can be a "non-prejudiced discriminator" (Merton, 1957)—one who expresses prejudice due to social pressure but has not internalized intolerant beliefs. As such, it might be better to distinguish between intolerant expressions (including politics, business policies, and so on) and intolerant individuals; the same individual might at one time express prejudiced ideas and at other times not. Drawing dotted lines, rather than hard connections, between attitudes and behavior helps to explain Billig et al.'s (1988) dialectic. People may behave according to political correctness when in the presence of other groups (tolerant behavior) but may in fact harbor prejudiced feelings.[4] Whether behaviors are a common outgrowth of stances or are entirely indicative of one's stance, the assumption is the same:

4. (In)tolerances are manifested through communication.

However, to allow for the possibility that beliefs and internal states can be disconnected and inconsistent, the following is allowed:

5. The relationship between psychological (in)tolerances and communication may be imperfect.

Note that this assumption is *not* intended to divorce us from responsibility for our intolerant actions. To the contrary, it allows a focus on feelings, attitudes, *or* communicative behavior (regardless of intent)—or all at the same time.

A value-driven project. The fact that expressions of intolerance change according to what is socially accepted shows that some changes are possible in at least the expression of tolerance. Bennett (1986a) suggests that levels of ethnocentrism can be ascertained and that interventions of different sorts can make people less ethnocentric. And it has been stated that others must live with the consequences of our actions, which are often exclusionary. This hints at another assumption:

6. One's level of intolerance/appreciation can be identified and changed.

The first part of this assumption will receive little debate, for scholars have sought for many years and in many ways to measure (in)tolerance. The latter, however, suggests a value-based agenda for research. Some might suggest that this will obscure the results that are found. The first answer to this suggestion is that no science is value-free (Bernstein, 1976; Lincoln & Guba, 1985). It is important, therefore, to carefully choose and openly admit the values that drive the research. Burrel and Morgan (1979) place social science research on a continuum from subjective to objective. However, they list another continuum from social change to maintaining the status quo, a continuum that has sometimes been ignored. It is acceptable to use science for changing the status quo, though science must often examine things as they currently exist.

Second, in the case of (in)tolerance for diversity, this value is warranted. Few cultures in the contemporary world are homogeneous, nor are they melting pots. Instead, they are full of diversity (Barnlund, 1994)—diversity that often maintains its shape and form, despite the degree to which it takes on the flavor of the cultural *broth* around it. These cultures might be seen more as *stir-fry* cultures (King, 1991). Beyond being inevitable, diversity is desirable, in both relationships (Watzlawick, Beavin, & Jackson, 1967) and organizations (Harris & Moran, 1987).[5]

Layering and the concept of stances can help to facilitate change. For example, on the individual level, people adjust messages in line with the stances of others as much as possible. Social judgment theory suggests that messages can be aimed at the level of acceptance on particular issues (i.e., near their stance). Just as in dealing with people from other cultures, an attempt can be made to fit messages to others' perceptual grasps, taking into account the filters that may be involved in their encoding and decoding (Gudykunst & Kim, 1992). Thus not only is communication behavior attuned (communication accommodation theory; Gallois, Franklyn-Stokes, Giles, & Coupland, 1988) but also stance.[6] At a group level, those aspects of institutions, legal systems, and so on can be analyzed to see how they reproduce intolerance, and changes can be implemented at the societal or policy level.

Spheres

Spheres are *group-based identities upon which (in)tolerance is based.* For example, one can be intolerant of another based on social class, sexual orientation, gender, or political views. Byrd (1993), for example, discusses intolerance based on "race," sex, sexual orientation, age, and physical/mental disability. There can also be intolerance based on groups of a different nature, such as gang membership, region of origin (north/ south United States), division within an organization (students/faculty/ staff/administration, sales/research and development), levels of a hier- archy (owners/managers/workers), and so on. One can see world con- flicts based on intolerances such as religion (Northern Ireland), political party (Colombia), and ethnicity (former Yugoslavia, various Russian and African republics). These intolerances could be seen in terms of the various, sometimes conflicting "ingroups" to which people belong and through which they identify themselves (Tajfel, 1978a, 1981) and in the various ways and intensities with which they express those identities (Collier, 1994; Collier & Thomas, 1988; Hecht et al., 1993). A rhetori- cal or discourse-analytic perspective might look at how those ingroups are created (boundaries defined) and defined (characteristics elabo- rated) through private and public discourse and images. To more fully understand the spheres of (in)tolerance, we must look at their relation- ship to each other and to the stances.

The relationships between spheres. As noted in the introduction, many have recently argued that things such as "race," class, and gender are articulated together, yet are separate. That is, people create and pass on images (both in interpersonal communication and in mass media and popular culture) that reproduce ideas and structures that are often intermingled with one another: Welfare recipients or crime perpetrators may be perceived to be of certain ethnic groups; there are different stereotypes and status positions for women of color than for men of color; and so on. For an individual, or at a societal level, the stance toward one group can change for the better, such as with new historical and political developments, while the stance toward another group can remain the same or worsen. For example, Bennett and Woolacott pro- pose in *Bond and Beyond* that the James Bond myth in England "has been constantly re-presented to account for differing political actuali- ties within British and indeed world political and economic history" (in Blake, 1992, p. 49). The enemies change, as do the representations of a given enemy.[7]

Further, because representations, even of the same group, can change from region to region, from culture to culture, and from point to point in history, it is logical that there may be different manifestations of a given sphere. Sexism may be interpreted differently by women in Saudi Arabia than by women in France. There may be different "racisms," whether intrinsic versus extrinsic (Appiah, 1990), everyday racism versus the extraordinary incidents (Essed, 1991), or historically and culturally bound "racisms" (Gilroy, 1990; Goldberg, 1990, 1993). Further, in a given location, one may be "racist" toward different groups in different ways, revealing different "racisms" even at the same historical and cultural juncture. This leads to the following assumptions:

7. There are various areas of intolerance/appreciation based on group belonging, including (but not limited to) "race," sex, sexual preference, age, physical/mental ability, and socioeconomic status.

8. Spheres of intolerance can be looked at collectively, as many of the underlying components of them are the same, or separate from one another, as each has its own distinctness.

9. A sphere of intolerance (e.g., "racism") may be manifested differently from culture to culture, from one point of history to another, or even within the same point in culture and history.

The field of (in)tolerance is broad enough to focus on many different areas. Because each area of intolerance is different (intolerances), there is justification for someone to focus *only* on ethnocentrism (Levinson, 1982a), anti-Semitism (Levinson, 1982b), racism (McConahay, 1986), and so on. At the same time, because many intolerance(s) may be related or have similar underlying causes (psychological, structural, rhetorical, and so on), some can look at the relationships between them (Baldwin & Hecht, 1993; Byrd, 1993). Confirmatory and exploratory factor analyses support the distinction between different spheres such as sexism, ableism, and ageism (Baldwin & Hecht, 1993; Byrd, 1991), although there are correlations between these different "isms."

Spheres and stances. The idea that a collective or an individual can hold different stances toward groups at the same time (or, to borrow again from the dialectic idea, different stances toward the same group in different areas or contexts) contrasts with two predominant viewpoints in social science. One of these is Allport's (1979) view that people have "generalized prejudice"—if one is prejudiced toward Catholics, one will also probably be prejudiced toward communists. This is the perspective behind much of the social psychological work examining authoritarianism (Adorno et al., 1982) and closed-mindedness (Rokeach, 1960). Byrd (1993) supports the position that "attitudes towards outgroup people (termed tributary in [her] text) are highly correlated" (p. 153).

Yet Byrd's work (1991) and that of the authors Byrd cites (Bierly, 1985; Ray & Lovejoy, 1986) all leave "ample room for different types of prejudice to have different correlates" (Ray & Lovejoy, 1986, p. 564). Perhaps this view and the idea of layered perspectives can be synthesized by supposing that people have base levels of (in)tolerance, but that these can change depending on the sphere, context, and other factors.[8] To follow with this sphere metaphor, areas of intolerance are like globes with permeable boundaries—they operate each in its own trajectory, but their orbits affect one another and at times they overlap each other to large degrees. More simply, the following is assumed:

10. While two or more spheres may be related to each other, they need not be. Someone might be appreciative in some areas but not others.

The other view that contrasts with ours is that the forces of one sphere dictate those of other spheres. This is most clearly exemplified in the "class-race" debate, which is detailed below. Many hold that social class considerations are the ultimate determining factor—even if this is not at first apparent (Althusser, 1971)—and dictate what happens in spheres of "race," gender, and so on. It should be noted, however, that often under discussion is *not* intolerance based on social class but the desire to hold economic advantage (Marxists: the ownership of production) or political advantage (critical theorists: power over ideology), with these struggles ushering in or propagating the various spheres of intolerance.[9] Byrd (1993) proposed that a "racist" or other intolerant person "is not only prejudiced, but also holds membership in the power-dominant group, therefore [having] the potential of implementing discriminatory practices" (p. 135). This view works if "racism" (and other "isms") is equated with discrimination (in jobs or allocation of resources). However, while the majority of "ism" literatures look at the "ism" of the empowered over the disempowered, definitions of sexism, racism, and so on need to allow consideration of intolerance in those of any group toward those of another group. Further, there is a need to be able to account for those instances when people are intolerant of their own group. The strength of Byrd's approach is that it brings into focus important issues of power that are often deemphasized—indeed, many of the world conflicts noted above are based as much on issues of power as on group perception. However, power issues may not always be at play. Even if all acts of intolerance are in some way connected to a power struggle, they are acts that can be perpetrated by either side of the struggle (Steele, 1990).

11. Intolerance/appreciation is two way or multiway. That is, either women or men can be sexist; people of any "race" or ethnic group can be racist; and so on.

An understanding of spheres of intolerance should help us to understand those areas where greater intolerance is expressed; this will allow for an increased focus on how to reduce intolerance in those areas. As an example, Byrd (1991) found that items tapping "racial intolerance" are not consistently responded to by college students. But when a specific "race" is substituted into the scale (Baldwin & Hecht, 1993), consistency results. It seems that students' views toward those of different "races" vary in a given geographic region. In ongoing research, perceptions of both African and European American adults of "racist communication" they have experienced are being investigated.

Combining the first two elements of our perspective, several types of research questions are possible. These questions exhibit the strength of being able to layer spheres and stances. Some examples include the following:

- How are European American, southern U.S. prejudices toward Vietnamese fishermen and African Americans expressed and experienced differently? What prejudices do these groups have of the first group?
- What behaviors are perceived by different groups as being sexist, racist, and so forth?
- What forms of intolerance (if any) are expressed by those who are appreciative of cultural, racial, and other forms of diversity?
- How do expressions of intolerance change toward different groups when more blatant expressions become politically unacceptable?
- What are the similarities and differences in content of verbal and nonverbal expressions of various intolerances (e.g., racism, sexism, and heterosexism)?
- What communication strategies can be used with people who hold intolerant stances toward members of a certain sphere by members of the targeted group?

Levels of Analysis

Chaffee and Berger (1987) propose that there are various "levels at which communication can be conceptualized and studied empirically" (p. 143). These *levels of analysis* can be considered as *the loci where social phenomena occur and at which they should be studied.* Chaffee and Berger contend that scholars at the various levels focus only on one or two levels and "rarely consult with one another" (p. 143). Triandis et al. (1984), for example, seek to "explore individual systems of meaning so that we might discover common elements across individuals" (p. 1390). Hewes and Planalp (1987) argue that "the individual is the locus of social action" (p. 146) but that the role of the individual in communication has been oversimplified; a better understanding of the individual's role in communication will shed more light on the interactive nature of communication. On the other hand, in relational communication, Montgomery (1986) criticizes the research of Indvik and Fitzpatrick (1986), claiming it ignores the interdependent nature of communication among workers, acquaintances, friends, best friends, and intimates. Fitzpatrick and Indvik (1986) respond that both dyadic and individual levels of analysis are necessary to understand relational communication.

Duck and Sants (1983), however, argue that relationships are not simply the products of communicators' responses to each other or the combination of their attributes. Relationships are processes, and the study of them must include various aspects, such as role negotiation, discrepancy of participants' views of the relationship, and so on. Viewing the relationship as level of analysis is thus distinct from looking at individual messages or their interaction. Still others have argued for an inclusion of the macrosocial level of analysis. McLeod and Blumler (1987) argue that, while one must define and measure phenomena at their level of abstraction, there is a need for macro-level (community- or society-level) scholarship in communication. This would include power relationships, mass media influences, and other "institutional sectors in the social system" (p. 277). They note that "developments in semiotics and sociolinguistics have highlighted complex relationships between cultural forms and social identity" (p. 271). To this end, some have argued that social identity is central to an individual's intolerance (e.g., Tajfel, 1981). Baldwin (1994b) suggests that much of the literature in intergroup communication has focused on the individual level; although sociological aspects are often considered, they are considered only as they affect individual cognitions and predispositions. Macro-level factors should be given more attention in intergroup studies, Baldwin argues, but not to the exclusion of individual-level analyses.

Possible levels and their relationship to one another. The complexity of social reality and multiplicity of ontological and methodological perspectives have led Chaffee and Berger (1987) to conclude that "*at least* four levels need to be kept in mind" when looking at communication science (p. 143, italics in original): the individual level, the interpersonal or dyadic level, the network level, and the macrosocial level. Cappella's (1987) levels include zero-order inquiry (analysis of sets, types, and structures of behaviors), first-order inquiry (individual characteristics and dispositions), second-order inquiry (patterns of interaction), and third-order inquiry (the "linkage between relationship factors and interaction patterns" (p. 193). Hecht (1993) combines these approaches to arrive at four possible levels of analysis as they pertain to the enactment of identity. The *personal level* includes aspects of individuals "stored as self-cognitions, feelings about self, and/or a spiritual sense of self-being" (p. 79). The *enactment (dyadic) level* includes identities enacted through social interaction. The *relationship level* refers to the negotiation of identity as communication partners develop relationships, especially as a relationship gains its own identities or as certain relational roles (e.g., marital, employment, friendship) interact with personal identities. Consistent with Duck and Sants (1983), it is at this level that one would consider power relationships and discrepancies in perceptions of the relationship. Finally, at the *communal level*, "identities . . . are jointly held/remembered and taught to new members" through community action, rituals, institutions, and so on (Hecht, 1993, p. 80). This level can be expanded to include impersonal social actions, such as wars, government laws and constitutions, and organizational policies as they affect (in)tolerance. Thus there is concern with the cognitions, interpretations, feelings, and behaviors of individuals, the interactions (communication) and relationships between people, and the structure and collective memories of communities (Middleton & Edwards, 1990).

Hecht (1993) argues that the different levels "interpenetrate" one another. That is, they influence and interact with each other. As such, while some phenomena can be studied only at one level, often one must look at two, three, or four levels to understand a phenomenon. For example, exclusion of someone based on biological sex (sexism) or "race" (racism) might exist on the level of personal attitudes and communication behavior, in turn-taking and other dyadic behavior, in the construction of roles in relationships, and at the level of cultural norms ("don't invite 'them' over for dinner" role structures), institutions (laws forcing segregation, organizational policy), rituals (*Carnaval,* parades, celebrations), and popular culture (textbooks, romance novels, rock-'n'-roll lyrics). These, in turn, interact with each other in various ways to maintain or diminish such exclusions. In the language of the present perspective, the levels of analysis are layered. Thus the following is assumed:

12. Appreciation/intolerance can exist within individuals, in interaction, within relationships, and/or at the communal and societal levels.
13. These factors interact with and interpenetrate one another, making them all worthy of investigation both alone and in their interactions.

Levels, spheres, and stances. The levels serve as lenses of focus on social reality (or individual realities). They allow one to look at the various levels at which (in)tolerance (stance) toward a certain group (sphere) may exist or be reproduced. With all elements combined, the layered perspective allows examination of not only how the spheres overlap (interpenetrate) one another (e.g., sexism, racism, classism) but how appreciation or intolerance is experienced, built, and expressed at various levels (e.g., society, dyad), and how (in)tolerance at various levels relates to (in)tolerance at other levels. By combining these elements, one can investigate several areas of appreciation or intolerance:

- How can we understand people's stances in a specific sphere (e.g., What are the dynamics of ageism?)?
- How do people interact *about* the spheres and stances across boundaries (e.g., How would people with two different stances toward certain ethnic groups communicate about tolerance of those groups? What are the dynamics of metacommunication about various intolerances?)?
- What are the dynamics of individuals' relational development if they begin from stances of intolerance toward one another's group?
- What types of personal and professional relationships exist within and across spheres and stances?
- How will the dynamics of an organization be affected if two individuals who interact frequently are intolerant but in different spheres (e.g., sex and "race")?
- How might (in)tolerance of certain groups be shown in hiring or admission practices?
- How are communities within specific spheres and with specific stances organized through communication?
- How can a community or organization reproduce (in)tolerance through discourse, ritual, media, and other community-based behaviors?
- How might individuals or groups concerned with fighting intolerance help themselves or others to find strategies of resistance—ways to reinterpret messages or symbols in a positive light or to reduce or cope with expressions of intolerance?
- What communicative strategies (personal or mediated) are most effective in changing individual and societal structures toward appreciation or tolerance?

Types of Understanding

Because (in)tolerance can be understood at various levels, it is argued that no hard-and-fast operationalization of the concept be maintained. It is suggested that there are various valuable *types of understanding*, which include *different ways of seeing the world (ontology), human nature, and knowledge (epistemology).* Because different foci and ways of seeing the world require different tools, types of understanding *must also include different methodologies.* Crossing over all of these boundaries is the aspect of the different "disciplines" that address (in)tolerance. First, the relationship between ontologies, epistemologies, and methodologies will be investigated, then the nature of "disciplines" and their relationship to the above elements will be discussed.

Ontology, epistemology, and methodology. (In)tolerance can be experienced in different ways by different individuals (phenomenological), and yet there can be commonalities, derived through common experiences and shared symbols, between how individuals with common histories experience a reality (generalizable, empirical). Behavior can be both mindful (intentional; Langer, 1978) and yet influenced (determined). A full conceptualization of intolerance must take into account research from different ontological, epistemological, and methodological perspectives. The crux of layering, as stated earlier, is its reliance upon multiple perspectives and multiple methodologies. Researchers may use self-report inventories, interviews, critical and rhetorical analyses of artifacts, ethnographic descriptions, and other methods separately or in combination to understand these diverse phenomena. This approach is not intended to gloss over the different issues or difficulties with interpretive (Bostrom & Donohew, 1992), empirical (Lincoln & Guba, 1985), or critical research (Bernstein, 1976; Hammersley, 1992). Rather, the following is suggested:

14. The greatest understanding of intergroup (in)tolerance will come from dialogue between and among those of different "ontologies" and "epistemologies."
15. Triangulation of, or multiple methods of researching, (in)tolerance will yield the fullest understanding.

Historically, communication theories of intolerance and intergroup communication have leaned heavily on individual factors (Collier & Thomas, 1988; Gallois et al., 1988; Gudykunst, 1988; Stephan, 1985). A discussion of social structure and other factors may even seem foreign in some communication theories, perhaps, to continue Leeds-Hurwitz's (1990) historical contextualization of intercultural communication, because of the strong influence of cognitive approaches to interpersonal communication on intercultural studies in the last several years (Gudykunst & Kim, 1992; Gudykunst & Nishida, 1989). There are many factors and aspects of (in)tolerance, with each "discipline" looking through its own lens at the phenomenon.

"Types of understanding" and disciplines. The relationship between "disciplines" and the above elements is complicated. It is too simplistic to say that social psychologists are individualistic, for even those communication theories mentioned above that are *strongly* social psychological consider some elements of group influence. For example, Gallois et al. (1988) consider group norms and social and contextual factors; Gudykunst's new anxiety/uncertainty management theory (see Chapter 2, this volume) considers normative and institutional support. "Disciplines" thus seem best suited for various levels of analysis: Social biology is a convenient discipline for examining individual, dyadic, and relational levels; sociology, for dyadic, relational, and community; and so on. Boundaries for "disciplines," ontologies, and methodologies do not coincide: A social anthropologist can be objectivist or subjectivist (or somewhere in between, or both in different aspects). An ethnographer can be an anthropologist, a sociologist, or a communicationist, an objectivist or a critical theorist, and so on.

Theories, even metatheories, tend to offer alternative explanations for only some portions of the social world. But to sift through these to find the elements needed for more comprehensive explanations of social reality is sometimes difficult, as scholars in many areas do not cite scholars in other areas. Rather than derive from each area the specifics for a midlevel theory to explain all (in)tolerance, the objective here is to review some of the perspectives with which (in)tolerance is viewed, for the purpose of future theory building. The "containers" in which research and theory are "served up" are inconsistent: Some are perspectives (e.g., sociobiology, critical theory) that claim to be cross-disciplinary. Others (social psychology, sociology) fall more into current, socially constructed understandings of "disciplines." Slightly adapting Allport's (1979) six areas of theory, some of the viewpoints evident in sociobiology, social psychology, sociology, and rhetoric/critical theory are presented.[10] Figure 3.2 outlines the main approaches, their subdivisions as we see them, and their strengths and weaknesses.[11]

Sociobiological perspectives. Sociobiology, like many perspectives mentioned below, crosses both levels of analysis and disciplines. It seems to work best to explain individual behavior and relational communication behavior, and through these, dyadic behavior. Sociobiological theories look to inherited traits in some way. Some, such as the eugenicists of the early 1900s and the scholars who continue to hold that there are, indeed, actual differences between ethnic groups based on genetics (e.g., intelligence), focus on what is inherited through genetic makeup. (Most authors surveyed oppose this tendency: Franklin, 1991; Gould, 1981; Stepan, 1991; cf. Glass, 1986.) Others, who call

(text continued on page 84)

SOCIOBIOLOGY

• Genetic Focus/Eugenics[1]

Franklin, 1991 (−)   Glass, 1986 (+)
Gould, 1981 (−)   Martínez-Echazábal, 1988
West, 1982 (−)   Stepan, 1991

Tenets/Focus[2]
  • Characteristics, personality traits are inherited through genes.
  • Some "races" are genetically inferior to others in certain ways (e.g., intelligence), thus called by some "scientific racism."
  • Eugenics, an early form of genetic focus, held that either biology or environment can affect genes (depending on school). Countries should strive for "good" genetic line.
  FOCUS: INHERITANCE THROUGH GENES

• Evolutionary Theory

Barker, 1990 (−)   Ross, 1991 (+)
Goldberg, 1993 (−)   van den Berghe, 1986 (+)
Reynolds, Falger, & Vine, 1987 (+)

Tenets/Focus
  • Instinctual drives (fear of unknown, antipredator aggression, enforcement of solidarity) are root of prejudice.
  • People instinctually seek to preserve gene pool (inclusive fitness) or ingroup.
  • Humans share much of behavior with other animals.
  FOCUS: INHERITANCE THROUGH INSTINCTUAL DRIVES

Strengths and Weaknesses of Sociobiology
  + It might explain some of why intolerance persists despite efforts at change.
  + It might provide explanation at an even deeper level than psychological approaches as to why ingroups are so important and why prejudice is "natural" (Allport, 1954/1979).
  − More deterministic applications leave little hope of change, of reduction of intolerance.
  − Some strains have been used explicitly or implicitly to justify exclusions.
  − Some strains (e.g., "inclusive fitness") do not work well for non-"gene pool" intolerances.

SOCIAL PSYCHOLOGY

• Psychostructural Approach

Adorno et al., 1982   Rokeach, 1960
Allport, 1954/1979

Tenets/Focus
  • Underlying attributes and psychological needs are associated with prejudice (e.g., authoritarianism, ethnocentrism, rigidity, conformity, uncertainty, anxiety, expectations, closed-mindedness).
  • Some attention is paid to other factors as they influence personal needs, constructs (e.g., frustration).
  FOCUS: PSYCHOLOGICAL CONSTRUCTS (can be state or trait, biologically or socially derived)

Figure 3.2: Disciplines/Perspectives on (In)Tolerance

- Cognitive/Categorization

    Tajfel & Turner[3]   Billig[4]
    Stephan, 1986   Gudykunst[5]

    Tenets/Focus
    - We see, evaluate, and compare ourselves with others based on group belonging (Tajfel, Turner).
    - We (naturally) divide social world into categories (in-, outgroups) (Allport; Sherif, 1966).
    - Competing personal goals create contradictions within us (Billig).
    - Encoding/decoding of messages depends upon "conceptual filters" including prejudice and stereotypes (Gudykunst).
    FOCUS: CATEGORIZATION, IN-/OUTGROUPS

- Ethnicity and Communication

    Giles[6]   Hecht, Collier[7]
    Clément & Noels, 1992   Gumperz, 1982
    Weinreich, 1986   Edwards & Potter, 1992

    Tenets/Focus
    - Personal intentions, context, salience, vitality of languages (ethnolinguistic vitality), and other factors affect whether communication partners adjust or diverge communication styles (Giles).
    - How one perceives own and "other's" (ethnic) identity affects the communication process in areas such as conflict (Collier), strategies (Hecht), code-switching (Gumperz), and so on.
    - Ethnic (and other) identities are enacted in different ways at different levels (Hecht). Social identities are constructed through discourse (Edwards & Potter).
    - Identities are fluctuating and fluid: We have different identities that compete within us (Weinreich); these are "situated" in certain contexts (Clément & Noels).
    - More research in this branch uses interpretive research or discourse-analytic methods.
    FOCUS: HOW IDENTITIES ARE ENACTED IN/THROUGH COMMUNICATION

- Rational Choice

    Banton, 1986, 1987

    Tenets/Focus
    - Behavior is intentional and logical: Prejudiced acts result from personal goals.
    FOCUS: PERSONAL DECISIONS AND CHOICES AS THEY AFFECT BEHAVIOR

- Moral Exclusion

    Bandura, 1990   Opotow, 1990[8]
    Bar-Tal, 1990

    Tenets/Focus
    - Groups adopt a double standard, excluding certain groups from behavior that would be considered fair, just if applied to own group.
    - Primary concern is with exclusion.
    FOCUS ON EFFECTS OF MORAL DOUBLE STANDARD

Figure 3.2: Continued

Strengths and Weaknesses of Social Psychology
> + Approaches explain various types of intolerance with same principles (i.e., parsimonious).
> + It is one of most useful areas so far in intergroup communication, with much research produced (i.e., heuristic).
> + It is useful in explaining how individuals can differ within the same social and historical conditions.
> + Some forms (especially moral exclusion) allow us to look at intentions *and/or* processes.
> + Some branches are now focusing more on identity and its manifestations rather than objectifying group membership.
> + Its focus is on problematic elements of interaction.
> − It can neglect differences between specific types of intolerance.
> − Some forms can create the idea that most prejudice or discrimination is a result of personal (i.e., not structural) factors, when it is likely that these account for only a portion (Allport suggests 50%).
> − It can subordinate nonindividual factors so much that they do not receive appropriate attention, such as group processes by which "realities" are negotiated or held in place.
> − Some approaches do not allow for intentionality of human action.

STRUCTURE/SOCIOLOGY[9]

• Ethnicity Approaches

Mirandé, 1985	Robert Park (in Lal, 1986)
Parillo, 1980	Asante, 1987
Gunnar Myrdal (in Omi & Winant, 1986)	Omi & Winant, 1986

Tenets/Focus
> • Original theorists (Park, Chicago School) explained prejudice in terms of competition for resources (job, space) between groups, with boundaries drawn on (European) ethnic lines.
> • The 1960s saw resurgence in ethnic nationalism, with groups focusing on ethnic (as opposed to class) differences (Asante).
> • Many societies (e.g., United States; Omi & Winant) are structured at every level by "race"; we can trace the political and economic precursors to racial formation and reformation.

FOCUS: GROUP BELONGING (especially ethnicity) IS CORE TO PREJUDICE

• Marxist/Neo-Marxist Approaches

Marx (Tucker, 1978)	Miles, 1989[10]
Solomos, 1986	Hall, 1982, 1985, 1986
Wolpe, 1986	Gramsci, 1957/1983
Althusser, 1971	Williams, 1980

Tenets/Focus
> • "Strict" Marxism accounts for intolerances (e.g., "racism") based on the role of ownership of labor (mode of production) and the social relationships that this imposes (relations of production). For example, group divisions inhibit revolt by workers.

Figure 3.2: Continued

- Labor structures (base) are central to human existence. Mode and relations of production dictate rest of society (superstructure), such as religion, family structure, politics, education.
- Various forms of Marxism/neo-Marxism (Solomos counts five) differ in degree of autonomy seen between forces of production and other spheres of social life. Some forms are very nondeterministic.

FOCUS: SOCIAL CLASS, ECONOMIC FORCES, not group belonging, ARE CENTRAL TO PREJUDICE

- Weberian Approaches

  Weber (Gerth & Mills, 1946)   Rex, 1980, 1986

  Tenets/Focus
  - Distribution of resources (not their ownership), maintenance of social status (honor) are core.
  - In times of economic flux, socioeconomic level of a group *is* central to status; in times of stability, focus changes to "way of life."
  - There are a *variety* of economies, with different relations—not just owner and worker.

  FOCUS: AUTHORITY, STATUS, HONOR OF GROUPS IN COMPETITION

Strengths and Weaknesses of Structural/Sociological Approach
  + It is useful in explaining how differences in spheres, stances toward and between groups can relate to group-based demographic or structural variables (e.g., ethnic segregation, "glass ceilings").
  + Approaches look beyond individual factors to life circumstances in which individuals are situated and that can influence individual factors.
  + Ethnicity: It shows role of migration and immigration patterns, which helps explain (in)tolerance between groups of same ethnicity.
  + Marx: It reveals potential role of power and economic advantage, beyond mere dislike based on ignorance (Jackman & Crane, 1986).
  + Marx: Literature aids in understanding of rising trend in dialectic (Billig, 1976) and critical theory.
  + Weber: It explains intolerance between groups where money or labor relations do not seem to be an issue.
  + Weber: It is not as reductionistic, has more explanatory power than many Marxist theories.
  − It is not as useful in explaining why groups within a single circumstance have different spheres, stances of intolerance.
  − It does not explain role of language in prejudice.
  − Some forms rely only one lens of focus; for example, some neo-Marxist views see power or economics at play in all intolerance. This focus may blind us to other possible influences.
  − Macro-level focus may distance scholars from an understanding of how specific individuals experience or exhibit (in)tolerance.

CRITICAL/RHETORICAL

- Critical Theory (CT)[11]

  Kellner, 1989   Goldberg, 1990, 1993[12]
  Stepan, 1991   Essed, 1990, 1991
  McKerrow, 1989, 1991   Lacan, 1977

Figure 3.2: Continued

Lévi-Strauss, 1963
hooks, 1990
Warner, 1991, 1992
Habermas, in Golden, Berquist,
& Coleman, 1989

Althusser, 1971
Marcuse, 1974
Williams, 1980
van Dijk, 1984, 1987

Tenets/Focus

- CT is more a "perspective" than a theory—it has manifestations in many different fields, from architecture to communication to history; even within one field, there might be many approaches to the same thing (e.g., intolerance).
- Most forms offer a critique of some aspect of society. The role of social science is to bring reality in line with an ideal. In most cases, this ideal would include maximum freedom of action for all individuals. Thus CT holds that science is value laden and should be used for political ends.
- Key concepts include liberation, emancipation, such as from the structures and ideologies of those in positions of domination (e.g., "dominant" culture).
- In the context of intergroup communication, CT has its strongest voice in the field of rhetoric (Habermas, McKerrow), though it is also used in discourse analysis of racist communication (Essed, van Dijk).
- Connected to communication, some CT looks at the loose relationship between words and the "realities" they stand for (Lacan, Lévi-Strauss). Symbols like "British" and "family values" mean different things to different people (polysemy), with different groups trying to establish their meanings over those of others.

- Cultural Studies (CS)

Hall, 1982, 1985, 1986
Barker & Beezer, 1992
CCCS, 1982
Gilman, 1990

Grossberg, Nelson, & Treichler, 1992
Nakayama, in press
Schwichtenberg, 1989
Turner, 1990

Tenets/Focus

- CS is a major branch of CT. Like CT, it is multidisciplinary but has a large emphasis in rhetoric.
- CS looks at popular culture of a society and its "texts" (novels, billboards, advertisements, music videos, and so on). Some CS writers look at texts themselves, others at the various meanings the text has for audience members (Turner, 1990).
- These texts reproduce (continue the existence of) power structures and ideas that restrict freedom and oppress people. Many social realities and definitions for words are maintained in place by those whom they benefit.
- The purpose of much CS is to give new readings to texts that help people to resist them, that is, to emancipate people from dominant structures.
- Thus popular culture (and cultural values themselves) is a "site of struggle" where forces vie for "hegemony" (following Gramsci, 1957/1983).

Strengths and Weaknesses of Critical/Rhetorical Approach

+ It examines phenomena in their historical and cultural context more than some other approaches. This can lead to less culturally bound approaches toward (in)tolerance.
+ It attempts to be multidisciplinary, which would allow for several ways of understanding (in)tolerance.

Figure 3.2: Continued

+ Some aspects (cultural studies) give strong attention to the role of images and popular culture in the maintenance of structures and ideas that exclude others.
+ Literature is diverse, giving much attention to several "disempowered" groups, and offering a variety of potential explanations.
+ It has the goal of practicality: the application of principles learned to daily lives of people to empower them against or liberate them from forms of oppression.
− Some critical theorists (in Grossberg et al., 1992) feel CT has wandered from its original goals; this includes the importation of U.S. or British theory to other regions (Turner, 1990).
− In the same vein, some have accused CT of trying to impose yet another European theory (Marxism) on non-European groups (Asante, 1987).
− Some critical theorists are moving away from a multidisciplinary focus, choosing and privileging only certain methods.
− Many theorists privilege only "liberal" viewpoints—theory is not easily used to explain intolerance of "disempowered" groups toward "dominant" cultures.
− Many theorists have grown entrenched in academia, to the point that theory has lost a political and practical edge.
− Like other Marxist views, sometimes theorists can be blinded by "power" focus, precluding consideration of other explanatory factors.

NOTES: 1. This branch of theory, which only some sociobiologists follow (and may include some noted sociobiologists), seems most closely akin to Allport's (1954/1979) "deserved reputation theory": We are prejudiced toward certain groups because they have qualities that "merit" our disdain. Many in this perspective do not differentiate between sociobiology and evolutionary theory. Others see *sociobiology* as the broader term, with its more "racist" inclusions. Sociobiology, more than the others, has strong opponents, so we have indicated here the authors' stance (+/−) toward this approach.
2. Tenets listed may not describe all researchers within a tradition. For example, not all sociobiologists are interested in genetic superiority/inferiority.
3. Tajfel (1978a, 1981, 1982), Tajfel and Turner (1978), Turner (1987b).
4. Billig (1976), Billig et al. (1988), Howett et al. (1989).
5. Gudykunst (1986, 1988, in press), Gudykunst and Kim (1992).
6. Communication accommodation theory (CAT): Gallois, Franklyn-Stokes, Giles, and Coupland (1988); Giles, Bourhis, and Taylor (1977b); Giles and Coupland (1991); Giles and Evans (1986).
7. Collier (1994); Collier and Thomas (1988); Hecht, Collier, and Riebeau (1993); and various studies by Collier, Hecht, and others.
8. The entire issue (No. 1) of the *Journal of Social Issues* (Vol. 46, 1990) is dedicated to this. The fact that many of the authors cite each other but neither cite nor are cited in other bodies of literature leads us to think this is a "perspective" of its own, rather than authors from various perspectives responding to a call for papers on a specific topic.
9. In this line, one could also include political, economic, and institutional factors.
10. Miles and Phizacklea's work, which focuses on intolerance toward immigrant labor groups, is reviewed, along with other neo-Marxist approaches, in Solomos (1986).
11. The scope of critical theory is expansive, from the empiricism of Adorno (*The Authoritarian Personality*) and Horkeimer, to structuralism (Barthes, Lacan, Lévi-Strauss), to postmodernism (Baudrillard, Deleuze and Guattari, Foucault, Jameson, Lyotard), to New Crisis Theory (Habermas). Because all deal with power and ideology, all might be pertinent to a discussion of (in)tolerance. Here, however, we have only cited those we feel are most directly related.
12. Goldberg and Stepan do not clearly call themselves critical theorists, though some of their work is critical and they discuss some of the writers of this school.

Figure 3.2: Continued

themselves sociobiologists or evolutionary theorists, explain prejudiced behavior more in terms of instinctual, rather than specifically genetic, influences, such as fear of the unknown, preservation of one's own gene pool or ingroup, and enforcement of group solidarity. Writers have used sociobiology to explain a variety of outgroup intolerances (Reynolds, Falger, & Vine, 1987; Ross, 1991). While some accuse all sociobiology of being used for racist or exclusionary purposes (Barker, 1990), others defend it (van den Berghe, 1986; see Mason, 1986): If it is scientific truth, it should be accepted regardless of its popularity in academia.

Social psychological approaches. These approaches take or affect most of what is seen in interethnic or intergroup communication literature. There are at least five divisions of intergroup literature under this umbrella. The early psychologists (Adorno et al., 1982; Allport, 1979; Rokeach, 1960) were beginning to look at how social factors (e.g., group belonging, societal norms for aggression) affected intolerance. However, they frequently focused primarily on the elements of *psychological structure* such as rigidity, conformity, authoritarianism, and closed-mindedness (dogmatism), as these were developed in one's upbringing. Based on the work of these early psychologists, another group of writers took another focus: *cognitivism.* Tajfel and Turner (1978) developed their social identity theory, according to which we define and evaluate ourselves in terms of the groups we belong to (ingroups) but we compare ourselves—usually favorably—with those who are not in our "group" (outgroups). The roots of psychological structure and categorization systems mix in different ways in the intergroup theories of Gudykunst (1986, 1988) and Stephan (1985).

Many writers focus their theories on how *ethnicity or other group belonging is enacted* in communication processes (Giles, Bourhis, & Taylor, 1977b; Gumperz, 1982; Hecht et al., 1993) or how multiple, sometimes conflicting identities are balanced (Clément & Noels, 1992; Weinreich, 1986). Others focus on how social identities are socially constructed through discourse (Edwards & Potter, 1992; Howett et al., 1989). Still others look at the conflicting forces within individuals, largely as created through social interaction (Billig et al., 1988). Thus one must look at the "interaction between society and the individual" (Howett et al., 1989, p. 159), and not just individual personality constructs. In the same line, *rational choice theorists* hold that individuals' prejudices are based on personal choices that meet social needs (Banton, 1986, 1987).

Finally, a group of writers have united a great diversity of perspectives under the banner *moral exclusion.* This exclusion is the placing of other groups beyond the boundaries of what one would deem fair and appropriate for one's own group (Bar-Tal, 1990). Moral exclusion might be based on instincts, on psychological needs, or on categories and stereotypes as they are influenced by history and macrostructural phenomena (politics, economics). However, because most of the writers focus on ingroups and outgroups (a categorization), we place moral exclusion here.

Structural or sociological approaches. These have received much less attention in "traditional" intergroup communication literature, though their presence in critical theory (discussed below) is largely felt. Three main strains of structure-based intergroup theory (mostly regarding "race") were found. The first, the *ethnicity approaches*, differ from those approaches mentioning ethnicity above, in that they focus on ethnicities as groups. The emphasis is on group-based factors, such as immigration patterns, allocation of resources (space, jobs), and establishment of boundaries based on ethnicity or "race." Beginning with the work in the early 1900s by Robert Park and the Chicago School (Lal, 1986), this approach is now manifested in ethnic nationalism (Omi & Winant, 1986; e.g., Asante, 1987) and in the views of those who argue that "race," not class, is what divides many cultures. The question of interest becomes how those societies come to be "racially formed" or structured and how that formation is perpetuated (Omi & Winant, 1986).

A variety of *Marxist* and *neo-Marxist approaches* look to the relationship between the labor owners and workers (modes, relations of production) and the way those relations are replicated in other areas of society (base, superstructure). However, many who would call themselves Marxian have abandoned the more reductionistic view that Marx is assumed to have promoted (e.g., that intolerances are promoted by the owning class to divide the workers so they would not rebel). Power, economic advantage, forces vying for hegemonic power in various sites of struggle (Gramsci, 1983; Hall, 1982, 1986), dominant cultures maintaining their positions through control of ideology (Althusser, 1971; Hall, 1982, 1985)—all of these are mixed in a variety of ways in different forms of Marxist theory.[12] Max Weber, and those who take *Weberian approaches* to (in)tolerance, would not deny that labor forces are important, but would likely urge that they are important more as they pertain to status and honor. The chief operator in (in)tolerance is the maintaining of one's own group in a superior status position—but that position is not always marked by money, especially in times of relative economic stability. Further, Weberian approaches recognize several different possible social relations—not just workers and owners (Rex, 1980, 1986).

Even within these theories there is competition. Thus, based on the contact hypothesis notion that increased contact between nontypical members of groups under certain circumstances will produce better intergroup relationships, Hallinan and others (Hallinan & Teixeira, 1987; Hallinan & Williams, 1987, 1989) find that structural changes (how groups are formed in an elementary classroom; policies that promote noncompetition between students) are associated with higher numbers of interracial friendships formed. But Jackman and Crane (1986) conclude that, regardless of positive affect, white students still do not want to grant measures that would equalize power or status in the classroom.

Critical/rhetorical approaches. As stated above, the structural approaches, particularly Marxism, have had a major impact on critical theory and, through this, on cultural studies. There are certainly many rhetorical theories that might look at (in)tolerance that are not critical, but critical theory seems to be the best represented approach in rhetorical analyses of difference. Critical theorists are as diverse in their approaches as those in the areas mentioned above. There are structuralists and poststructuralists, postmodernists, feminists, queer theorists, and others (Kellner, 1989). Many are informed by the Marxist writers mentioned above, such as Gramsci (1983; hegemony, sites of struggle) and Althusser (1971; control of ideology). Others are influenced by the structuralists such as Lacan (1977) and Lévi-Strauss (1963), who note the frequently loose connections between symbols and what they stand for. For example, a brown uniform in South Africa can be for many a symbol of intolerance and oppression.

One outgrowth of critical theory is *cultural studies*, which looks at popular culture—novels, newscasts, music lyrics, posters, films—to see how certain interpretations (ideologies) or social structures are reproduced or propagated. Some in this school look at different meanings (polysemy) that can be given to a text, often seeking to provide ways of reading a text that can empower those whom the text oppresses (Turner, 1990). Others provide their own meaning. Regardless, cultural studies writers have in common with other critical theorists that the goal of their research is to change individuals and society—individuals so that those oppressed can resist, and society so that structures that oppress can be challenged and changed.[13]

Integration of the layers of understanding. It seems that each of these perspectives holds an important piece of the (in)tolerance puzzle. The question is this: How do the pieces relate to each other? Allport's (1979) telescoping model of theories of prejudice seems to indicate (though he does not articulate this) that history and situation affect sociology, which affects psychology, which affects cognition. This is to say that social factors and norms affect the psyche, which, in the last instance, is where prejudice lies. The prejudiced personality will, in turn, express intolerance through verbal and nonverbal activity. We agree with this. Many factors (individual and social) influence one's desire to adapt communicative patterns to a perceived other. What the layered perspective adds to this solid framework is the recursive nature of influence and the possibility that items can influence one another directly instead of through only one factor—for example, through the psyche, through economic structures, and so on (Blalock, 1982a; see Figure 3.3 for potential interrelationships between "disciplinary" types of understanding). The layering concept increases awareness of the complex interrelatedness of aspects; it allows for the compounding effects of aspects through time (i.e., process); and it allows for the interpenetration of the elements with each other. Not only are rhetorical and cognitive influences interrelated, for example, but media images help construct and reproduce the category systems of those who receive them; yet certain images are produced based on individual views that media creators hold. These individual views, however, are socially enhanced and shaped through discourse.

If someone wanted to argue that the ultimate foci of analysis—those directly preceding communication—are psychological and cognitive, we would agree. But it cannot be stated that those are the *most* important. One is led to ask, looking at many of the linear and individualistic models in communication, if personal needs can affect categorization. Can one's personal experience (phenomenology as opposed to cognitive psychology) affect personal needs? Certainly how one experiences the world and personal needs will lead to communication, but how does that person's own communication, interaction, and relationships with others, and exposure to symbols and texts, affect that person's cognition and psyche? As people symbolically co-create reality, how do their messages influence history and social structure? Can social structures affect history, and history social structures (Becker, 1992)?

At the next level of complexity, one also asks questions concerning how elements in the model are jointly enacted (e.g., How is Eurocentrism enacted after viewing a movie on oppression while in the presence of friends from the empowered group?) and how knowledge gained on one level is played out at other levels (e.g., How are media constructions of "race" reflected in individual thought patterns?). One can also ask about the dynamic tensions between and among layers (e.g., How do people reject media images of "race"? How do groups work to liberate themselves or others from hegemonic influences?). In short, it is proposed that research be approached from a variety of perspectives and, we hope, from more than one at a time.

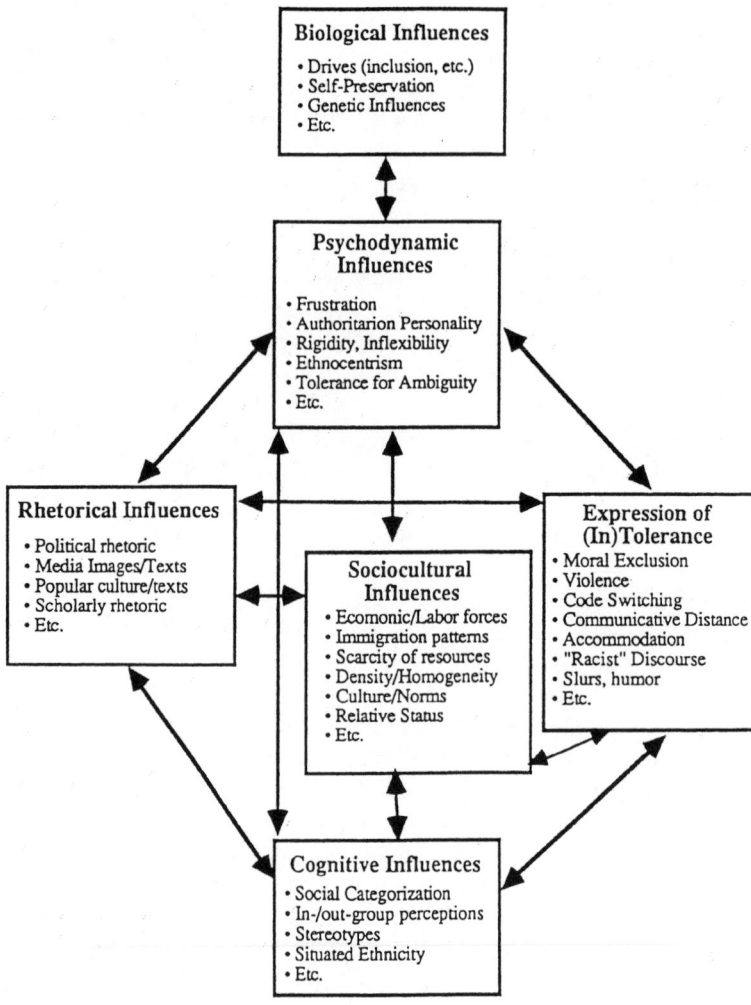

Figure 3.3: A Visual Model for the Levels of Analysis and Their Potential Interrelationships

Because of the complexity and circular nature of causality, especially in the case of (in)tolerance (Riedl, 1984; Watzlawick, 1984a, 1984b), this chapter has not ventured to state exact hypotheses. Rather, we hope that this perspective will lay groundwork for future dialogue between scholars of many areas. Each layer or interpenetration could be grounds for planting a new theory or line of research.

CONCLUSION

The notion of layering implies that there are several overlapping and interpenetrating layers of appreciation or intolerance. Not only do the spheres overlap and interpenetrate, but so do the levels of analysis. An individual's level of appreciation will interact with that person's role in interactions, relationships, and the community. The expressions of intolerance or appreciation that are shared in a community will in turn affect future social structures and cognitions, which will affect future communication. A complete understanding requires the peeling of different layers, much like an artichoke. As the layers are peeled back, one might find differences in personal, sociocultural, economic, and other influences that lead to the frequent contradictions in (in)tolerance between spheres. In these cases, types of analysis can be juxtaposed (triangulated) to see what each has to offer to understanding. What is still unclear is how to describe the artichoke "heart."

Not only are the factors of intolerance/appreciation layered, but the methodologies for investigating them are as well: The layered research method would, of necessity, use multiple methods (if not in a single study then in a research line) and incorporate a variety of perspectives (e.g., multiethnic and/or multidisciplinary research teams; juxtaposing the experiences of cultural group members with "experts" such as poets and novelists). One may use self-report inventories, experimental methodology, interview, critical and rhetorical analyses of texts, ethnographic descriptions, and other methods separately or in combination to understand these diverse phenomena.

The implications for theory of this perspective are that, even if one chooses to focus on one level of analysis or one area of the (in)tolerance puzzle, the individual should be familiar with other areas and integrate them when possible, looking for their value. Any theory of (in)tolerance must be complex, and not monistic. No one theory or study will incorporate all levels, spheres, stances, and types of understanding, but studies should build in as many of these as possible and expedient for the purposes at hand. Some studies will remain on one level or in one sphere, but studies need to be done also to show the connections between the elements. Theorists and studies should indicate the connections to the other layers and consider the implications of reductions that lead to exclusions.

This chapter has sought to lay groundwork for the development of a layered perspective of (in)tolerance(s) that integrates the strengths of these past areas of research on prejudice. The intent has been to provide a framework that can guide not only individual studies but theories and lines of research. One example of such a line of research would be first to see how "race" and "racism" are constructed structurally for individuals (using qualitative methods) (Baldwin, 1994a; Niles & Baldwin, 1994). One could then use critical, rhetorical, and/or social scientific methods to compare this with structural formations of "race" and "racism" (e.g., Ezorsky, 1991; Franklin, 1991), such as that found in the court systems (Zatz, 1987) or media. Then, one could see what behaviors are perceived to be racist and how racism is expressed, comparing societies that do not sanction such expression with those that do (to find out whether social sanctions really eliminate racism). Experimental methodology could be used to see if providing certain rhetorical readings of texts indeed helped people resist racist messages, or to see if certain educational programs or field experiences had short- or long-term effect on either one's racist attitudes or on one's behavior that others could perceive as racist.

This approach argues against firm methodological and disciplinary boundaries. It suggests instead that each type of research has something to add to a greater understanding of (in)tolerances. Unfortunately, many research programs that do consider the role of prejudice, stereotypes, and expressions of intolerance are limited in their methodological focus (kinds of understanding), their theoretical perspective on where the key factors of intolerance lie (levels), the targets of intolerance (spheres), or the conceptualizing of prejudice/tolerance into a dichotomy. The investigation of this perspective will require collaborative research by scholars from different fields and different groups. This sort of research should address the complexity of the issues surrounding intolerance and, we hope, pave the road for appropriate interventions at individual and societal levels to make the world a more tolerant—even a more appreciative—place to live.

NOTES

1. Following many current writers on "race" (e.g., Goldberg, 1990; Stepan, 1991), we believe that "race," while perhaps based on supposed biological differences, is a social construction; people's understanding of what "race" is has changed throughout history (Banton, 1987). Guillaumin (1980) and Outlaw (1990) give a thorough justification for this. To highlight its social constructedness, we have, except where to do so would twist the intended meaning of the authors we are citing, placed it in quotation marks. For stylistic reasons, we did not do this for sex, age, and so on, but the same argument applies. In addition, we have placed "disciplines" in quotations to note their social constructedness; what they include and how they are structured are historical and culturally varied.

2. To date, there is not a good word for this idea. *(In)tolerance* allows the reader to understand that tolerance and intolerance are sides of the same coin; to discuss one is to discuss the other. While we will shortly introduce the idea of appreciation, *appreciation/intolerance* is bulky. Thus we will use *(in)*tolerance to refer to the range of acceptance, from appreciation to rejection, based on a perceived Other's group belonging. We use intolerance*(s)* to indicate that, while there may be a certain level of intolerance at the individual or cultural level toward many groups, the nature of that intolerance differs. We

will elaborate on both of these as we discuss the theory in detail. While we recognize different forms of intolerance (intolerances), for ease of reading we will not continue to bracket the "s."

3. This is not to assume that all ethnography is subjective. Ethnography is, in fact, a method and can be approached from a "naive realistic" point of view (Hammersley, 1992), a "critical" point of view (Clough, 1992), or a subjective point of view, in which the ethnographer realizes and admits that the tale is her or his own construction of what was observed.

4. We realize we have oversimplified Billig, who sees the dilemma as one not merely of self-presentation but of the desire to be rational.

5. Some suggest that similarity facilitates relationships (Rychlak, 1965) and reduces uncertainty (Berger & Calabrese, 1975). We feel that dissimilarity can be good. It can stimulate relationships (McCarthy & Duck, 1976) and is even necessary for them, as expressed in Baxter's (1990) dialectic perspective.

6. As such, some of the same limitations of attuning as laid out in communication accommodation theory might also apply here (e.g., "overattuning," situational constraints).

7. The idea that spheres can be held at the individual as well as the societal level contrasts with the view that intolerance is an individual rather than a group phenomenon. If intolerance is seen only as an internal construct, then this would be true. But if actions can express intolerance regardless of intent, then cultural (group-based) values, norms, and behaviors, as well as society-level actions, images, and collective memory, can contain expressions and ideas that exclude, regardless of the individual intents of many actors. Further, these society-/culture-level phenomena can be at work reproducing (in)tolerance in individuals. A focus only on the internal would reproduce the social psychological emphasis in much of our field, and it is one of the chief functions of this theory to give us more ways of looking at the world.

8. As we are presenting a perspective for the conceptualization of (in)tolerance and not a specific theory to account for all possible variables of a type of intolerance, we will not elaborate on the factors here.

9. We do not intend to oversimplify either Marxism or critical theory. We will elaborate more on these under "types of understanding."

10. This order is not intended to privilege those views that come first; the order is not important. Our presentation differs from Allport's (1979) in the following ways, based on our view of current theory and research: Deserved reputation is subsumed as part of the *sociobiological theories*; phenomenological (cognitive) and psychodynamic theories are placed under *social psychological theories*; sociological influences remain as Allport conceptualized them. And *critical/rhetorical approaches* take in the situational/historical uniqueness of certain intolerances as well as studies of media and other forms of discourse.

11. In this section, as in any abbreviation, we have taken great liberties in summarizing the perspectives and authors. Our purpose is not to fully explain the intricacies of each theory but to show how it fits in the overall picture. We ask all authors to excuse our reduction. Also note that, in this section, we have attempted to include minimal citing. More references to the work we have reviewed for this chapter are found in Figure 3.2. We apologize that, both here and in the figure, a bulk of the sources relate to the interethnic or interracial sphere of intolerances—that is only because this is our own area of interest and research.

12. Solomos (1986) details at least five strains of Marxist theory as it pertains to racial intolerance. Other reviews of the literature appear in Banton (1986, 1987), Franklin, (1991), Omi and Winant (1986), and Rex (1986).

13. One critique of critical theory is that it is a European theory (in that it is Marxist) used to liberate those disempowered by European/American hegemony (Asante, 1987).

4

Toward a Differential Demand Model of Sojourner Adjustment

JEFFREY C. ADY • *University of Hawaii at Manoa*

Those who experience extended cross-cultural sojourns may notice themselves undergoing a process of becoming accustomed, to varying degrees, to the new environment in which they find themselves. Sojourner adjustment is both a task and a process faced by those studying abroad, those on foreign assignment as part of their job responsibilities, and many others who experience extended stays in a culture different than their own. The important consequences for sojourners adjusting— and those for sojourners not adjusting, such as poor academic and job performance, serious physical and mental illness, premature return, and the loss of resources and funds that support the sojourners' travel—have been established by a number of writers (Black, Mendenhall, & Oddou, 1991; Copeland & Griggs, 1985; Spradley & Phillips, 1972; Tung, 1982). Many studies have both conceptually and empirically explored sojourner adjustment in relation to its antecedents, correlates, processual nature, and consequences. Yet, perhaps in part due to the multidimensional nature of sojourner adjustment, the phenomenon has been conceptually and operationally approached in different ways to such an extent that no consensus has developed over the past four decades on what sojourner adjustment is or how it is best measured (Black et al., 1991; Church, 1982; Parker & McEvoy, 1993; Spradley & Phillips, 1972). This chapter seeks first to examine the sojourner adjustment literature across a variety of disciplines and identifies several general trends in the conceptual and operational definition of sojourner adjustment. Next, general comments are made on the relative strengths and weaknesses of those trends. Finally, this chapter presents an alternative model of sojourner adjustment that is based on discrepancy theory, incorporates many of the lessons learned by researchers in subjective well-being, offers many advantages in measurement, and may provide important new directions in the exploration of sojourner adjustment.

DEFINING SOJOURNER ADJUSTMENT

Sojourner adjustment is a relatively short-term, individually and time-based process that is conceptually distinct from cultural or ethnic assimilation, adaptation, and intercultural communicative competence. This chapter follows Brein and David (1971) in defining sojourner adjustment as the psychological adjustment of relatively short-term visitors to new cultures whose permanent settlement is not the purpose of the sojourn. While Gudykunst (1984, p. 404) classifies a *sojourner* as "a traveler, a visitor, not a person who has come to the host community to reside," this chapter allows for a possibly extended stay such as that frequently characteristic of international students or employees of foreign/multinational organizations who are on foreign assignment; the distinctive feature of the sojourner is that he or she does not intend to stay permanently in the host culture. *Sojourner adjustment*, thus defined, is viewed as different than other terms frequently taken to be synonymous in the literature (e.g., *cultural* or *cross-cultural adjustment, cultural* or *ethnic assimilation, cultural adaptation*) because those very terms "are ambiguous or suggest a more permanent assimilation to the host culture" (Church, 1982, p. 540). Sojourner adjustment is also seen as an individually based process, in contrast to acculturation, which involves groups of people moving from one cultural setting to another (Berry, 1980). Sojourner adjustment is also viewed as a process of change to a new environment that is separate from others' views of the adjusting individual as engaging in appropriate and effective communication, which is the basis of Spitzberg and Cupach's (1984) model of communicative competence. Grove and Torbiörn (1985) argue that the sojourner is adjusted when he or she engages in behavior that is socially acceptable and interpersonally effective, and define adjustment in terms of competence in contrast to numerous publications that conceptualize sojourner adjustment as more general change to a new environment. The relationship between adjustment and competence may admittedly be a riddle of the "chicken-and-egg" variety; the argument can be made, for example, that an individual is adjusted when competence has been built through time. In Spitzberg and Cupach's (1984) words, adjustment is viewed "as an end state of having developed competence in interactions generally" (p. 35). Conversely, adjustment can be viewed as a time-based process (as distinct from an end state in the former case), at the culmination of which the individual engages in competent communicative behavior (Grove & Torbiörn, 1985). This chapter assumes the latter position.

TRENDS IN THE CONCEPTUALIZATION
OF ADJUSTMENT FOUND IN THE LITERATURE

Literature on sojourner adjustment has conceptualized the phenomenon in a variety of ways, but the multiplicity of views can be reduced to six general trends in definition: general satisfaction, process, interaction, psychopathology, adjustment to change, and competence. Table 4.1 details all six general areas of definition in chronological order. The literature review undertaken for this chapter, although not exhaustive, is representative of the work done across a number of disciplines on sojourner adjustment.

Numerous authors have defined sojourner adjustment in terms of general satisfaction with one's life in a new environment (Church, 1982; Diggs & Murphy, 1991; Dunbar, 1992; Hammer, 1987; Hawes & Kealey, 1981; Lysgaard, 1955; Ruben & Kealey, 1979; Searle & Ward, 1990; Sewell & Davidsen, 1956; Ward & Searle, 1991; Ying & Liese, 1990, 1991). These definitions generally describe sojourner adjustment in terms of feelings of well-being or satisfaction with one's general environment or with primary facets of one's life. Table 4.1 presents detailed listings of these authors' particular definitions of sojourner adjustment.

Other writers have cast sojourner adjustment in terms of its nature as a time-based process. Oberg (1960) described adjustment as the successful progression through four stages of culture shock. Gullahorn and Gullahorn (1963) further elaborated the four-stage approach into the U- and W-curves of culture and reentry shock. Adler's (1975) five-stage model took the sojourner from lower self- and cultural awareness to higher states of both. Grove and Torbiörn (1985) recast the four-stage model in terms of the sojourner's progress toward optimal behavioral applicability and perceptual clarity.

Several studies have defined sojourner adjustment as involving interpersonal interaction in the host culture. Bochner, Lin, and McLeod (1980, p. 266) wrote that the U- and W-curves and the view of adjustment as an intrapsychic variable leave "the interpersonal determinants of adjustment remaining mostly implicit." Brein and David (1971) defined sojourner adjustment as effective interpersonal functioning dependent upon "the development of understanding between the sojourner and host" (p. 224). Tucker, Raik, Rossiter, and Uhmes (1973) defined adjustment simply as intercultural interaction. Mendenhall and

TABLE 4.1 Trends in Sojourner Adjustment Conceptualization by Trend, Author(s), and Conceptual Definition

General Satisfaction	
Lysgaard (1955)	". . . not defined in any precise way; the concept is used as a convenient reference to the respondent's subjective reports on their feelings of satisfaction with different aspects of the stay" (p. 46)
Hawes & Kealey (1981)	Adjustment, satisfaction
Church (1982)	Emotional well-being and satisfaction
Hammer (1987)	Satisfaction and report of how well one functioned while living in a host culture
Searle & Ward (1990)	Psychological adjustment (feelings of well-being and satisfaction)
Ying & Liese (1990)	"Adaptation" incorporates emotional well-being (process oriented, involving an experiential, internal, private state; the level of distress experienced while engaged in the process of making the adjustment)
Diggs & Murphy (1991)	Satisfaction with experiences abroad
Ward & Searle (1991)	Psychosocial adjustment (feelings of well-being and satisfaction)
Ying & Liese (1991)	Emotional well-being (an affective phenomenon)
Dunbar (1992)	General satisfaction
Ruben & Kealey (1979)	Psychological adjustment: general psychological well-being, self-satisfaction, contentment, and comfort with and accommodation to a new environment after the initial perturbations that characterize culture shock have passed
Process	
Oberg (1960)	Adjustment is the successful progression through the four stages of culture shock
Gullahorn & Gullahorn (1963)	The "U"- and "W"-curves of adjustment
Church (1982)	Stage models of adjustment
Interaction	
Brein & David (1971)	Effective interpersonal functioning; depends on the development of understanding between sojourner and host
Bochner et al. (1980)	U- and W-curves and the intrapsychic variable of adjustment leaves out the interpersonal determinants of adjustment remaining mostly implicit
Mendenhall & Oddou (1985)	Others-Oriented Dimension: relationship development and willingness to communicate
Psychopathological	
Schram & Lauver (1988)	Vulnerability, loneliness, loss of identity, helplessness, desire for dependence, fear, bewilderment, hostility, and alienation (powerlessness, meaninglessness, and social estrangement) named as characteristics of the adjustment period
Armes & Ward (1989)	Various emotional states

(continued)

TABLE 4.1 Continued

Abe & Zane (1990)	Maladjustment: psychotic disorders (schizophrenia, affective psychosis, reactive or acute psychosis, major depression, and anxiety)
Rogers & Ward (1993)	(Lack of) psychological distress
Ward & Kennedy (1993)	Psychosocial adjustment: stress and coping
Adjustment to Change	
Spradley & Phillips (1972)	Accommodating cultural differences
Ruben & Kealey (1979)	A subset of adaptation
Church (1982)	Typologies of sojourner characteristics or patterns of adjustment
	Culture learning (operant conditioning)
Mendenhall & Oddou (1985)	Self-Oriented Dimension: reinforcement substitution, stress reduction, and technical competence
	Perceptual Dimension: attributional and evaluative flexibility and "looseness"
	Cultural-Toughness Dimension: relative cultural distances
Kim (1988a)	The term *adaptation* is used as a broad concept that accommodates subjective, objective, assimilative, acculturative, and adjustive aspects of acculturation
Black & Stephens (1989)	General, interaction, and work adjustment (cf. other Black studies)
Black (1990)	Literature suggests that adjustment is generally measured from the perspective of the individual experiencing the transition and that adjustment could be measured in terms of adjustment to the general environment, to the work situation, or to interacting with host nationals
Searle & Ward (1990)	Sociocultural adjustment (the ability to "fit in" or negotiate interactive aspects of the host culture)
Ying & Liese (1990)	"Adaptation" incorporates adjustment (result oriented, reflective of stage consequent to attempts to cope with the challenges of life in a new country; a cognitive appraisal of one's life)
Ward & Searle (1991)	Sociocultural adjustment (the ability to "fit in" or negotiate interactive aspects of the host culture)
Ying & Liese (1991)	Adjustment (cognitive process)
Black (1992)	Adjustment to (a) the job, (b) interacting with host nationals, and (c) the general nonwork environment; adjustment is a function of having higher levels of accurate or met expectations (rather than undermet or overmet expectations)
Stening & Hammer (1992)	Adaptation
Ward & Kennedy (1993)	Sociocultural adjustment: culture learning
Parker & McEvoy (1993)	Adjustment to (a) the job, (b) interacting with host nationals, and (c) the general nonwork environment (following Black's series)
Competence	
Grove & Torbiörn (1985)	Behavior that is applicable to the environment (socially acceptable and interpersonally effective) and a clear frame of reference

Oddou (1985) defined adjustment in part as relationship development and willingness to communicate.

Other scholars have focused on the psychopathological consequences of the lack of adjustment. Adjustment, or the lack thereof, has been defined as vulnerability, loneliness, loss of identity and other emotional disturbances (Schram & Lauver, 1988), and disturbances in various emotional states (Armes & Ward, 1989). Furthermore, sojourner (mal)adjustment has been conceptualized in terms of depression (Searle & Ward, 1990), various psychotic disorders (Abe & Zane, 1990), psychological distress (Rogers & Ward, 1993), and stress (Ward & Kennedy, 1993).

A comparatively large body of research has conceptualized sojourner adjustment in terms of changes sojourners must make to new environments and their feelings of comfort with those changes (Black, 1990, 1992; Black & Stephens, 1989; Black et al., 1991; Church, 1982; Holmes & Rahe, 1967; Kim, 1988a; Mendenhall & Oddou, 1985; Parker & McEvoy, 1993; Ruben & Kealey, 1979; Searle & Ward, 1990; Spradley & Phillips, 1972; Stening & Hammer, 1992; Ward & Kennedy, 1993; Ward & Searle, 1991; Ying & Liese, 1990, 1991). See Table 4.1 for a detailed listing of these researchers' definitions of sojourner adjustment.

Finally, Grove and Torbiörn (1985) defined sojourner adjustment in terms of the adjusted individual (a) engaging in behavior that is acceptable and interpersonally effective and (b) feeling that his or her frame of reference is accurate, complete, clearly perceived, and practically useful. While Grove and Torbiörn's position on sojourner adjustment may arguably be reduced to one of general adjustment to a new environment, it is similar to Spitzberg and Cupach's (1984) model of communicative competence, except for the important fact that it does not stipulate that the crux of acceptability and effectiveness is the judgment made by others regarding the degree of acceptability and effectiveness.

TRENDS IN OPERATIONALIZATIONS OF ADJUSTMENT FOUND IN THE LITERATURE

Literature on sojourner adjustment has operationally defined the phenomenon in a variety of ways that are similar to that of sojourner adjustment conceptualization, but that variety can be reduced to five general areas of operationalization: general satisfaction, interaction, psychopathology, adjustment to change, and competence. Table 4.2 details all five general areas of operationalization in chronological order. The relative merits and weaknesses of each general area of operationalization will be discussed as they are enumerated in Table 4.2.

TABLE 4.2 Trends in Sojourner Adjustment Operationalization by Trend, Author(s), and Operational Definition

General Satisfaction	
Lysgaard (1955)	Satisfaction and emotional reactions to the host country
Sewell & Davidsen (1956)	The Index of Affect, measuring the positivity of overall attitudes toward the host country
Ruben & Kealey (1979)	Open-ended questions probing levels of comfort, acceptance, and satisfaction with various aspects of life, work, and self in Kenya
	Three words written summarizing how respondents felt generally about experience
Hawes & Kealey (1981)	Personal feelings of satisfaction (self-rated)
Hammer (1987)	One question on how satisfied subjects were with stay in foreign culture (six-point Likert-type scales ranging from very satisfied to very dissatisfied)
	One question on how well subjects felt they functioned while living in the host culture (six-point Likert-type scales ranging from very well to not well at all)
Armes & Ward (1989)	Five-point bipolar self-report scales measuring happiness and satisfaction
Dunbar (1992)	Overall measure of satisfaction with living abroad (Hawes & Kealey, 1981)
Stening & Hammer (1992)	Satisfaction (measured by six-point self-report ratings)
Tanaka et al. (1994)	Sojourn satisfaction
Interaction	
Schram & Lauver (1988)	Social Contact Scale (out-of-class contact time)
Stening & Hammer (1992)	Intercultural Communication (ability to initiate interaction, meaningful dialogue, resolution of misunderstandings)
	Intercultural Relationship (ability to develop satisfying relationships, maintain satisfying relationships, understand others' feelings, empathize with others, effectively work with others) (measured by six-point self-report ratings)
Tanaka et al. (1994)	Affiliation motive and attitude toward Japanese manners of behavior
Psychopathological	
Ruben & Kealey (1979)	Six-item alienation index measuring powerlessness, meaninglessness, normlessness, cultural estrangement, social estrangement, and estrangement from work
	Observation ratings of psychological adjustment by a trained psychologist (Kealey)
Schram & Lauver (1988)	University Alienation Scale (powerlessness, meaninglessness, and social estrangement)
Armes & Ward (1989)	Five-point bipolar self-report scales measuring anxiety, boredom, depression, frustration, helplessness, isolation, and loneliness

(continued)

TABLE 4.2 Continued

Abe & Zane (1990)	Maladjustment measured by the Personal Integration subscale of the Omnibus Personality Inventory
Searle & Ward (1990)	Psychological adjustment: Self Rating Depression Scale (affective, psychological, and physiological components of depression)
Ying & Liese (1990)	Emotional well-being: CES-D postarrival scores
Ward & Searle (1991)	Profile of Mood States (proprietary-ETS): self-report of symptoms of tension, depression, anger, vigor, confusion, and fatigue
	Self-report of difficulty subjects have dealing with everyday social situations
	UCLA Revised Loneliness Scale measuring quality of IP relationships, together with self-report estimates of amount of time spent weekly with host nationals, fellow nationals, and internationals
Ying & Liese (1991)	Minimal depressive symptomatology was measured by CES-D
Rogers & Ward (1993)	Beck Depression Inventory; Spielberger State Anxiety Inventory
Ward & Kennedy (1993)	Profile of Mood States: self-report of symptoms of tension, depression, anger, vigor, confusion, and fatigue
	Self-report of difficulty subjects have dealing with everyday social situations
Tanaka et al. (1994)	Perceived stress, loneliness, emotional state, and stress coping methods
Adjustment to Change	
Holmes & Rahe (1967)	Social Readjustment Rating Questionnaire: "Social readjustment measures the intensity and length of time necessary to accommodate to a life event, regardless of the desirability of this event." (p. 213)
Spradley & Phillips (1972)	The intensity and length of time necessary to accommodate to a cultural difference, regardless of the desirability of that difference; 33 items of cultural difference (self-report ratings of "average amount of readjustment required by most people to a list of cultural differences")
Szapocznik et al. (1978)	Self-report scores compared between two cultures on behavioral acculturation (1978) scale (33 items) and value acculturation (22 situations)
Hawes & Kealey (1981)	Professional/cultural adjustment (self-report), adjustment/ family adjustment, and satisfaction (self-report)
Searle & Ward (1990)	Sociocultural adjustment: 16-item self-report questionnaire in which respondents rate level of difficulty with everyday life situations

(continued)

TABLE 4.2 Continued

Ying & Liese (1990)	Adjustment: five-point self-report answers to three questions: (a) How do you feel about studying in the United States? (b) How well do you feel about living in the United States? and (c) How well are you adjusting to living in the United States?
Diggs & Murphy (1991)	Self-report ratings of problems, including social adjustment of children, school adjustment of children, and domestic problems
Parker & McEvoy (1993)	Black's 14-item scale (work, general living, and host national interaction adjustment), self-report of "degree of adjustment" subjects felt toward each of the three adjustment domains in specific
Black & Stephens (1989)	General: seven-point Likert self-reports of "adjustment to" living conditions in general, housing conditions, food, shopping, cost of living, entertainment/recreation facilities and opportunities, and health care facilities
	Interaction: seven-point Likert self-reports of "adjustment to" socializing with host nationals, interacting with host nationals on a daily basis, with host nationals outside of work, and speaking with host nationals
	Work: seven-point Likert self-reports of "adjustment to" specific job responsibilities, performance standards and expectations, and supervisory responsibilities
Black (1990)	Six items measuring general adjustment (self-report), four measuring adjustment to interaction with host nationals, and three measuring work adjustment
Black (1992)	Repatriation adjustment was measured by an adaptation of the multifaceted measure of expatriation adjustment (Black & Stephens, 1989)
	Adjustment to the job, interacting with host nationals, and the general nonwork environment were assessed via self-report items
Stening & Hammer (1992)	Intercultural Stress Management (ability to deal with frustration, stress, political systems, anxiety), measured by six-point self-report ratings
Competence	
Stening & Hammer (1992)	Perceived effectiveness (measured by six-point self-report ratings)

Sojourner adjustment has been operationally defined by a number of researchers in terms of one's general satisfaction with life in a new environment. Lysgaard (1955) measured satisfaction and emotional reactions to the host country; Sewell and Davidsen (1956), the positivity of attitudes toward the host country; Ruben and Kealey (1979), comfort, acceptance, and satisfaction; Hawes and Kealey (1981), personal feelings of satisfaction; Hammer (1987), satisfaction with one's stay in a foreign culture; Armes and Ward (1989), happiness and satisfaction; Dunbar (1992), satisfaction with living abroad; and Stening and Hammer (1992), attitudinal satisfaction. Tanaka, Takai, Kohyama, and Fujihara (1994) measured satisfaction with one's sojourn. Global assessments of one's subjective well-being are viewed by some researchers as possible and sufficiently valid (Veenhoven, 1991) and have the possible advantage of working as efficient single-item measures. The case can be made, however (and will be discussed later in this chapter), that serious methodological problems exist with the strategy of asking respondents to provide global assessments of subjective well-being (Andrews & Whithey, 1976; Campbell, 1981; Headey & Wearing, 1991; Schwarz & Strack, 1991; Veenhoven, 1991). Many studies operationalize sojourner adjustment according to general satisfaction. Later in this chapter, an alternative approach will be presented.

Several efforts have operationalized sojourner adjustment in terms of intercultural interaction; Schram and Lauver (1988) measured foreign students' out-of-class contact time with host nationals; Stening and Hammer (1992) measured international students' self-reported abilities to initiate interaction, engage in meaningful dialogue, resolve misunderstandings, develop and maintain satisfying relationships, understand others' feelings, empathize with and effectively work with others. Tanaka et al. (1994) tested exchange students' affiliation motive and attitude toward Japanese manners of behavior. It is noteworthy that the ability measurements are self-report in nature; while more direct measures of social interaction are likely to be prohibitively demanding, self-reports of social interaction yield different results depending on whether they measure number, frequency, depth, or range of encounters (Church, 1982). In addition, the theoretical link between social interaction and adjustment may be one of necessity but not sufficiency; interaction in the host environment is no guarantee that adjustment to that environment will follow, given the many pitfalls endemic to intercultural communication (Church, 1982).

Sojourner adjustment has been operationally defined in terms of psychopathology by a number of studies (Abe & Zane, 1990; Armes & Ward, 1989; Rogers & Ward, 1993; Ruben & Kealey, 1979; Schram & Lauver, 1988; Searle & Ward, 1990; Ward & Kennedy, 1993; Ward & Searle, 1991; Ying & Liese, 1990, 1991; Tanaka et al., 1994). Table 4.2 offers a detailed listing of specific researchers' operationalizations. The psychopathological approach to the operationalization of sojourner adjustment assumes a fundamental relationship between psychopathology and adjustment: If the pathology exists, the sojourner must not be adjusted; conversely, if the pathology is absent, the sojourner must be adjusted. But this logic may have its own difficulties. An individual's adjustment is being conceptualized as the lack of something, which is not quite the opposite of adjustment. Many subjective well-being researchers have noted that well-being is at least bidimensional in affect (Argyle, 1987), with positive and negative affect having differential effects on well-being. Loneliness, for example, is a psychopathology frequently measured in connection with sojourner adjustment; yet loneliness contributes to one's experienced negative affect without affecting positive affect, which is the basis of satisfaction; the same holds true for neuroticism and depression (Argyle, 1987). Headey, Holström, and Wearing (1984a) have demonstrated that well-being and ill-being are distinct, though not orthogonal, dimensions, in that "the correlates and causes of well-being are somewhat different from the correlates and causes of ill-being" (p. 115). The frequently assumed inverse relationship between psychopathology and adjustment, therefore, may not be as valid a measure of sojourner adjustment as might have intuitively been supposed. Why then the focus on psychopathology? Several rather atheoretical reasons for many scholars' choice of psychopathology as a measure of sojourner adjustment may be (a) the gravitational pull of extant measures and (b) the funding practicalities of grantsmanship and the popularity of the pathological turn in North American psychology. Many of the measures specified in Table 4.2 under psychopathological operationalization have long histories and large followings. It is interesting to note that many of the studies listed under the "Adjustment to Change" heading (Ruben & Kealey, 1979; Searle & Ward, 1990; Stening & Hammer, 1992; Ying & Liese, 1990, 1991) and one study listed under "General Satisfaction" (Ward & Searle, 1991) in Table 4.1 are operationalized according to the pathological model in Table 4.2, which may be further evidence of the pull such measures exert.

Scholars have also operationalized sojourner adjustment in terms of general adjustment to a new environment or broad facets of one's life in a new environment (Black, 1990, 1992; Black & Stephens, 1989; Diggs & Murphy, 1991; Hawes & Kealey, 1981; Holmes & Rahe, 1967; Parker & McEvoy, 1993; Searle & Ward, 1990; Spradley & Phillips, 1972; Stening & Hammer, 1992; Ying & Liese, 1990). Table 4.2 details those operationalizations. A strong commonality among most of these studies is that they measure adjustment using sojourners' self-reports of whether they "adjusted" to the new culture in a global sense or to several broad domains of life in the new culture. Many of these studies actually use the term *adjustment* itself, asking respondents to rate how well they "adjusted." The extent to which the words *adjustment, adjusting,* and *adjust* (a) evoke consistent denotative meanings across individuals and across within-subject measures and (b) evoke meanings reflective of the researchers' conceptualizations of sojourner adjustment provides a psychometric justification for such a choice of stimulus materials. But, in this author's reading, no exploration or report provides any evidence suggesting that this is in fact the case. "Adjustment" is therefore often taken as a prima facie measurement of itself.

Among the articles reviewed for this chapter, Stening and Hammer's (1992) work was the only research measuring sojourner adjustment in terms approximating communicative competence. Their work assessed sojourners' perceptions of their own effectiveness in terms of items from Hammer, Gudykunst, and Wiseman's (1978) scale measuring the dimensionality of intercultural effectiveness. A significant feature of this and related studies (see also Abe & Wiseman, 1983; Hammer, 1987; Hammer et al., 1978) is that factor-analytic studies of self-reports of this nature have generally yielded a dimensional model of intercultural effectiveness that involves sojourners' abilities to manage stress, communicate effectively, and maintain relationships. This model may have important bearing on the sojourner adjustment process. But using sojourners' own estimates of their abilities is different than using behavioral measures, particularly in speaking of effectiveness in behavioral terms. Spitzberg and Cupach's (1984) model involves others' ratings of sojourners' behavior. In addition, Stening and Hammer's (1992) use of the attitudinal satisfaction variable as a measure of adjustment (see Table 4.2 and the discussion of general satisfaction above) may also have weaknesses, as will be discussed further.

CONCLUSIONS REGARDING THE SOJOURNER
ADJUSTMENT LITERATURE ACROSS DISCIPLINES

Although the preceding review of the extant literature on sojourner adjustment should not be taken to be exhaustive, several conclusions emerge. First, much conceptual and operational confusion exists; even the latest published studies give no evidence of change over previous observations by researchers (Black et al., 1991; Church, 1982; Parker & McEvoy, 1993; Spradley & Phillips, 1972). This confusion may be due, in part, to the multidimensional nature of sojourner adjustment (Church, 1982). In addition, research on sojourner adjustment has been largely atheoretical (Black et al., 1991).

Second, a strong predilection for conceptually and operationally defining sojourner adjustment in terms of happiness or satisfaction exists. Many studies have defined sojourner adjustment in terms of happiness or satisfaction of either global or domain-specific nature. While happiness or satisfaction may evidence some relationship to adjustment, the content validity of that relationship has never been fully established. Furthermore, such a relationship may be psychometrically problematic.

Third, the relationship between various psychopathologies and sojourner adjustment seems not to be as simple as that required by extant psychopathological views and measures of adjustment. If psychopathologies are viewed as indicators of a lack of sojourner adjustment, the logical difficulties outlined above may call into question the validity of such a measure. Furthermore, the complex nature of the interaction between personality and situational factors (Church, 1982; Spradley & Phillips, 1972) may introduce potentially confounding variables not adequately explained by measures of psychopathology alone.

Fourth, a good number of studies operationalize adjustment in a circular fashion (i.e., asking subjects to rate their adjustment to something). The content validity of such measures is uniformly taken for granted while evidence for that validity appears to be lacking. Admittedly, it is difficult to establish the content validity of a measure, particularly so when dealing with cross-cultural research (Irvine & Carroll, 1980) and with research on subjective well-being (Michalos, 1991). However, this writer is not content with what seems to be the prima facie acceptance of "adjustment" as a measure of adjustment. If a uniformly accepted, concise, and cogent definition has not emerged in the sojourner adjustment literature, it is unlikely that sojourners themselves will react uniformly to the word *adjustment* as a stimulus.

LESSONS FROM THE SUBJECTIVE WELL-BEING LITERATURE: TOWARD A DIFFERENTIAL DEMAND MODEL OF SOJOURNER ADJUSTMENT

Some lessons learned by scholars in subjective well-being may be particularly helpful in view of the problems identified above. Global measures of satisfaction, happiness, and well-being may be too problematic to be practically useful for assessing sojourner adjustment; domain-specific measures of adjustment may be far more powerful than global measures in terms of explaining variance and providing a better indicator of sojourner adjustment across both time and environmental features. A gap-theoretic approach to sojourner adjustment may better conceptualize sojourner adjustment in terms of the discrepancies between felt environmental and personal demands. A promising array of research activities follow from that approach.

The Problems Faced by Satisfaction and Happiness Measures

The bulk of subjective well-being measures take the form of questions regarding happiness and/or satisfaction with life or with specific areas of one's life (Glatzer, 1991; Schwarz & Strack, 1991; Veenhoven, 1991). Work done in this area has been labeled research in subjective well-being, social indicators, and quality of life (Glatzer, 1991). Many subjective well-being writers have identified weaknesses in asking respondents about their satisfaction and happiness. First, most objective life circumstances account for less than 5% of the variance in measures of subjective well-being; measures of subjective well-being have yielded low test-retest reliabilities, usually falling near .40 and not exceeding .60 when the same question is asked twice during the same one-hour interview (Schwarz & Strack, 1991). Schuman and Presser (1981) also found subjective well-being measures to be highly sensitive to influences from questions asked earlier in a questionnaire or interview. Andrews and Whithey (1976) have estimated that error accounts for about half the variance in reports of happiness; Veenhoven (1991) explains this by noting that respondents may not have a definite opinion on their happiness in mind and therefore "engage in an instant [re]assessment which is then influenced by situational characteristics . . . those who do have a definite opinion hold a rather global idea and will not think in terms of a ten point scale. Hence, their precise score may vary " (p. 12).

In addition, happiness and satisfaction measures have yielded surprisingly ironic twists. Well-known studies have shown that economically disadvantaged people are sometimes happier than their wealthier counterparts, including those who win large sums of money in lotteries (Easterlin, 1974); that postoperative cancer patients were happier than a healthy control group (Irwin, Allen, Kramer, & Danoff, 1982); and that paralyzed victims of automobile accidents were happier than might be expected given their circumstances (Brickman, Coates, & Janoff-Bulman, 1978).

The implication of these findings for sojourner adjustment measurement is that questions about sojourner satisfaction and happiness tend to be unstable and open to situational influences that have little to do with the sojourner's actual adjustment.

The Problems of Global Measures of Subjective Well-Being and the Advantages of Domain-Specific Measures

Angus Campbell (1981), regarded as a pioneer in subjective well-being research (Schwarz & Strack, 1991), has argued that the use of social indicators measures is based on the assumption that all the countless experiences people go through from day to day add to . . . global feelings of well-being, that these feelings remain relatively constant over extended periods, and that people can describe them with candor and accuracy. (p. 23)

Yet those assumptions regarding the globality, stability, and reportability of feelings of well-being have been questioned by other writers (Schwarz & Strack, 1991; Veenhoven, 1991). One possible reason for the instability of global measures of satisfaction and well-being is their very globality. It may mean asking subjects to do something they cannot do. Schwarz and Strack (1991) claim that " 'taking all things together' is a difficult mental task . . . it asks something impossible from the respondent" (p. 29). Schwarz and Strack (1991) elaborate:

Evaluations of general life satisfaction pose an extremely complex task that requires a large number of comparisons along many dimensions with ill-defined criteria and the subsequent integration of the results of these comparisons into one composite judgment. . . . Facing this complex task, people may rarely engage in it. Rather, they may base their judgment on their perceived mood at the time, unless the informational value of their current mood is discredited. (p. 29)

It is for this reason that global measures of satisfaction, happiness, and well-being may be too problematic to be practical for assessing sojourner adjustment because subjects must respond in terms of counter-intuitive global assessments of well-being and in reference to things other than their well-being. According to Schwarz and Strack (1991), transient affective states confound the measure.

Domain-specific measures eschew global considerations of subjective well-being in favor of polling respondents on certain aspects or facets (called "domains") of life. The exit offered by Schwarz and Strack (1991) to the problems they identify with global measures is a domain-specific approach, because respondents have at their disposal numerous bases of comparison by which they can evaluate specific areas of their lives. Comparison judgments in subjective well-being can involve comparisons with the way life was at some time in the past, with the way it should be ideally or in the future, or with what other people have or do (Argyle & Martin, 1991). These judgments are seen as superior in validity to immediate affective state as indicators of subjective well-being (Schwarz & Strack, 1991). The advantages of approaching well-being through multiple domains over addressing it globally have also been noted by other researchers (Lewinsjohn, Redner, & Seeley, 1991; Michalos, 1991).

Some extant sojourner adjustment research has, in part, taken advantage of domain-specific measurement. Research by Black (1990, 1992), Black and Stephens (1989), and Parker and McEvoy (1993) all follow a model stipulating three dimensions of expatriate adjustment: adjustment to work, interaction with host nationals, and the general nonwork environment. While this represents a departure from most sojourner adjustment research in that a multidimensional view of adjustment is taken, the "general nonwork environment" dimension may be too broad, particularly given observations of a gap in reported satisfaction between public (in this case, work) and private (interaction and general nonwork environment) domains of life (Glatzer, 1991). But when is an identified domain sufficiently "narrow" to allow respondents a stable basis for evaluating their well-being? Such a question may not be answerable at present but might be addressed by examining the stability of domain-specific evaluations over time and within subjects. Domain schemes identified thus far by subjective well-being scholars include family life, marriage, financial situation, housing, job, friendship, health and leisure activities (Campbell, Converse, & Rodgers, 1976); marriage/partnership, family life, household management, job, division of household tasks, living standard, housing, leisure, household income, health, social security, education, church, public safety, and environmental protection (Glatzer, 1991); work, leisure activities, neighborhood, family life, marriage, and competence (Lewinsjohn et al., 1991); and friendships, health, and financial security (Michalos, 1991).

A Differential Demand Model of Sojourner Adjustment

To review the claims made about the nature of sojourner adjustment thus far in this chapter, sojourner adjustment is a relatively short-term, individually and time-based process that is conceptually distinct from cultural or ethnic assimilation, adaptation, and intercultural communicative competence. Further observations can be made on the basis of evidence from domestic adjustment and quality-of-life work. Adjustment can be defined by degree in terms of discrepancies between personal and environmental needs and how those needs are met; Dawis and Lofquist (1984) take this approach when examining adjustment to changes in work. To elaborate this definition, adjustment is defined as the gap between the relocated worker's needs and how the work environment meets them ("satisfaction") in addition to the gap between the work environment's demands and the individual's ability to meet them ("satisfactoriness"). The narrower the totaled two gaps are, the more adjusted the individual is considered to be. Dawis and Lofquist's (1984) conceptualization has already been theoretically related to expatriate international adjustment (Black et al., 1991) and is attractive in that the role ambiguity, role novelty, and role conflict characteristic of domestic work relocation (Dawis & Lofquist, 1984) are certainly important stressors for sojourners, at least for those who work and in their work-related roles (Black et al., 1991). Such an approach to measuring subjective well-being is known as a "gap-theoretic" approach. Michalos (1991) describes gap, or discrepancy, theory in the following manner:

> The basic idea behind [gap or discrepancy theory] is that satisfaction or happiness is an emergent property resulting from the particular relationships or mixtures of other properties. In other words, in these theories satisfaction or happiness is analyzed and understood as the effect or result of something else, something more primitive. While utilitarian philosophers and economists have used satisfaction or happiness as the basis or basic building block of their theories, gap theory in general . . . is a theory designed to analyze and explain that basis. It is a theory designed to go beyond satisfaction or happiness, to get to its sources or causes. (pp. 30-31)

Michalos (1991) further asserts that the gap- or discrepancy-theoretic approach is consonant with person-environment fit theory, which has enjoyed a long history and wide empirical support from numerous studies (see Michalos, 1991, p. 55, for a listing of review articles enumerating these findings).

In sum, then, this chapter defines sojourner adjustment as *a function of the extent to which the sojourner judges he or she is meeting environmental demands and the extent to which the sojourner judges his or her needs are being met in the new environment.* Figure 4.1 illustrates this definition of adjustment. This model can be further developed through several axioms:

Axiom 1: Sojourner adjustment is multidimensional. This is so in that subjective well-being is experienced differentially across a wide variety of domains (Glatzer, 1991; Lewinsjohn et al., 1991; Michalos, 1991; Schwarz & Strack, 1991); the sojourner adjusts to many domains in the new environment that differ from those in the old (see Figure 4.2).

The nature of the multiple dimensions of adjustment, as described by extant literature on sojourner adjustment and life changes in general, is amorphous both in terms of the enumeration of domains and in terms of how those domains may interact with each other in the totality of the adjustment experience. Partitioning life into domains discrete enough to avoid the pitfalls to which global assessments of adjustment are subject is difficult; the number of areas of life that may have possible

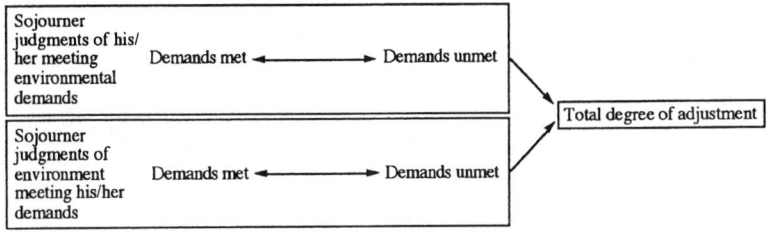

Figure 4.1: Person-Environment Demands and Sojourner Adjustment

significance in the sojourner adjustment experience is endless. It is not the task of this chapter to develop a domain scheme for a differential demand model of sojourner adjustment. But a few clues from existing literature are helpful in suggesting what *general classes* of domains, at a minimum, one should include in this view of adjustment. Recalling that work by Black (1990, 1992), Black and Stephens (1989), and Parker and McEvoy (1993) follows a model stipulating three dimensions of expatriate adjustment (adjustment to work, interaction with host nationals, and the general nonwork environment), one may argue that the domains of adjustment fall into the categories of *task* domains (employment and daily tasks that tend to structure the majority of one's waking hours), *social support* domains (including interaction with host nationals, friendships, and other facets of social support), and *ecology* domains (physical characteristics and human-made features of the new environment with which the sojourner must deal to function effectively). Domain enumeration in many studies on quality of life and environmental psychology includes areas of life from these three categories (see, e.g., Andrews & Whithey, 1976; Chamberlain, 1985; Emmons & Diener, 1985; Headey, Holström, & Wearing, 1984a, 1984b; Lance & Sloan, 1993; Leelakulthanit & Day, 1993; Mastekaasa, 1984; Michalos, 1980, 1985; Milbrath & Sahr, 1975; Ostroot, Shin, & Snyder, 1982; Poloma & Pendleton, 1990; Vermunt, Spaans, & Zorge, 1989; Walter-Busch, 1983; Wood & Johnson, 1989). Table 4.3 details the domains examined in these studies. It is notable that these studies enumerate what might be termed "things one has to get used to" domains (in other words, environmental demands). More notably, sojourner-oriented or egocentric domains (in other words, sojourner demands)—important to any consideration of what the sojourner might face when handling the challenge of meeting his or her own needs—are also viewed as important. Including the latter in any operationalization of sojourner adjust-

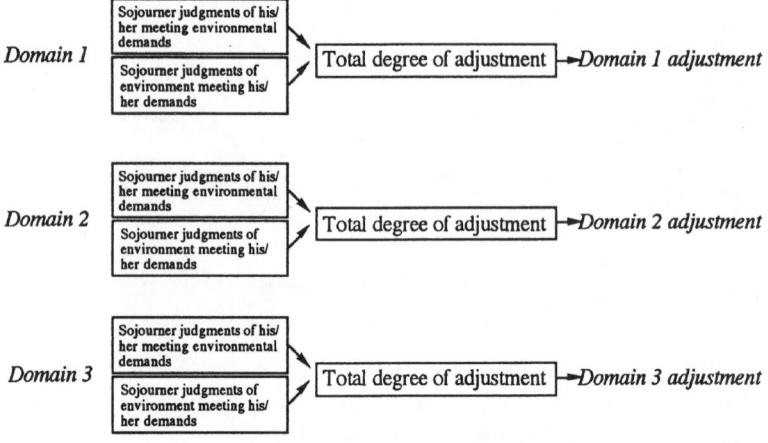

Figure 4.2: The Multidimensional Nature of Sojourner Adjustment

ment may be necessary if the differential demand model is to be followed. What emerges, then, is a general domain scheme that includes task, social support, and ecology domains that are experienced in terms of environmental and sojourner demands being met to varying degrees.

Axiom 2: Adjustment is differential across domains and over time. The sojourner does not fully adjust to every novel feature in the new environment at once. Features that are *less different* may be adjusted to sooner than features that are *more different*. "Felt" adjustment to a particular feature may decrease sharply as the sojourner learns more about that feature. Furthermore, domains may interact with each other over time to exert even more influence on adjustment (see Figure 4.3). A classic example of how one domain may exert influence on another is that of language and relational quality—as the sojourner becomes more fluent in the host language, conversation with the users of that language becomes more efficient and rewarding. Or, in terms of the general domain scheme proposed above, adjustment in terms of a task or ecology domain may influence adjustment in terms of a social support domain—for example, learning how to use the transportation system efficiently may mean more time (and energy) for developing friendships. The latter example shows, in addition, how meeting environmental demands can feed back positively to the meeting of sojourner demands—within and across domains (and, possibly, how met sojourner demands can relate positively with the meeting of environmental demands).

TABLE 4.3 Enumerations of Domains in Selected Studies

Andrews & Whithey (1976)	*Chamberlain (1985)*	*Davis & Fine-Davis (1991)*
Self	Prosperity	Housing
Family	Self-actualization	Neighborhood
Money	Environment	Health
Fun	Personal relationships	Health services
Housing	Personal harmony	Life in general
Family activities	Family	
Leisure activities	Leisure	
National government		
Consumer services		
Health		
Job		

Emmons & Diener (1985)	*Heady, Holström, & Wearing (1984a)*	*Headey, Holström, & Wearing (1984b)*
Friends	Social networks	Organizations you belong to
Love life	Reliable alliances	House
Family	Friendships	Leisure
Recreation	Intimate attachments	Suburb
Housing	Satisfaction with life concerns	Friends
Standard of living	Leisure	Marriage
Religion	Friends	Standard of living
Physical attractiveness	Marriage	Sex life
Courses	Standard of living	Job
Grades	Sex life	Health
Future career	Job	
	Health	

Lance & Sloan (1993)	*Leelakulthanit & Day (1993)*	*Mastekaasa (1984)*
Job	Life in general	House/apartment
Friendships	Family	Local community
Marriage	Self	National government
Family	Material possessions	Job
Global	Work	Finances
Health	Social life	Leisure/hobbies
Neighborhood	Personal health	Marriage/family
Leisure	National government	Friends
	Local government	Health
	Life in this country	
	Personal health	
	Health care	
	Recreation	
	Consumption	
	Spiritual life	

(continued)

TABLE 4.3 Continued

Michalos (1980)	Michalos (1985)	Milbrath & Sahr (1975)
Health	Health	Happy human relations
Financial security	Financial security	Upward striving
Family life	Family relations	Consumption
Job	Paid employment	Outdoor style living
Friendships	Friendship	Natural environment
Housing	Housing	Quality of home environment
Area you live in	Area you live in	Security
Free time activity	Recreation activity	Environmental excitement
Self-esteem	Self-esteem	Public services
Ability to get around	Transportation	Utilities
Education	Education	Transportation and travel
Secure from crime	Religion	

Ostroot, Shin, & Snyder (1982)	Poloma & Pendleton (1990)	Vermunt, Spaans, & Zorge (1989)
Medical care	Religion	Health
Neighborhood	Employment	Money
Housing	Friends	Family/relatives
Work	Health	Paid job
Quality of own education	Homework	Friendship
City	Household members	Housing
Standard of living	Living in (Akron)	Partner
Leisure	Marital status	Leisure time
Police protection	Neighborhood	Philosophy of life
Amount of own education	Schooling	Self-esteem
Security walking at night	Standard of living	Transportation
Municipal services		Training
Public schools		

Walter-Busch (1983)	Wood & Johnson (1989)
Beauty of site	Health
Beauty of built-up environment	Family
Personal housing conditions	Spouse
Local housing in general	Friends
Entertainment facilities	Housing
Shopping facilities	Esteem
Schools	Life
Social services	Happiness
Medical care	
Mentality of inhabitants	
Average level of salaries	
Public transportation	
Private transportation	
Level of taxes	
Variety of job opportunities	
Career opportunities	
Job security	
Proficiency of local government	
Facilities for children	
Unrest of daily life	
Quietness, absence of noise	

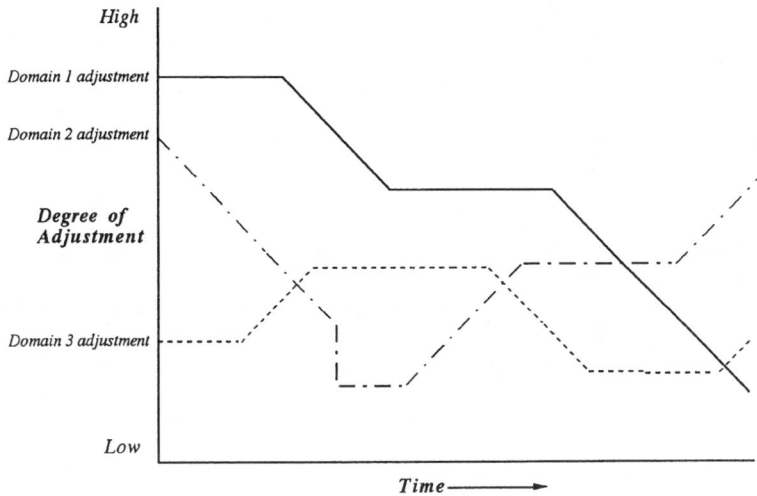

Figure 4.3: The Differential Nature of Sojourner Adjustment Across Domains and Over Time

Axiom 3: Sojourner adjustment is crisis-intensive in apperception. The sojourner's evaluation of his or her adjustment is likely to be affected by experiences of adjustive stress *relative to those domains placing stressful demands on the sojourner at that time*, while domains whose demands the sojourner has learned to meet are largely out of the sojourner's awareness.

Axiom 4: Sojourner adjustment is nongestalt in apperception. A sojourner's estimation of his or her adjustment is likely to be less an arithmetic mean across environmental features than a judgment of the criticality of currently stressful features, particularly given that some domains of subjective well-being, especially family and living standard domains, are weighted more heavily than others by respondents (Glatzer, 1991). Axioms 3 and 4 imply that the sojourner's perception of the salience of a particular domain ought to be at least as important as the perception of whether demands are being met. In the case of quantitative measures of sojourner adjustment, importance ratings should accompany ratings of the degree to which environmental and sojourner demands for each domain are met.

Taken together, the above definition of sojourner adjustment and the four axioms that follow it suggest a "differential demand" label for the model, whereby sojourner adjustment is conceptualized as sojourner and environmental demands being met to varying degrees across differential domains and time.

CONCLUSIONS AND CALL FOR FUTURE WORK

This chapter attempted a cross-disciplinary review of writing on sojourner adjustment. While not exhaustive, this review is representative of work on this topic. This chapter identified general trends in defining and measuring sojourner adjustment. While the shape of these trends may be, in part, a function of the writer who identifies them, strong patterns in conceptualization and operationalization are apparent. Various strengths and weaknesses of the general satisfaction, interaction, psychopathological, adjustment, and competence approaches to measuring sojourner adjustment have been suggested, and conceptual and methodological weaknesses have been identified. Rich literature on subjective well-being offers helpful insights on the psychometry of subjective well-being in general and sojourner adjustment in particular; based on this research, a differential demand model was generated that defines sojourner adjustment in terms of sojourner and environmental demands being met to varying degrees across differential domains and time.

The differential demand approach to sojourner adjustment may offer important advantages in that it allows for the measurement of multiple domain adjustment. It offers what may be a dramatically more valid and stable basis from which sojourners can evaluate their adjustment; and it allows for the exploration of domain-specific adjustment as a function of time, which is particularly important because empirical findings regarding the U- and W-curves of adjustment are sparse and contradictory (Church, 1982).

The differential demand model of sojourner adjustment awaits confirmation by empirical testing. Future work should involve the identification of the domains of adjustment for specific types and durations of sojourns. Future work should also attempt to profile degrees of sojourner adjustment across specific domains over time, which involves the longitudinal study of sojourner adjustment—in contrast to the cross-sectional approach taken by the majority of extant work on adjustment. In addition, outcome measures for sojourner adjustment should be used in regression-type explorations to test how different domains may be weighted in sojourners' evaluations of their adjustment.

The differential demand model of sojourner adjustment takes the conceptualization of sojourner adjustment to the basic foundations of a general movement in social science theory—person-environment fit—and moves measurement of the construct to something that may be more situationally adaptive and meaningful to sojourners.

5

Accommodating Intercultural Encounters
Elaborations and Extensions

CYNTHIA GALLOIS • *University of Queensland*
HOWARD GILES • *University of California, Santa Barbara*
ELIZABETH JONES • *Griffith University, Brisbane*
AARON C. CARGILE • *University of California, Santa Barbara*
HIROSHI OTA • *University of California, Santa Barbara*

As the need for sophisticated theories of intercultural communication grows increasingly important, Communication Accommodation Theory (CAT) has been shown to provide insight into many of the critical phenomena and processes involved. Consider, for example, the interactions between Koreans and African Americans reported by Hutchinson (1991, p. 554). Members of both cultural groups complained that the other often failed to speak "English" with them. Such linguistic practices and perceptions have contributed significantly to difficult episodes and poor relations. Other intercultural interactions, however, are far more favorable. When traveling abroad, one American coauthor of this chapter (AC) found French hosts to be friendly and receptive when, despite a lack of fluency, he attempted to communicate in their native tongue. As these examples illustrate, communication in intercultural settings can take many different forms, with a variety of outcomes.

Communication Accommodation Theory contributes to our understanding of interactions like these by focusing attention on the language, nonverbal behavior, and paralanguage used by interlocutors to realize moves of speech *convergence* and *divergence*, that is, linguistic moves to decrease and increase communicative distance. When we acknowledge that communication involves this constant movement toward and away from others, which is called *accommodation* in this theory, we can begin to explain why it takes the forms that it does—for example, why an African American's English may sound more "black" at times, and why even dysfluent French may be well received by native speakers, as our coauthor found.

Perhaps even more important than recognizing the currents of convergence and divergence in conversation, CAT has explored, and continues to elaborate, reasons that speakers may behave as they do. For example, our coauthor's attempt to sound like the French is differently motivated than the behavior of Daniel Day-Lewis. From the "posh" side of town, his first role and accent accommodation was performed not on stage, but in real life: the role of the working-class lad. For him, speaking like the others was deemed an essential ingredient of everyday, interactional management (in Corliss, 1994, p. 66). By uncovering such links between language, situation, and identity, CAT aims not only to explain episodes of intercultural communication but also to predict them based on features of the communicators and the context. The theory focuses on actual communication, is heuristic, and has received broad empirical support (see Coupland & Giles, 1988; Giles & Johnson, 1987). Thus this chapter presents an approach to CAT in the intercultural context, together with some of its major propositions, revised for this context. Along with this, we describe some recent empirical work on intercultural communication that tests and extends CAT and that has clarified several important problems. At the same time, we point to a number of theoretical and methodological issues that must be addressed in the intercultural context, and that should be part of the research agenda in this area for the coming years.

In doing this task, we draw throughout on older and more recent work on CAT, its predecessor Speech Accommodation Theory (SAT), Ethnolinguistic Identity Theory (ELIT; see Giles & Johnson, 1987), Ethnolinguistic Vitality Theory (ELV; see Harwood, Giles, & Bourhis, in press), and, relatedly, Social Identity Theory (see Tajfel & Turner, 1986). CAT is a cross-contextual theory that emphasizes the communality in motivation, communication strategies, and reactions to the behavior of others that characterize communication across all kinds of intergroup encounters. On the other hand, each context (including the intercultural one) has its own unique features, and in this chapter we argue for the importance of considering and theorizing about them in any work on intergroup or interpersonal communication.

A BRIEF HISTORY OF CAT

CAT comes directly from work begun by Giles (1973) and ultimately named Speech Accommodation Theory (SAT); an extended report of the course of that work can be found in Giles and Coupland (1991) and Giles, Coupland, and Coupland (1991). SAT represented a reaction against then-current approaches in sociolinguistics (e.g., Fishman, 1971; Labov, 1966), which posited a causal role for the context in determining the communicative moves of speakers that overshadowed most other variables. SAT, on the contrary, proposed that the *motivation* of the speaker was the main determinant of the language and communication codes chosen by speakers.

Giles and colleagues argued that speakers move through their linguistic repertoire so as to *converge* to their conversational partners (i.e., make some aspect or aspects of their speech more like that of their partner) to gain approval or identify; to *diverge* from the partner (i.e., make their speech more different from the partner's, usually in ways that accentuate their own group membership) to distinguish themselves from the partner; or to *maintain* their own speech style, which is usually perceived as divergence (Bourhis, 1979). These two motives—*to gain approval* (mainly by showing one's similarity to the partner; see Byrne, 1971) and *to show distinctiveness*—along with a third motive, *to achieve clearer or smoother communication*—have remained the main speaker motivations proposed by CAT (see Meredith, submitted). In addition, the strategies of convergence, divergence, and maintenance have been the most extensively studied of all those proposed (see Giles & Coupland, 1991).

In 1987-1988 SAT was expanded to include a wider range of communication contexts, motives, strategies, and behaviors, and was renamed *Communication* Accommodation Theory (Giles, Mulac, Bradac, & Johnson, 1987). Soon after that, Coupland, Coupland, Giles, and Henwood (1988) presented a new predictive model, situated in the context of intergenerational communication. Their model moved CAT to explore discourse in more detail and, as a consequence, made a number of additions and changes.

First, the motivational component was expanded to incorporate the initial *sociopsychological states* of speakers, or the extent to which speakers are motivated at the outset of an interaction to converge or diverge, as well as the specific goals of speakers already elucidated in SAT. Second, speaker strategies were reconceptualized as resulting from *addressee focus*, or the way in which one speaker pays attention to the needs or behaviors of another. Convergence, divergence, and maintenance were renamed *approximation strategies*, resulting from an addressee focus on the productive language and communication of the other person. Three new *nonapproximation* strategies were added. The first of these was interpretability, resulting from an addressee focus on the skills and competence of the partner, or stereotypes about it, and leading among other things to slower or simpler speech, more use of questions to check understanding, and the choice of familiar topics. The second nonapproximation strategy, discourse management, results from an addressee focus on the partner's conversational needs, and leads among other things to sharing of topic choice and development, as well as shared conversational register. Finally, interpersonal control results from an addressee focus on the role relations in the interaction and leads to use of interruptions, honorifics, and the like, to keep the other person in role or to allow the other the freedom to change roles. All these strategies can be used to make interactants closer and more equal (*accommodation* or *attuning*) or to emphasize intergroup or interpersonal differences (*nonaccommodation*). Since 1988 other addressee foci have been proposed, not least of which is the emotional state of one's interlocutor (Williams, Giles, Coupland, Dalby, & Manasse, 1990).

Third, Coupland et al. (1988) expanded the conceptualization of reactions to speaker behavior. In their model, reactions are divided into (a) labeling of the behavior as accommodative or not and (b) attributions about why the behavior occurred (see also Giles & Johnson, 1987); these communicative classifications and social attributions provide crucial situational information, and hence are hypothesized as usually preceding any evaluations of the speaker *per se*. Overall, the model is dynamic, in that the reactions by one speaker feed back into subsequent and contingent behavior by the other speaker. Nevertheless, the model presents a path, starting with the psychological orientations of speakers toward each other, going through goals, behavior, and reactions to it, and finishing with speakers' evaluations of each other. Since 1988 this model has been tested and expanded in a number of studies in the intergenerational context (e.g., Coupland et al., 1988; Harwood & Giles, 1993; Williams et al., 1990). The work has highlighted the importance of stereotypes held by one speaker about another in determining addressee focus, strategies, and reactions to the other's behavior (see Fox & Giles, 1993; Harwood, Giles, Fox, Ryan, & Williams, 1993).

Gallois, Franklyn-Stokes, Giles, and Coupland (1988) recast the Coupland et al. (1988) model specifically into the context of intercultural communication. In doing this, they also made several additions. First, they incorporated the predictions of Ethnolinguistic Identity Theory (ELIT; Giles & Johnson, 1987) into a component of *initial orientation*, using the concepts of dependence and solidarity on one's ingroup (see below). This component includes propositions about the extent to which speakers, before an intercultural encounter, are predisposed to view the encounter as solely intergroup, solely interpersonal, or both intergroup and interpersonal (Giles & Coupland, 1991; see also Tajfel & Turner, 1986). In addition to dependence and solidarity for the ingroup, intergroup and interpersonal orientations are theorized by ELIT and CAT to be influenced by several ethnolinguistic variables. These include the *ethnolinguistic vitality* of the two groups (or cultures; see below for details), the extent to which *ethnolinguistic boundaries* between the groups are perceived to be hard and closed (as opposed to soft and permeable), the extent to which the sociostructural relations between the groups are perceived to be *legitimate* (as opposed to illegitimate), and the extent to which relations between the groups are perceived to be *stable* (as opposed to being likely to change for the worse or the better). Moving on from the available empirical work, Gallois et al. made predictions about members of minority and majority speech communities; subsequent research, however, has maintained the focus on members of minority communities and from there language survival (Giles, Leets, & Coupland, 1990; Leets & Giles, in press).

Second, Gallois et al. (1988) made more explicit the impact of the *situation* on behavior in intercultural encounters. A number of studies testing SAT and CAT had revealed the interaction of situational and motivational factors (e.g., Ball, Giles, Byrne, & Berechree, 1984; Genesee & Bourhis, 1982, 1988; Giles & Johnson, 1986) and in particular the impact of norms. In their model, Gallois et al. stressed the extent to which a situation is threatening, as a result of norms emphasizing status or the presence of conflict, in predisposing speakers toward a more intergroup orientation. More recent researchers have continued to argue for the importance of the situation. For example, Gallois and Callan (1991) pointed out that situational norms put constraints on the behaviors with which accommodative moves, as well as the extent of communicative (if not psychological) accommodation, that can occur (Bourhis, 1991, makes an analogous point in the organizational context). In addition, Giles and colleagues have argued for a more situated concept of identity in CAT and ELIT (e.g., Cargile, Giles, & Clément, in press). In this chapter, we present a further expansion of the role of situation on communication accommodation.

Finally, Gallois et al. (1988) expanded the later part of the CAT model to include an *evaluation* that interlocutors take away with them, and that influences their future orientation both toward the other person and toward other members of that person's group. Based on labeling of the other person's behavior and attributions about it, evaluations may be positive or negative. In addition, the other person may be seen as *typical* or *atypical* of his or her group. The evaluation of the person is much more likely to spread to other members of the outgroup, and thus to have an impact on social identity, if the other person is perceived as a typical group member (Hewstone & Brown, 1986; see also Turner, 1987a, for a discussion of the role of prototypicality in social identity theory). In this chapter, we have revised the 1988 propositions about the impact of the context.

A COMPARISON OF CAT AND OTHER THEORIES OF INTERCULTURAL COMMUNICATION

An important issue for any theory of communication is its relation to and overlap with other theories in the same domain. Before addressing some theoretical issues that are specific to CAT and presenting our revised model, we felt it would be informative to discuss CAT in the light of five other theoretical frameworks formulated for understanding intercultural communication, which are all influential in the field. After sketching the theories very briefly, we compare them with CAT on several dimensions. In this way, we will see that CAT provides a perspective on intercultural interactions that is not only richly complementary but also unique. Readers new to this field may not find this discussion as relevant as those more seasoned in intercultural theory, and indeed may prefer to skip the ensuing section and arrive at the heart of CAT below. Nonetheless, this admittedly very brief coverage will be available as a resource for readers, once they are more familiar with other theoretical perspectives in the intercultural arena. First, the five theories.

Coordinated Management of Meaning

First developed by Pearce and Cronen (1980) as a general theory of communication, Coordinated Management of Meaning (CMM) has been elaborated to help explain the process and demands of intercultural communication (Cronen, Chen, & Pearce, 1988). According to the theory, communication is simultaneously regulated by, yet constitutive of, structure. Structure, in the form of relationships, roles, self-image, ritual, and so forth, shapes talk that in turn creates structure. For example, the relationship between a husband and wife guides the former's interpretation of her remark, "You are special." At the same time, that remark also helps develop in his mind what he perceives their relationship to be. In this way, the theory highlights rules that both tell people how to behave and are created through those same behaviors.

By focusing on rules and structure, CMM can provide insight into episodes of intercultural communication. In the terms of this theory, culture is understood best as patterns of sense-making and performance—a structure created, maintained, and transformed through communication. These patterns, however, are realized only by particular people in specific circumstances. Culture is neither static nor universal. Thus, because it exists embedded in material circumstances, culture is just one of several structures that compete to prefigure interaction between people. Interlocutor behavior must be responsive not only to culture but also to the perceived shape of interpersonal relations, self-image, and the episode. CMM then views intercultural communication as a process that demands the coordination of rules at multiple levels.

Communicative Resourcefulness

Just as CMM emphasizes coordination, so too does the theory of communicative resourcefulness (Ting-Toomey, 1993). This theory, however, focuses exclusively on coordination between interlocutor *identities*, by defining competent intercultural communication as effective identity negotiation. Accordingly, effective identity negotiation is realized through managing the dialectics of identity security-vulnerability and inclusion-differentiation. In Ting-Toomey's view, identity security-vulnerability is the primary dialectic of human existence. People need to be secure in their self-conceptions, yet not so secure that they fail to feel alive and experience a potential for change. Relatedly, a secondary dialectic of existence concerns inclusion and differentiation. As social creatures, humans have a need to be included among others, yet too much inclusion can inhibit a necessary personal sense of space and identity.

When people are successful in managing identity dialectics, the theory states that the resources necessary for effective intercultural communication will be available. Such resources include "the cognitive knowledge and the affective and behavioral predispositions to act appropriately, effectively, and creatively in any novel situation" (Ting-Toomey, 1993, p. 90). These resources are, of course, learned. Thus effective identity management will not create these resources but, instead, will bring them to bear during interaction, thereby allowing individuals to communicate with the highest degree of competence possible. In this manner, the process is reflexive. As people come to manage their identities, they make available a host of resources that, in turn, help coordinate intercultural communication and allow for continued effective negotiation of identity, even with culturally different others.

Communication Theory of Ethnic Identity

The third theory of intercultural communication has similarities with the previous two. The communication theory of ethnic identity, developed by Hecht, Collier, and Ribeau (1993), defines competence as the successful enactment of identity and is based upon a reflexive relationship between communication and structure. Unlike CMM, however, structure in this theory centers on identity and not rules. Identity is a way of understanding and behaving that simultaneously prescribes modes of conduct and arises out of them. The emphasis of this theory is on differentiating and integrating four frames of identity: personal, enacted, relational, and communal. As the authors explain, these four frames define the "location" of identity. "Identity is 'stored' within individuals, relationships, and groups, and is communicated within and between relational partners and group members" (Hecht et al., 1993, p. 164).

The frames of identity act as "lenses" with which to interpret the social world. They not only are useful to the social scientist but also provide ways in which laypeople conceptualize their own identities; for example, "I am an artist" (enacted identity) or "I am a wife" (relational identity). These frames do not exist in isolation but operate jointly or in a dialectical fashion. Understanding the full nature of identity in these terms and the reflexive relationship that identity has with interaction then allows us to develop a more complete understanding of intercultural communication. Communication is so thoroughly saturated with issues of identity that these four frames should facilitate interpretation of intercultural episodes.

Communication and Cross-Cultural Adaptation

A fourth theory offering insight into intercultural communication has been developed by Kim (1988a, in press-a) and concerns itself largely with cross-cultural adaptation. Unlike the previous three theories, that emphasize conceptions of social life belonging to symbolic interactionism (Mead, 1934) and other related schools of thought (e.g., North American pragmatism), Kim's theory of communication and cross-cultural adaptation relies on a different metatheoretical perspective, namely, general systems theory (see Boulding, 1956/1977; Ruesch & Bateson, 1951/1968). From this vantage point, a person is seen as an open communication system that interacts with and adjusts to the environment. When interacting with individuals from the same culture, little adjustment is required, because both interlocutors have already learned to communicate similarly through the same socialization process. Adjustments are required, however, if we are to interact effectively with those culturally different others who constitute foreign environments.

According to the theory, when people enter environments in which they no longer function effectively, they will attempt to change through a process of stress-adaptation and growth. This occurs entirely through communication. During intercultural interaction, interlocutors who recognize themselves to be outside their environment will become stressed with the experience of confusing and ineffective communication. Consequently, they will try to adapt by learning new elements of the host culture that will allow them to communicate like people from that culture while, simultaneously, unlearning the respective elements from their own culture. In this way, communicators grow in a constant process of trying to achieve a beneficial "fit" with those who make up their environment, by developing the communication competence of hosts. Thus, in Kim's view, understanding intercultural communication involves looking at who is learning, or not learning, what elements of which culture.

Anxiety/Uncertainty Management Theory

The final theory considered here is anxiety/uncertainty management theory (AUM), developed by Gudykunst (1985a, 1988, 1993, this volume). According to this theory, effective communication has two basic causes: anxiety and uncertainty. Anxiety is an affective response, a feeling of being uneasy, whereas uncertainty is a cognitive state describing one's inability to predict and explain people's behavior (Berger & Calabrese, 1975; see also, in an intergroup context, Hogg & Abrams, 1993). Both anxiety and uncertainty must be maintained within certain limits if effective communication is to occur. When either is too high, we lose the ability to understand and relate to others in a manner necessary for effective communication. When either is too low, we lose our motivation to do those same things.

Although anxiety and uncertainty are the basic causes of effective communication, their relationship with communication is moderated by "mindfulness" (Langer, 1989). Mindfulness is essentially the activity of being aware—thinking hard about and attending carefully to an interaction. Accordingly, anxiety and uncertainty must not only be managed, but managed mindfully, for misunderstandings to be minimized. In turn, effective communication does not begin with anxiety and uncertainty. Instead, the theory outlines a host of "superficial causes." These factors affect an interlocutor's levels of anxiety and uncertainty, which in turn influence communicative outcomes. The relationships between variables here are laid out in a number of different axioms, to which several more have been added to account for cultural variations in the relationships. Together, the 94 axioms spell out the details of intercultural communication in terms centered on people's states of anxiety and uncertainty.

Having presented the five theories, we now examine them and compare them with CAT with regard to four important dimensions: theoretical foci, intergroup/interpersonal features, culture, and context. Such a comparison will highlight lacunae in the field as well as give a context to the complementary value of CAT.

Theoretical Foci

As Gudykunst and Nishida (1989) have discussed, one useful way of comparing theories is to situate them along a dimension from objective to subjective. Objective theories are those that focus on predicting communicative outcomes, such as competence or adaptation, while subjective theories focus on understanding the interactive process of communication. Within the study of intercultural communication, objective theories belong primarily to the effectiveness tradition (e.g., Hammer, Gudykunst, & Wiseman, 1978), and subjective theories to an ethnographic approach (e.g., Hymes, 1972).

On this dimension, the intercultural communication theories by Ting-Toomey, Kim, and Gudykunst may be situated toward the objective end of the continuum, whereas those by Hecht et al. and Cronen et al. are subjective. In comparison, CAT is well positioned, because it recognizes both objective and subjective features in intercultural communication. Like other objective theories, CAT is concerned with prediction. Its predictions, however, are not situated within a static input-output model of interaction. The essential vocabulary used in the other objective theories tends to reduce interaction to a state of individual achievement: Ting-Toomey (mobilized resources), Kim (communication competence), and Gudykunst (anxiety and uncertainty reduction). CAT, however, predicts the motivated communicative *processes* of convergence and divergence, thus making it an objective theory that highlights subjective dimensions of intercultural interactions.

Intergroup/Interpersonal Features

Much of the complexity inherent in intercultural encounters occurs because they have two different but equally important facets; they are both intergroup and interpersonal (Giles & Coupland, 1991; Tajfel & Turner, 1986). Interactants from different cultures come together in the light of a history of relations between their cultural groups, which may include rivalry, conflict, and social inequality and almost always involve some degree of prejudice (cf. Hewstone & Brown, 1986). At the same time, intercultural encounters can also involve the coming together of two or more individuals to form a relationship, to complete a task, or perhaps both. They may like or dislike each other, and the task at hand may be either important or trivial to them. Indeed, the interpersonal aspects of the encounter may be so important that they completely override the intergroup aspects, or vice versa.

Thus, to do justice to the multiple and interacting influences on any intercultural interaction, theories must at least take account both intergroup and interpersonal factors and must give equal importance to each of them (see Gudykunst & Ting-Toomey, 1988). Although several of the intercultural theories reviewed above include features of intergroup communication, all five attempt to understand the process primarily as an *interpersonal* undertaking. CAT, however, represents a bridge, by providing an account of interpersonal interactions, with their motivations, antecedents, and consequences, in intergroup settings, including intercultural ones.

Culture

At the same time that culture is a category of group membership, it also prescribes certain modes of existence. Interactants from different cultures will, to a greater or lesser extent, endorse different and perhaps incompatible values, different relationship styles, and different communication styles and rules. The possibilities for miscommunication and misunderstanding arising from these differences have long been studied (e.g., Banks, Gao, & Baker, 1991; Furnham & Bochner, 1986; Hall, 1959). Thus, because culture influences interaction, theories of intercultural communication must incorporate features of cultural variability. This task, however, depends on the definition of culture being used. As Cronen et al. (1988) and Hecht et al. (1993) similarly view it, culture is defined by changing, discursive patterns emergent in communication. Because the evolving and processual nature of communication is emphasized, such a definition resists attempts to include culture as a predictive axiom in theory. Nonetheless, this can be done when, like Gudykunst (this volume), Ting-Toomey (1993), and Kim (in press-a), culture is treated as the behavioral norms, attitudinal tendencies, and beliefs shared among people from the same group.

Research has identified several dimensions of culture, including individualism/collectivism, power distance, uncertainty avoidance, and masculinity-femininity (Hofstede, 1980, 1991), and they have been successfully employed in accounting for variation in a host of communication-related phenomena and processes (see Gudykunst & Ting-Toomey, 1988). Until this point, CAT has neglected such dimensions (see, however, Giles, Coupland, & Coupland, 1991). Recognizing the importance of cultural variability, we attempt in this chapter some modest theorizing about the impact of individualism/collectivism on accommodation. This move should make CAT more robust, especially because, unlike many other intercultural theories, it does not limit culture to the nation-state. Rather, CAT acknowledges the variety within ethnic subgroups, gender groups, age groups, and the like. Moreover, CAT can deal with culture both as a predictor of communication and as something manifest in the processes of communicating (i.e., language, vocabulary, accent).

Context

Because communication does not occur in a vacuum, the role of context must also be theorized. Context impinges on interaction at two different levels. First, the *sociostructural context* pertains to macrofactors such as historical, political, economic, and religious intergroup relationships (see Albrecht, 1994), the receptivity of the host culture, host conformity pressures (Kim, 1988a, in press-a), and the demographic factors represented by groups' network size and strength (Giles, Bourhis, & Taylor, 1977b; Gudykunst, this volume; Kim, in press-a). Second, the *immediate social context* addresses the nature of situations, for example, the degree of formality or informality of encounters and the cooperative structure of the goals (Gallois et al., 1988; Gudykunst, this volume). CAT acknowledges the importance of context in intercultural communication and takes more account of the sociostructural context than most other theories. As noted above, Gallois et al. (1988) included normative constraints as well as the impact of threat and formality as influences on accommodation. The incorporation of ELIT in CAT and the distinction between majority and minority groups in their propositions also deals with sociostructural factors. In the model presented here, we make a further distinction between long-term contextual and sociostructural factors on the one hand and the features of the immediate encounter on the other.

The concept of *ethnolinguistic vitality*, which is now included in CAT, represents a further account of interethnic and intercultural communication from a macroperspective. Giles et al. (1977b) defined vitality as that which makes a group likely to behave as a distinctive and active collective entity in intergroup situations. Subjective vitality (Bourhis, Giles, & Rosenthal, 1981; Harwood et al., in press) is assessed by three factors (see Willemyns, Pittam, & Gallois, 1993, for confirmatory factor-analytic support for this configuration): status of a group (e.g., economic power, social prestige, sociohistorical status, status of the language and culture locally and internationally); demographic factors (e.g., number of the group, population distribution in various areas); and institutional support (e.g., representation in and control over religious, educational, political, media, and cultural contexts). At least two groups' present, past, and future vitality are measured, and hence a historical perspective is incorporated. Bourhis and Sachdev (1984) argue that individuals who perceive higher vitality in their language use it much more and in a greater variety of settings than those who perceive lesser vitality. Moreover, when individuals perceive their ethnolinguistic vitality to be low, they use the outgroup language in communication with people from other groups (but see below for some contradictory evidence on the impact of low vitality).

Overall, CAT is a multifunctional theory that conceptualizes communication in both subjective and objective terms. It focuses on both intergroup and interpersonal features and, as we shall see, can integrate dimensions of cultural variability. Moreover, in addition to individual factors of knowledge, motivation, and skill, CAT recognizes the importance of power and of macrocontextual factors. Most important, perhaps, CAT is a theory of intercultural communication that actually attends to communication.

THEORETICAL ISSUES FOR CAT

As CAT has extended its complexity and predictive range, a number of theoretical and metamethodological issues have assumed increasing importance. All of them are important in understanding intercultural communication, and the model of CAT presented in this chapter reflects our thinking about them.

The Nature of Accommodation

The first theoretical issue concerns the nature of accommodation itself, that is, what counts as "accommodation." Giles and colleagues (e.g., Giles, Coupland, & Coupland, 1991) have differentiated three dimensions of accommodation: psychological (or motivational), linguistic (or communicative), and subjective (perceived) versus objective (actual behavior). A speaker may be convergent on some of these dimensions, yet divergent on others. Given its motivational starting point, CAT posits the primacy of subjective and psychological accommodation over objective and linguistic accommodation, although discrepancies among these dimensions can represent an important source of miscommunication.

Long-Term and Short-Term Accommodation

A second theoretical issue involves the time span of accommodation. Originally, SAT conceptualized accommodation as occurring within the space of a single interaction. Soon, however, it became clear that the same motivations that underlie accommodation within an interaction can also provoke convergence to the speech of a new group across a longer time period. For example, Trudgill (1986) explored the role of long-term convergence across dialects and suggested that the motivation to converge to the speech of another community is a central factor in dialect change. Others (e.g., Gallois & Callan, 1988, 1991; Shockey, 1984) have examined the impact of long-term convergence by immigrant speakers on the reactions of members of the dominant language community. Recently, Niedzielski and Giles (in press) have considered the influence of long-term convergence on languages in contact. To date, however, CAT has not explicitly theorized a distinction between long-term and short-term accommodation; the model in this chapter does so.

Intergroup and Interpersonal Accommodation

A third theoretical issue to emerge concerns the distinction between intergroup and interpersonal accommodation. In earlier work, it was assumed that speakers accommodate interpersonally to their interlocutor, although accommodation is likely to take place on group-marked variables like language and accent. As time went on, however, purely interpersonal accommodation was examined, on variables such as speech rate (e.g., Street, Brady, & Putman, 1983), lexical diversity (e.g., Bradac, Mulac, & House, 1988), paralinguistic behaviors (e.g., Natale, 1975), gaze (e.g., Mulac, Studley, Wiemann, & Bradac, 1987), and even song registers (e.g., Yaeger-Dror, 1994), albeit not always from a CAT perspective (for theoretical alternatives, see Burgoon, Dillman, & Stern, 1993). Sometimes, this research produced unexpected results. For example, Bilous and Krauss (1988) found that men and women converged on some variables in mixed-sex interactions but simultaneously diverged on others; results like these highlight the primacy of psychological convergence.

Gallois et al. (1988) made the interpersonal/intergroup distinction somewhat more explicit, by suggesting that accommodation based on group membership is likely to occur on some behaviors (particularly language, accent, and register), while interpersonal accommodation is more likely on other behaviors (particularly nonvocal behaviors like gaze and gesture). To date, their predictions in this area have not really been examined empirically. Recently, Cargile et al. (in press) have theorized intergroup and interpersonal *motives* for accommodation, which can influence convergence or divergence. The distinction between intergroup and interpersonal accommodation in motives and in behavior has particular importance, because it situates CAT as an intergroup theory of interpersonal communication.

Cultural Variability and Accommodation

Acknowledging cultural influences on accommodation is important, considering their propensity to be involved in intergroup communication breakdowns (e.g., Coupland, Giles, & Wiemann, 1991). As mentioned above, the implications of one aspect of cultural variability, individualism/collectivism, will be discussed for CAT, because this powerful dimension has garnered the most research attention (see Gudykunst & Ting-Toomey, 1988).

Broadly speaking, *individualism* represents a cluster of values that emphasize a pursuit of one's own personal goals and uniqueness, while *collectivism* gives priority to harmonious relationships within a group, and thereby fosters more of a "we" than an "I" identity (Ting-Toomey, 1989b). Triandis (1993) argues that both individualistic and collectivistic tendencies exist in any single nation, but one tends to predominate over another: individualism in many Western societies and collectivism in the East. Verbal communication in more collectivistic cultures is referred to as a verbal contextual style (Gudykunst & Ting-Toomey, 1988), which emphasizes role relationships. People in these cultures often use more politeness strategies (Brown & Levinson, 1978; Ting-Toomey, 1989b) and more formal language than do individualists when facing outgroup members, so as to demonstrate the distance between them (Mizutani, 1981; Okabe, 1983; Yum, 1988). On the other hand, speakers from individualistic cultures typically use informal expressions. They use a verbal personal style (Gudykunst & Ting-Toomey, 1988), which "emphasizes personhood" (p. 109), and try to converge linguistically even with outgroup members. Particularly in intergroup situations, cultural collectivism and individualism can play important roles in the strategies of accommodation people adopt.

One distinctive feature of collectivism/individualism is ingroup/outgroup differentiation (Triandis, 1990). Collectivists belong to few ingroups, and they identify with these strongly on a long-term basis. In this way, group identity (Tafjel & Turner, 1986) is likely to be emphasized. In contrast, individualists tend to belong to multiple ingroups, many of which they are affiliated with on a relatively short-term basis. Hence identity grounded in groups is relatively attenuated, and, instead, personal identity (Turner, 1987a) may emerge as predominant. In intergroup communication situations, collectivists tend to make sharp distinctions between ingroup and outgroup (Gudykunst, Yoon, & Nishida, 1987). This phenomenon is probably due to a relative emphasis on social, rather than personal, identity in collectivistic cultures.

Strong beliefs about ingroup identification and loyalty are very likely to be perpetuated in the socialization processes of collectivistic communities. Kelly (1993) argues that "strong group identification brings the social world into sharper focus by promoting clear distinctions between 'us' and 'them' " (pp. 76-77). Indeed, the sharper ingroup/outgroup distinctions in collectivistic than in individualistic cultures may be attributed to the higher ingroup identification or social identity in the former than the latter (Grant, 1993; Gudykunst, 1989a). Furthermore, Hinkel and Brown (1990) argue that collectivism promotes more intense modes of intergroup comparison (i.e., how do "we" fare, say in terms of vitality, compared with "them") than does individualism, with Brown et al. (1992) finding strong correlations in this regard.

Intergroup comparisons are made along various cognitive dimensions (Hinkel, Taylor, Fox-Cardamone, & Crook, 1989; Turner, 1987a), a relevant one in intercultural contexts being valued ethnolinguistic boundaries (see above), and within the latter, a distinctive language and/or communicative style (Cargile et al., in press; Giles, 1979). Because collectivists tend to identify strongly with the ingroup, and make sharper differentiations between themselves and relevant outgroups, it can be argued that they assume "harder" ethnic boundaries. For instance, the Japanese have a "hard and closed" ethnic boundary, given the ideology that their language is impenetrable for most foreigners (Hildebrandt & Giles, 1983; Suzuki, 1975). Ross and Shortreed (1990) found that their Japanese sample believed that responding in Japanese even to highly proficient non-native Japanese speakers was not empathic and was largely inappropriate. In contrast, individualists' ethnic boundaries can be relatively soft, because of sometimes fuzzier ingroup/outgroup identities. The multiculturalism often institutionalized and practiced (to varying degrees of success, of course) in certain individualistic cultures (e.g., Australia, Canada, Northern European nations) may exemplify their openness to outgroups.

Thus an approach from another speaker is treated in different ways depending on the cultural background of the listener in intergroup and intercultural situations. Individualists may react to convergence from outgroup interlocutors in a relatively positive manner, and converge toward the outgroup speaker reciprocally. With oftentimes softer group boundaries, their thresholds for allowing linguistic penetration by outgroup members may be lower. Conversely, people from collectivistic cultures, who perceive harder group boundaries, may react to attempts at communicative convergence from outgroup members more negatively, and may diverge from them more if they perceive the convergence as overstepping a valued cultural or national boundary. In general then, speakers who come from a collectivistic culture are likely to diverge more from outgroup interlocutors, both psychologically and linguistically, than their individualistic counterparts. The model presented below reflects these considerations and incorporates cultural variability as an important macrocontextual factor.

Metamethodological Issues

In addition to the theoretical issues described above, a number of metamethodological issues have arisen from research on CAT. The first of these concerns the extent to which the CAT model is predictive, as opposed to a description of intergroup and intercultural encounters. The original model in SAT, as well as the expansions that came later (Coupland et al., 1988; Gallois et al., 1988; Leets & Giles, in press; Williams et al., 1990), all propose a predictive path linking initial orientation and contextual factors to linguistic and behavioral outcomes. On the other hand, much recent research has involved discourse or other forms of qualitative analysis, which do not easily lend themselves to path analysis or predictive patterns. The model we present below is intended as both heuristic and predictive. Thus we present propositions that can be tested using quantitative methods. In addition, researchers analyzing the discourse in intercultural encounters can also use this model to guide them to the most important variables.

Second, and related, there has been work on operationalizing all the variables in the model as completely as possible in the intercultural context. This task is huge, given the large number of behaviors and contextual specificity involved, particularly for the nonapproximation strategies. In addition, the distinctions between long-term and short-term accommodation, and between intergroup and interpersonal accommodation, imply an even larger array of behaviors on which accommodative action may occur. The work presented below continues this mammoth job of operationalization and shows the ways in which convergent methodologies (experimentation, survey, discourse analysis) contribute to it. Nevertheless, further operationalization remains an important area for future research.

RECENT EMPIRICAL DEVELOPMENTS

Ethnolinguistic Differentiation, Identity, and Vitality

Several articles (Giles, Coupland, Williams, & Leets, 1991; Giles et al., 1990; Leets & Giles, in press) have explored the consequences of dependence and solidarity on the ingroup's beliefs about linguistically differentiating or diverging from outgroups (Gallois et al., 1988). *Dependence* on a group, as a part of social identity, refers to the extent to which one needs that group to provide a positive identity, and is linked to the number of alternative satisfying group memberships available to the person (cf. Thibaut & Kelley, 1959, and their concept of comparison level for alternatives). Highly dependent people need their group to maintain a positive sense of self-esteem, and are thus more likely to conform to group norms and to defend their group from perceived threats. *Solidarity* refers to the benefits one receives from group membership, in terms of status or other rewards (cf. Thibaut & Kelley's concept of comparison level). People with high solidarity are likely to feel proud of their group and to be motivated to frame its interests competitively against the interests of other groups.

Giles, Leets, and colleagues have put forward motivational and sociolinguistic profiles of high dependence/high solidarity (high/high) and low dependence/low solidarity (low/low) individuals (see Giles, Coupland, Williams, & Leets, 1991, for details). These profiles amount to a more intergroup and divergent initial orientation for high/high people, and a more interpersonal, convergent orientation for low/low people, in terms of motivation, addressee focus, and tendency to use particular linguistic strategies. Leets and Giles (in press), in a survey of Spanish and English use and motivation to maintain Spanish among Hispanic students in California, showed the validity of this conceptualization. High/high students were more oriented to the maintenance of Spanish, and low/low students were more oriented to the acquisition of English, although there were some complications to this picture. The hardness of ethnolinguistic boundaries, and the stability and legitimacy of the interethnic situation, were all contributors to language maintenance or loss, as ELIT and CAT predict. Their results have been incorporated into the propositions presented below.

A related series of European studies have examined the relationship of perceived ethnolinguistic vitality (Bourhis et al., 1981) to ethnolinguistic identity and CAT for a number of minority language groups. These results have shown once again that the perceived vitality of one's language group is an important predictor of a more intergroup or a more interpersonal orientation. The studies also highlight the role of contextual factors. In particular, and contrary to predictions, low rather than high perceived vitality, together with a strong sense of identity, were found to lead to a stronger desire to promote and maintain one's language when talking to members of a contrastive ethnolinguistic group (Giles & Johnson, 1987; Giles & Viladot, 1994; Ytsma, Viladot, & Giles, 1994). It was argued that when those in an ethnic group who are committed to the membership of it feel that the vitality of their ingroup tongue has diminished, their energy will be directed at restoring positively valued distinctiveness (see Kraemer & Olshtain, 1989). These results, although not predicted, complement earlier ones suggesting that threat is an important mediator of language identity (e.g., Sachdev, Bourhis, Phang, & D'Eye, 1987). Like the work described above, these studies showed that linguistically differentiating from a cultural outgroup was a function not only of strong ingroup identification and strong perceived intergroup boundaries but also of a belief that the social position of one's group could change in the near future. Overall, this work has led to the call for more use of the concept of situated identity (see Clément & Noels, 1992) in CAT (Cargile et al., in press; Coté & Clément, 1994).

Operationalization of CAT in the Intercultural Context

A recent project in Australia has made a systematic attempt to operationalize the variables in the CAT model and to test some of its predictive paths, with respect to communication accommodation between Australians (individualistic culture) and Chinese (collectivistic culture) overseas students in academic contexts. In one part of the project, videotaped simulations of conversations between Chinese or Australian students and faculty members were shown to judges, who were themselves Australian students, Chinese students, and Australian faculty members. The actors on the tapes engaged in accommodating or nonaccommodating behavior, using discourse management and interpersonal strategies to treat the other person more as an equal individual or to put down the other person and his or her group. Judges labeled the nonverbal behavior of the actors on the videotapes (from "too little" to "too much" of a number of behaviors, including smiling, gaze, and vocal loudness) as well as the appropriateness of the behavior in general. They also made attributions for the behavior and evaluated the actors on power and solidarity.

Results indicated, first, that behavior was by far the strongest influence on evaluations of the actors; nonaccommodating students and faculty members, as predicted, were rated less favorably than accommodating ones (Gallois, Barker, Jones, & Callan, 1992; Jones, Gallois, Barker, & Callan, 1994b). On the other hand, the interlocutors of nonaccommodating actors were generally rated more favorably in contrast. Next to behavior, the role of actors was the biggest influence on ratings of them; faculty members were rated as more powerful than students who behaved in the same way, and also tended to be rated higher than students on solidarity when they accommodated. The impact of ethnic group on evaluations was subtle; in general, ingroup actors were rated in much the same way as outgroup members.

Another set of results from this study are of particular interest here. Following the CAT model, ratings of nonverbal behavior, the appropriateness of the actor's behavior, and evaluations of the actors were included with ethnicity and sex of the actors in a path analysis (Jones, Gallois, Barker, & Callan, 1994a). Although there were some unpredicted paths, in general the relationships proposed by CAT held up; labeling of nonverbal behavior (both vocal and nonvocal) predicted ratings of appropriateness, which in turn predicted evaluations of the speakers. This part of the study showed that accommodation was partly reflected in specific nonverbal behaviors and, in addition, that perceptions of behavior at least partly mediated more global judgments of the person, as CAT predicts.

The project included a second phase, which involved two-person same-sex conversations between Chinese overseas students, Australian students, and Australian faculty members. First, open-ended and structured written measures of subjects' initial orientation and goals for the interaction were taken. These indicated that Chinese students were more conscious of their ethnicity than were Australians, and more oriented to issues of interpretability. The goals of faculty members also showed that they were concerned with the interpretive skills of Chinese students more than were Australian students. As neither verbal nor nonverbal behavior was controlled in these interactions, a series of measures were developed to operationalize the strategies in the CAT model (see Jones, 1994, for detailed discussions of these measures). As had been accomplished in previous studies (e.g., Bilous & Krauss, 1988; Gallois & Callan, 1988), approximation (convergence and divergence) was operationalized by measuring the similarity of vocal behavior (including pauses, turn length, and turn latency) and nonvocal behavior (smiling, gestures, and so on) between interactants across time.

Results indicated little convergence in the conversations, although this may have been because convergence occurred very early in the interactions, before measurement began. Chinese and Australian students showed objectively similar vocal behavior, indicating probably that Chinese students had accommodated long term to Australian conversational norms. There was also a good deal of similarity in nonvocal behavior. Chinese students, however, showed the greatest differences in nonverbal behavior between interactions with students and interactions with faculty members, which may reflect their home-country norms about formality in staff-student interactions, rather than interpersonal accommodation. In addition, Chinese students' ratings indicated that they perceived greater differences in their behavior as a function of who they were talking to than actually appeared in their nonverbal behavior, as well as perceiving greater differences between their behavior and that of Australians than was measured objectively. These results once again reflect the kinds of differences that appear between subjective and objective accommodation, and the need to measure both.

A number of subjective and objective measures of the nonapproximation strategies were developed (Jones, 1994). Among these were turn-by-turn measures of the interaction process, including the use of questions versus statements and positive (jokes, laughter, agreement) versus negative (sarcasm, hostility, disagreement) speech forms. In addition, the course of conversational episodes was examined, including measures of topic initiation, development, and change. Finally, the content of the conversations was examined, in particular to determine the extent to which speakers shared a common perspective on the issues they discussed, and to look for the extent of talk relevant to students, to overseas students, and to academic settings.

As these analyses progressed, it became clear that many of the behaviors were being used in connection with one or more of the strategies. Topic development, for example, could be dominated by one person so as to block the participation of the other (a form of nonaccommodation in discourse management; see Coupland et al., 1988). This same behavior, however, was also used to allow one person (usually an overseas student) to talk about familiar topics (interpretability) or to keep one or both speakers in their student or staff roles (interpersonal control). In addition, different types of dyads appeared to employ the same strategy with different behavior. For example, when speaking with an overseas student, female Australian students emphasized interpretability by adjusting their response latency and pause length; faculty members chose topics with which Chinese students were likely to be familiar; and male Australian students made greatest use of questions to check for understanding.

These results, and others like them, indicate the need to separate strategies from behavior in the CAT model, as we have done in this chapter. The strategies are closely linked to addressee focus, are partly motivational in character, and last for a significant part of the interaction. Behavior, on the other hand, is highly dynamic and tactical (i.e., occurs largely as a reaction to the behavior of the other person) and can only reflect strategy to the extent that the speaker's repertoire and understanding of the situation permit. In addition, situational norms constrain the behavior that can flow from any of the strategies.

A final phase of this project once again tests the predictive paths in the CAT model. In this phase, Australian and Chinese overseas students watched the videotaped interactions and gave structured ratings of goals, strategies, behavior, and evaluations. These ratings of naturalistic conversations, as opposed to the scripted behavior in the earlier study (Jones et al., 1994a, 1994b), also show that the path from goals to evaluations predicted by CAT holds up but that the role (student or faculty member), gender, and ethnicity of the speakers and judges all exert influences on perceived accommodation.

Taken together, these results go some way to fleshing out the variables in CAT in one type of intercultural interaction, and they show the validity of combining qualitative and quantitative measures of verbal and nonverbal behavior to do this. In addition, they point to the importance of measuring both subjective and objective accommodation and show clearly that multiple group memberships interact and combine with interpersonal factors to produce the behavior in an interaction. In the context of this project, where conflict and threat were low but the potency of the academic setting was high, student or faculty role was probably the most salient, but gender and ethnicity still played their part. It is clear that theories of intercultural communication must take account of the impact and variable salience of multiple roles, and that considering ethnic or cultural group alone is not sufficient to capture the complexities of these encounters.

A REVISED CAT MODEL AND PROPOSITIONS

In this final section, we attempt to coalesce, in as parsimonious a fashion as possible, the current status of CAT and our thinking about it. We present a revised heuristic model (after Gallois et al., 1988), which we believe can guide quantitative and qualitative research in this area. As we go through the model, we present some propositions, which will form the core of CAT in the intercultural context, to be tested further in the future. Figure 5.1 shows the model.

Sociohistorical Context

Intercultural interactions, as noted above, take place within a socio-historical context, and the CAT model starts with them. This macro-level context includes first the perceived and "actual" sociostructural relations between the groups. In addition, contextual factors include societal norms for intergroup contact, for example, whether it is appropriate for members of one group to use the dialect or language of the other. Cultural variability, and in particular important cultural values like collectivism/individualism, appear here too. As can be seen in Figure 5.1, contextual factors have a two-way or reciprocal link to the second box, "accommodative orientation."

Accommodative Orientation

This part of the model shows the strong emphasis on subjectivity in CAT. The accommodative orientation box includes three subboxes that deal with an individual's ongoing tendency to perceive encounters with members of an outgroup in intergroup terms, interpersonal terms, or both, as well as to converge or diverge psychologically. It is worth noting here that, although we describe this box in the context of an encounter between people from two different cultures, the variables in it are also relevant to talk about an outgroup that takes place between ingroup members. Indeed, sometimes the role of intergroup factors is much clearer in the latter case than in face-to-face intercultural interactions, because of situational norms (see below).

The first subbox is labeled "intrapersonal factors." It includes an individual's social identity, conceptualized here mainly as dependence on and solidarity for the ingroup, as well as relevant parts of personal identity, particularly the extent to which the person is oriented toward interpersonal relationships (as opposed to task oriented). Much previous research on group processes leads to the prediction that relationship-oriented individuals are more likely to be interpersonally convergent than more task-oriented people. The intrapersonal factors subbox is linked two way (reciprocally) to a subbox called "intergroup factors," which reflect the individual's orientation to the outgroup. This subbox includes perceived ingroup vitality, perceived intergroup boundaries, and the perceived stability and legitimacy of the intergroup relations.

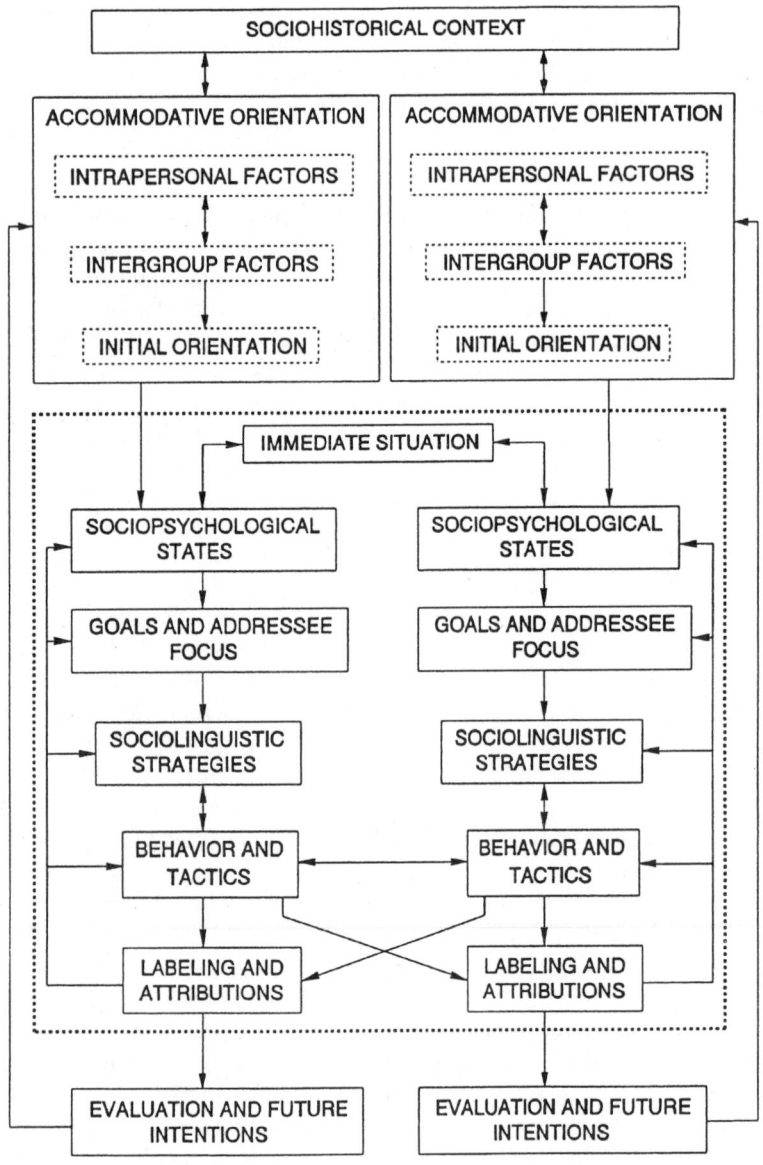

Figure 5.1: Communication Accommodation Theory in Intercultural Contexts
NOTE: This figure represents two interactants, to reflect the dynamic nature of such communication; there may, of course, be more than two people.

Note that the impact of these factors is likely to be different for members of dominant and subordinate groups, as the propositions show. This subbox leads to the third one, "initial orientation." This subbox includes the intergroup salience of any encounter, the perceived potential for conflict and threat of encounters with members of the outgroup, and, importantly, *the long-term motivation to accommodate to the outgroup.*

These two boxes capture the situation for individuals before they interact with members of the outgroup, or the longer-term situation. They lead to our first group of propositions (which, it should be noted, are not in the form of hypotheses, although hypotheses can easily be derived from them). First, the sociostructural relations between groups, as well as important cultural values, determine the extent to which encounters between their members are perceived in intergroup or interpersonal terms. In particular,

> *Proposition 1:* A history of rivalry or conflict between groups, particularly for cultures with an important value of collectivism, leads to interactions being perceived by many people in the group as more intergroup than interpersonal, and thus to a long-term motivation to diverge.

Each group in a society has norms about the appropriate and competent sociolinguistic behaviors for its ingroup and for outgroup members, which are influenced by intergroup relations and core cultural values. Thus, other things being equal,

> *Proposition 2:* Many members of collectivistic cultures are more likely to subscribe to norms of nonaccommodation to outgroup members than are members of individualistic cultures, and to negatively sanction outgroup members who converge to them.

On the other hand, much research indicates that perceptions by members of a dominant group about the vitality and strength of a subordinate group, and about the stability of the intergroup situation, are an important influence on the normative climate. When people in dominant groups have an insecure sense of identity or feel threatened by the vitality of subordinate groups, they may create a climate that is intolerant of any deficiencies in accommodation by members of subordinate groups, for example, in their attempts to learn the language of the dominant group (cf. Genessee & Holobow, 1989). Thus

> *Proposition 3:* Members of dominant groups with an insecure sense of identity and who perceive potential threat or conflict from subordinate groups

are likely to subscribe to strict sociolinguistic norms and to evaluate attempts at convergence by members of the subordinate group negatively and in more intergroup terms, compared with members of dominant groups with more secure identity.

Contextual factors, including important cultural values, are important to social and personal identity:

> *Proposition 4:* Many members of collectivistic cultures are more likely to show higher dependence on their ingroup and its sociolinguistic markers than members of individualistic cultures.

In terms of the second box, personal identity has an impact on the intergroupness of an individual's overall communicative orientation. Thus

> *Proposition 5:* Relationship-oriented individuals are likely to perceive all interactions, including intergroup ones, in more interpersonal terms than task-oriented individuals.

When social identity is considered, people who are highly dependent on their group and feel high solidarity for it are oriented to perceive stability, legitimacy, and boundaries in more intergroup terms than individuals who are low on dependence and solidarity. In particular,

> *Proposition 6a:* Individuals who are highly dependent on their group and feel high solidarity for it, and who are members of subordinate groups, are likely to perceive intergroup relations as illegitimate and unstable with the possibility of change for the better, especially when ethnic and communicative boundaries are perceived as soft and permeable,

while

> *Proposition 6b:* Individuals who are not dependent on their group and feel little solidarity with it, and who are members of subordinate groups, are likely to perceive relations as stable and legitimate in these contexts.

> *Proposition 7a:* Individuals who are highly dependent on their group and feel high solidarity for it, and who are members of dominant groups, are likely to perceive intergroup relations as legitimate but unstable with the possibility of change for the worse, especially when ethnic and sociolinguistic boundaries are perceived as soft and permeable,

while

Proposition 7b: Individuals who are not dependent on their group and feel little solidarity for it, and who are members of dominant groups, are more likely to perceive relations as stable and legitimate in these contexts.

Thus

Proposition 8a: Individuals who are highly dependent on their group and feel high solidarity for it, and who are members of either subordinate or dominant groups (especially collectivistic ones), are likely to perceive intergroup encounters in intergroup terms, to perceive intergroup encounters as threatening and conflictual, and to be motivated long term to emphasize the linguistic markers of their own group,

while

Proposition 8b: Individuals who are not dependent on their group and feel little solidarity with it, and who are members of either subordinate or dominant groups (especially individualistic ones), are likely to perceive intergroup encounters in interpersonal terms, to perceive intergroup encounters as nonthreatening and friendly, and to be motivated long term to accommodate to the linguistic markers of the other group.

Two aspects of Propositions 6, 7, and 8 should be kept in mind. The first is that one of the major variables to which they are relevant is the acquisition of the outgroup language. Propositions 6a, 7a, and 8a lead to individuals' refusal to use the outgroup language or to learn the language to fluency. On the other hand, Propositions 6b, 7b, and 8b lead to predictions of fluency in the outgroup language and use of it by individuals, as well as the potential disappearance of the ingroup language (see Leets & Giles, in press). Second, unlike Gallois et al. (1988), no propositions have been put forward for people with low dependence and high solidarity, or the converse. This is because there is still too little research at the present time to ground such propositions clearly, except to say that such individuals are likely to perceive intergroup encounters in both interpersonal and intergroup terms.

A return to Figure 5.1 shows that the model at this point takes up the immediate intercultural contact situation. A one-way link from accommodative orientation leads into the next box, "sociopsychological states."

Sociopsychological States

This box describes the sociopsychological orientation of individual speakers in an intercultural encounter (see Coupland et al., 1988). It includes the speaker's immediate intergroup/interpersonal orientation as well as the short-term motivation to accommodate to the other person (or people). It also includes any other salient group memberships for the speaker. This box is linked reciprocally to the one above it, "immediate situation," showing the extent to which individual and situational factors impinge on each other.

Immediate Situation

This box is intended to capture the immediate situational variables that are likely to affect anyone in the encounter. These variables include perceived situational norms for interpersonal contact and accommodation as well as norms for other salient roles or group memberships in the situation. For example, in an academic context like that in the Australian studies reviewed above, norms for behavior by students and faculty members clearly exerted a strong influence, often stronger than the influence of the interethnic context. In other cases, ethnic group membership would overwhelm the influence of other roles and norms.

Situational norms, and especially the extent to which the situation is status stressing and formal, place constraints on the forms accommodation can take, and even whether communicative convergence or divergence (as opposed to psychological accommodation) is possible (Gallois & Callan, 1991; Ryan, Giles, & Sebastian, 1982). On the other hand, speakers clearly perceive the situation and its norms at least partly as a function of their own orientations. In many cases, especially where their intergroup orientation is strong, they may perceive very different norms for members of the ingroup and outgroup (McKirnan & Hamayan, 1984; Platt & Weber, 1984). Thus this box is influenced directly by speaker states and indirectly by the overall accommodative orientation of speakers.

The variables associated with speaker states and situational factors lead to another set of propositions. First, situational norms place constraints on the forms accommodation can take. In particular,

> *Proposition 9:* In formal and status-stressing situations, many speakers are likely to converge to the sociolinguistic markers and behavior of the dominant group.

In addition,

> *Proposition 10:* In face-to-face intergroup encounters (which are formal and status stressing in particular), many speakers are likely to converge interpersonally, especially on communicative behaviors not strongly marked for, or symbolically/stereotypically associated with, either group.

As noted above, initial orientation affects the interpretation of situational norms. Thus

> *Proposition 11a:* Intergroup-oriented individuals, especially where they are task oriented and collectivistic, are likely to perceive narrower, more constraining norms for the behavior of outgroup members and wider, more tolerant norms for ingroup behavior,

while

> *Proposition 11b:* Interpersonally oriented individuals, especially when individualistic and where they are relationship oriented, are likely to perceive similar norms for ingroup and outgroup members.

The next part of this model follows closely the older versions of CAT (see Gallois et al., 1988; Giles & Coupland, 1991) and links goals, addressee focus, strategies, behavior, and labeling of and attributions about the other person. As Figure 5.1 shows, the box on sociopsychological states leads to the next box, "goals and addressee focus"; thus the immediate situation and the speaker's long-term accommodative orientation have an indirect influence here too.

Goals and Addressee Focus

In this box are included several short-term motivations that are salient in intercultural (and other intergroup) encounters: gaining approval, identifying with the other person, differentiating self from the other, achieving clear and smooth communication, and other task and relationship motives. In addition, this set of factors includes the addressee foci that speakers can adopt toward each other, including attending to the productive performance (behavior) of the other person, attending to the other's conversational competence, conversational needs, role relations, emotional and relational needs, and so forth (see Coupland et al., 1988; Williams et al., 1990, for more details). This box leads to the next one, "sociolinguistic strategies."

Sociolinguistic Strategies

As noted above, speakers can adopt a number of strategies to guide their behavior. At present, four main strategies have been theorized by CAT: approximation, interpretability, discourse management, and interpersonal control. Future research will no doubt point to other analogous strategies. It should be noted that, while there is an association between particular addressee foci and particular strategies (for example, attending to productive performance is likely to lead to the use of approximation strategies), there is no necessary connection. In any case, strategies lead to the next box, "behavior and tactics."

Behavior and Tactics

The variables in this box reflect the dynamics of ongoing interactions, as they are represented in verbal and nonverbal behavior. As a result, the list of behaviors is long and includes language, accent, paralanguage, nonvocal behaviors, topic and content, conversational style and register, and so forth. Once again, while there is some association between strategies and behavior (for example, discourse management is often reflected in topic development and the management of turn-taking), there is no necessary connection. Indeed, in principle, any strategy can be reflected in any behavior. In addition, the reciprocal link between the behavior of two interactants represents the tactical character of these variables. Much of the behavior in an interaction occurs as a direct response to the behavior of another person (a good example of this is the close coordination of turn-taking in conversations).

The relations between goals, strategies, and behavior form the basis for our next set of propositions:

Proposition 12a: When speakers desire the social approval of their interlocutors or to identify with them or their groups, desire a high level of communication clarity and comprehension, desire to meet the perceived communicative, relational, or emotional needs of their interlocutors, or desire equal-status role relations with their interlocutors, they are likely to attempt to attune positively (converge) to the communicative characteristics they believe to belong to their interlocutors,

but

Proposition 12b: When speakers desire to communicate a contrastive self- or group image to that of their interlocutors, desire to dissociate personally from their interlocutors, desire to signal differences in experience, communicative competence, or communication style from their interlocutors, or desire to achieve or maintain a high-status role relative to their interlocutors, they are likely to attempt to counterattune (diverge) or not to attune to the perceived communicative characteristics of their interlocutors.

Proposition 13a: When interpersonal concerns are salient in an intergroup encounter, speakers are likely to attempt to attune to their interlocutors (or to counterattune) primarily through approximation, interpretability,

discourse management, and interpersonal control strategies, using behavior relevant to idiolectal (personal identity) or ongoing stylistic
features relevant to the immediate interaction,

whereas

Proposition 13b: When intergroup concerns are salient, speakers are likely
to attempt to attune (or to counterattune) to their interlocutors through
approximation, interpretability, discourse management, and interpersonal control strategies, using group-marked behavior and behavior
relevant to group differences and intergroup role relations.

The extent to which speakers are able and motivated to attune their
behavior is influenced by a number of contextual and individual factors:

Proposition 14: The extent of attuning depends upon the extent of speakers'
communicative repertoires, norms about the minimum and maximum
limits of conversational attuning in the speech community, and the
extent to which their interlocutors' actual communication in the interaction matches speakers' beliefs about it.

At this point, the model takes up the reactions of interactants to the
behavior of their interlocutors as well as the impact this has on future
interactions and identity. As can be seen from Figure 5.1, this reaction
occurs in at least two stages.

Labeling and Attributions

For behavior to have an impact, it must be perceived and labeled. In
addition, a long tradition of social psychological research suggests that the
impact will be different if the behavior is attributed internally to the person
rather than externally to the situation. As can also be seen from Figure 5.1,
labeling and attributions are theorized to feed back to behavior, strategies,
goals, and even sociopsychological states. Thus interactants continue to
construct and reconstruct their identities with respect to each other in a
fluid way throughout the interaction. This recognition of the dynamic
nature of interactions, including intercultural ones, shows the subjectivist
aspect of CAT. This box also leads to the next one, "evaluation," and thus
out of the interaction and into future identities.

Evaluation and Future Intentions

CAT, along with social identity theory and a number of other communication theories, also aims to theorize the impact of particular interactions

on longer term identity and future interactions with the interlocutor and other members of his or her group. As interactants construct their identities within the interaction, they also reconstruct their own identities afterward. Thus this box leads back to speakers' long-term accommodative orientations. Following ELIT and SIT, we come to the last set of propositions:

Proposition 15a: When recipients perceive their interlocutors' behavior to be positively attuned (convergent), in terms of their own or their group's perceived or stereotyped communication style, or when they perceive it to adhere to a valued communication norm, especially when they attribute to their interlocutor high effort, high choice, and benevolent intent, recipients are likely to evaluate their interlocutors' behavior positively (as friendly, attractive, and so forth),

but

Proposition 15b: When recipients perceive their interlocutors' behavior to be counterattuned (divergent) or badly attuned, in terms of their own or their group's perceived or stereotyped communication style, or when they perceive it to depart from a valued communication norm, especially when they attribute to their interlocutor high effort, high choice, and malevolent intent, recipients are likely to evaluate their interlocutors' behavior negatively (as hostile, unattractive, and so forth).

Finally,

Proposition 16a: When interactants in intergroup encounters evaluate their interlocutors positively, and the interlocutors are perceived as typical of their group, they are likely to evaluate other members of the group positively and to be motivated to interact in future both with the interlocutor and with other members of the interlocutor's group,

but

Proposition 16b: When interactants in intergroup encounters evaluate their interlocutors negatively, and the interlocutors are perceived as typical of their group, they are likely to evaluate other members of the group negatively and to be motivated not to interact in future either with the interlocutor or with other members of the interlocutor's group.

On the other hand,

Proposition 17: When an interlocutor is perceived as atypical of the group, evaluations of the interlocutor will not change interactants' original long-term accommodative orientation toward members of that group or the speaker's original intentions to interact with them.

CONCLUSION

The model we have presented here is an attempt to capture and draw together many research programs, both from within the tradition of Communication Accommodation Theory and from outside it. As our comparison with other theories of intercultural communication suggests, CAT deals with both individual and sociostructural levels of communication and, importantly, with motivation as well as with overt behavior. As such, CAT is a large-scale theory and provides a framework rather than a tightly interlocked set of predictions. Arguably, it is unique vis-à-vis the other frameworks presented earlier in this chapter—as well as other potent approaches (e.g., Carbaugh, 1990). We have seen ways—yet have frankly resisted them for this context at least—of amalgamating other theories' tenets (that is, building on notions of anxiety, resourcefulness, and so on). Clearly, we would not wish to be seen as imperialistic. This could yield a hopelessly irrefutable grand theory when minitheories—whose boundaries should judiciously and comparatively be drawn—are perhaps ideal for the current state of the development of our art. In any case, we would not wish to fall ourselves, needlessly, into the trap of perpetuating intergroup rivalries in intercultural communication theory. Hence we invite testing those CAT propositions readers find particularly relevant to their own ideological tastes in as many different intercultural settings as feasible. For as the above indicates, any research program is likely to test only one part of the theory, and to test it in only one kind of context.

6

Toward a Theory of Conversational Constraints

Focusing on Individual-Level Dimensions of Culture

MIN-SUN KIM • *University of Hawaii at Manoa*

In a previous paper, M. Kim (1993) *explained* cross-cultural differences in the selection of communicative strategies, based on the assumption that many communication acts are influenced by a set of conversational constraints. In everyday social interaction, people have various social goals (e.g., gaining compliance, affinity-seeking, seeking favors, seeking information, revealing information). To achieve these goals, people must have strategic competence—the procedural knowledge necessary to reach their goals. This chapter puts forward the notion of *conversational constraints* that guide the choice of communication tactics and the general assessment of communication competence. The different priorities given to the constraints will give rise to different approaches to achieving interaction goals, and ultimately to overall impressions of intercultural strategic competence.

Focusing on culture-based conversational constraints, M. Kim (1993) outlined a theoretical perspective to understand and predict differential conversational strategy choices made by members of different cultural groups. Specifically, two conversational constraints (face concern and clarity) were theoretically linked to an important dimension of culture, that is, individualistic-collectivistic orientation. The essential idea is

AUTHOR'S NOTE: The author gratefully acknowledges constructive comments and suggestions from Drs. William B. Gudykunst, Richard L. Wiseman, and Narayan S. Raja on earlier drafts of this chapter. Correspondence concerning this manuscript should be sent to Dr. Min-Sun Kim, Department of Speech, University of Hawaii at Manoa, Honolulu, HI 96822.

that the collectivism-individualism construct systematically affects the salience of face support and clarity of conversational strategies. These conversational constraints, as generators of strategy preferences, in turn, influence the choice of strategies and the assessment of cross-cultural competence.

This prior model of conversational constraints has proven to be useful and has received empirical support. For example, it was found that there are systematic cross-cultural differences in the perceived importance of these constraints (see M. Kim, 1994) as well as in the mean and rank ordering of request tactics along these constraint dimensions (Kim & Wilson, 1994). The prior theoretical framework, however, involved only the cultural level, that is, those factors that lead people in one culture to communicate similarly to or differently than people in other cultures. The model focused only on how culture influences individual behavior. However, a solid theory of intercultural communication should be based on individual- as well as culture-level explanation. For a theory to be broadly applicable, it must be supported by individual-level as well as culture-level data (Leung, 1989). The individual-level approach has received minimal attention in theoretical work on intercultural communication.

Recently, the use of broad cultural variability dimensions has been criticized by many authors for its lack of explanatory power (e.g., Kagitcibasi, 1987; Schwartz, 1990; Singelis, 1994). When broad dimensions such as individualism-collectivism or high versus low context are invoked to account for cultural differences, it is uncertain exactly how or why these differences occur. The use of culture as a post hoc explanation of observed differences does little to help us understand the underlying causes of behavior. Given the complexities of the influence of culture on communication behavior, it is necessary to find relevant intervening variables to understand what it is in culture that accounts for cultural differences. Surely, the division of the world into individualist and collectivist cultures is a broad-brush simplification that deserves a more systematic and detailed examination (Schwartz, 1990).

In intercultural communication research, there may be a bias toward preferring to use "culture" as the only explanatory variable. Most studies tend to *assume* an individual-level approach and focus on the culture level. The problem stems from the fact that researchers rely on cultural differences as an antecedent variable to explain cultural differences in communication behavior, without knowing for certain that cultural differences correspond to individual-level differences. The use of mediating variables has the advantage of reducing the likelihood of bias as an explanation for a coherent pattern of cultural differences. Little has been done to study intercultural communication patterns by means of individual-level analyses. Many theoretical approaches in intercultural communication at some point invoke individual-level processes (e.g., self-concept, identity) as an explanation of cultural differences (see Collier & Thomas, 1988; Cronen, Pearce, & Tomm, 1985). However, there is a conspicuous lack of empirical evidence about the specifics of the self-systems of people from different cultural backgrounds. Individual-level conceptualizations and data are definitely needed to substantiate these formulations.

The use of culture as the sole explanatory variable for cultural differences is not satisfactory; culture must be unpacked. One might claim that an individual-level approach is best suited to psychological rather than cultural phenomena. However, many theoretical approaches in intercultural communication invoke some individual-level factors, such as self-conception and face. A universally applicable theory should concern itself with individual-level as well as culture-level issues. Convergence between individual- and culture-level explanations would support the universality of the theory. This chapter integrates the individual-level analyses (focusing on those factors that motivate us to communicate and influence the way we create and interpret messages), based on the assumption that cultural and individual levels are interrelated.

To summarize, the purpose of this chapter is to provide a theoretical framework for illuminating the relationship of individual-level culture variables (several elements of self-structure) to the perceived importance of conversational constraints, which are guiding motives or criteria for selecting conversational strategies. The ability to deal with individual-level variables of culture dimensions should be a useful tool in determining whether previously established cultural differences match up with corresponding individual-level differences.

The following three elements constituting self-structure, that is, individual-level variables, were chosen: (a) two dimensions of self-concept, that is, independent and interdependent self construals explicated by Markus and Kitayama (1991); (b) need for approval and need for dominance; and (c) psychological gender, that is, masculinity and femininity. These individual-level variables have corresponding cultural dimensions and seem to be fundamental for understanding cultural differences in communication. Theoretical predictions should generalize across cultures and across types of interaction (e.g., intracultural and intercultural conversations). The current theory can be applied to a wide variety of primary goals (e.g., criticisms, apologies, refusals, seeking information, eliciting promises). In addition, this theory can be tested with a wide variety of populations from differing linguistic and sociocultural backgrounds.

The remaining sections of this chapter are organized as follows: First, the three conversational constraints are introduced. Next, several mediating variables relating to an individual's self-system are linked to the perceived salience of conversational constraints. Specific theoretical propositions are derived from this discussion. Finally, the theoretical implications and future directions for research are discussed.

CONVERSATIONAL CONSTRAINTS

Conversation is typically viewed as a goal-directed action requiring coordination with others. According to Street and Cappella (1985), interaction goals are classified into two types: (a) global or cross-situational goals and (b) situation-specific goals. Cross-situational goals are distinguished from situation-specific goals in that the former are operative during almost all social encounters, while the latter become individually operative given situational exigencies. The primary, or situation-specific, goals include gaining compliance, escalating relational intimacy, and remedying a faux pas (see M. Kim, 1993).

Conversational constraints, as cross-situational goals, are best viewed as criteria for making a choice of conversational strategy. They are fundamental concerns regarding *the manner in which a message is constructed* and tend to affect the general character of every conversation one engages in, and an individual's conversational style in general. Thus they contribute to consistent conversational performances across varying contexts (Wilensky, 1983). M. Kim (1993, 1994) posits that conversational constraints would be of two general kinds: (a) concern with face support, interpersonal relations, needs of others, and of one's relationship with them (concern for not hurting the hearer's feelings, concern for minimizing imposition) and (b) concern with getting one's own way (clarity). These constraints represent a "meta" concern in the mind of the individual while pursuing interaction goals. Based on past research by M. Kim and others (M. Kim, 1994; M. Kim, Sharkey, & Singelis, 1994; M. Kim & Wilson, 1994), two social-relational constraints (imposition and concern for other's feelings) and one task-oriented constraint (clarity) are identified.[1] In the following section, the three conversational constraints are defined.

Concern for Clarity

Clarity, as applied to conversational behavior, is the likelihood of an utterance making one's intention clear and explicit. That is, the concern for clarity controls the degree to which the intention of the message is explicitly and unambiguously communicated to a listener (Blum-Kulka, 1987). Applied to conversational behavior, the constraint (or preference) for clarity therefore is a concern for achieving an outcome in the most direct way possible. Movement toward increased clarity typically results in the choice of more pointed and direct tactical means. For example, if one's primary goal is to request an action, direct imperative forms (e.g., "Repay the loan" or "Lend me your book") will make the speaker's illocutionary point explicit. For instance, in hint strategies, illocutionary force is not derivable from the literal meaning of the utterances. In such strategies as imperatives, the requester's intention is marked explicitly, making little inferential demand. In the past, several authors have suggested similar conversational constraints that are motivating forces in communication: "be[ing] clear" (Lakoff, 1977), "concern for clarity" (Greene & Lindsey, 1989), and "directness" (Blum-Kulka, 1987). Grice (1975) also put forward the "maxim of manner" in the use of language (e.g., be clear, be brief, try to avoid obscurity), which can be seen as guidelines for direct communication. Brown and Levinson (1978) also posit such a want as the desire to be efficient or indicate urgency.

Concern for Avoiding Hurting the Hearer's Feelings

When planning to achieve interaction goals, people may also take into account how their projected actions might affect the hearer's feelings. "Concern for the other's feelings" relates to the speaker's perceived obligation to support a hearer's approval-seeking or the hearer's positive self-image (Brown & Levinson, 1978; Ting-Toomey, 1988). Research on politeness focuses on strategies for minimizing threats to others' face, and reinforces the importance of the concern for others' feelings in conversational behavior (Brown & Levinson, 1978; Lakoff, 1977; Leech, 1983; Scollon & Scollon, 1981). Researchers have used various other names for this constraint (concern for the hearer's feelings), including "the want to maintain the hearer's positive face" (Brown & Levinson, 1978), "identity goals" (Wilson & Putnam, 1990), and "concern with support" (need to show concern for other's feelings; Greene & Lindsey, 1989). Bald imperatives (e.g., "Give me the money!") involve more risk of hurting the other's feelings than hints (given the same situational contingencies). The former, with their lack of request mitigation, may convey the implicit message that the speaker is not concerned about the relationship but only with accomplishing the instrumental outcome (e.g., getting the money back).

Concern for Minimizing Imposition

This constraint pertains to the degree to which an utterance avoids imposing on the hearer or interfering with the hearer's freedom of action (Brown & Levinson, 1978). An act of communication may threaten the hearer's negative face to the extent that it imposes on her or his right to autonomy (Scollon & Scollon, 1981). This type of concern has been referred to in more abstract terms, such as "negative politeness" (Brown & Levinson, 1978) or "deference politeness" (Scollon & Scollon, 1981), which avoid making imposition on others. Thus concern for minimizing imposition has primarily been conceived as a means of protecting the hearer's negative face. Several authors (Blum-Kulka & House, 1989; Scollon & Scollon, 1981; Ting-Toomey, 1988) argue that the notion of politeness is usually associated in the Western world with "negative" or deference strategies: The show of deference is expressed by trying not to be heard as imposing on the hearer, by leaving the hearer options for noncompliance, and by not assuming cooperation. While the salience of this constraint might differ between cultures, prior research confirms the importance of minimizing imposition in many cultures (Blum-Kulka & House, 1989; Holtgraves & Yang, 1990, 1992).

In summary, the above three conversational constraints may serve as general motivating forces in the selection of conversational strategies and tactics, and thus serve as important determinants of "cultural ways of speaking" (Katriel, 1986). While the salience of each constraint might differ across cultures, prior research confirms the importance of all of them in conversational performance (M. Kim, 1994; M. Kim & Wilson, 1994; M. Kim et al., 1994).

A growing body of cross-cultural studies of the self-concept (Cross & Markus, 1991; Markus & Kitayama, 1991; Triandis, 1989) reveals that an exclusive focus on culture-level generalizations is no longer appropriate for studying intercultural communication styles. It is necessary therefore to identify the theoretical elements or processes that explain these cultural differences. Self construal may be one such powerful factor. Recent cross-cultural research on the self has suggested that self-concept is an important mediator of cultural behavior patterns (Ting-Toomey, 1989b; Triandis, 1989). The concept of self may be linked to many of the communication styles previously associated with cultural dimensions, such as individualism and collectivism. The notion of self-concept may permit us to better specify what precisely is the role of the self in mediating and regulating preferences for conversational styles. The following section discusses the relationship between conversational constraints and individual-level culture dimensions.

Content of Self in Different Cultures:
Independent and Interdependent Construals of Self

The notions of "individualism" and "collectivism" have been used to account for differences in communication style between cultures. A typical general conclusion is that members of individualistic cultures prefer direct communication styles, while members of collectivistic cultures prefer indirect communication styles. Despite the popularity of individualism and collectivism as major cultural dimensions, their psychological validity is not well established. Triandis (1989) proposed an explanation of culture's influence on behavior. He employed the concept of self as a mediating variable between culture and individual behavior. Among other things, self-concept is a powerful force in shaping perceptions, evaluations, and behaviors (Geertz, 1975; Markus & Kitayama, 1991). Our self-conceptions influence how we communicate with others and our choices (both conscious and unconscious) of those with whom relations are formed (Gudykunst, 1993). The self can be construed, framed, or conceptualized in different ways. There is evidence that the notion of self is different across cultures (Marsella, DeVoss, & Hsu, 1985). Triandis (1989) suggested that collectivistic cultures encourage the development of many cognitions that refer to a group or collective, thus increasing the chances that these cognitions will be sampled frequently by the individual. On the other hand, individualistic cultures nurture the growth of cognitions that refer to the individual's traits and states.

Recently, Markus and Kitayama (1991) delineated two types of self construals (independent and interdependent) and argued for the systematic influence of these differing self-concepts on cognition, emotion, and motivation. These two images of self were originally conceptualized as reflecting the emphasis on connectedness and relations often found in "non-Western" cultures (interdependent) and the separatedness and uniqueness of the individual (independent) stressed in "the West." In the *independent* construal, most representations of the self (i.e., the ways in which individuals think of themselves) have as their referent an individual's ability, characteristic, attribute, or goal ("I am friendly" or "I am ambitious"). These inner characteristics or traits are the primary regulators of behavior. This view of the self derives from a belief in the wholeness and uniqueness of each person's configuration of internal attributes (Johnson, 1985). The normative imperative of such cultures is to become independent of others and to discover and express one's own unique attributes (Marsella et al., 1985; Miller, 1988). Thus the goals of persons in such cultures are to "stand out" and to express their own unique internal characteristics or traits. This orientation has led to an emphasis on the need to pursue personal self-actualization or self-development. Individual weakness, in this cultural perspective, is to be overly dependent on others or to be unassertive (Bellah, Madsen, Sullivan, Swidler, & Tipton, 1985).

By contrast, in the *interdependent* construal, the self is connected to others; the principal components of the self are one's relationships to others. This is not to say that the person with an interdependent view of the self has no conception of internal traits, characteristics, or preferences that are unique to him or her but that these internal, private aspects of the self are not primary in directing or guiding behavior. Instead, behavior is more significantly regulated by the desire to maintain harmony and appropriateness in relationships. Within such a construal, the self becomes most meaningful and complete when it is cast in the appropriate social relationship. So one's behavior in a given situation may be a function more of the needs, wishes, and preferences of others than of one's own needs, wishes, or preferences. As a result of this interdependent construal of the self, one may attempt to meet the needs of others and to promote the others' goals. Weakness in this perspective is to be headstrong, unwilling to accommodate the needs of others, or self-centered (Cross & Markus, 1991).

According to Markus and Kitayama (1991), from the standpoint of an independent, "self-ish" self, one might be led to romanticize the interdependent self, which is ever attuned to the concerns of others. Yet, in many cases, responsive and cooperative actions are exercised only when there is a reasonable assurance of the "good intentions" of others, namely, their commitment to continue to engage in reciprocal interaction and mutual support. "Clearly, interdependent selves do not attend to the needs, desires, and goals of *all* others. Attention to others is not indiscriminate; it is highly selective and is most characteristic of relationships with 'in-group' members" (Markus & Kitayama, 1991, p. 229). The distinctions between independent and interdependent construals must be regarded as *general* tendencies that may emerge when the members of the culture are considered as a whole. For instance, even in American culture, there is a theme of interdependence that is reflected in the values and activities of many of its subcultures. Religious groups, such as the Quakers, explicitly value and promote interdependence, as do many small towns and rural communities (Bellah et al., 1985).

Relationships Between Self Construals and Preferences for Conversational Constraints

These general cultural differences in self-concept have implications for cross-cultural preferences in conversational styles. The degree of interdependent self-orientation of an individual may systematically affect the perceived importance of the two face-related conversational constraints (concern for the other's feelings and concern for nonimposition) that guide the communicative behavior. What is focal in an interdependent self is not the protagonist him- or herself but the protagonist's relationships to other actors (Hamaguchi, 1985).

An interdependent self construal is defined as a flexible, variable self that emphasizes (a) external, public features such as status, roles, and relationships; (b) belonging and fitting in; (c) occupying one's proper place and engaging in appropriate action; and (d) being indirect in communication and reading another's mind (Markus & Kitayama, 1991). According to Markus and Kitayama (1991), relationships, rather than being means for realizing various individual goals, will often be ends in and of themselves. In some cases, meeting the other's goals, needs, and desires will be a necessary requirement for satisfying one's own goals.

Within each particular social situation, the self can be differently instantiated (Markus & Kitayama, 1991). Similarly, Triandis (1989) argued that aspects of the self are differentially sampled in different situations. Sampling of collective (interdependent) self is more likely when the ingroup is distinctive in the particular situation. Furthermore, although most prior attempts to measure individualism-collectivism have assumed it to be a single bipolar dimension (Triandis, McClusker, & Hui, 1990), the two aspects of self can coexist. Recently, Singelis (1994) confirmed the notion of "dual" selves by showing the strength of an individual's independent and interdependent self construals as separate dimensions. These data confirmed the existence of two distinct dimensions of self construal, as opposed to the bipolar conceptualization of individualism-collectivism. Singelis concludes that, when the unit of analysis is the individual, one must consider these dimensions separately.

These ideas, as applied to conversational constraints, would mean that individuals using interdependent self have, as an overall goal, the desire to avoid loss of face and to be accepted by ingroup members, which strengthens their preference for "prosocial" means (by not imposing and by avoiding hurting the other's feelings) for achieving primary goals. The requirement is to "read" the other's mind and thus to know what the other is thinking or feeling.

Thus we may expect those using interdependent selves to be more attentive and sensitive to others than those with independent selves. This should result in a relatively greater concern for relational constraints in the choice of conversational strategies. That is, regardless of

one's primary goal(s) in any specific encounter, the concern for minimizing imposition and concern for not hurting the other's feelings will
be more important considerations when an individual samples interdependent views of the self to a greater extent. Based on this reasoning,
the following propositions are formulated:

> *Proposition 1:* Activation of interdependent self construal will give rise to
> higher perceived importance for *not hurting the hearer's feelings* in the
> pursuit of primary goals.
> *Proposition 2:* Activation of interdependent self construal will give rise to
> higher perceived importance for *minimizing imposition to the hearer*
> in the pursuit of primary goals.

In a previous theoretical perspective (M. Kim, 1993), the author
argued that the predominant forms of communication in individualistic
cultures call for clear and direct communication, exemplified by expressions such as the following: "Don't beat around the bush" and "Get to
the point." Therefore, an individualist orientation systematically increases the importance of directness concerns in guiding tactical choices.
Similar to the notion of individualistic cultural orientation, independent
self construal is defined as a bounded, unitary, stable self that is separate
from social context. The constellation of elements composing an independent self construal includes an emphasis on (a) internal abilities,
thoughts, and feelings; (b) being unique and expressing the self; (c)
realizing internal attributes and promoting one's own goals; (d) being
direct in communication (Markus & Kitayama, 1991). The independent
construal of self gives rise to processes like self-actualization, realizing
oneself, expressing one's unique needs, rights, and capacities, or developing one's distinct potential in contrast to the interdependent self "as
interdependent with the surrounding context, [where] it is the 'other' or
the 'self-in-relation-to-other' that is the focal in individualistic experience" (Markus & Kitayama, 1991, p. 225).

The independent self-image places a higher priority on maintaining
independence and asserting individual needs and goals. It is the individual's responsibility to "say what's on her or his mind" if she or he
expects to be attended to or understood (Markus & Kitayama, 1991).
For a person oriented toward the independent construal of self, the
general tone of social interaction may be more concerned with being
direct, clear, unambiguous, and concise in the choice of verbal tactics.
Therefore, independent self construal may systematically increase the
importance of the clarity concern in guiding choices of conversational
strategies. Consequently, the following proposition is formulated:

Proposition 3: Activation of independent self construal will give rise to higher perceived importance for *clarity* in the pursuit of primary goals.

Consequences of "Dual" Selves on Preferences for Conversational Constraints

According to Markus and Kitayama (1991), on the average, relatively more individuals in Western cultures will hold independent self construals than will individuals in non-Western cultures. Within a given culture, however, individuals will vary in the extent to which they are "good" cultural representatives and construe the self in the typical way. Thus not all people who are part of an independent culture will possess primarily independent self construals, nor will all those who are part of an interdependent culture possess primarily interdependent self construals. Within independent and interdependent cultures, there will be great diversity in individual self-definition, and there can also be strong similarities across cultures.

Cross and Markus (1991) also found support for two dimensions of self in their study of stress and coping behavior among American and East Asian exchange students. East Asian students who viewed the interdependent or collective aspects of the self as less important, and had elaborated the independent aspects of the self, reported less stress. When asked to indicate the importance of the independent and interdependent facets of the self, the East Asian exchange students placed much more importance on the interdependent dimension of the self than did the American students, but importance scores on the independent dimension did not differ between the groups. Therefore the Asian exchange students appeared to have elaborated an internal, private, autonomous self-system while continuing to retain the interdependent aspects of the self. This suggests the development of a bicultural self-system, in which the collective, interdependent components of the self coexist with private, or independent, self-conceptions.

According to Singelis (1994), we need not presuppose the development of one self to the exclusion of others. Circumstances, such as having parents from different cultures, or intercultural experience, may contribute to the development of both the private and the collective self. Bhawuk and Brislin (1992) found that one measure of cultural sensitivity was an individual's ability to modify his or her behavior according to the cultural context—collectivist or individualist. This ability to switch between collectivist and individualist modes suggests the existence of two well-developed self-concepts among some individuals. The point to be made is that some individuals may have two well-developed self-concepts. The coexistence of two well-developed self construals is not necessarily problematic and may be quite useful when moving between cultures.

According to Kline (1984), it appears that construct system development is connected with the selection of different kinds of strategies. Messages generated by less differentiated individuals, that is, Low Construct Differentiation (LCD), posited a well-defined social order structured by explicit roles and mutually understood rules. In contrast, highly differentiated individuals, that is, High Construct Differentiation (HCD), tended to define communication tasks in a way that incorporated the face wants of the persuadee into the goal structure of the situation. Their messages attended to the persuasive task *and* to the persuadee's face wants simultaneously. Similarly, persons who have well-developed independent as well as interdependent selves (bicultural) may be considered highly differentiated individuals and may be more cognizant of both clarity and relational constraints. They may also be able to modify their behavior appropriately and successfully, depending on situational contingencies or when moving from one culture to another. Their awareness of the conversational constraints may also be high. This vision of people as multifaceted seems to coincide with such concepts as "intercultural person" (Y. Kim, 1988a), "universal person" (Walsh, 1973), "multicultural person" (Adler, 1976), and "international person" (Lutzker, 1960). Adler (1976), for example, explains the multicultural person as one who is neither totally a part of, nor totally apart from, her or his culture. Such a person may be capable of reconciling the conflicts posed by competing conversational constraints and achieving a high level of communication competence. She or he may be better able to make deliberate choices in various situations and to maintain a dynamic balance rather than being bound by the culturally imposed emphases on various conversational constraints.

Production of two well-developed selves appears to be an important antecedent of intercultural communication competence. While recognition of the importance of conversational constraints does not by itself mean that one's message will address all those constraints, it still reflects one's flexibility in strategy choice depending on situational contingencies. A certain level of adherence to the clarity concern is as essential for the successful achievement of interactional balance as is maintaining good interpersonal relationships. The particular set of trade-offs arrived at for a given situation may depend on other factors such as the importance of primary goals, relational outcome values, and nature of the situation.[2]

Presumably, tendencies toward independent construal prevent speakers from being maximally indirect (e.g., use of mild hint), whereas tendencies toward interdependent construal prevent speakers from being maximally direct (e.g., use of imperatives). Thus, individuals with two well-developed selves may be able to find clear as well as relationally sensitive strategy choices, rather than totally abandoning one constraint in favor of another. On the other hand, individuals with poorly developed self construals may not internalize either collective or private selves and may not be strongly guided by any of the conversational constraints. As Craig (1986) notes, communication competence is often defined as the ability to satisfy all goals and constraints in an optimal manner. As conflicts occur between constraints, individuals with two well-developed selves may focus on the more important constraint, yet try to modify at least some of their actions to satisfy the other constraint to the limited extent possible. However, this flexibility may not always be possible for culture-typed individuals; they may abandon one constraint in favor of the other (as prescribed by their particular culture). Thus it seems plausible that more frequent sampling of the interdependent as well as independent selves will lead to higher concern for all the conversational constraints. That is, given that multiple aspects of the self can exist within an individual, the more a person samples both private and collective selves, the more likely it is that she or he will have regard for clarity as well as relational concerns.

> *Proposition 4:* Individuals with high independent as well as simultaneously high interdependent self construals will show high concern for relational as well as clarity constraints, whereas individuals with either low-independent/high-interdependent or high-independent/low-interdependent self construals will tend to favor one set of constraints at the expense of the other.
> *Proposition 5:* Individuals with low-independent as well as low-interdependent self construals will attach less importance to relational as well as clarity constraints than individuals with either low-independent/high-interdependent or high-independent/low-interdependent self construals.

Need for Social Approval and Need for Dominance as Other Elements of Self-System

The independent versus interdependent construals of self are among the most general and overarching schemata of the individual self-system (Markus & Kitayama, 1991). The need for approval (the degree to which an individual is concerned about what others might think of his or her actions; Salzman & Hunter, 1983) and need for dominance (the degree to which an individual desires to control and dominate social situations; Salzman & Hunter, 1983) are also parts of self-concept that may have consequences for the perceived importance of constraints. Concern regarding feelings of others and negative evaluation by others seems to be at the heart of such interdependent (collectivistic) characteristics as need for approval. Similarly, the extent of the need for social approval seems to closely coincide with the cultural dimension of other orientation or social orientation (Yang & Ho, 1988). *Other orientation* refers to sensitivity to others' opinions about oneself and hence to a concern for impression management. Similarly, Yang (1981) defines *social orientation* as a predisposition toward behavior patterns such as submission to social expectations and concern about others' opinions so as to avoid punishment, embarrassment, rejection, and ridicule. Need for social approval is related to the notion of social orientation.

The desire to create and sustain positive identities in the eyes of others may induce people to manage the interaction in such a way as to project a desired self-image (Wilson & Putnam, 1990). Other-directed people (contrasted with inner-directed people) are said to have a paramount need for social approval and direction from others, and hence to have the tendency to act in conformity with others. Other-directed people actively seek approval and popularity (Ho, 1993). If the main concern is to be socially accepted, the imperative during conversation is to avoid disapproval or rejection by the other. Consequently, such persons must be sensitive to social norms and to others' needs.

As a person's concern for social approval increases, others will be assigned much more importance and will be relatively focal in the person's own behavior. Meeting others' goals, needs, and desires will be a necessary requirement for satisfying the person's own goals, needs, and desires. Thus, with the need for approval, successful communication must be attentive to the feelings of others as well as to potential impositions on the interactional partner. One of the normative goals for the personality characteristic of need for approval is to fit in and assimilate. As concern for the reactions of others increases, so may the importance of conversational constraints such as concern regarding the hearer's feelings, and minimizing imposition.

> *Proposition 6:* The higher an individual's need for approval, the higher the perceived importance for that individual's concern for the hearer's feelings in the pursuit of primary goals.
>
> *Proposition 7:* The higher an individual's need for approval, the higher the perceived importance for that individual of minimizing imposition on the hearer in the pursuit of primary goals.

On the other hand, concern for clarity, as a general guideline in the choice of conversational action, seems to serve the need for social dominance. A major aspect of the need for dominance involves breaking away, pushing ahead, and gaining control over surroundings, rather than fitting in and accommodating to existing realities. This individual dimension seems consistent with cultural dimensions such as person-over-nature orientation ("the mastery-over-nature view") and activity orientation (the "Doing" culture) (see Kluckhohn & Strodtbeck, 1961). The person-over-nature orientation takes the view that all natural forces or situations can be overcome or controlled by active intervention. Similarly, the "Doing" activity orientation may be based on individuals' belief that through controlling and dominating situations they can cause things to happen. Prior research has shown that persons with high assertiveness, high need for control, and high self-confidence tend to be more concerned with clarity (i.e., Frese, Stewart, & Hannover, 1987). Similarly, individuals with a heightened need for dominance in social situations tend to assert their needs with direct, clear, and nonambiguous communication strategies, making the speaker's intention transparent to the hearer. Based on the above reasoning, the following proposition is formulated:

Proposition 8: The higher an individual's need for dominance, the higher the perceived importance of clarity for that individual in the pursuit of primary goals.

Consequences of Psychological Gender on the Perceived Importance of Conversational Constraints

The self-concept derives not only from the relational self-schema but from the complete configuration of self-schemata, including those that are a product of gender culture. Sex roles would be the equivalent of the cultural dimensions of masculinity and femininity (see Gudykunst, 1993, p. 71). A growing body of psychological theory, based on analyses of women's experiences, suggests that women's sense of self is best characterized by an emphasis on caring (Gilligan, 1982), and "being-in-relationship" (Miller, 1984), rather than by an autonomous and independent self. Stewart and Wheeless (1981) have listed dominance, aggressiveness, competitiveness, and independence among the traits of masculinity and suggested that being sensitive to the needs of others is a valued feminine trait.

For Bem (1974), the characteristics of masculinity may be viewed as instrumental, cognitive in focus (job completion/problem solving), and agentic (concern for the self as an individual). In contrast to this, the characteristics of femininity for Bem are exemplified as expressive (concern for group harmony and the welfare of others) and communal (the relationship between self and others). Psychological gender is a crucial part of an individual's self-concept. The perceived importance of various conversational constraints in a given situation is therefore likely to be influenced by psychological gender. Many past studies have attempted to link communication style with physical gender (for a review, see Canary & Hause, 1993). However, hardly any studies have examined the relationship between communication style and psychological gender, that is, the traits of femininity and masculinity (Whitley, 1988). When researchers focus on physical gender as the independent variable, they find more similarities than differences in communication style, or they find nothing at all (Canary & Hause, 1993). The traits of masculinity and femininity, while not as easy to assess as physical gender (male or female), may be of greater value to communication researchers.

Female-male miscommunication has been interpreted in a number of ways, most notably as an innocent by-product of different socialization patterns and gender cultures (Maltz & Borker, 1982). Tannen applies a cross-cultural approach to cross-gender conversation, in which men and women, boys and girls, can both be seen to accomplish and display coherence in conversation, but from different cultural perspectives. Similarly, Maltz and Borker (1982) claim that gender differences can be understood as cultural differences. Gender-based differences in language use have been discussed in countless studies (see Sheldon, 1990). The general claim is that men's speech and women's speech seem to have different content and to serve different purposes. Male speech is characterized as competition oriented or adversarial. On the other hand, female speech is characterized as collaboration oriented or affiliative. At this point, it is still unclear how cultural femininity and masculinity are related to conversational styles. The mechanisms underlying the influence of cultural gender have not been verified at a cognitive level.

While independent and interdependent construals of self are very general cultural self-schemata, the gender orientation applies to a given individual's view of self deriving from gender history. An important perspective on gender and the themes of affiliation and independence comes from the work of Gilligan (1987). Awareness of and sensitivity to others are described as significant features of the psychology of women. As Gilligan (1987) claimed, a willingness and an ability to care are standards of self-evaluation for many women. Gilligan's portrayal of women's self-concept is similar in many ways to the characteristics of feminine cultures. Similarly, according to Hofstede (1980), feminine cultures emphasize interpersonal cooperation, a friendly atmosphere, and sympathy for the weak; by contrast, masculine cultures emphasize achievement, recognition, and challenges. Cultures high in femininity include Sweden, Norway, and the Netherlands; cultures high in masculinity include Japan, Austria, and Venezuela. Leung, Bond, Carment, Kirshnan, and Liebrand (1990) found that Dutch subjects (feminine culture) preferred harmony-enhancing procedures more, and confrontational procedures less, than did Canadian subjects (masculine culture).

In a similar vein, the gender image individuals have of themselves affects the way they communicate with others, and their self-concept of maleness or femaleness affects how they perceive themselves as communicators. The justice orientation focuses on autonomy (Gilligan, 1987). Terms used to describe this orientation are *agency, self-assertion,* and *individuality* (Eagly, 1987). This orientation tends to appeal to a universalist point of view, rather than to the particular concerns and needs of others and of one's relationship with them. A person who operates from the justice orientation (a) frames conflict in terms of individual rights that must be respected in the relationship; (b) values detachment, independence, and autonomy; (c) assumes separation and the need for an external structure of connection; (d) steps back from the situation and appeals to a rule, or reasons from a principle, to resolve conflict, valuing logic, rationality, and control and often losing sight of the needs of others; and (e) attends to rights and respect.

The care orientation, associated with female style, focuses on maintaining the connection between oneself and others in intimate groups, and defines the self in the context of the relationship (Gilligan, 1987). Terms such as *communication, affiliation, empathy, interdependence,* and *involvement* have been used to describe this focus (Bakan, 1966; Eagly, 1987). This perspective pays more attention to the needs of others. According to Gilligan (1987), a person who operates from the care orientation (a) assumes connection between the self and others, and frames conflict resolution in terms of the relationship; (b) shows greater tolerance of, compassion for, and responsiveness to others; (c) emphasizes understanding and communication through listening and speaking, and hearing and being heard; (d) seeks agreement and tries to respond to everyone's needs; (e) shows less legalistic elaboration; and (f) appeals more to a particularistic understanding of others and less to a universal point of view. Thus a female focus on relationships serves to enhance communication and respond to the needs and feelings of others, whereas a male focus on the self shows through in the insistence on getting one's own way as well as the appeal to self-serving rules. If the stereotype is true that men (i.e., masculine cultural orientations) use language "to assert a position of dominance" by coming directly to the point (clarity), whereas women (i.e., feminine cultural orientations) use language to create and maintain relationships of closeness, then this should also be reflected in an individual's differential preference for conversational constraints. Consequently, the following propositions are formulated:

> *Proposition 9:* The more masculine an individual's psychological gender, the higher the perceived importance of clarity for that individual.
>
> *Proposition 10:* The more feminine an individual's psychological gender, the higher the perceived importance for that individual not to hurt the hearer's feelings.
>
> *Proposition 11:* The more feminine an individual's psychological gender, the higher the perceived importance for that individual of avoiding imposition on the hearer.

DISCUSSION

This chapter attempts to disentangle the cultural and psychological aspects of cultural communication styles. Using this individual-level approach to cross-cultural differences in conjunction with our prior culture-level approach (M. Kim, 1993), hypotheses can be examined both intraculturally and cross-culturally, so that explanatory variables may be tested at two levels (Berry & Dasen, 1974). Following the terminology of Leung and Bond (1989), this correspondence (between individual-level and culture-level dimensions) is called a "strong etic" relationship, and a theory based on this relationship is called a "strong etic theory." The theoretical framework proposed here, combined with the prior culture-level approach (M. Kim, 1993), allows the examination of effects at both levels (individual and culture levels) simultaneously, and the comparison of their relative importance.

The proposed theory integrates literature from the areas of cross-cultural communication and social cognition. This approach promises to be an exciting and fruitful marriage of culture and cognition. It may demonstrate how theoretical and empirical benefits can accrue by combining literature and data from different specializations. The focus on self-systems (e.g., independent versus interdependent selves) may provide a means of integrating research on a large number of separate personality constructs. Because self-concept provides a link between the norms and values of a culture and the everyday behavior of individuals, it is a promising means of explaining conversational styles in different cultures. The notion of self-concept brings broad cultural variability dimensions to the individual level. At the individual level, the problematic categorization of people as either individualists or collectivists is ameliorated (Singelis, 1994). The nature of divergent self-systems permits us to better specify the precise role of the self in mediating and regulating communication behavior.

Several major cultural dimensions (e.g., individualism and collectivism, masculinity and femininity) emerge from the literature as high-order psychological concepts that can help explain cross-cultural differences in behavior over a wide range of situations. In many cases, a broad concept is invoked to explain major aspects of the behavior of an entire cultural population. However, high-level concepts such as individualism and collectivism tend to be loosely defined. It is also difficult to ascertain their validity, because the delimitations of these broad concepts (i.e., the boundaries between aspects of behavior that are covered by the concept and those that are not) remain unclear. Self-structure may prove to be a strong intervening variable that can help explain how culture affects behavior. To more precisely understand the processes by which culture influences behavior, several elements of the self-system are proposed in this chapter. However, this is not to argue that high-level concepts (e.g., individualism and collectivism) are invalid dimensions. Rather, this approach shows that a more parsimonious and precise explanation (of the kinds of cross-cultural differences ascribed to cultural variability dimensions) is possible by resorting to certain mediating variables.

Merely identifying cross-cultural differences is not sufficient. A more important goal is to render such differences interpretable by explaining the relationship between cultural differences and individual processes. The theoretical framework proposed here incorporates individual-level equivalents of different dimensions of cultural variability. The author's prior theoretical analysis (M. Kim, 1993) was on the cultural level. The theory would be incomplete without the individual-level analysis. Methodologically, attempts should be made to verify whether individual-level and culture-level variables produce the same effects.

To try to understand the origins of cultural preferences for specific conversational strategies, this chapter proposes that certain *conversational constraints* influence people's choice of conversational tactics. As people pursue interaction goals such as gaining compliance, seeking information, or altering relationships, they generate messages within a variety of constraints. Regardless of one's interaction goal, there exist higher level concerns regarding how one will achieve that interaction goal. Given that global constraints contribute to consistent conversational performances across varying contexts (Street & Cappella, 1985), understanding the importance of these higher level goals (i.e., conversational constraint) is essential to explain and/or predict the choice of conversational strategies across cultures.

To gain a more complete understanding of how actors deal with the multiple constraints of communication, future theoretical endeavors will need to incorporate situational factors as well. Factors such as situational contingencies (intimacy, ingroup versus outgroup, long-term relational consequences, and so on) appear to mediate the actual choice of strategies. The benefits of optimizing clarity or relational constraints, versus the costs of doing so, depend on the importance of the primary goal to the actor. Even if similar goals (e.g., requesting) are being pursued, differences in situational contingencies (e.g., relational consequences, perceptions of urgency) can lead to very different strategy choices. Irrespective of culture, emergency situations are likely to lessen concerns for relational constraints and heighten the concern for clarity (e.g., "Your clothes are on fire!").

Future theoretical developments should focus on investigating the combined effect of context and individual-level cultural dimensions. According to Ting-Toomey (1989b), context includes components such as situational and relational context (*relational context* refers to the influence of family or friendship networks). One's self-system depends heavily on the context in which the encounter takes place. How one constructs and presents a self in a relationship is, to a large degree, situation dependent (see Ting-Toomey, 1989b; Triandis, 1989). While beyond the scope of this chapter, how situational variables, cultural contexts, and the importance of constraints are interrelated is an important question. Cross-cultural studies of situations (Detweiler, Brislin, & McCormack, 1983; Forgas & Bond, 1985) have shown significant differences in the way situations are perceived across cultures. However, researchers have yet to agree on well-defined and measurable variables or dimensions that are necessary to integrate situations into the theoretical framework. Another limitation of our theoretical framework is that it focuses on preferences rather than on actual strategy choices. Clearly, people sometimes may be unable to make strategy choices based solely on their preferences. On the other hand, knowledge helps performance; the current theory focuses on how perceptions of conversational constraints may differ across different self-systems associated with various dimensions of culture.

The relationship of conversational constraints and other culture-relevant personality constructs deserves further investigation. A number of constructs drawn from social psychological literature, such as those dealing with self-monitoring (e.g., Snyder, 1974), public versus private self-consciousness (Fenigstein, 1984), and cognitive complexity (e.g., Wiseman & Abe, 1986), can also be related to the perceived importance of conversational constraints. For instance, one might expect a positive correlation between relational constraints and the other-directedness factor of the Self-Monitoring Scale (Hoyle & Lennox, 1991).

The concept of conversational constraints can help explain cultural differences in judgments of communicative competence. The idea that conversational constraints may function differently across cultures offers a useful framework for explaining intercultural misunderstanding. Prevailing culture determines whose speech style will be seen as normal; who will be required to learn the communication style, and interpret the meaning, of the other; whose language style will be seen as deviant, irrational, and inferior. Also, due to differing implicit theories about conversational styles, the two groups may disagree about appropriate choices of conversational strategies. Thomas (1983) introduced the notion of "cross-cultural pragmatic failure" and argued that, in different cultures, different pragmatic rules may be invoked. Pragmatic failure stems from cross-culturally different perceptions of what constitutes appropriate linguistic behavior.

An individual's beliefs about the importance of conversational constraints are apt to affect what conversational tactics and strategies she or he chooses as well as what inferences she or he makes about her or his own and others' behavior. Strategic competence involves the ability to select an *effective* means of performing a communicative act, enabling the listener to identify the intended meaning. It may be that different cultural groups have drastically different ideas about what constitutes an *effective* strategy or tactic. This could lead to misjudgments regarding the conversational partner's communicative competence. Failure to produce effective strategies might be seen as reflecting a general knowledge deficit or as communicative incompetence (see M. Kim, 1993). It would be interesting to study cross-cultural perceptions of the communicative competence of a speaker in relation to his or her linguistic choices and self-concepts.

It is important to point out that the general processes included in this theory should generalize across cultures and across different primary goals. The implications of the notion of different self-systems (e.g., independent versus interdependent construals) are enormous. Individual-level research has the potential to generate new concepts and frameworks that are not likely to be discovered with culture-level data. The manifestations of different self-structure can be examined in the areas of acculturation, intercultural conflict negotiation, and organizational behavior. The current theoretical approach is part of an ongoing program of research attempting to link general cultural orientations with individuals' perceptions and choices of conversational strategies.

NOTES

1. The previous data (M. Kim, 1994) indicated that cultural variability does indeed influence the perceived importance of three of the five conversational constraints. There were no cross-cultural differences in the importance ratings for two of the five constraints: avoidance of negative evaluation and concern for effectiveness. Thus, in this theoretical framework, we will use only the former three constraints (minimization of imposition, concern for the other's feelings, and concern for clarity).

2. How the importance of constraints will translate into actual strategy choices depends on many factors. First, at times, maximal activation of independent and interdependent self construals, and corresponding choices of maximally clear and maximally relational strategies, are not pragmatically possible. In other words, occasions exist in which being truly independent or interdependent are just not possible. Second, at times, maximal interdependence and maximal independence, even if theoretically possible, are not preferred.

7

Cross-Cultural Adaptation
An Integrative Theory

YOUNG YUN KIM • *University of Oklahoma*

Millions of people change homes each year, crossing cultural boundaries. Immigrants and refugees resettle in search of a new life, side-by-side with temporary sojourners finding employment overseas as artists, musicians, writers, accountants, teachers, and construction workers. Diplomats and other governmental agency employees, business managers, Peace Corps volunteers, researchers, professors, students, military personnel, and missionaries likewise carry out their work overseas for varying lengths of time. Individuals such as these are, indeed, contemporary pioneers venturing into an unfamiliar cultural terrain where the "business-as-usual" ways of doing things quickly lose their relevance. Even relatively short-term sojourners must be at least minimally concerned with building a healthy functional relationship to the host environment in a way similar to the native population. They confront their cross-cultural predicaments and engage in new learning for an improved "goodness-of-fit" to handle their daily transactions with a greater ease and heightened sense of efficacy. Accompanying this process is an increased self-awareness, which, in time, facilitates the development of an identity that reaches beyond the original cultural perimeters.

This description points to the phenomenon of the cross-cultural adaptation being theorized. Broadly, the present theory offers (a) a description of the *process* of cross-cultural adaptation as it unfolds over time and (b) an explanation of the *structure* of this process and the key constituent factors that influence the degree (or rate) in which individuals adapt to a new and unfamiliar culture.

BACKGROUND

The author's work in the field of cross-cultural adaptation began almost two decades ago. As a graduate student from Korea working on doctoral research in communication, I was drawn to this field partly by a personal interest in understanding the various changes that I and others had experienced. What happens when individuals born and reared in one culture (or subculture) settle into another unfamiliar culture? What role does communication play in this process? And why are some individuals more successful than others in meeting cross-cultural challenges?

The doctoral research began to address these issues through a survey among Korean immigrants in the Chicago area (Y. Kim, 1976, 1977a, 1977b, 1978a, 1978b). I have since conducted studies among other immigrant and refugee groups in the United States, including Japanese (Kim, 1978b), Mexicans (Kim, 1978b), and Southeast Asian refugees from Vietnam, Cambodia, and Laos (Y. Kim, 1980, 1989, 1990). More recently, my research subjects have been extended to the adaptation experiences of American Indians to a predominantly Anglo cultural milieu (Kim, Lujan, Shaver, & Boyle, 1991) and to Japanese managers temporarily assigned to the United States by their company headquarters in Japan (Kim & Paulk, 1994a, 1994b).

While the basic research issues stated above have remained the same throughout these studies, my methodological perspective has undergone a change from the initial linear-causal approach exemplified in the "path model" developed through the doctoral research to a more interactive and integrative "systems" perspective incorporated into my subsequent work. This methodological shift in the later work was partly due to my recognition of the apparent divergence among various social science approaches to cross-cultural adaptation, and a need to find a way to integrate the existing approaches into a more cohesive, comprehensive, and thus more realistic theoretical account of the phenomenon.

The systems perspective, indeed, has provided a metatheoretical framework based on which this investigator attempts to integrate a number of previously separate and divergent approaches. Among the various approaches that are consolidated in the present theory are (a) the long-term adaptation of immigrants (e.g., Berry, 1990; Y. Kim, 1990) and short-term adaptation of temporary sojourners (e.g., Church, 1982; Furnham & Bochner, 1986; Torbiörn, 1982), (b) the macro-level analyses of cultural/institutional changes or interethnic relations in anthropology and sociology (e.g., Glazer & Moynihan, 1975; Mead, 1964; Shibutani & Kwan, 1965; Spicer, 1968; Zenner, 1987) and the micro-level psychological analyses of the adaptive change in individuals (e.g., Berry, 1990; Taft, 1988), and (c) the "melting-pot" ideology reflected in many of the traditional studies of immigrants in the United States and the pluralist ideology of multiculturalism driving some of the more recent studies. (For a discussion of ideological influences on studies of ethnic groups and individuals, see Gordon, 1981; Pettigrew, 1988; Roosens, 1989; Root, 1993.)

The short-term and long-term categories, for example, have been replaced with a single continuum of the length of residence in the host environment. Some of the macro-level (cultural, institutional, and structural) factors have been incorporated into the present theory as key conditions of the host environment. Also, the value assumptions in assimilationist and pluralist ideologies have been merged into a single factor by treating them as differing levels of adaptive motivation.

An initial attempt at developing a comprehensive, integrative theory was presented in *Communication Yearbook 3* (Kim, 1979), followed by the editing of two multidisciplinary anthologies, *Interethnic Communication: Current Research* (Kim, 1986b) and *Cross-Cultural Adaptation: Current Theory and Research* (Kim & Gudykunst, 1988). Presenting diverse conceptualizations and research reports from anthropological, communication, and social psychological perspectives, these anthologies helped lay a groundwork for the author's subsequent full articulation of an interdisciplinary theory in *Communication and Cross-Cultural Adaptation: An Integrative Theory* (Kim, 1988a). This theoretical presentation has since been further refined and elaborated in a revised edition (Y. Kim, in press-a) and is briefly highlighted below.

ORGANIZING PRINCIPLES: AN OPEN-SYSTEMS APPROACH

The present theory is predicated on a set of "open-systems" assumptions about the nature of humans as adaptive living entities (see Bertalanffy, 1956; Ford & Lerner, 1992; Ruben & J. Kim, 1975; Ruesch & Bateson, 1951/1968).

Assumption 1: Humans have an inherent drive to adapt and grow. Adaptation is a fundamental life goal for humans, something that people do naturally and continually as they face the challenges from their environment (Slavin & Kriegman, 1992). The introduction of every new experience, particularly one that is drastic and disorienting, leads to transformation throughout one's life. From the first frustrations of early childhood to the later changes in life circumstances, people go through a series of graduated sink-or-swim situations. For the most part, such challenges are successfully handled by people without a complete breakdown in their internal system. Their natural adaptive drive is reflected in an instinct of curiosity and the power of initiative in pursuit of a "feeling of efficacy," a sense of being an agent in the living of their lives.

Adaptation in turn brings about a succession of relatively enduring internal changes. Such changes occur in the direction of increase in the complexity of a person's structural and functional characteristics while maintaining his or her inner coherence and unity (Ford & Lerner, 1992). In this view, a person is never a "finished product" but, instead, is in the business of growing or maturing. Personality changes are possible, as individuals continually refine and revise themselves.

Assumption 2: Adaptation to one's social environment occurs through communication. Adaptive changes in individuals continue as long as they are engaged in a given sociocultural environment with which they send (encoding) and receive (decoding) messages. In this process, communicators continually engage in generating "information output" to the environment as well as generating meaning for the "information input" or "feedback" internally (Geyer, 1980). Here, input and output messages are not limited to linguistic or other explicitly coded symbols such as traffic signs, mathematical symbols, and computer languages but also include more spontaneous and expressive nonverbal messages that are often unintentional and implied. This means that all actions and events (as well as nonactions and nonevents) have continuous and pervasive communicative interface, as pointed out in the axiom of Watzlawick, Beavin, and Jackson (1967): "One cannot not communicate." This also means that individual adaptation activities occur as long as one lives in a given social environment (Dance & Larson, 1976).

Assumption 3: Adaptation is a complex and dynamic process. Because the person and the environment coparticipate in the person's adaptation through a continual give-and-take, adaptation must be conceived as a phenomenon that consists of multiple dimensions and facets. In this person-environment interface lies both the internal (intrapersonal) and the external (social/environmental) conditions and, as such, both must be taken into account when describing and explaining the course of that person's adaptation. The person's adaptive process, furthermore, is multifaceted, in that various parts of his or her internal system and the environment are engaged simultaneously and interactively, mutually influencing one another. Change in one part is likely to have functional consequences in many other parts.

Based on these open-systems assumptions, the present theory is designed to achieve a maximal theory-reality correspondence by emphasizing (a) the dynamic, evolutionary nature of the process of adaptive change and growth over time; (b) the multidimensional, multifaceted, and interactive nature of the forces, both internal and external to the individual, that operate in the adaptation process; and (c) the functional interdependence and bilateral causal influences between the components of an open system and its environment. As such, the present approach moves beyond the common practice of applying independent and dependent variables to explaining cross-cultural adaptation based on the underlying assumption of linear causality (e.g., Gao & Gudykunst, 1990; Gudykunst, 1988; Kim, 1977a).

Definitions and Boundary Conditions

The definitional incoherence among existing approaches to cross-cultural adaptation is viewed as at least partly stemming from the employment of concepts that often overlap in meaning. In developing the present theory, attempts have been made to achieve maximum generality by employing concepts of higher order abstraction and thus of greater parsimony.

Among the various general concepts employed in the present theory are two central terms: *adaptation* and *stranger*. These two terms are chosen for their broad generality and as a "master concept" or "superordinate category" (White, 1976, p. 18) that help define the domain of the present theory. *Cross-cultural adaptation* embraces other similar but narrower terms, from *assimilation* (the acceptance of "mainstream" cultural elements of the host society by the individual) and *acculturation* (the process commonly defined as the acquisition of some, but not all, aspects of the host cultural elements), to coping and adjustment (both of which are often used to refer to the psychological responses to cross-cultural challenges), as well as to integration (mainly defined as social participation in the host society).

Along with the term *cross-cultural adaptation*, the term *stranger* incorporates in it a wide range of cross-cultural resettlers and sojourners. Initially employed by the German sociologist Simmel (1908/1950), this concept has served as one of the most heuristic and parsimonious concepts for analyzing the social processes of individuals who confront a new and unfamiliar milieu. As such, the notion of *strangers* clearly offers a most inclusive term that integrates other, more specific terms such as *immigrants, refugees,* and *sojourners* who resettle for various lengths of time, as well as members of ethnic groups who cross subcultural boundaries within a society. (See Gudykunst & Kim, 1992, and Levine, 1979, for an elaboration of this concept.)

All of these individuals are included in the present definition of *strangers,* as they commonly share the experience of beginning their adaptation processes as cultural "outsiders" and of moving in the direction of cultural "insiders" over time. As such, the present theoretical domain is broadly defined, limited only by three *boundary conditions*: (a) The strangers must have had a primary socialization in one culture (or subculture) and have moved into a different and unfamiliar culture (or subculture); (b) the strangers are at least minimally dependent on the host environment for meeting their personal and social needs; and (c) the strangers are engaged in continuous, firsthand communication experiences with that environment. As such, the present domain is broad, general, and comprehensive without being delimited by either the specific reasons for, or the lengths of, contact with the new environment (e.g., long-term or short-term exchange students, business employees, immigrants, or refugees).

Included in this domain are the adaptive experiences of those who face significant changes in domestic sociocultural environment, either through voluntary relocations (e.g., American Indians leaving an Indian reservation to find employment in a predominantly Anglo urban environment) or through the demographic changes in the surrounding environment through incoming and outgoing population movements (e.g., a significant increase in Asians and Hispanics in Los Angeles). Also included in the present domain are the situations of reentry (Austin, 1983; Brabant, Palmer, & Gramling, 1990) into one's original culture. Generally, of course, the process of readapting to one's original culture is less demanding with regard to new cultural/language learning than the process of adapting to a foreign culture. Yet, to the extent that the returnee has been changed by the sojourn experience, and to the extent that the original cultural (subcultural) milieu has changed during the sojourn, he or she must, once again, go through the cross-adaptation process upon returning "home."

The situation of young children accompanying their parents to a new culture (or subculture), on the other hand, cannot be properly included in the present domain due to the fact that the formation of their cultural identity (or identities) is still in progress and that both the receiving culture and the subculture of the parents at home influence this process. A more appropriate theorizing effort can be found in the psychological and sociolinguistic literature on bilingual/bicultural development and education (e.g., Arnberg, 1987; Fantini, 1985; Phinney & Rosenthal, 1992; Wolfgang, 1975).

THE PROCESS OF CROSS-CULTURAL ADAPTATION

How, then, do strangers adapt to new cultural challenges? The first part of the present theory addresses this issue by providing a description and explanation of the process of cross-cultural adaptation from an open-systems perspective.

Deculturation and Acculturation

Throughout the socialization process, children become adapted to the fellow members of their cultural group, which, in turn, gives them their status and assigns to them their role in the life of the community. Culture, indeed, is imprinted in its members as a pattern of knowledge, attitudes, values, mind-sets, perceptions, and behaviors that permeate all life activities. The mere fact that children grow up to be cultural beings bears witness to the fundamental fact of human pliability and the pervasive role of culture in shaping individual behavior.

Upon entering a new and unfamiliar culture, strangers set in motion the process of enculturation all over again. But this time, they are faced with situations that deviate from the familiar and internalized original cultural script. Strangers become more aware of the previously taken-for-granted habits of mind because, as Boulding (1956/1977) noted, the human nervous system is structured in such a way that "the patterns that govern behavior and perception come into consciousness only when there is a deviation from the familiar" (p. 13). Now, strangers discover that they lack a level of understanding of the communication system of the new host society, and must learn and acquire many of its symbols and patterns of activities.

The process of *learning* and acquiring the elements of the host culture is commonly called *acculturation* (Shibutani & Kwan, 1965). This secondary socialization, or reenculturation, does not occur so smoothly as their childhood enculturation because of the distinct cultural identity and communication competence already internalized in strangers. As new learning occurs, *unlearning*, or *deculturation*, of at least some of the old cultural habits occurs—at least in the sense that new responses are adopted in situations that previously would have evoked old ones. The cost of acquiring something new is inevitably the "losing" of something old in much the same way as "being someone requires the forfeiture of being someone else" (Thayer, 1975, p. 240).

The Stress-Adaptation-Growth Dynamic

Because cross-cultural adaptation necessitates both acculturation (learning) and deculturation (unlearning), and because a stranger's cultural identity and attributes are placed against the backdrop of the systemic forces of the host culture, the cross-cultural experiences of newcomers are unsettling indeed. The experiences of acculturation and deculturation inevitably produce forms of temporary personality disintegration, or even breakdown in some extreme cases. As parts of their internal organization undergo small changes, the strangers are, at least temporarily, in a state of disequilibrium, which is manifested in many emotional "lows" of uncertainty, confusion, and anxiety.

In the present open-systems perspective, such disruptive experiences of a person reflect *stress*, or the generic response that occurs whenever the capabilities of individuals are not adequate to the demands of the environment. Indeed, the challenges of handling daily activities are most severe during the initial phases, as has been shown in many culture shock studies. Humans are characteristically homeostatic, attempting to hold constant many variables in their internal structure to achieve an integrated whole. Under stress, a so-called defense mechanism is activated in strangers to hold the internal structure in balance by some form of protective psychological maneuvering. They attempt to avoid or minimize the anticipated or actual "pain" of disequilibrium by selective attention, self-deception, denial, avoidance, and withdrawal as well as by hostility, cynicism, and compulsively altruistic behavior (Lazarus, 1966, p. 262).

Defensive (or protective) stress reactions such as these, however, are generally temporary and counterproductive to the strangers' effective functioning in the host environment. They must, and generally do, accompany *adaptation* responses as well. This is possible because strangers strive to "meet" and manage the challenge by acting on and responding to the host environment. Or in Piaget's (1963) terms, the adaptive activities consist of the two subroutines of assimilation (acting on the environment so that aspects of it may be incorporated into their internal structure) and accommodation (responding to the environment by adjusting their internal conditions to the corresponding external realities). Through assimilative-accommodative activities, the strangers sooner or later learn to deal with the impending cross-cultural challenges and, in time, work to improve their functional relationship with the host environment.

What follows the stress and adaptation responses is a subtle internal transformation of *growth*. The periods of stress will pass in time as the strangers work out new ways of handling problems through sources of strength in themselves and in their social environment. A crisis, once managed by the strangers, presents an opportunity for a strengthening of their coping abilities. The stress-adaptation experiences bring about

Adaptation

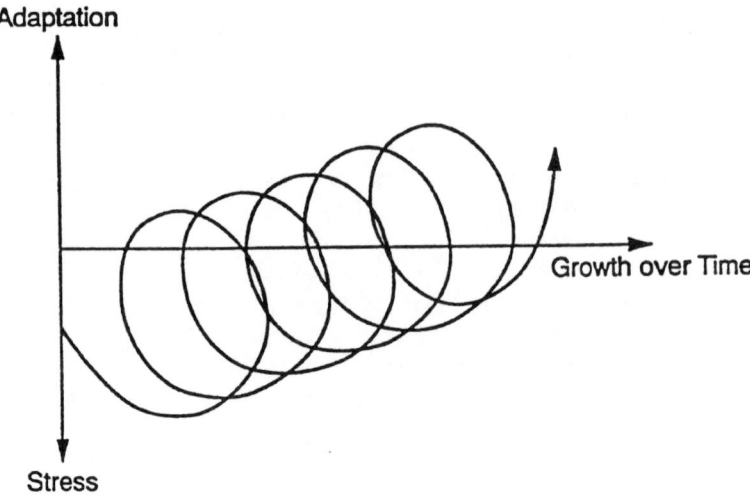

Figure 7.1: Stress-Adaptation-Growth Dynamics

change and growth—the creative responses to new circumstances. Over time, the stress-adaptation-growth dynamic plays out not in a smooth, linear progression but in a cyclic and continual "draw-back-to-leap" pattern similar to the movement of a wheel depicted in Figure 7.1. Each stressful experience is responded to by strangers with a "draw back," which then activates their adaptive energy to help them reorganize themselves and "leap forward." It presents a dialectic relationship between push and pull, or engagement and disengagement, in the psychological movements of strangers.

The process of cross-cultural adaptation, then, is essentially one of the continual resolution of internal stress, and one that facilitates a qualitative psychic transformation. Even those who interact with the natives with the intention of confining themselves to only superficial relationships are likely to become, given sufficient time, at least minimally adapted to the host culture "in spite of themselves" (Taft, 1977, p. 150). Large and sudden adaptive changes are more likely during the initial phase of exposure to a new culture. Such drastic changes are themselves indicative of the severity of adaptive difficulties and disruptions.

Intercultural Transformation

As strangers experience a progression of internal change, they are likely to undergo a set of identifiable transformations in their habitual patterns of cognitive, affective, and behavioral responses. Through the processes of deculturation and acculturation, some of the "old" cultural habits are replaced by new cultural habits. They acquire increasing proficiency in self-expression and in fulfilling their various social needs.

Three interrelated aspects of the strangers' intercultural transformation are specified in the present theory as the key outcomes of the cross-cultural adaptation process. The first aspect is an increased *functional fitness*. Through the repeated activities resulting in new cultural learning and internal reorganizing, strangers in time achieve an increasing "synchrony" (Hall, 1976; Y. Kim, 1993) between their internal responses and the external demands in the host environment. Successfully adapted strangers have accomplished a desired level of proficiency in communicating and developing a satisfactory relationship with the host society—particularly with those individuals and situations that are of direct relevance to their daily activities.

The development of the strangers' functional fitness in the host society has been documented extensively. The studies of both sojourners and immigrants have shown an increase over time in various subjective indicators of functional fitness such as life satisfaction, positive feelings toward one's life in the host society, sense of belonging, and greater congruence in subjective meaning systems (Szalay & Inn, 1987), as well as such objective socioeconomic indicators as occupational and income status (Kim, 1976, 1980, 1989, 1990).

Closely associated with the increased functional fitness is increased *psychological health* in relation to their host environment. The psychological health of strangers is directly linked to their ability to communicate and the accompanying functional fitness in the host society. Most strangers have been observed to achieve a higher level of psychological health and a subsiding level of disturbance in dealing with the host environment. Extensive data in support of this increasing trend in the strangers' psychological well-being are documented in culture shock studies and similarly in the studies of mental health/illnesses among immigrants and refugees (e.g., David, 1969; Dyal & Dyal, 1981; Hurh & K. Kim, 1988; Kino, 1973).

The development of functional fitness and psychological health in strangers is likely to accompany an emergent *intercultural identity*. Adversarial cross-cultural experiences bring about the experiences of what Zaharna (1989) calls "self-shock," a "shake-up" of the strangers' sense of connection to their original cultural group and an accompanying growth beyond the perimeters of the original culture. The psychological movement of strangers into new dimensions produces "boundary-ambiguity syndromes" (Hall, 1976, p. 227), in which the original cultural identity begins to lose its distinctiveness and rigidity while an expanded and more flexible definition of self emerges (Kim, in press-b; Kim & Ruben, 1988). In Adler's (1976) words, this emergent intercultural identity is based "not on 'belongingness' which implies either owning or being owned by a single culture, but on a style of self-consciousness that situates oneself neither totally *a part of* nor totally *apart from* a given culture" (p. 391).

THE STRUCTURE OF CROSS-CULTURAL ADAPTATION

Building on the above description and explanation of the cross-cultural adaptation process, the theory now moves to identifying the structure and its constituent factors that help explain the differential rates (or speeds) at which this process plays out across different individuals. Once again, the basic open-systems assumptions noted earlier help find the explanatory factors in the stranger-environment interface through communication. Within this framework, strangers' communication activities are conceptualized in two basic, interdependent dimensions: *personal communication*, or "private symbolization" and all the internal mental activities that occur in individuals that dispose and prepare them to act and react in certain ways in actual social situations, and *social communication*, or the "public symbolization" that underlies "intersubjectivization" and occurs whenever two or more individuals interact with one another, knowingly or not.

Personal Communication

The successful adaptation of strangers is realized only when their personal communication systems sufficiently overlap with those of the natives. The capacity of strangers to appropriately and effectively receive and process information (decoding) and to design and execute mental plans in initiating or responding to messages (encoding) is labeled here as *host communication competence*.

By definition, the strangers' host communication competence facilitates their cross-cultural adaptation process in a most direct and significant way. It serves as an instrumental, interpretive, and expressive means of coming to terms with the host environment. It enables strangers to develop their understanding of the way things are carried out in the host society and the way they themselves need to think, feel, and act in that environment. Until strangers have acquired a sufficient level of host communication competence, they are handicapped in their ability to meet their physical, psychological, and social needs and goals.

The key elements that generally constitute the concept of communication competence, including the present host communication competence, can be grouped into three commonly recognized categories: (a) cognitive, (b) affective, and (c) operational (Dinges, 1983; Hammer, 1989; Imahori & Lanigan, 1989; Kim, 1991; Spitzberg, 1989; Wiseman & Koester, 1993). *Cognitive competence* includes such internal capacities as the knowledge of the host culture and language including the history, institutions, worldviews, beliefs, mores, norms, and rules of interpersonal conduct, among others. Language/culture learning is accompanied by a development of cognitive complexity, that is, the structural refinement in an individual's internal information processing ability. Along with cognitive competence, *affective competence* facilitates cross-cultural adaptation by providing an emotional and motivational capacity to deal with the various challenges of living in the host environment. Included in this competence is the strangers' willingness for new learning and making changes in their own native cultural habits. Also included in affective competence is their ability to understand and empathize with, and participate in, the natives' aesthetic and emotional sensibilities reflected in their experiences of beauty, fun, joy, despair, anger, and the like.

Interactively linked with the cognitive and affective components of host communication competence is *operational competence* (Taft, 1977), otherwise referred to as behavioral competence or the "enactment tendencies" (Buck, 1984, p. vii). This competence facilitates the strangers to enact, or express, their cognitive and affective experiences outwardly. As they try to come up with a mental plan for action, therefore, they must base the decision on their current knowledge and cognitive capacity to process information about the host culture as well as their motivational and attitudinal capacity to meaningfully appreciate and join in the natives' emotional and aesthetic experiences. The strangers' operational competence thus enables them to choose a "right" combination of verbal and nonverbal behaviors so as to achieve a smooth and harmonious interface with the host milieu.

Social Communication

The strangers' host communication competence is directly and reciprocally associated with their participation in the interpersonal and mass communication activities of the host society. A stranger's host social communication experiences are constrained by his or her host's communication competence. At the same time, every host social communication event offers the stranger an opportunity for cultural learning.

Host interpersonal communication, in particular, helps strangers to secure vital information and insight into the mind-sets and behaviors of the local people, thereby providing them with points of reference for a check and validation of their own behaviors. Most strangers in a new culture must begin to form a new set of relationships as they find themselves without an adequate support system when they are confronted with highly uncertain and stressful situations. The crucial importance of host interpersonal communication activities in facilitating cross-cultural adaptation has been acknowledged and demonstrated widely and repeatedly across the social sciences (Kim, 1986a). In some cases, the degree of host interpersonal communication has been accepted as an indicator of cross-cultural adaptation itself (e.g., Gordon, 1973; Nagata, 1969; Spicer, 1968).

Similarly, *host mass communication* has been observed to facilitate the adaptation of strangers (Subervi-Velez, 1986). While the interpersonal channel of communication offers opportunities for more personalized and thus "meaningful" involvement with members of the host culture, mass communication channels help them participate in vicarious learning through "para-social interactions" with the host environment at large beyond the ordinary reaches of their daily lives (Horton & Wohl, 1979, p. 32). Compared with interpersonal communication activities, mediated communication activities may be governed by a lesser sense of mutual obligation and effort. Thus, while host mass communication renders less opportunity for feedback than do interpersonal communication situations where a quick exchange of information is maximal (Rogers, 1979; Schramm, 1979), it serves as an important source of cultural and language learning, particularly during early phases of the adaptation process when strangers have less direct access and less likelihood to succeed in communicating with the natives face-to-face.

In many countries today, most strangers' interpersonal and mass communication activities involve their coethnics or conationals and home cultural experiences as well. Whether we speak of British compounds in India, American military posts in West Germany, Puerto Rican barrios in New York City, Chinatown in Tokyo, or a Japanese student association in a Canadian university, ethnic communities provide strangers with access to their original cultural experiences. Many aliens have organized some form of mutual aid or self-help organizations that render assistance to those who need material, informational, emotional, and other forms of social support (DeCocq, 1976). In the case of many larger ethnic communities, mass media (including newspapers, radio stations, and television programs) perform various informational, educational, entertainment, and social services for their members.

These *ethnic interpersonal* and *mass communication systems* serve adaptation-facilitating functions for new immigrants and sojourners during the initial phase of their adaptation process (Kim, 1987). Because many strangers initially lack host communication competence and do not have access to resources to become self-reliant, they tend to seek and depend heavily on ethnic sources of informational, material, and emotional help and thereby compensate for the lack of support they are capable of obtaining from host nationals. Due to the relatively "easy" or stress-free communication experiences in dealing with their own ethnic individuals and media, intraethnic communication experiences offer temporary refuge. In the case of certain temporary residents, such as American military personnel stationed overseas, their daily duties confine their social communication activities almost exclusively to other Americans at the military base.

Beyond the initial phase, however, ethnic social communication has been found to be important for group identity maintenance (Boekestijn, 1988) and negatively associated with adaptation into the host culture (J. Kim, 1980; Kim, 1976, 1977b, 1980, 1986a, 1989, 1990; Shah, 1991; Walker, 1993; Yang, 1988). Whether by choice or by circumstance, the strangers' heavy and prolonged reliance on coethnics sustains their original cultural identity and limits their opportunities to participate in the social communication activities of the host society (Burgess, 1978). Implied in this observation is that strangers cannot remain strongly ethnic in their communication activities and, at the same time, become highly adapted to the host cultural environment. They are likely to remain poor in their functional fitness in the host environment, which, in turn, hinders their intercultural transformation.

Environment

To the extent that strangers participate in the social (interpersonal, mass) communication activities of the host society, the host society exerts influence on their adaptation process. The nature of such influence, in turn, is shaped by the various characteristics of the host society and, for many, their social environment includes fellow coethnics as well.

Given the mixed nature of the environment in which many strangers find themselves, three environmental conditions are identified in the present theory as affecting the individual stranger's adaptation process: (a) host receptivity, (b) host conformity pressure, and (c) ethnic group strength. *Host receptivity* incorporates the meaning of other similar terms such as *interaction potential* (Blau & Schwartz, 1984; Hallinan

& Smith, 1985; Kim, 1979) or *acquaintance potential* (Cook, 1962) and refers to the degree to which a given environment is structurally and psychologically accessible and open to strangers. Different locations in a given society may offer different levels of receptivity toward different groups of strangers. For example, Canadian visitors arriving in a small town in the United States are likely to find a largely receptive host environment. On the other hand, the same small town may show less receptivity toward visitors from a lesser known and vastly different culture such as Turkey or Kenya.

Along with receptivity, *host conformity pressure* (Zajonc, 1952) varies as well across societies and communities. Here, *conformity pressure* refers to the extent to which the environment challenges strangers to adopt the normative patterns of the host culture and its communication system. In particular, the conformity pressure of a host environment is often reflected in the expectations the natives routinely have about how strangers should think and act, thereby exerting pressure on the strangers to adapt to the host cultural milieu. Different host environments show different levels of tolerance to strangers and their ethnic/cultural characteristics. For example, heterogeneous and open host environments such as the United States generally tend to hold a more pluralistic political ideology concerning cultural/ethnic differences and thereby exert less pressure on strangers to change their habitual ways. Within the United States, ethnically heterogeneous metropolitan areas such as Los Angeles and Miami tend to demand less that strangers conform to the dominant Anglo-white cultural practices than do small, ethnically homogeneous rural towns. Further, even within a city, certain neighborhoods may be more homogeneous and thus expect more conformity from strangers.

The degree to which a given host environment exerts receptivity and conformity pressure on a stranger is closely influenced by *the strength of the stranger's ethnic group* relative to the host environment at large. An insight into ethnic group strength has been provided by a number of investigators such as sociologists Clarke and Obler (1976), who describe ethnic communities developing from the stages of initial economic adjustment and community building to the subsequent stage of aggressive self-assertion and promotion of identity. An additional insight has been offered in Breton's (1964) model of institutional completeness and the social psychological concept of ethnolinguistic vitality (Giles, Bourhis, & Taylor, 1977a). These and related theoretical descriptions point to an observation that a strong ethnic group offers its members a strong informational, emotional, and material support system within the larger host environment, facilitating the cross-cultural adaptation of strangers during the initial phase. In the long run, however, a strong ethnic community is likely to exert stronger social pressure to conform to its own cultural practices and to maintain the strangers' ethnic group identity. This, in turn, discourages their participation in the host social communication activities that are necessary for their adaptation to the larger society. A comparison of social communication activities of Korean immigrants in two locations with differing levels of ethnic group strengths has provided empirical support for this theoretical reasoning (Inglis & Gudykunst, 1982).

Predisposition

Along with the above-described host and ethnic environmental conditions, the process of cross-cultural adaptation is affected by the internal conditions of the strangers themselves prior to resettlement in the host society. To the extent that strangers differ in their backgrounds, such differences help set the perimeters for their own subsequent adaptive changes.

First, strangers come to their new environment with differing levels of *preparedness*, that is, the mental, emotional, and motivational readiness to deal with the new cultural environment including understanding of the host language and culture. Affecting their preparedness are a wide range of formal and informal learning activities they may have had prior to moving to the host society. Included in such activities are the schooling and training in, and media exposure to, the host language and culture, and the direct and indirect experiences in dealing with members of the host society as well as the prior intercultural adaptation experiences in general. In addition, the strangers' preparedness is often influenced by the level of positive expectations toward the host society and of willingness to participate in it voluntarily. Voluntary, long-term immigrants, for example, are more likely to enter the host environment with a greater readiness for making adaptive changes in themselves compared with temporary sojourners who unwillingly relocate for reasons imposed on them.

Strangers also differ in cultural, racial, and linguistic backgrounds. The term *ethnicity* is used here as an inclusive term to refer to various characteristics of strangers pertaining to their distinctiveness as a people. As such, the Japanese sojourners and immigrants bring to a given host society common physical, linguistic, and cultural features that are different than, say, Mexicans or the French. Such ethnic characteristics play a crucial role in the cross-cultural adaptation process, as it affects the ease or difficulty with which the stranger is able to develop communication competence in a given host society and participate in its social communication activities. For instance, many of the Japanese business executives in the United States are likely to face a lesser amount of host receptivity in overcoming their physical, linguistic, and cultural barriers than are their British counterparts. This suggests that strangers of different ethnic backgrounds embark on their cross-cultural journey with different levels of advantage or "handicap" (Phinney & Rosenthal, 1992, p. 145). Empirical evidence shows, indeed, that the extreme stress reactions in the form of escapism, neurosis, and psychosis are most frequently witnessed among those whose native culture radically differs from that of the host community (David, 1969; Kino, 1973; Krau, 1991; Williams & Westmeyer, 1986).

Along with ethnic backgrounds, strangers enter a host environment with a set of more or less enduring *personality* traits. They begin the challenge of the new environment within the context of their existing personality, which serves as the basis upon which they pursue and internalize new experiences with varying degrees of success. Of particular interest to the present theory are those personality resources that would help facilitate the strangers' adaptation by enabling them to endure stressful challenges and to maximize new learning, both of which are essential to their intercultural transformation.

Openness is such a personality construct. In the systems theoretical perspective, openness is defined as an internal posture that is receptive to new information (Gendlin, 1962). Openness minimizes resistance and maximizes a willingness to attend to new and changed circumstances. Openness further enables strangers to perceive and interpret various events and situations in the new environment as they occur with less rigid, ethnocentric judgments. As a theoretical concept, openness is employed in the present theory as varying in degrees among strangers. It is a broad term that incorporates other similar but more specific concepts such as open-mindedness, intercultural sensitivity, empathy, and tolerance for ambiguity (Ruben & Kealey, 1979; Tamam, 1993). Also, the present meaning of openness includes the optimism and affirmative orientation in the strangers' basic outlook on life as well as their fundamental "self-trust" in the face of adverse circumstances. It is a dimension of personality that enables strangers to continually seek to acquire new cultural knowledge and to cultivate greater intellectual, emotional/aesthetic, and behavioral compatibility with the natives.

Strength is an additional personality trait that is vital to cross-cultural adaptation. Like openness, personality strength is a broad concept that represents a range of interrelated personality attributes such as resilience, risk-taking, hardiness, persistence, patience, elasticity, and resourcefulness.

Personality strength thus means the inner quality that absorbs "shocks" from the environment and bounces back without being seriously damaged by them. Low levels of personality strength are seen in tendencies to be shy, fearful, and easily distressed by uncertain or stressful situations. On the other hand, individuals with high levels of personality strength tend to be stimulated by new challenges and remain effervescent and confident (Lifton, 1993).

The above two broad concepts, openness and strength, help define the strangers' overall personality predisposition to "push" themselves in their adaptation process. Strangers with greater openness and strength are less likely to succumb and more likely to take on the challenging situations in the host society. Their personality predisposition serves as an inner resource for working toward developing the host communication competence, so as to facilitate their own intercultural transformation and growth. A serious lack of openness and strength, on the other hand, would weaken their adaptive capacity and would serve as self-imposed psychological barriers against their own adaptation.

A Structural Model

Collectively, the six dimensions of factors identified above and summarized in Table 7.1 help explain the fact that not everyone is equally successful in making cross-cultural transitions. We began with the dimension of personal communication, which is most central to strangers' adaptation. The cognitive, affective, and operational facets of the strangers' host communication competence (Dimension 1) serve as the very "engine" that pushes them along the adaptation process. Inseparably linked with host communication competence are the activities of host social communication (Dimension 2), through which strangers participate in the interpersonal and mass communication activities of the native population. Ethnic social communication (Dimension 3) adds the distinct, subcultural experiences of interpersonal and mass communication with fellow coethnics. Interacting with personal and social (host, ethnic) communication are the conditions of the host environment (Dimension 4) such as the degree of the receptivity and conformity pressure of the local population as well as the strength of the stranger's own ethnic group. The stranger's predispositional factors (Dimension 5) such as preparedness for the new environment, difference/similarity of the stranger's ethnicity to that of the natives, and personality factors such as openness and strength have been explained as influencing the subsequent unfolding of the stranger's personal and social communication activities.

TABLE 7.1 Dimensions and Constructs of Cross-Cultural Adaptation

Dimensions	Constructs
1. Host Communication Competence	Host Cognitive Competence
	Host Affective Competence
	Host Operational Competence
2. Host Social Communication	Host Interpersonal Communication
	Host Mass Communication
3. Ethnic Social Communication	Ethnic Interpersonal Communication
	Ethnic Mass Communication
4. Environment	Host Receptivity
	Host Conformity Pressure
	Ethnic Group Strength
5. Predisposition	Preparedness
	Ethnicity
	Personality
6. Intercultural Transformation	Functional Fitness
	Psychological Health
	Intercultural Identity

Together, these five dimensions and the corresponding constructs constitute the structure of cross-cultural adaptation, according to which strangers' intercultural transformation (Dimension 6) is facilitated (or impeded) and manifested in increased functional fitness, psychological health, and intercultural identity.

The model presented in Figure 7.2 illustrates the overall structure of cross-cultural adaptation, with all of the linkages between and among its constructs indicated in terms of bidirectional (or mutual) functional dependence. The nature of each theoretical linkage in the model is specified as a theorem, that is, generalizable and predictive statements of functional relationships, for example, "The greater the host communication competence, the greater the participation in host social (interpersonal, mass) communication" (Theorem 1). (Due to the space limitations, readers interested in the full explication of axioms and theorems are referred to Kim, 1988a, and Kim, in press-a.)

RESEARCH CONSIDERATIONS

So far, the process and the structure of cross-cultural adaptation have been theorized based on an open-systems perspective. The theorizing process has taken a back-and-forth movement between the conceptual

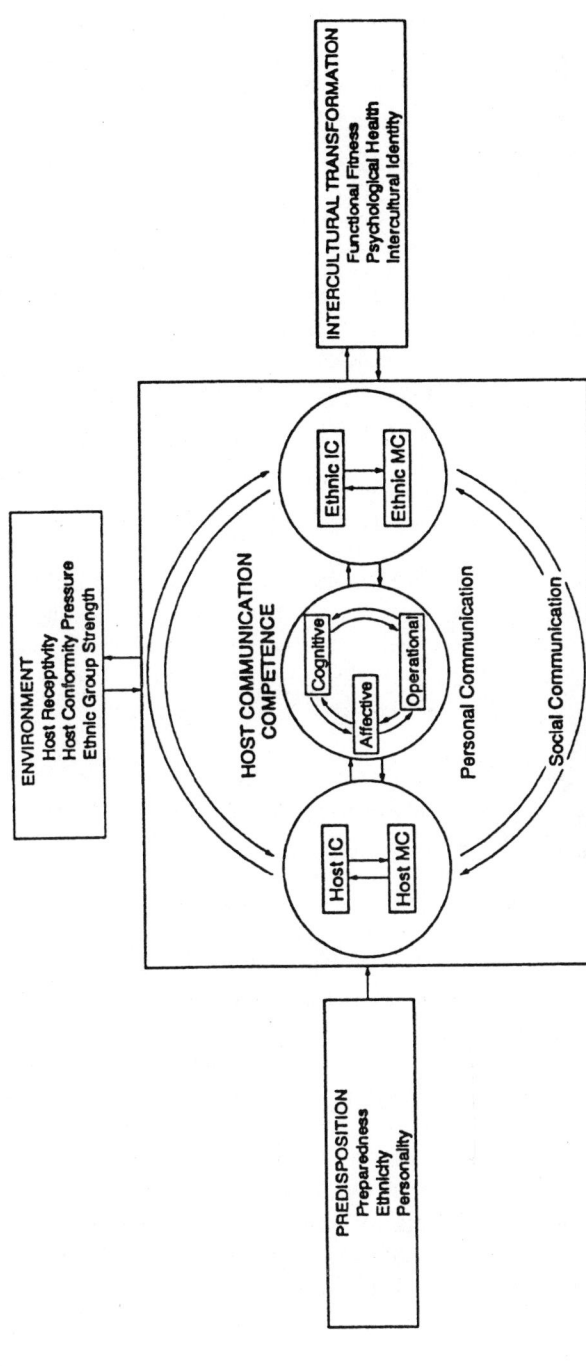

Figure 7.2: A Communication Model of the Structure of Cross-Cultural Adaptation
NOTE: IC = interpersonal communication; MC = mass communication.

189

realm of logical deduction and the empirical realm of proofs available in social sciences. Although the theory is not restricted by available empirical data, new research can offer a more systematic test of the validity of the way the present theory describes and explains cross-cultural adaptation.

Testing the Process Model

The present description of the process of adapting to a new cultural environment—from being a cultural outsider to increasingly becoming a cultural insider—is rooted in the natural drive of human beings to adapt whenever new environmental challenges threaten their internal equilibrium. At the heart of the present description of the cross-cultural adaptation process is the stress-adaptation-growth dynamic (Figure 7.1). This dynamic process acts as the prime "mover" of strangers in the evolutionary journey of intercultural transformation. The stress-adaptation-growth dynamic presents a dialectic relationship between push and pull, or engagement and disengagement, in the experiences of the individual. It affirms that challenges to one's internal system perform a necessary condition for its continued, progressive evolution, requiring it to muster a creative courage and resourcefulness so as to discover new symbols and new patterns of life from which a new, intercultural identity emerges.

Although few studies have directly examined the process of cross-cultural adaptation as presently theorized, many "snapshots" of evidence are available to support the present description of the stress-adaptation-growth dynamism and the spiral form of evolution. Supportive insights have been provided, for example, in the findings that indicate a U-curve process of sojourner adaptation over time (Church, 1982; Deutsch & Won, 1963; Lysgaard, 1955). Other studies also indirectly provide evidence for the relationship between stress and adaptation, including the report by Eaton and Lasry (1978) that the stress level of more upwardly mobile immigrants was greater than that of those who were less upwardly mobile. Likewise, among Japanese Americans (Marmot & Syme, 1976) and Mexican American women (Miranda & Castro, 1977), the better adapted immigrants had initially experienced a somewhat greater frequency of stress-related symptoms such as anxiety and a need for psychotherapy than the less adapted group. Additionally, some of the findings from the study of Ruben and Kealey (1979) suggest that, even in the case of Canadian technical advisers in Nigeria, those who were the most effective in their new environment underwent the most intense culture shock during the initial transition period (Ruben, 1980).

Cross-sectional analyses of data comparing various adaptation indices of immigrants and sojourners based on the length of residence have further shown that, once the initial phase has been successfully managed, people almost always develop more refined and positive views toward the host society and toward themselves. These analyses have also found that the individuals develop, over time, more behavioral abilities to manage themselves and function effectively and experience less feelings of alienation and hostility in relation to the host environment. While new immigrants have been reported to point out differences between their original culture and the new culture, they become increasingly in tune with similarities between the two cultures over time (Kim, 1976, 1977a).

Ideally, empirical evidence for the dynamic process of cross-cultural adaptation described in the present theory must be found in *longitudinal data*. The cross-sectional analysis can only indicate a rough estimate of the adaptation process, and needs to be further validated and elaborated by longitudinal research (Menard, 1991) involving repeated observations of a "panel" sample consisting of the same individuals over a prolonged period using *in-depth case studies* (Yin, 1984). There is, of course, an awareness of the constraints of time and resources that discourages longitudinal research. Yet, it is important to recognize that the intricate and subtle process of intercultural adaptation is the work of the human mind, which can be best revealed through intimate and continual observation (Brewer & Hunter, 1989; Denzin, 1989; Fielding & Fielding, 1986; Kirk & Miller, 1986; Weller & Romney, 1988). In the absence of systematic and longitudinal research data, personal testimonials, anecdotes, and biographies available in nonacademic sources can serve as informal but useful data providing a basis for generating more systematic research. (See, for example, Abramson, 1992; Keene, 1994; Y. Kim, 1994.)

Testing the Structural Model

The second part of the present theory deals with the structure of cross-cultural adaptation (Figure 7.2). Integrating factors both external and internal to the stranger, the present model offers a comprehensive conceptual "map" that consists of six dimensions and the key constructs thereof. These dimensions and constructs are theorized to work interactively and collaboratively to facilitate or impede the stranger's adaptive transformation. Like a locomotive engine, the workings of each unit operating in this process are explained to affect, and are affected by, the workings of all other units.

As previously noted, each of the theorized relationships between/ among the dimensions and constructs has been articulated based on both deductive reasoning and available empirical evidence. Future studies can provide a more systematic and detailed test of the structural relationships between and among the dimensions and constructs articulated in the present theory. Given the multidimensional-multifaceted nature of the structure of cross-cultural adaptation, testing the structural relationships may be varied in the degree of conceptual correspondence to the domain depicted in Figure 7.2. A limited test, for example, can be focused on the relationship between only one or two of the six dimensions included in the theory (e.g., host social communication and environmental conditions) and assess the nature of the interrelationships between and among some or all of the relevant constructs identified. A more ambitious research plan would, of course, involve most or all of the six dimensions and their constructs, thereby increasing what Fielding and Fielding (1986) call "a greater empirical and conceptual accountability on the part of the research" (p. 90).

The comprehensive nature of the structure of cross-cultural adaptation theorized in the present theory is ideally suited for an *integrative, multimethod research design*, in which quantitative-analytic and qualitative-holistic styles of gathering and analyzing evidence are used. As advocated by an increasing number of investigators (e.g., Brewer & Hunter, 1989; Cahn & Hanford, 1984; Fielding & Fielding, 1986; Strauss & Corbin, 1990), the integrative methods allow statistical tests of specific axioms and theorems to be complemented by in-depth, naturalistic assessments of various dimensions and constructs without the constraints of controlled quantification. The goal of maximizing the benefits of the two approaches and minimizing their respective shortcomings can be achieved, for example, by conducting a large-scale survey involving quantitative assessments of relevant factors, followed by smaller scale in-depth interviews and participant observation (Dyal & Dyal, 1981, p. 320). The sequence may be reversed: One may begin with smaller-scale in-depth interviews and/or observations, and then proceed with a large-scale quantitative assessment.

CONCLUSION

The present theory portrays cross-cultural adaptation as a collaborative effort, in which a stranger and the receiving environment are engaged in a joint venture. As such, one cannot overemphasize the important role that the host society can play to embrace the stranger and facilitate his or her adaptive effort. Ultimately, however, cross-cultural adaptation is, and must be, "the gift of the individuals" (Steele, 1990, p. 171). It is neither reasonable nor practical to expect any large population to significantly modify its own cultural habits with the sense of urgency that is required of a newcomer. The main power and responsibility for change has to reside in the stranger who, in the end, is responsible for his or her own psychological and social welfare.

Indeed, most strangers under most conditions appear to understand this reality and to accept their cross-cultural predicaments as part and parcel of living in an unfamiliar cultural milieu. They are not only willing but also able to make necessary self-corrections, recognizing that doing so is in their own self-interest (Cornell, 1988). Such is the case in the experiences of many of the former Peace Corps volunteers, diplomats, missionaries, and exchange students, not to mention the countless immigrants and refugees who have ventured through experiential territories seldom thought possible or even desirable. Their successful adaptation experiences are represented by Japanese American writer Jeanne Wakatsuki Houston (1981), who offers a personal intercultural transformation:

> Now I entertain according to how I feel that day. If my Japanese sensibility is stronger, I act accordingly and feel OK. If I feel like going all American, I can do that too and feel OK. I've come to accept the cultural hybrid of my personality and recognize it as a strength, not as a weakness.

Personal testimonials such as this bear witness to the remarkable human capacity to carry on life even under the conditions of an extreme cultural estrangement. Cross-cultural adaptation as depicted in this theory thus is not an extraordinary phenomenon that only exceptional individuals achieve. Rather, it is simply an incident of the normal human mutability manifesting itself in the work of ordinary people "stretching" themselves out of the old and familiar. In their individual stories, the present theory finally rests.

8

Cross-Cultural and Intercultural Applications of Expectancy Violations Theory

JUDEE K. BURGOON • *University of Arizona*

That all cultures have communication expectancies seems patently obvious. Whether cast as cultural display rules (Ekman & Friesen, 1969) or cognitive schemata for processing social information (Planalp, 1985; Schank & Abelson, 1977; Taylor & Crocker, 1981), every culture has guidelines for human conduct that carry associated anticipations for how others will behave. The question for communication scholars is whether greater understanding of human relations within and between cultures can be achieved by examining the effects of people's adherence to and deviations from those expectations.

One theory that answers the question in the affirmative is expectancy violations theory (EVT; Burgoon, 1978, 1983, 1986, 1992, 1993; Burgoon & Hale, 1988; Hale & Burgoon, 1984). EVT frames interpersonal communication patterns and outcomes within the context of expectancies and their violations. Considerable communicological, sociological, and psychological literature has implicitly or explicitly endorsed the importance of confirming or disconfirming expectations. For example, in his prolific sociological writings on self-presentation, Goffman (1959) asserted that successful performances depend upon discerning the norms or expectations for a given situation and conforming to those expectations. Further, he claimed that failure to conform would result in stigmatization and spoiled identities. Most training manuals and programs preparing employees for international work implicitly embrace the same assumption by enumerating a given culture's norms and

AUTHOR'S NOTE: I would like to express my appreciation for the helpful comments Cindy White and Pamela Koch provided on this chapter.

advising workers to abide by them. Seemingly bolstering the same conclusion is research documenting the negative consequences of committing nonverbal violations such as personal space invasions (see Burgoon & Jones, 1976).

Yet, some psychological and marketing work has argued just the opposite, that violating expectations can be beneficial. For example, the multiple plausible causes framework (summarized in Eagly & Chaiken, 1993) proposes that unexpected persuasive messages are more successful than expected ones. Marketing researchers have similarly concluded that customer satisfaction is maximized by positively violating customer expectations rather than confirming them (Brandt, 1988; Cadotte, Woodruff, & Jenkins, 1987; Oliver, 1980; Sirgy, 1984; Swan & Trawick, 1981; Tse & Wilton, 1988).

The importance of framing communication events according to expectancies is thus tacit in a wide array of research. What has yet to be resolved is when expectancy violations are harmful or helpful and whether conclusions about the effects of violations generalize beyond Western cultures.

To date, EVT principles have rarely been applied or tested beyond the scope of mainstream U.S. culture (for exceptions, see Burgoon, 1992, 1993; Gudykunst & Ting-Toomey, 1988; Lobdell, 1990). My objectives in this chapter are (a) to articulate some of the key principles of EVT and (b) to consider their universality in predicting and explaining interpersonal interactions within and between disparate cultures. Because I have addressed elsewhere the possible implications of EVT for emotional expression (see Burgoon, 1993), I will confine the current analysis to four other communication functions: relational communication, conversational management, impression management, and social influence.

EXPECTANCY VIOLATIONS THEORY

The focal constructs in the theory that have special relevance for cross-cultural and intercultural interactions are expectancies, expectancy violations, communicator valence, and behavior valence.

Communication Expectancies

Communication expectancies are enduring patterns of anticipated verbal and nonverbal behavior (Burgoon & Walther, 1990). Expectancies comprise (a) socially normative patterns of behavior applicable to an entire speech community or subgroup plus (b) person-specific knowledge related to another's typical communication patterns. When individuating information is absent or open to interpretation, expectancies tend to be stereotypical (Hamilton, Sherman, & Ruvolo, 1990). Inasmuch as most stranger and intercultural interactions entail very little personalized knowledge about other interactants, expectancies revert to cultural or subcultural norms and stereotypes.

There are actually two different senses of "expected." One reflects the regularity with which a behavioral pattern occurs, that is, its central tendency. *Expectancy* in this sense refers to communicative acts that are modal (most typical) in a given culture or subculture. The other meaning of *expectancy* reflects the degree to which a behavior is regarded as appropriate, desired, or preferred. It refers to idealized standards of conduct rather than actual communicative practice. Staines and Libby (1986) label these two conceptualizations, respectively, *predictive* and *prescriptive expectations*.

Like expectancy-value theories in the social influence arena (e.g., Fishbein & Ajzen, 1975), EVT assumes that expectancies (and beliefs) entail both a predictive and a prescriptive component. This permits arraying expectancies on a valenced continuum from good to bad. Jackson (1966), in an insightful analysis of social norms and roles, showed that behaviors occurring most frequently are often, but not always, the most preferred. Thus the relationship between a behavior's frequency and its evaluation need not be linear. For example, although moderate proximity may be the modal pattern in noncontact cultures, close proximity may be preferred, especially with favorably regarded others. Operationally, this means that understanding communication through an expectancy lens requires knowing both a behavior's typicality and its valence.

Predictive communication expectancies are shaped by three classes of factors—those related to individual communicators, those related to the relationship between sender and receiver, and those related to the communication context itself. *Communicator* factors include all those salient features of individual actors, such as sociodemographic factors, personality, physical appearance, social skills, language style, and so on that are the basis for categorizing people and that carry associated anticipations about how such people will communicate. For example, females are expected to be more affiliative than males. *Relationship* factors include interpersonal characteristics such as degree of familiarity, liking, attraction, similarity, or status equality that also lead to anticipated communication patterns. For example, where status or power asymmetries exist, the less powerful person is expected to show deference toward the more powerful one. *Context* characteristics include environmental constraints and definitions of the situation—such as its privacy, formality, or task requirements—that prescribe or proscribe certain interaction behaviors. These three classes of elements combine to form primary interaction schemata that should be activated in all human encounters, irrespective of culture.

The presence of such expectancies does not imply that expectancies will be identical across cultures. To the contrary, the *content* of each culture's interactional expectancies will vary substantially along such cultural dimensions as collectivism-individualism, uncertainty avoidance, power distance, masculinity-femininity, ascription versus achievement orientations, time and activity orientation, universalism-particularism, degree of face concern, and high- versus low-context communication (see Gudykunst & Y. Kim, 1992; M. Kim, 1993). Collectivist cultures such as Japan and China may expect greater verbal indirectness, politeness, and nonimmediacy than individualistic cultures such as the United States, Canada, and Australia (Baker, 1989; M. Kim, 1993). People from cultures that are more expressive and assertive (e.g., Australians, Indians, Pakistanis, Iranians, Israelis, Spaniards) may expect others to be more talkative and dominant than will people from cultures that are more inexpressive and reticent conversationally (e.g., Japanese, Koreans, Swedes, Norwegians, and the British; Ito, 1989b; Matsumoto & Ekman, 1989). Noncontact cultures may expect greater interaction distances than contact cultures (Hall, 1966, 1976), and so forth. But each culture will have its own set of expectancies for a given type of encounter.

Cultures may also vary in the extent to which expectancies are rigidly or loosely defined. This might be conceptualized statistically as the size of the confidence interval around the mean expected behavior. However, because expectancies are better conceived as ranges than point estimates, the diffuseness or precision of the expectancies might be better visualized as the size of the tolerance range for a given act beyond which the act is considered a violation and may invoke sanctions or disapprobation. An example is gum chewing—an act that is commonplace in the United States, frowned upon in Germany, and illegal in Singapore. It may be that ideological societies, which rely on rules and laws to minimize conflict, may have more narrow expectancy bandwidths than human relations societies, which are more concerned with group harmony than with conforming to prescriptions and principles (Ito, 1989a, 1989b). Alternatively, human relations cultures may be more restrictive given the importance they place on obedience, status differentials, and interpersonal harmony (Chu, 1988). In line with this latter possibility, Gudykunst and Ting-Toomey (1988) conjectured that cultures low in power distance and uncertainty avoidance (such as the United States) have fewer rules and norms regulating proxemic behavior than do cultures high in power distance and uncertainty avoidance (such as Japan). Although the empirical evidence leads me to disagree that proxemic norms are minimal in the United States (see, Burgoon, Buller, & Woodall, 1989; Hayduk, 1978), it may be that, relatively speaking, such cultures are less norm-bound. Regardless of which cultures have narrower or wider tolerance ranges, the larger principle here is that cultures are not uniform in the degree to which communication behavior is regulated by rules and social norms.

Where rules and norms are less explicit, cultures may also vary in the degree of tentativeness or certainty with which communication expectancies are held. Japanese, for example, have greater attributional confidence about how strangers from their own and disparate cultures will behave than do North Americans (Gudykunst & Nishida, 1984). Too, cultures may differ on the degree of intracultural homogeneity. For example, if distinctly different expectancies are held for different subgroups, a single expectancy cannot be identified that has culturewide applicability. The different expectancies for ingroups and outgroups in Greece is illustrative: Ingroup members are expected to be warm, cooperative, polite, reliable, and truthful, while outgroup members are expected to be hostile, competitive, untrustworthy, and deceitful (Broome, 1990).

As a counterpoint to all these claims for cultural differences, it must be recognized that, at some fundamental level, there must be some commonalities present that enable shared meanings and coordinated interchanges. Without them, communication would be impossible. These commonalities reflect collective norms or expectations about communicative practices, many of which transcend culture (see Graumann, in press). Further systematic study of the foundations of communicative exchange may reveal many points of similarity. If so, expectancy-based predictions will not require as much culture-specific adjustment.

Regardless of how well defined and homogeneous or heterogeneous the predictive expectancies are, all expectancies theoretically should have an associated valence that defines their prescriptive aspect. Predictive components of expectancies are arrayed on a frequency continuum; prescriptive components are arrayed on a valence continuum. The answer to the question, Is the expected range of behavior viewed as good, bad, or neutral? dictates where on the valence continuum the range is located. Its size reflects the latitude of acceptable variability (i.e., the magnitude of departure from the midpoint of the range that is tolerated before the valence changes).

Expectancy valences may vary significantly from one culture to the next. To illustrate, collectivist cultures place more positive value on communicative indirectness and restrained expressiveness than do individualistic cultures. Hence they may be more distressed by forthrightness and flamboyance than would individualistic cultures. Japanese, for example, suppress emotional expressiveness so as to avoid insulting the group (Matsumoto, 1993). Valences may also be specific to particular communicator, relationship, or context characteristics within cultures. In Mediterranean cultures, for instance, public hand-holding is a positive and accepted display of friendship when exhibited by same-sex friends but unacceptable when displayed by heterosexual pairs; in North America, the opposite is true (Morris, 1971). Even though our current state of knowledge is such that the valences for many communicative behaviors are unrecognized or ambiguous at present, they are theoretically subject to empirical verification.

To summarize, despite variability in the content, stability, intracultural homogeneity, and evaluations associated with expectancies, predictive and prescriptive communicative expectancies should be ubiquitous *within* cultures.

But what about communication expectancies between cultures? If expectancies are a fundamental principle of social organization or social information processing, it follows that they should also exist for interactions between unfamiliar and dissimilar people. The form such intercultural expectancies take probably coincides with the character of most intergroup interactions, such that people respond primarily to one another according to social categories and ingroup-outgroup distinctions (Tajfel, 1981). The degree to which a culture is individualistic or collectivistic is known to affect perceptions of, and interactions with, ingroup versus outgroup members (Gudykunst, Gao, Schmidt, et al., 1992). Prior experience with a given group should also determine the extent to which communication expectancies are grounded in stereotypes or whether any well-formulated expectancies even exist (Manusov & Hegde, 1993). With highly limited knowledge, expectancies may be very tentative and/or aligned with whatever outgroup the individual appears to most closely resemble. To the extent that expectancies are linked to outgroup stereotypes, they may also be more negatively valenced than expectancies for those from familiar or similar cultural backgrounds.

With repeated interactions, intercultural expectations presumably should shift from heavy reliance on cultural- and sociological-level data to greater emphasis on psychological, particularized, and idiosyncratic data; that is, they should evolve from being "noninterpersonal" to "interpersonal" (see Miller & Steinberg, 1975). If such interactions follow uncertainty reduction theory principles, greater familiarity simultaneously should foster increased certitude associated with the expectancies (Gudykunst, 1985c; Gudykunst & Nishida, 1984). Thus intercultural expectancies should parallel longitudinally the evolution of expectancies among strangers within the same culture.

Expectancy Violations

Expectancy violations refers to actions sufficiently discrepant from the expectancy to be noticeable and classified as outside the expectancy range. In psychology, such behavior is frequently referred to as *behavioral disconfirmation.* Just as rules are partly defined by their exceptions, so are expectancies partly recognized by their violations. Thus, if cultures have expectancies, by definition they must also have expectancy violations. In some cases, such violations may even invoke legal sanctions or other social means of enforcement, but more often they are "legislated" tacitly. Cultures vary in how deviant a behavior must become before it is recognized as a violation. For example, cultures high in uncertainty avoidance are intolerant of deviant behavior (Hofstede, 1980). Such cultures should be quicker to declare a given nonnormative behavior as a violation than cultures that are more tolerant of individual variability.

The manner in which people respond to violations should also differ. Gudykunst and Ting-Toomey (1988), for instance, theorize that individualistic cultures will respond to proxemic violations with aggressive behavior while collectivistic cultures will respond to such violations with withdrawal. EVT proposes a more complex set of predictions that are a function of the valencing of the violation.

Of course, expectancy violations are not just within-culture phenomena. Because intercultural interactions typically fall at the heterogeneous end of a homogeneity-heterogeneity continuum (Sarbaugh, 1979), they are prototypical cases of potential expectancy violations. Fundamental differences in philosophies, values, and social organization, coupled with widespread ignorance about cultural differences, make intercultural encounters prime candidates for colliding expectancies. The countless anecdotes about misunderstandings and failed communication often translate into pitting one culture's norms against the quaint, peculiar, or "deviant" acts of another culture (Yousef, 1976).

Communicator Valence

A key premise of EVT is that communication expectations are influenced by communicator characteristics and, more specifically, the valences attached to those characteristics. We know from the proxemic literature, for example, that close proximity is regarded as desirable when interacting with attractive and familiar interactants but not when interacting with unattractive others or strangers. With the former, proximity may communicate such positive meanings as liking, interest, and approval-seeking but, with the latter, may be seen as threatening and/or overbearing. The communicator's positive or negative characteristics are posited to moderate how distance and other violations are interpreted and evaluated.

The salient aspect of communicator characteristics is encapsulated in EVT as *communicator reward valence* or, more simply, *communicator valence*. That communicator characteristics affect communication practices is no news flash to communication scholars. But social scientists have had great difficulty prioritizing communicator variables in terms of importance or impact. The stance taken in EVT is that what unifies innumerable and disparate communicator characteristics is their net valence—whether, on balance, a communicator is deemed rewarding or not and, by extension, whether an interaction with that person is expected to be pleasurable or not. The importance of communicator valence is echoed by social exchange and attraction theories (e.g., Byrne, 1971; Thibaut & Kelley, 1959), which postulate that communicators size up the costs and rewards associated with another and attempt to maximize rewards relative to costs.

Just as communicator, relationship, and context factors are posited to affect expectancies, so are they also posited to govern communicator valence. All prior knowledge or observable information about a communicator, plus that individual's behavior during the interaction, feeds into the communicator valence quotient. For example, an individual may be reputed to have task expertise (a preinteractional, externally attributed communicator characteristic) or may actually demonstrate that task knowledge during the interchange (an internally derived, interactional characteristic). Although features inevitably will vary in how heavily they are weighted for each given circumstance, the key point is that they yield a net positive or negative valence assigned to the communicator.

To date, factors that have been operationalized and verified as relevant components of communicator valence within U.S. culture include physical attractiveness, task expertise and knowledge, socioeconomic status, giving positive or negative feedback, possession of appealing personal attributes, similarity, familiarity, and status equality (Burgoon & Hale, 1988).

Apart from the direct effects that communicator valence exerts on communication patterns and outcomes (which is by no means unique to EVT), its special importance in EVT arises from its moderating role in valencing communication behaviors generally and violations specifically. It does so by influencing one or both parts of an interpretation-evaluation process.

Behavior and Violation Valence

Deviant and unexpected behaviors, by virtue of their novelty or unusualness, are known to be alerting or arousing and to trigger finer grained information processing (Burgoon & Hale, 1988; Heinemann, Pellander, Vogelbusch, & Wojtek, 1981; Hilton, Klein, & von Hippel, 1991; Langer & Imber, 1980; Le Poire & Burgoon, 1995; Newtson, 1973). This attention-diverting feature of expectancy violations is posited to intensify responses relative to expectancy confirmations by potentiating communicator valence and activating an otherwise latent interpretation-evaluation process. Specifically, attention should be drawn to the violator and the violation act itself. The heightened awareness of communicator characteristics should magnify their positive or negative value. At the same time, the increased attention to the violation behavior should instigate an appraisal process to "make sense" of the violation. This appraisal process is postulated to include assessment of (a) the meaning(s) associated with a given violative act (*interpretation*) amid the range of possible meanings and (b) the act's desirability (*evaluation*).

Interpretations and evaluations hinge partly on constraints imposed by the context but also partly on who has committed the violation, that is, on communicator valence. When a violation's meaning is ambiguous or subject to multiple interpretations, communicator valence may influence which interpretations are selected. An abrupt departure, without the usual leave-taking ritual and no available situational information to explain it, is a violation. If committed by a person who is highly regarded, it may be perplexing but the perceiver may make more charitable attributions about its cause than if the act is committed by a poorly regarded communicator. For example, the departure may be excused as necessitated by some urgent problem, an attribution that would further reinforce the communicator's perceived power and status. It is unlikely to be interpreted as an intentional slight (unless the receiver suffers from low self-esteem). However, the same act committed by a disliked other may be interpreted as an affront, as rude, or as indicative of the communicator's social incompetence. Thus, when alternative readings are possible, the "who" committing the act becomes an essential factor in narrowing the range of interpretations considered plausible.

Communicator valence may also moderate evaluations, with or without having affected interpretations. In the leave-taking example, even though the act itself is normally not evaluated positively, the fact that it is committed by someone held in high regard may result in it being evaluated neutrally. By contrast, the same act by the poorly regarded communicator is more likely to be evaluated severely and classified as a negative violation of expectations. Gaze serves as another example. A high degree of gaze generally carries positive interpretations and evaluations in Western cultures (Burgoon, Coker, & Coker, 1986). But such gaze from a stranger, if prolonged, is likely to become disconcerting and to be judged as unpleasant.

The interpretive analysis of communicative behaviors may precede evaluation, follow it, or occur simultaneously and instantaneously with it. Regardless of the temporal ordering, the end result of this appraisal process should be a valence, ranging from positive to negative, that is attached to the violation. (Expected behaviors are also assumed to undergo an appraisal process over the course of their numerous instantiations but their interpretations and evaluations are likely to remain at a much more subconscious level as long as the interaction is "humming along.")

The current state of knowledge of what interpretations and evaluations are attached to various behaviors until now has rested largely on an anecdotal and intuitive base. To give expectancy- and violation-based predictions the necessary empirical grounding, my own work within U.S. culture has been investigating systematically the expectations, meanings, and evaluations associated with various nonverbal behaviors and composites (Burgoon, 1992; Burgoon, Buller, Hale, & deTurck, 1984; Burgoon & Hale, 1988; Burgoon, Manusov, Mineo, & Hale, 1985; Burgoon & Newton, 1991; Burgoon & Walther, 1990; Burgoon et al., 1986). Similar undertakings are needed within other cultures and for intercultural interactions. Our results so far have shown that some behaviors have consensual interpretations and evaluations while others are moderated by communicator valence (Burgoon, 1992; Burgoon et al., 1986). For example, nearly constant gaze is interpreted as dominant when exhibited by a highly regarded male but as submissive when exhibited by a highly regarded female. An open, relaxed posture is also viewed as dominant when exhibited by an attractive same-sex partner but submissive when exhibited by an unattractive one. Various forms of touches are evaluated differently depending on the attractiveness of the communicator, and proximity is evaluated differently depending on the status equality or inequality between participants (Burgoon & Walther, 1990). Michael Burgoon's research program has similarly confirmed that communicator credibility and gender moderate the evaluations of language choices and compliance-gaining strategies (M. Burgoon, 1974; Burgoon, Birk, & Hall, 1991). In many other cases, communicator valence has an additive effect on evaluations; that is, the more rewarding the communicator, the more desirable his or her behavior is judged to be.

Although far less is known currently about how various communicative acts are interpreted and evaluated in other cultures, knowledge of linguistic and nonverbal norms (e.g., Burgoon, Newton, Walther, & Baesler, 1989; M. Kim, 1993) may permit drawing inferences about which kinds of violations might be positively or negatively valenced and hence produce positive or negative consequences within different cultures. To illustrate, Gudykunst and Ting-Toomey (1988) contend that high-context, ambiguous, and indirect communication typifies collectivist cultures. Such behavior presumably is also preferred. If so, verbal directness and immediacy may constitute negative violations that lead to unpleasant interactions and outcomes.

The same kind of inferential analysis can also be applied to intercultural interactions. Take, for example, an American working in Japan. Politeness is expected and preferred, but a Japanese businessman may expect (stereotypically) a U.S. businessman to be very forthright and opinionated. If, instead, the U.S. businessman displays a great deal of tact and forbearance, this may serve as a positive violation. The result should be more agreeable interaction than had the American been expected to be polite in the first place. As another illustration, consider an interchange between an American and an Israeli. Although Americans and Israelis both value "straight talk" as sincere, Americans have an upper threshold beyond which candor is seen as rude and overbearing. Israelis, for whom a highly direct speech pattern known as *dugri* is normative (see Katriel, 1986), may find themselves committing negative violations when interacting with North Americans because their discourse is overly direct. The severity of such violations is likely to be even greater when interacting with Japanese or Chinese.

Despite myriad differences cross-culturally on what communicative behaviors qualify as positive or negative violations, there may be some superordinate forms of communication that prompt universally positive or negative evaluations. Chinese and North Americans are highly similar in how they display discontent when disputed, wronged, or disappointed (Ma, 1990), for instance. It seems plausible that many communicative acts that are negatively valenced in this culture—betrayals of trust, insults, excessive familiarity by a stranger, or angry outbursts—would be negatively valenced in most other cultures as well. Similarly, some positively valenced communication acts—compliments, gift giving, humor, unexpectedly positive feedback—should generalize beyond North American culture.

Because of the predilection to assign more socially desirable interpretations and evaluations to the behaviors of positively valenced communicators, the probability might appear much higher for them to engage in more positive violations than negatively valenced communicators. But this is an empirical question, and two factors mitigate against this always occurring. One is that positive-valence communicators are granted a wider latitude in deviating from social norms before their behavior is regarded as unexpected. This larger bandwidth of expected behavior (akin to idiosyncracy credits in the small groups literature) means that positive-valence communicators may have to engage in more extreme behaviors before their acts qualify as violations. Second, the standards of conduct for positive-valence communicators may be much higher than for negative-valence communicators. If expected and enacted behaviors are placed along a continuum from extreme positive valence to extreme negative valence, then the gap between what is expected and enacted might be quite small for a positive-valence communicator, but quite large for a negative-valence one, making it easier for a negative-valence communicator to commit a positive violation. High expectations also make it easier for a positive-valence communicator to commit a negative violation. Thus positive violations are not uniformly associated with positive-valence communicators, or negative violations, with negative-valence ones. It is quite possible for positive-valence communicators to commit negative violations and negative-valence communicators to commit positive violations.

EVT APPLICATIONS TO COMMUNICATION FUNCTIONS

The relationship between violation valences and their effects on interaction patterns and interaction outcomes is as follows: Positive violations are predicted to yield more favorable interactions and outcomes than conforming to expectations while negative violations are predicted to yield more unfavorable consequences than conforming to expectations. In the remaining sections of this chapter, I want to outline briefly how these predictions apply to four communication functions, two of which are related to interaction processes themselves—relational communication and conversation management—and two of which are related to interaction outcomes—impression management and social influence. I will review some of the empirical research on these functions and speculate on how EVT principles and findings might "translate" cross-culturally and interculturally.

Interaction Processes: Relational Communication and Conversation Management

Relational communication refers to messages, exchanged between two or more people, that define the nature of their interpersonal relationship. Statements or behaviors that convey liking, friendship, dominance, formality, distrust, or animosity are all relational statements. For example, eye contact connotes such meanings as affection, interest, composure, informality, and dominance. Many scholars believe relational communication is present as a subtext in all human interchanges (see Burgoon et al., 1984; Watzlawick, Beavin, & Jackson, 1967). Although often transacted by nonverbal means while the verbal channel simultaneously transmits the "ostensive" content, relational messages can take either nonverbal or verbal form.

Relational communication has typically been viewed as an outcome of an interaction because it is measured postinteractionally. Yet, it can also be understood as synonymous with the interpretation part of the violation valencing process during an interaction. Here, I want to consider it in this light. Expectancy violations are posited to elevate relational implicatures from background to foreground by drawing attention to the relational import of a violative act. Given that people typically rely on nonverbal channels to conduct relational business, the greater importance a culture invests in nonverbal forms of expression, the greater the chances of violations reinforcing the relational interpretations associated with them. Hence collectivist and homogeneous cultures (e.g., China, Japan) that are oriented toward interpersonal relationships, characterized by ambiguous language, and highly dependent on nonverbal cues, may be especially subject to violations having relational implications. For example, one of the cardinal principles of Confucianism is promoting warm human feelings and "proper social relationships" (Yum, 1988). Indirection, commonly used as a means of preserving face and minimizing conflict, forces greater reliance on nonverbal behavior (Doi, 1973; Reischauer, 1977). Yet even an individualist, heterogeneous culture such as the United States exhibits high consensus on the relational meanings associated with certain nonverbal cues (Burgoon & Newton, 1991). We can surmise, then, that expectancy violations may affect relational communication in all cultures, albeit to different degrees, even though the content of those messages will vary from culture to culture. A self-effacing act that is interpreted as appropriate deference in one culture may be interpreted instead as spineless sycophancy in another. The particular meanings associated with violations, then, will be culture specific, but relational interpretations of some sort will still be attached to the interactional behaviors.

One question that arises is whether cultures with rigid role and rule structures ever assign positive interpretations to violations and hence valence them positively. In discussing proxemic violations, Gudykunst and Ting-Toomey (1988) contend that, in high power distance and collectivist cultures, a high-status person engaging in a personal space violation would be behaving totally outside ascribed role behavior and that such an action would inevitably produce stress and anxiety—a negative outcome. The implication of this example is that all forms of violations would carry negative relational attributions in such cultures. This is an empirical question, and the speculation runs counter to common intuition that unexpected acts such as shows of kindness or affiliativeness might be viewed as liking or approval—a positive relational interpretation likely to lead to other positive outcomes. While we cannot assume that what constitutes a positive violation in U.S. culture will be a positive violation elsewhere, EVT makes no such an assumption. It only postulates that if (a) an act is unexpected, (b) it is assigned favorable interpretations, and (c) it is evaluated positively, it will produce more favorable outcomes than an expected act with the same interpretations and evaluations. Making predictions within any given culture requires knowing what interpretations and evaluations are assigned to communicative behaviors *in that culture.*

In intercultural encounters, an additional factor may need to be taken into account: uncertainty. Dissimilarities between participants may heighten ambiguities associated with the relational meaning of violations. A study of sojourners reentering their home culture is illustrative. Lobdell (1990) examined friends' and family's reactions to sojourners who return from their travels with new mannerisms, dress, and values at odds with those of their home culture. These expectancy violations, which may be analogous to the situation confronting interactants in intercultural encounters, proved to be a source of uncertainty and were often evaluated negatively. White (1989), in analyzing the role of expectancy violations in relationship development, similarly found that violations, especially negative ones, typically increase uncertainty. Thus, to the extent that violations increase rather than decrease relational ambiguities and are accompanied by discomfort or negative affect, they may lead to unfavorable relational attributions.

However, this need not be the case. White (1989) conjectured that unexpected behavior, especially in newer relationships, may also create opportunities to learn more about another. This would be especially true of intercultural interchanges, which are often an occasion for gaining greater knowledge about another culture and lifestyle. Under such circumstances, violations may take on positive rather than negative valence. Interactants may be inclined to give more favorable "readings" to the other's behaviors, or they may suspend relational interpretations until more information is forthcoming. Because of the greater uncertainty associated with intercultural interactions, participants may also give those from a different culture a "wider berth" to deviate from expectations without regarding the others' behavior as a violation. That is, the expectancy bandwidth may be expanded to tolerate a wider range of behavior. How long interactants are willing to remain in an elevated state of uncertainty before reverting to their own culture's expectancies and relational interpretations would determine the longevity or transience of favorable reactions to the novelty and uncertainty. It is possible that, as the newness of interacting with an unfamiliar other wears off, the expectancy bandwidth may also lose its elasticity such that behaviors once tolerated would now fall outside the acceptance region, and behaviors initially interpreted as "quaint" might now be seen as annoying. These conjectures argue for more empirical investigation of what expectancies people hold for interactions with those from dissimilar cultures and what range of interpretations they are willing to assign to dissimilar communication patterns.

A second communication function related to interaction processes is conversation management: creating a coordinated interchange and regulating the flow of conversation. Interactions that are progressing smoothly should exhibit, among other things, synchronization of verbal and nonverbal activity between speaker and listener, rapid turn-switches between speakers, and reciprocity of communication styles (see Bernieri & Rosenthal, 1991; Burgoon, Stern, & Dillman, in press).

Within this arena, EVT has been applied specifically to predicting conditions under which interactants adapt their interaction behaviors to one another in the form of reciprocity or compensation (Burgoon, Le Poire, & Rosenthal, in press; Burgoon, Olney, & Coker, 1988; Hale & Burgoon, 1984; Le Poire & Burgoon, 1994). Like communication accommodation theory (Giles, Coupland, & Coupland, 1991, pp. 1-68), EVT posits that, under some circumstances, interactants will converge toward or match each other's communicative behavior (reciprocity) and in other circumstances, diverge (compensation). The pattern depends on the valences of the communicator and the violation. For example, increased involvement by a rewarding partner is hypothesized to be reciprocated because it is a behavior pattern with positive connotations that is welcomed from such a partner. Decreased involvement by the same partner is hypothesized to elicit compensatory increases in involvement because low involvement connotes disinterest or dislike, is unpleasant, and should motivate the person to restore the interaction to its previous involvement level. With a nonrewarding partner, the reverse should be true. Increased involvement should be unwanted, thus prompting a compensatory response, whereas decreased involvement, the preferred pattern, should prompt a reciprocal decrease in involvement. The net effect is that interactants should follow another's lead when that person moves the interaction in a desired direction but resist when that person moves it in an undesired one. This general prediction should hold true regardless of which culture is involved and whether the interaction is between or within cultures.

The interaction predictions have yet to be tested outside U.S. culture. Before doing so, it may be useful to consider two shortcomings of the theory noted by Burgoon, Stern, and Dillman (in press). First, EVT does not fully account for the overwhelming prevalence of reciprocity that has been found in interpersonal interactions. Second, it is silent on whether communicator valence supersedes behavior valence or vice versa when the two are incongruent (such as when a disliked partner engages in a positive violation). As a corrective, Burgoon et al. (in press) have begun to develop a new theory, Interaction Adaptation Theory, that builds upon many EVT principles but also incorporates biological and sociological pressures toward reciprocity as part of its explanatory calculus. Additionally, expectancies are supplemented by personal requirements and desires in predicting initial interaction patterns and responses to discrepant partner behaviors. The new theory, which is currently being tested in an intercultural context, still makes predictions compatible with EVT in that interactants from both similar and dissimilar cultures are hypothesized to adopt interaction styles that maximize their needs, preferences, and expectations. They are hypothesized to do so by reciprocating behavior that is more positively valenced than anticipated and compensating behavior that is more negatively valenced than anticipated. The behavior patterns that are positively and negatively valenced, however, are theorized to differ depending on whether the interaction is between people from similar or dissimilar cultures. If the theory is supported, it may argue for revising EVT or for supplanting expectancies with a more comprehensive construct comprising required, expected, and desired behaviors, when the objective is to predict communication patterns themselves.

Interaction Outcomes: Impression Management and Social Influence

Two other interrelated communication functions that have been examined in testing EVT are impression management and social influence. Because impression management often has as its end objective maximizing credibility and attraction, it is often seen as the means by which one can achieve persuasion and compliance.

According to EVT, positive violations are theorized to produce more positive impressions of a communicator and to effect more influence than conformity to expectancies. By contrast, negative violations are theorized to be detrimental relative to expectancy confirmation. These predictions have been tested under varying circumstances, with most centering on communicator evaluations rather than influence as the dependent measure.

The first test (Burgoon & Jones, 1976) manipulated conversational distance as the violation. Confederates gave positive or negative feedback (positive and negative communicator valence, respectively) while adopting one of four interaction distances during a sentence completion task. Subsequent ratings of the confederates showed that positive-valence communicators were generally perceived as more credible and attractive at violation distances (close, extremely close, or far), while negative-valence communicators were rated most favorably at the expected (normative) distance. The next several experiments (Burgoon, 1978; Burgoon, Stacks, & Woodall, 1979; Stacks & Burgoon, 1981) used similar distance manipulations but different operationalizations of reward. Later tests expanded violations to include gaze (Burgoon et al., 1985; Burgoon et al., 1986), immediacy and involvement (Burgoon & Hale, 1988; Burgoon & Le Poire, 1993; Burgoon, Newton, Walther, & Baesler, 1989), vocalics (Buller & Burgoon, 1986), and touch (Burgoon, Walther, & Baesler, 1992). Throughout these experiments, results showed that some kinds of violations enhanced credibility and attraction regardless of communicator valence, whereas the effects of other kinds of violations were moderated by communicator valence. Positive violations were also found to intensify evaluations of positive-valence communicators relative to enacting behaviors that confirmed expectations.

The first, indirect test to include influence as a dependent measure (Woodall & Burgoon, 1981) examined the effects of self-synchrony on message persuasiveness, perceived speaker credibility, and message comprehension. *Self-synchrony* refers to the degree that gestural and facial activity is coordinated to the speaker's verbal-vocal stream. The experiment created conditions in which gestures and facial expressions were (a) coordinated with the verbal-vocal presentation, (b) out of sync with it, or (c) absent. The dissynchronous presentation, which would qualify as a negative violation, was the least persuasive and credible. It also was the most distracting, was comprehended the least, and triggered the most source derogation.

A second, direct test (Burgoon, Stacks, & Burch, 1982) employed two positive-valence or two negative-valence confederates who interacted with a third, naive participant. While arguing the prosecution or defense case from an actual criminal trial, one of the confederates committed a proxemic violation by moving much closer or farther away than normal, while the other confederate remained stationary. Positive-valence confederates were found to be more persuasive and credible when engaging in either a close or a far violation, but especially a far one. This was true both in comparison with their own persuasiveness and credibility when they instead conformed to the norm *and* in comparison with the other nonviolating confederate, who was of equally high reward valence. Conversely, negative-valence confederates undermined their own persuasiveness and credibility and conferred more credibility on their opponent by engaging in a violation. Thus violating expectations was a particularly efficacious strategy for a positively valenced interactant but conformity was the best strategy for a negatively valenced one.

The last studies to examine influence-related outcomes were three field experiments testing effects of distance violations on helping behavior (Burgoon & Aho, 1982). In two experiments, confederates posed as high- or low-status customers with an intent to purchase an expensive or inexpensive item. In the third, confederates posed as experts or nonexperts conducting interviews on consumer behavior. The violations consisted of close or far conversational distance (as compared with normative distance). Although only reward valence affected behavioral compliance in the first two experiments, and the third experiment was confounded by confederate differences, the effects of distancing on nonverbal behaviors across the three studies revealed that violations increased behavioral activation and apparent distraction.

At this juncture, the findings from my own research can probably best be summarized as follows. Expectancies exert significant influence on people's interaction patterns, on their impressions of one another, and on the outcomes of their interactions. Violations of expectations in turn may arouse and distract their recipients, shifting greater attention to the violator and the meanings of the violation itself. People who can assume that they are well regarded by their audience are safer engaging in violations and more likely to profit from doing so than are those who are poorly regarded. When the violation act is one that is likely to be ambiguous in its meaning or to carry multiple interpretations that are not uniformly positive or negative, then the reward valence of the communicator can be especially significant in moderating interpretations, evaluations, and subsequent outcomes. Examples of this type of violation include, in the nonverbal realm, conversational distance and various types of touch. In other cases, violations have relatively consensual meanings and valences associated with them, so that engaging in them produces similar effects for positive- and negative-valenced communicators. Examples of this type of violation are gaze and nonverbal involvement.

But we need not rely on this program of research alone to support EVT. Numerous other investigations, summarized in Burgoon (1983), have provided tangential support when recast in EVT terms. Similarly, M. Burgoon et al.'s (1991) program of research on violating linguistic expectations has produced results consistent with EVT. For example, it has shown that patients generally expect male physicians, who are highly credible, to use moderately aggressive compliance-gaining strategies such as giving directives and information. Yet patients are much more likely to comply when the physician adopts either highly aggressive strategies or highly nonaggressive, comforting, empathic ones than moderately aggressive ones. In other words, either type of violation is more effective than expectancy confirmation.

Additional corroboration comes from work on expectation states theory (Berger, Conner, & Fisek, 1974; Ridgeway & Berger, 1986), a theory that originated to explain influence in task groups. According to the theory, external status cues or internal behavioral ones such as dominance behaviors are weighted and aggregated to form expectations for certain kinds of performances. This is identical to the EVT concept of net communicator valence. Like EVT, these characteristics are posited to become the basis for power, prestige, and favorable evaluations, enabling such individuals to have more opportunities to contribute to task execution and to influence group decisions. Status characteristics are posited to take on reward value through shared referential beliefs about the characteristics, abilities, and accomplishments typically associated with occupants of valued status positions. Empirical work has confirmed that high-status communicators profit from committing violations. Consistent with other literature showing that males are accorded higher credibility and status than females, Ridgeway and Jacobson (1977) found that males were rated as slightly more desirable coworkers and ranked as somewhat more influential than women; that is, they were more positively valenced than women. They also achieved more actual influence than females on a group task, *especially when they were nonconforming*. Thus violations were a better strategy than conformity for the more positively valenced group members. (Nonconforming females were also more influential than conforming ones even though they seemed to engender more resentment from group members when deviant than when conforming.) Ridgeway and Jacobson (1977) concluded that "nonconformity may have acted as a perceptual marker for a subjects' [*sic*] response, attracted his groupmates' attention both to his competence and his yeoman effort to secure points for the group" (p. 423). The "perceptual marker effect" is completely isomorphic with the EVT principle of violations heightening attention to and reinforcing the positive attributes of violators. Another experiment demonstrated that competent confederates (i.e., ones who made relevant contributions to the task) who were status equals enhanced their influence on a group through nonconformity, whereas nonconformity ultimately undermined influence for incompetent, low-status members. Those who were competent but with low status were most successful adopting intermediate nonconformity (Ridgeway, 1981). If competence and status are combined to array participants on a reward continuum, these findings match EVT predictions: Violations should be most beneficial for those of highest reward value (i.e., competent/high-status members), moderately beneficial to those of mixed reward value (competent but low status), and a liability for those of lowest reward value.

Ridgeway's (1981) conclusion could be an endorsement for EVT:

> Conformity is not by itself an aid to influence and status attainment in task groups. Nonconformity, on the other hand, can be an asset in achieving influence both because it attracts attention and because it is self-assertive, which can enhance perceived competence when it accompanies a task contribution. (p. 346)

In sum, the evidence is persuasive that expectancy violations can be more efficacious than expectancy confirmations when the objective is to enhance self-image and influence another. But will violations be equally efficacious in different cultures or in intercultural interchanges? Ridgeway and Berger (1986) contend that high-status members' greater license to violate group norms does not include violating status-linked performance expectations. They claim there is greater risk violating those behavioral expectations that are markers of status and affirm the legitimacy of a status position (e.g., participating more, influencing the group, speaking with a firm voice, and looking at others directly while talking). This qualification might apply to other cultures as well, although the status-linked cues themselves would vary. However, the previous EVT findings implicitly challenge the necessity of powerful and high-status people adhering to these stereotypical profiles. Ultimately, the answer will lie in further research. If favorable impressions and influence are attainable by virtue of violations galvanizing attention to positive or negative qualities of communicators and their behavior, then positive violations should gain more desirable consequences and negative violations should gain less desirable ones, regardless of culture.

CONCLUSION

This brief review of expectancy violations theory offers a sampling of the theory's potential to gain greater understanding of interpersonal communication within and between cultures by framing encounters according to expectancies and expectancy violations. The confluence of findings and theorizing from different disciplinary tributaries on some of the theory's propositions is encouraging and endorses the heurism gained from an expectancy perspective. Further cross-cultural and intercultural research will ultimately provide the litmus test for the universality of EVT predictions and explanations. It is hoped that the current chapter will stimulate research in that direction.

III

THEORIES ON INTERCULTURAL
COMMUNICATION CONTEXTS

9

Intercultural and Cross-Cultural Health Communication

Understanding People and Motivating Healthy Behaviors

KIM WITTE • *Michigan State University*
KELLY MORRISON • *Michigan State University*

An urgent need exists for effective intercultural and cross-cultural health communication strategies. Thousands of children die daily in developing countries because of lack of adequate nutrition, clean water, and immunizations (Graeff, Elder, & Booth, 1993). Hundreds of people suffer needlessly from misdiagnosis, unnecessary treatments, or the use of risky procedures due to misunderstandings arising from poor communication (Haffner, 1992). To promote health and prevent disease, intercultural health communication research must focus on two central issues—understanding and motivation.

Understanding and motivation can be promoted through effective communication, which is mutually constructed between people in social interactions. Any communication process takes place in a context into which participants bring their own personal experiences, knowledge, and beliefs. Meaning, or understanding, is influenced by the communication context and the interpretive assumptions that each person holds. In the health context, members of different cultures often bring different sets of interpretive assumptions to a communication interaction. For health professionals to help their patients or audiences, they must understand the interpretive frameworks within which their clients communicate.

Effective communication is a necessary first step to understanding, particularly where matters of health are concerned. Practitioners and

216

public health officials must understand patients' concerns, worldviews, and medical complaints in order to diagnose, heal, or prevent disease. Likewise, patients must understand practitioners' questions and recommendations if they are to be healed or if diseases are to be prevented. Mutual understanding comes about when people have *the same definitions of verbal and nonverbal messages.*

Communication problems are exacerbated and understanding between people is reduced when the patient and practitioner are from different cultures (Fitzgerald, 1988). The first part of this chapter examines empirical concepts related to intercultural health understanding and offers a theoretical perspective on how to promote effective communication, and hence understanding, between physicians or public health practitioners and their patients.

Effective communication and mutual understanding between practitioners and patients is a necessary, but not sufficient, condition to promoting health and preventing disease. Once mutual understanding of a health issue is achieved, people must be motivated to act in appropriate ways. Much research has been conducted on how to motivate individuals to act in healthy ways. However, the wholesale application of these Western-based theories to other cultures may be inappropriate, and in some cases actually cause more harm than good. Culturally based theories are desperately needed. While it is probable that there are universal variables that influence health-related decision making across cultures, it is also probable that there are unique and idiosyncratic variables in each culture that must be addressed if effective health communication is to occur. The second part of this chapter identifies culturally universal and culturally specific empirical variables to consider when motivating patients to adhere to medical regimens or when motivating target audiences to change their behaviors in health promoting or disease preventing ways. Additionally, a theoretical framework is offered as a starting point for developing culturally specific behavior change theories.

DEVELOPING MUTUAL UNDERSTANDING

Health communication in general, and intercultural health communication in particular, necessitates a return to the basics of communication. To communicate effectively, people must have agreed-upon definitions of words, codes, symbols, and gestures. Communication is difficult enough between members of the same culture with common codes and symbols, but when the cultural component is added to the process, misunderstandings and miscommunications become rife. For example, something as simple as nodding or shaking one's head—commonly agreed upon gestures in most Western cultures indicating "yes" for the former and "no" for the latter—can have different meanings for members of different cultures and result in miscommunication. For example, "an American physician may mistake the meaning of a lateral movement of the head. Instead of nodding, East Indians use head shaking to denote 'yes' or to make a positive assertion" (Ramakrishna & Weiss, 1992, p. 268). Similarly, when people hold different definitions for the same words, miscommunication and misunderstandings ensue. Sometimes miscommunication leads to adverse health outcomes, as was the case with a young, pregnant Hispanic women who began to lose weight after being asked by her physician to take sitz baths.

> The young woman said, "They are very tiring, but I have been doing them for 20 minutes twice a day." I ask her to tell me what she was doing because I wonder how a bath could be so tiring. Very seriously, she explains, she would fill the bathtub with water and get in and sit down. Then she would stand up, sit down, stand up, sit down, stand up, sit down—for 20 minutes at a time. No wonder she was tired! (Haffner, 1992, p. 258)

This example is a case of the effect differing definitions have on the mutual understanding between healer and patient. For health professionals to effectively communicate and promote mutual understanding, they must comprehend the interpretive assumptions, or worldview, within which patients or audiences process health-related messages. This section offers a healer-patient model for effective communication, followed by an outline of the most common areas of misunderstanding and miscommunication between people of different cultures.

Worldviews

Culture is defined as

> a set of guidelines [both explicit and implicit] which individuals inherit as members of a particular society, and which tells them how to *view* the world, how to experience it *emotionally*, and how to *behave* in it in relation to other people, to supernatural forces or gods, and to the natural environment. (Helman, 1990, pp. 2-3)

At its most basic level, culture shapes the interpretation and transmission of verbal and nonverbal messages. Therefore health care and public health officials must learn how members of other cultures define verbal and nonverbal messages if they are to communicate effectively with them. Culture is the lens through which we view the world. Each person has his or her own unique worldview developed from his or her culturally based experiences.

Figure 9.1 illustrates a healer-patient or practitioner-audience intercultural communication model. According to this model, the practitioner and the patient are separately entrenched in their own worlds. This is diagrammed by the two sets of concentric squares, each set representing the practitioner's and patient's separate worldviews. The most inner square (square 1) represents personal characteristics such as personality, physical characteristics (e.g., hair color, body build, attractiveness), age, sex, race, personal experiences, and genetic background (e.g., predisposition to disease). This square symbolizes all of those factors that occur within the person's mind or constitute the self. Square 2 represents the social characteristics of the person. This square includes all of the above personal characteristics but is expanded to include the patient's interpersonal relationships with others, such as family, peers, reference groups, and coworkers. Square 3 represents environmental characteristics, which comprise both the social landscape (square 2) and personal factors (square 1) as well as specific environmental characteristics including geographic considerations, time and historical elements, the weather, structural elements of society and where that person fits into the structure (e.g., socioeconomic status, chances for upward mobility), and economic conditions. Environmental characteristics are those factors that are beyond a person's immediate control.

Thus both a patient and a practitioner encounter health and disease with certain personal, social, and environmental characteristics in place. These worldviews have a profound and pervasive influence on their interpretation and transmission of health-/disease-related messages. "No matter how acculturated a person appears, at times of great stress, such as illness or death, early-learned ideas resurface and structure responses" (Barker, 1992, p. 251). The more similar participants are in an interaction, the more effective the communication between them. For instance, if there is low cultural distance between patient and healer, then the communication path is likely to be straight and unfettered, leading to high mutual understanding (Figure 9.1). Conversely, if there is high cultural distance between the interactants, then the communication path is likely to be difficult, full of obstacles leading to a twisted and crooked path resulting in low mutual understanding. Communication researchers have found:

> Other things being equal, the higher the degree of similarity of perception that exists among a number of individuals, the easier communication among

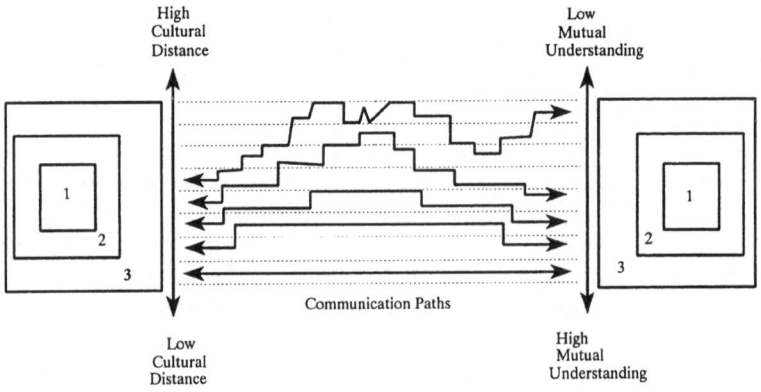

Figure 9.1: A Healer-Patient (or Practitioner-Audience) Intercultural Health Communication Model

them is likely to be, and the more communication among them is likely to occur. Conversely, where there is little or no communication among individuals there tends to be a decrease in similarity of perception, which in turn tends to make further communication more difficult. (Singer, 1987, p. 61)

Thus the closer the patient and practitioner's cultural background, the better the chances for effective communication and, hence, mutual understanding. Conversely, large differences in cultural backgrounds lay the foundation for miscommunication and misunderstanding. Empirically, Bochner (1983) found that the cultural distance between doctors and patients affected the quantity and quality of information exchanged. Doctors appeared to be more comfortable and willing to exchange information with patients with a high socioeconomic status. These patients were presumably closer socioculturally to the doctors than those patients with low socioeconomic statuses. "In general, those patients having a greater cultural affinity with their doctors, tended to be less confused about their roles than those more distant from the ethos of the medical profession and its middle-class assumptions" (Bochner, 1983, p. 137). Public health practitioners face the same problems that physicians do. They must understand why people are engaging in risky behaviors, understand the cultural milieu in which any health-risk behaviors are occurring, and develop effective public health messages that audiences can easily understand and apply to themselves.

If worldviews are similar, then when communications about health take place, each party is likely to have similar definitions for verbal and nonverbal messages. However, if worldviews differ, then misunderstandings can occur due to different definitions for the same message. In Figure 9.1, people with dissimilar worldviews tend to have different definitions for the same nonverbal and verbal messages. In this case, miscommunication leads to misunderstanding, which can lead to adverse health outcomes. In contrast, people with similar worldviews tend to have the same definitions for the same nonverbal and verbal messages. It is the practitioner's burden of proof to learn about the patient or audience's worldview and frame health- and disease-related messages within that person's worldview. In other words, the onus is on the health practitioner to understand the patient's view and develop messages that the patient or audience can understand.

There appear to be at least 11 distinct but interrelated categories where miscommunication can occur regarding health-related messages due to differences in definitions of verbal and nonverbal messages (Barker, 1992; Clark, 1983). Following is a brief description of each category.

Ethnomedical systems. An important part of one's worldview is one's medical belief system, or ethnomedical system. *Ethnomedical system* is defined as "the culturally unique beliefs and knowledge about health and disease held by the culture's members" (Witte, 1991). There are three main types of ethnomedical systems: personalistic, naturalistic, and Western (scientific; Foster & Anderson, 1978). Non-Western medical systems tend to be personalistic and/or naturalistic and focus on the "whole" person. Western medical systems tend to focus on the physiological aspects of health and disease.

In the personalistic medical system, people view supernatural beings (deities), nonhumans (ghosts, ancestors, evil spirits), or certain people (sorcerers) as causing disease. This type of medical system is usually found among indigenous tribal peoples around the world. When a person becomes sick, he or she is believed to be the victim of some alien or supernatural power. To restore health, shamans or sorcerers chant or perform ritual dances and negotiate with demons or gods to leave the sick person. For example, the Mien people of Laos are healed through "sipmmien" ceremonies, in which "ancestor spirits are called to protect living family members or evil spirits are called to appease them" (Gilman, Justice, Saepharn, & Charles, 1992, p. 313).

In the naturalistic medical system, illness is explained in impersonal, systemic terms. Health prevails when there is equilibrium in the body. Hot-cold food systems, a balance between yin and yang, and herbal practices all are characteristic of naturalistic medical systems. For example, an elderly East Indian with a naturalistic medical belief system "was convinced his relative's mental illness was due to excess heat resulting from an overconsumption of garlic" (Ramakrishna & Weiss,

1992, p. 268). Examples of naturalistic medical systems include humoral pathology, traditional Chinese medicine, Hispanic folk medicine, Ayurvedic medicine (India), and Anani medicine (Arabia). For instance, in the Hispanic folk medical system, a lack of balance leading to illness can be caused by the improper mixing of foods (e.g., too many hot or too many cold foods) or by experiencing extreme emotions (e.g., intense anger or jealousy).

Finally, in the Western medical system, objective, physical, chemical data are emphasized (e.g., laboratory tests, X rays). The body is viewed analytically and physiological explanations are sought for illnesses. The mind and body are separated and traditionally only the body is treated. For example, in Western medicine, if children have repeat bouts of tonsillitis, their bodies are "fixed" by removing the tonsils. Little attention is given to any causal factors that may have led to tonsillitis. Psychosocial factors such as stress are only beginning to receive attention in Western medicine. Previously, Western medicine had been criticized for its overemphasis on "objective" data and its neglect of the mind-body connection.

Many cultures combine medical belief systems. For example, Afghans combine personalistic and naturalistic medical beliefs.

Traditional Afghan medical beliefs emphasize the humoral concepts of Arabic-Persian medicine. . . . "hot" and "cold" are qualities of food, drink, and medicinal herbs, of individual human nature—related to age, sex, and temperament—and of illnesses. Illness results from humoral imbalance and is classified as either hot or cold. Hot illnesses, such as fever or measles, are treated with a diet emphasizing cold foods and medicines; cold illnesses, which include arthritis, malaria, and chickenpox, are treated with hot foods and medicines. (Lipson & Omidian, 1992, p. 273)

These naturalistic beliefs are accompanied by personalistic beliefs. For instance,

The evil eye, *nazar*, is the belief that someone can cause illness or harm by looking at another person. . . . *Nazar* can be unintentionally caused by expressing excessive admiration or love for another without remembering to say a preventive phase, such as "In the name of God." . . . Susceptible people, such as children, beautiful women, or fortunate people, can be protected through charms or amulets, such as blue stones or beads. (Lipson & Omidian, 1992, p. 274)

Mind-body connection. The mind-body connection is a fundamental component of most non-Western medical systems as well as most naturalistic and personalistic medical systems. Characteristic of this approach is Ayurvedic medicine, practiced primarily in India. In Ayurvedic medicine, "mind, body, and soul are interconnected components of a system in which malfunctioning in one component . . . disturbs the harmony of the whole system. This disequilibrium causes sickness" (Ramakrishna & Weiss, 1992, p. 267). Not only are the mind and body connected but the mind, body, and universe are seen as one interrelated system. Specifically:

> The term "ayurveda" indicates a positive attitude toward health. An interrelationship between the universe and the body is a fundamental principle of Ayurveda. The universe contains five elements (*pancabhuta*): water, fire, earth, wind, and ether. Three of these universal elements, *tridosa*, have analogues in the body as humors: fire (as bile), water (as phlegm), and wind (as wind). When a delicate balance of these humors is achieved, a person is healthy, whereas a disturbance of this homeostatic condition causes illness. (Ramakrishna & Weiss, 1992, pp. 266-267)

This mind-body-universe connection is also seen in various permutations in Native American, African, and Chinese medical systems. For example, Southeast Asians do not differentiate between physiological, psychological, or supernatural causes of disease (Gold, 1992, p. 292). Similarly, "there has never been a split between psyche and soma in Japanese thinking and both physicians and patients readily attribute nonspecific somatic complaints, symptoms of depression and other 'psychosomatic' symptoms to 'stress' " (Lock, 1983, p. 28).

Role of religion. In most non-Western cultures, religious beliefs cannot be separated from health beliefs and medical practices. For example, the healing ceremonies of the Mien in Laos "are an essential part of Mien traditional religion" (Gilman et al., 1992, p. 313). Navajos categorize illness by its supernatural cause rather than by its signs and symptoms. Certain illnesses are believed to be caused by witchcraft, others by a "breach of tabu," and all require different religious cures or healing rituals. Similarly, in Afghan culture, "illness may be interpreted as the will of God" and "is thought to result from not adhering to the principles of Islam" (Lipson & Omidian, 1992, p. 273). Prayer is used in treatment or healing rituals.

Individualism-collectivism. For many non-Westerners, the family or collective's needs are placed above individual needs (Hui & Triandis, 1986; Triandis, Brislin, & Hui, 1988). This collectivist orientation contrasts sharply with an individualist orientation in which each person watches out for him- or herself and is expected to have full autonomy with regard to taking care of his or her health needs. For example, in

Vietnamese families, "individualism is discouraged, whereas collective obligations and decision making are emphasized" (Gold, 1992, p. 290). Health-related decisions are made differently for members of collectivist cultures as compared with members of individualist cultures.

Role of the family. Related to individualist or collectivist orientations is the role of the family in health and disease practices. In many cultures, the position and role the family plays in an individual's life influences health beliefs and practices to the degree that physicians must broaden their conceptions from dyadic "physician-patient" interactions to "physician-patient-family" interactions. For example, in most non-Western cultures, the family expects to receive diagnoses and make treatment-related decisions, not the individual. In Japanese culture, "it is customary for a physician to tell the family and not the patient about a poor prognosis" (Lock, 1983, p. 28). Similarly, a Middle Eastern "patient's family acts as clearinghouse for information and often intervenes forcibly to block communication about a grave illness" (Lipson & Meleis, 1983, p. 55). Additionally, "the role of the family is to insist that a patient receive the best care possible from health personnel. Demanding behavior is prescribed by the culture and shows that the family cares about the patient" (Lipson & Meleis, 1983, p. 54). For the majority of non-Western cultures, a collectivist orientation means that the family makes treatment and health-related decisions, not the patient.

Gender. Women hold subordinate roles in many non-Western cultures. For example, in China, "the accepted formula is of 'thrice obeying' (*sam sing*), that as a young girl she must answer to her father, as a wife she answers to her husband, and as a mother she answers to her son" (Mo, 1992, p. 261). Similarly, "in rural Hispanic culture, the hierarchy is strict, with authority running from older to younger and from male to female" (Haffner, 1992, p. 257). In patriarchal cultures, males expect to receive diagnoses and make treatment decisions regarding any female relatives. More specifically, "among certain cultures, married females have no right to make decisions for themselves, but must defer to their husbands. Similarly, adult unmarried women must defer to their parents or older brothers for decisions regarding their care and treatment" (Rasinski, 1993, p. 170).

Communication patterns. Language barriers, translation and translator problems, misinterpretation of nonverbal messages, and normative politeness behaviors are significant areas of miscommunication leading to misunderstanding in the health context. First, language barriers are an obvious hindrance to effective communication and understanding. For those who speak the health professional's language as a second language, misunderstandings may occur when the patient takes the health professional's words literally (indicating different definitions for the same words). For example:

> A woman had previously signed a consent for an elective tubal ligation after her delivery and is scheduled to have the procedure in half an hour . . . it is quickly obvious that the patient has not fully understood that the sterilization is essentially permanent. A tubal ligation has been described to her as having her tubes "tied." She has consented, but with the idea that she can later change her mind—thinking the procedure is easily reversible. If her tubes can be "tied," she reasons, they can be "untied." She does not fully understand the answers in English but was having doubts. After I interpret the answers to her questions, she declines the procedure. (Haffner, 1992, p. 258)

Alternatively, it is sometimes difficult for members of diverse cultures to articulate their symptoms and feelings in the nonnative language. For example,

> often Middle Easterners express vague symptoms, giving generalized and global descriptions of their health status. Vague physical symptoms substitute for anxiety or depression because Middle Easterners lack concepts that distinguish mental states from physical states, and their experience does not permit them to carefully describe signs and symptoms as they are associated with different parts of the body. (Lipson & Meleis, 1983, p. 54)

Second, for those who do not speak the health professional's language, the use of translators may occasionally increase misunderstanding through miscommunication. Inaccurate transmission of messages through translators may occur for several reasons. First, translators may edit messages and only report what the translator thinks is medically important, when, in fact, health professionals gather clues about disease causation from all of the messages a patient expresses. Many physicians have reported the experience of "asking a patient whose language you do not speak, 'How do you feel?' The translator then spends five to ten minutes in discussion with the patient and comes back and says, 'Fine' " (Fitzgerald, 1988, p. 65). Second, translators may edit out important medical information. For example, translators "are sometimes reluctant to translate what they think is ignorance or superstition on the part of the patient" (Fitzgerald, 1988, p. 65). Third, translators with only technical proficiency in a language may not accurately interpret a patient's message. Cultural interpreters (i.e., translators familiar with the meanings of verbal and nonverbal messages within a certain culture) are needed because literal translations often do not convey the true meaning of a communicator's message (Haffner, 1992). Fourth, the common practice of using children as translators for their parents is fraught with problems. Children may be unable or unwilling to convey bad news to their parents. Conversely, parents may be reluctant to express embarrassing symptoms—especially those having to do with the reproductive or waste system—to their children. Haffner (1992) notes "the modesty of many Latino women can be a serious problem. . . . Latino women are often reluctant to reveal personal or private problems if their children are used to interpret" (p. 256). One 50-year-old female Mexican woman whose 35-year-old son typically interpreted for her suffered a great deal before the physician actually discovered what was the matter with her. A cultural interpreter explains what happened:

> This time I am called because the son has to leave to go to work. Before going into the room, the physician expresses to me his concern about whether the health problems claimed by this woman are real or imagined. She has been in the clinic three times before, each time with different vague and diffuse complaints, none of which make medical sense. As we learn, the poor woman has a fistula in her rectum. In her previous visits, she could not bring herself to reveal her symptoms in the presence of, and therefore to, her son as he interprets for her. She tells me that she has been so embarrassed about her condition that she has invented other symptoms to justify her visits to the physician. (Haffner, 1992, p. 256)

Because strict gender, age, and role divisions exist in many cultures, children should not be expected to translate for their parents. Young children may be especially traumatized by being forced to interpret for a health professional—especially when bad news is expected to be conveyed (Haffner, 1992). Again, a cultural interpreter familiar with the meanings of verbal and nonverbal messages for a particular culture would be the ideal option.

Third, nonverbal messages are among the most difficult to interpret because of diverse meanings for the same message across cultures. For example, the use of space differs greatly across cultures with Middle Easterners preferring close conversational distances (2 feet) and Americans preferring moderate-to-far distances (about 5 feet; Lipson & Meleis, 1983, p. 52). Middle Easterners may perceive American health professionals as uncaring and cold while Americans may perceive Middle Easterners as being pushy and aggressive. The use of touch is viewed as warm and friendly in some cultures, and as intrusive and inappropriate in others. Similarly, smiling is viewed positively by some and negatively by others. For example, "East Indian patients may not know how to respond to the American physician's social smiles. In India, smiles are only exchanged between social equals and in informal situations" (Ramakrishna & Weiss, 1992, p. 268). Time is viewed differently by members of different cultures. For example, time boundaries are flexible in Middle Eastern culture. "A patient might be late for an appointment, or not come at all, because another matter immediately at hand was seen as more important than the previously scheduled appointment" (Lipson & Meleis, 1983, p. 52). Nonverbal message meanings are among the most difficult to interpret. Competent cultural translators who can accurately interpret nonverbal messages are invaluable in a health care setting.

Fourth, differences in communication styles between healers and patients, especially in terms of politeness behavior, also may lead to miscommunication and misunderstandings. In many cultures, authority figures cannot be disagreed with, challenged, or contradicted. Noncompliance with medical regimens may occur unintentionally or intentionally due to these politeness norms. Noncompliance occurs unintentionally when patients do not understand health professional's instructions but fail to express this because it would be impolite to do so. For example, "Latinos feel they should agree with physicians out of politeness and respect, even when they really disagree or do not understand the issues involved. They expect physicians to make the decisions for them and do not understand why they are asked to make choices. They are used to, and seem to prefer, deferring to experts" (Haffner, 1992, p. 257). Noncompliance occurs intentionally when patients understand what health professionals want them to do, but do not want to follow prescribed regimens. They agree to comply because of politeness norms but in actuality have no intention of complying. For example, for Mexican Americans, "directly contradicting a physician is considered rude or disrespectful. Thus, a physician may think that a patient and the patient's family are in agreement with the plan of action when in fact they are strongly opposed to it" (Klessig, 1992, p. 321). Similarly, "Middle Easterners appear to comply with health regimens and professional advice, but in fact may ignore advice . . . [A]greeing to heed personally unacceptable advice can be a face-saving mechanism that hides a sense of powerlessness in making the suggested changes" (Lipson & Meleis, 1983, p. 55). Health professionals should be especially alert to politeness norms so as to assess true understanding and/or agreement with prescribed medical practices.

In sum, miscommunication leading to misunderstanding occurs most often due to language barriers or misinterpretation of verbal and/or nonverbal messages. Using cultural translators who are familiar with the nuances of a culture's verbal and nonverbal messages may improve the communication process. In addition, awareness of appropriate nonverbal behaviors and knowledge of politeness norms may help health professionals to assess the real meanings behind expressed messages.

Practitioner-patient relationship expectations. An additional factor that can influence whether or not understanding is achieved in health contexts is the expectations patients have of physicians. Many patients come into health encounters with culturally prescribed conceptions and expectations of a physician's behavior and/or the medical encounter. Unfortunately, there is often great within-group diversity, which makes it difficult for health professionals to know the best communication strategies even for members of the same culture. For example, while some East Indians prefer that physicians conduct a complete physical examination and acquire a thorough medical history from the patient, others may resent the in-depth questions that are usually required to ascertain a thorough medical history. High-status patients often expect preferential treatment, including "no waiting, detailed explanations, and convenient appointments" while low-status patients will not enter an encounter with similar expectations (Ramakrishna & Weiss, 1992, p. 265).

Two key issues impede the communication process with respect to individuals' expectations of physician behavior. First, many non-Westerners expect physicians to have a personal relationship with them and prefer indirect messages and questions. For example, members of many cultures are reluctant to divulge personal information to strangers or acquaintances (Lipson & Meleis, 1983). "Middle Easterners may be offended by the American proclivity to immediately talk about the business at hand instead of taking the time to establish a relationship" (Lipson & Meleis, 1983, p. 52). For these people, it is important to establish rapport or a friendship before moving on to health-related business. Additionally, members of many cultures are offended by direct and explicit messages and prefer indirect and implicit messages. For example,

> Afghans, like Middle Eastern immigrants, have a cultural communication style that is often misinterpreted by American physicians as being devious or insincere. . . . Afghans avoid saying "no" directly and do not like to hear "no" being said to them. Histories are difficult to take "efficiently" from Afghans, who communicate by means of stories. (Lipson & Omidian, 1992, p. 274)

Second, many patients expect physicians either to prescribe oral medication or, preferably, to give injections, during a medical encounter. For example, "a visit for a checkup without medication does not fit

Chinese patients' expectations. This feeling of incompleteness may progress into a lack of confidence in the physician" (Mo, 1992, p. 262). Similarly, "Middle Eastern patients may complain that 'the doctor didn't do anything,' if they have not received a prescription. Injections are preferred over medicines in liquid and tablet form, colored pills are preferred over uncolored and larger [pills] over smaller ones" (Lipson & Meleis, 1983, p. 53). For East Indians, "medication potency may be judged by its reputation and appearance. Capsules are thought to be stronger than tablets. . . . [I]t is widely believed that most illnesses cannot be cured without resorting to injections" (Ramakrishna & Weiss, 1992, p. 269). Discovering patient expectations with regard to a medical encounter may go a long way toward improving patient satisfaction.

Etiology/treatment relation. Individuals from different cultures have different beliefs about what causes disease (Burgoon & Hall, 1994). Across all cultures, people treat the *perceived* cause of their illness— which may be different than the true *cause* of their illness. Thus all treatments are logically related to their perceived causes. If individuals believe bacteria is causing them illness, then they will treat the bacteria (perceived cause) with antibiotics. Likewise, if individuals believe that an evil spirit is invading their body and causing them to feel ill, they will ask a sorcerer to exorcise it. When health professionals treat patients, it is important for the professionals to ascertain what the patients think caused their ill health. Patients may not adhere to the physician's recommended course of action if they do not believe it addresses the (perceived) cause of the illness. For example, "medicines, whether over-the-counter or prescription, are considered effective only if they 'fit' the illness for which they are intended. . . . If a prescription drug is not congruent with popular categories this will directly affect how, or whether, it is used" (Mitchell, 1983, p. 40).

Medical pluralism. An outcome of perceiving various disease etiologies (i.e., supernatural versus natural) within a culture is that medical pluralism, the use of multiple cures or treatments, often exists across cultures. This can have important implications for treatments, such as when an herbal folk treatment may counteract or enhance the effect of Western allopathic medicine. It is important to note that "herbal medications are not necessarily ineffective or 'harmless.' The potential for overdose, improper use, and drug interaction is real" (Barker, 1992, p. 251).

Medical pluralism is common across most cultures today. For example, North Americans typically use a medical doctor, a chiropractor, and perhaps have their priest pray for them when treating a back problem. In Malaysian culture, because illness stems from multiple causes, multiple combinations of treatments such as Western allopathic medication, massage, spells, and prayers are used. For many East Indians who believe in hot and cold humoral balances, doctors will be asked whether medicine should be taken with hot or cold water, and if certain foods should be included or removed from diets. Navajos often combine both Western and ceremonial medicine, and Ethiopians use traditional and Western medicine simultaneously. Practitioners should take care to discover other types of remedies being used and who else the patient has seen. In some cultures, traditional and modern healers have begun to work together to treat patients in the most effective manner possible (e.g., Africa).

Within-group diversity. Adding to the complexity of achieving a multicultural health orientation is the within-group diversity existing in many cultures. Grouping all Chinese into one category or all Afghan refugees into another will not provide effective diagnosis or treatment of health problems. Within any culture, many factions exist in which language and religions vary, as well as personal health beliefs and practices. For example, the "Vietnamese refugee population is made up of three distinct subgroups—the first-wave elite, the boat people, and the ethnic Chinese. These three groups . . . retain many social and cultural differences and have developed fairly disparate patterns of adaptation to the United States" (Gold, 1992, p. 290). Similarly, Ramakrishna and Weiss (1992) note that "diversity is the rule" in India, where "there are 16 recognized languages" (p. 265). Care must be taken to avoid lumping all members of one ethnic group into a single category because they may hold different health and disease beliefs.

Summary

Before physicians can effectively treat patients, they must understand what is wrong—both subjectively and objectively. Similarly, before public health practitioners can promote health and prevent disease, they must first understand what is impeding health and what is leading to disease. Mutual understanding is an obvious but often neglected concept. When a message is interpreted based on one's own worldview, the interpretation may not be in the manner intended by the communicator. Misunderstanding occurs because we misinterpret what the communicator is trying to express. Different meanings for the same codes, words, and gestures make communication a difficult task for members of different cultures.

One may think, given the vast socio-cultural-linguistic differences between health practitioners and patients, that effective communication is doomed. However, with ethnic and cultural sensitivity, and training and awareness on the health professional's part, effective health communication and mutual understanding can occur. To communicate effectively with people from diverse cultures, health professionals must enact a three-step process. First, they must be committed to discovering the patient's or public's (a) perception of the cause of the health problem (e.g., "What do you think causes AIDS?" "Why do you think you have an upset stomach?"), (b) perception of the "best" treatment for that health problem, and (c) appropriate standards of etiquette—particularly in terms of decision-making structure and nonverbal messages. Table 9.1 provides a basic list of normative beliefs for members of diverse cultures. Of course, there is great within-culture diversity, so care should be taken not to assume that everyone who falls within a certain cultural group has the beliefs outlined in Table 9.1. Additionally, health professionals must think of diverse strategies for discovering patients' or the public's perception of disease causation and treatment because asking the patients would be frowned upon in some cultures—the physician should "know" what caused the health problem and should not have to ask the patient. In a public health environment, focus groups can be used to ascertain salient beliefs about disease causation, preferred treatments, and preferred message strategies (e.g., preferred source, channel, type of message). In a clinical setting, a cultural interpreter who is familiar with the subtleties of both verbal and nonverbal messages is invaluable. Asking patients to repeat back treatment directions or procedures enables practitioners to detect any misunderstandings and clarify confusing statements.

MOTIVATING ADHERENCE
TO HEALTH-RELATED MESSAGES

Promoting mutual understanding between health professionals and patients or the public is a necessary first step in the ultimate goal of promoting health. Motivating people to adhere to health promotion and disease prevention messages is an equally important goal for health communicators. Interpersonally, physicians try to motivate patients to comply with treatment regimens. At the public health level, practitioners try to motivate individuals to avoid risky behaviors. Motivation is the second key construct in intercultural health communication.

Much research has gone into identifying factors that motivate people to protect themselves against health risks. However, most of this research has been conducted in Western industrial nations (Graeff et al., 1993, is a notable exception). Health professionals must be careful not

TABLE 9.1 Cultural Beliefs About Health, Disease, and Healers

Afghan Refugees
Practice indirect communication, avoid saying "no" directly, communicate by stories, ritual courtesy between people of differing status, will shop around for doctors, expect injections or pills at medical visits, may not admit to traditional beliefs and practices.

African Americans
Classify illness according to "natural" and "unnatural." Combine practical, magical, and religious beliefs. Illness may be viewed as "an attack" on the body and may involve beliefs relating to blood and flow (i.e., blood/flow is too thick, too thin, too much, too little). May seek traditional healers instead of, or in addition to, biomedical help.

Chinese
May be reluctant to seek physician care. Expect to receive medication at visit and may lack confidence in physician who does not dispense medication. Individual concerns are subordinate to what is best for the whole community or family. Religion is central to beliefs.

East Indians
Reluctant to disagree or contradict those with high status. May say "yes" even when they do not understand. Multidrug therapy is common and they like colored medication. Injections are popular. The "hand quality" of the physician is important and they may prefer to have their medication handed to them by the physician. Family is involved in patient care. Women and children typically will not visit a physician unaccompanied by a chaperon who will be present during the exam. Reluctant to have blood drawn or to donate blood. Medical pluralism exists, but they may be somewhat resistant to use of Western medicine.

Ethiopians
Traditional medical beliefs consist of "indigenous magicoreligious practices and beliefs" (Beyene, 1992, p. 330). May use both traditional cures and Western biomedicine. Family, friends, and religion are important. Many times physicians are expected to communicate through family members rather than directly with the patient. Concern is with medical diagnosis rather than prognosis. Trust is a major factor in physician-patient relationships. May evaluate a physician in terms of his or her warmth and manners. Most want to be reassured by the physician that they will make it through their medical crisis.

Filipinos
Very receptive to modern medicine, yet still retain indigenous disease beliefs. Place a high value on proper social conduct, avoiding unpleasantries, confrontations, and discourtesies. Practice proper respect for authorities. Often delay seeking medical attention. Prefer Filipino practitioners or folk practitioners and value personalism. May be receiving multiple treatments and take multiple medications (i.e., herbs and medicinal drugs) at once. Role of family is ultimately important, thus it may help to have a family member or close friend present during the encounter. Often are reserved and overly compliant. Value harmony. Group is more important than the individual.

(continued)

TABLE 9.1 Continued

Gypsies

Illness is a social experience, with family and friends supporting the sick person. They do not like to be alone. May be expected to consult with older relatives in treatment decisions. Traveling, good luck, cleanliness, and being overweight are all linked with good health. Avoid nongypsies and hospitals but will seek out the "best" medical care. Will try multiple cures for an illness, including nongypsy practitioners, gypsy remedies, and faith healers. Illness can be caused by spirits or the devil.

Hispanics

May have to seek eldest member of family for treatment consent. Expect authoritarianism, formal friendliness, and respect. Neglecting to shake hands is an insult. May be very respectful, nodding and saying "yes" even if they don't agree, and will avoid directly contradicting physician.

Jamaicans

Symptoms are believed to be identical to disease, therefore if there are no symptoms, no disease exists. Similarly, treatments are evaluated in terms of how quickly the symptoms disappear. There are specific beliefs about what causes illness (Hippocratic humoral concepts and germ theory), and a treatment must "fit" the illness for it to be used by the patient or considered effective. Self-medication is common.

Japanese

Readily report large amounts of information concerning their problems during encounters. Patient and family are often responsible for healing. Poor prognosis should be communicated to family, not patient. Often seek medication for a wide array of daily problems and may expect it to be dispensed in large quantities. Social groups take precedence over individual needs. Value harmony.

Koreans

Clients often visit clinics in groups of family or friends. Expect a relationship of trust (mutual harmony or unity) between patient and practitioner. May be dissatisfied with diagnoses that are not the result of laboratory tests, impressed by diagnostic machinery.

Malaysians

Categorize illnesses according to "usual" and "unusual." Will seek different healers for different illnesses. Relationship with healer must be harmonious otherwise treatment will not be effective. Will seek other healers/practitioners if treatments do not work or if relationship is not harmonious.

Mien

Family and religion are central to health beliefs. Expect medication, and injections are extremely popular, thus multidrug therapy is common. Traditional healing is common, and many therapies are related to diet. Believe that you must understand illness causation before you can effectively treat it.

(continued)

TABLE 9.1 Continued

Navajos
Silence is highly valued, signals respect and attentiveness. Traditional Navajos prefer to be addressed by kinship titles (mother, father) rather than names. Value hand shaking. May be offended by being rushed, interrupted, or practitioners not listening. Have a tendency not to ask questions or confront others. Expect to take time in their communication and establish rapport, avoid directness. Should avoid speaking of death.

Russian Émigrés
Have trouble understanding the concept of "preventive medicine" because in Russia "you don't think about your health until after you are ill" (Brod & Heurtin-Roberts, 1992, p. 334). Possess grand expectations for "American" medicine, to the extent that miracles can occur. Many do not comprehend biological causes of illness because they perceive "macrosocial" causes of illness, such as "war, immigration, political difficulties, and a poor medical system" (Brod & Heurtin-Roberts, 1992, p. 334). Appreciate physician's personal attention and efforts to explain and answer questions.

Southeast Asians
To some, the head is sacred and should not be touched. Similarly, because the feet are the lowliest part of the body, they should not be pointed at the patient because this is seen as an insult. Direct gaze between people of different status is avoided. Many adhere to politeness rules and will agree whether or not they understand, and avoid the use of "no." May delay seeking medical help and expect authoritarianism among physicians.

Vietnamese
Religion is central to health beliefs. Believe in both "good" and "evil" spirits. Obligation to family takes priority over self. Place great importance on harmony and maintaining self-control. May appear calm on the outside when actually are very upset. Practice ritual politeness, courtesy, and respect, especially to higher status individuals. Touching another's head and pointing feet toward another should be avoided; women may not shake hands but shaking hands is typically acceptable among men; direct eye gaze is avoided because it signals disrespect. Prefer indirect communication. Accept multiple causes of illness and may combine traditional and Western medicine. May delay seeking medical attention because of value placed upon stoicism and endurance. May be resistant to surgery, and fear loss of blood.

SOURCES: Anderson (1983); Beyene (1992); Bowser (1992); Brod and Heurtin-Roberts (1992); Calhoun (1986); Chin (1992); Fitzgerald (1988); Gates-Williams, Jackson, Jenkins-Monroe, and Williams (1992); Gilman et al. (1992); Gold (1992); Klessig (1992); Laderman (1991); Levy, Neutra, and Parker (1987); Lin (1983); Lipson and Omidian (1992); Lock (1983); Mitchell (1983); Mo (1992); Muecke (1983); Muller and Desmond (1992); Pang (1989); Ramakrishna and Weiss (1992); Snow (1983); Stern (1986); Stern, Tilden, and Maxwell (1986); Stroup (1993); Sutherland (1992).

to assume that the motivation for people in Western cultures is also the motivation for people in other cultures. Culture-specific theoretical work is desperately needed. While it appears there are certain "universal variables" that operate consistently across cultures, some idiosyncratic variables unique to each culture are also likely to operate. The following pages review five major health decision-making approaches. Then, based on the review of these approaches, we identify three variables and one issue believed to be universal across cultures given their widespread empirical and theoretical support in studies conducted over the decades. Next, we propose two non-Western variables that appear to be important influences on health behaviors. Finally, we propose a theoretical framework for motivating healthy behaviors as an initial starting point for developing culturally based theories.

Dominant Health Communication Theoretical Approaches

Five major approaches dominate much of the health communication research conducted today. The first three focus on the cognitive processes leading to healthy behaviors. The fourth uses a behavioral approach while the fifth identifies separate stages of audience readiness for health communications. Each is described briefly below.

The Health Belief Model. According to the Health Belief Model (HBM), preventive health behaviors (e.g., getting immunizations, eating healthily, wearing seat belts) are influenced by five factors:

a. perceived barriers to performing the recommended response (e.g., beliefs about psychological, physical, or financial "costs");
b. perceived benefits of performing the recommended response (e.g., beliefs about whether the recommended response will work and/or lead to such rewards as risk reduction, injury prevention, anxiety reduction);
c. perceived susceptibility (e.g., subjective probability of experiencing a hazard);
d. perceived severity (e.g., beliefs about the seriousness of the hazard); and
e. cues to action (e.g., advertisements).

Perceived susceptibility and perceived severity work together to motivate action regarding a health threat, perceived benefits provide direction regarding which path of action is best to take, and perceived barriers inhibit action (Rosenstock, 1974). Cues to action stimulate action either internally, as when a lump is discovered in a breast and a patient seeks medical care, or externally, as when mass media messages highlight the risks of breast cancer and the benefit of screening mammograms. The HBM has received much empirical support over a variety of health topics (Janz & Becker, 1984).

Social cognitive theory. Albert Bandura's Social Cognitive Theory (sometimes called Social Learning Theory) focuses on the role of perceived self-efficacy in health behaviors. *Self-efficacy* is defined as "people's beliefs that they can exert control over their motivation and behavior and over their social environment" (Bandura, 1989, p. 128). In other words, perceived self-efficacy is one's beliefs about one's ability to perform a certain action (one's perceived self-effectiveness). Self-efficacy is the driving force behind human behavior, according to Bandura (1977). Outcome expectations is another important construct in Bandura's theory. *Outcome expectations* refers to an individual's belief that a certain behavior will lead to a certain outcome (e.g., "If I use a condom I won't get infected with HIV"). Outcome expectations are what one thinks will happen if one takes a certain action, while efficacy expectations are one's beliefs about whether one is able to perform a certain action. According to Bandura (1977), only when efficacy expectations are high will people protect themselves against health risks.

Fear appeal theory: The Extended Parallel Process Model. Fear appeal research tries to explain the decision processes individuals go through when faced with a health threat. A recently developed fear appeal theory that integrates many previous theoretical and empirical perspectives, and can trace its lineage back to the Health Belief Model, is called the Extended Parallel Process Model (Janis, 1967; Leventhal, 1970; Rogers, 1975, 1983; Witte, 1992a). Fear appeals, commonly known as "scare tactics," are common persuasive strategies in the health communication arena. According to the EPPM, when people are faced with a health threat, they either control the danger (i.e., the actual health threat) or control their fear about the danger (Witte, 1992a, 1992b). They weigh their risk of actually experiencing the health threat (e.g., getting cancer) against actions they can take that would minimize or avert the health threat (e.g., "Does sunscreen really work?" "Can I really use it every time I'm in the sun?"). Thus the important variables in the EPPM are perceived threat, comprising perceived susceptibility to the threat (e.g., "Am I at risk for experiencing X?") and perceived severity of the threat (e.g., "Are the consequences of the threat severe?"), and perceived efficacy, comprising perceived response efficacy (e.g., "Will the recommended response avert the threat?") and perceived self-efficacy (e.g., "Am I able to perform the recommended response?"). When perceived threat and perceived efficacy are high (e.g., "I'm at risk for a terrible disease but if I do X I can protect myself against it"), people are motivated to control the danger by adhering to the message's recommendations. When perceived threat is high but perceived efficacy is low (e.g., "I'm at risk for a terrible disease and there's nothing I can do to keep myself from getting it"), people are motivated to control their fear by rejecting the recommended responses through defensive avoidance or denial of the threat.

Applied behavioral analysis. Behavioral analysis is a learning theory approach using rewards and reinforcements. It is different than the other approaches in two key ways. First, it has been used primarily in developing countries—mostly to promote child survival through the HEALTH-COM project (a multiyear, multicountry, U.S. AID-sponsored project). Second, "behavioral analysis emphasizes observable behavior-consequence relationships, whereas other theories focus more on cognitions and antecedent-behavior relationships" (Graeff et al., 1993, p. 26). According to this approach, any health communication team should consider the ABCs:

> *antecedents*—enabling knowledge and skills and physical materials necessary to perform the behavior; *behavior*—the specific sequential steps required to perform the behavior correctly; and *consequences*—both natural consequences that result when a behavior is performed and ideas for planned consequences that could be temporarily introduced. (Graeff et al., 1993, p. 40)

Theoretically, behavioral triggers (or antecedents) initiate a health promotive behavior while consequents strengthen, stop, or weaken a behavior. Target or ideal behaviors are carefully analyzed in terms of their distance from current behaviors as well as for their discrete behavioral steps (e.g., "How many discrete steps are there to hand washing after each toilet usage?").

Overall, applied behavioral analysis is a learning theory approach in which barriers are identified and removed and efficacy—particularly self-efficacy—is emphasized in skills training. This approach has received little attention in the Western world but appears very promising.

Prochaska's Stages of Change Model. Finally, though not a theoretical model per se, Prochaska's (1979) transtheoretical model offers important guidelines for any health communication professional. In his model, Prochaska (1979) identifies four separate and independent stages of health promoting/disease preventing behaviors. People in the precontemplation stage have not thought about performing or changing a target behavior. In the contemplation stage, individuals consider adopting the target behavior or making a behavioral change. Those in the action stage actually adopt the target behavior. Finally, the target behavior is continued indefinitely in the maintenance stage. Relapse to the contemplation or precontemplation stages can occur in either the action or the maintenance stage. Each stage calls for a distinct campaign strategy and style. Ideally, distinct campaigns should be developed for people in each stage. For example, a knowledge and awareness campaign would be appropriate for those audience members in the precontemplation stage. In contrast, a motivational persuasive campaign is needed for those in the contemplation stage.

Summary: Identification of universal variables. Across these health behavior change models, three key universal variables emerge as important influences on individuals' health and/or health-related behaviors: (a) Perceived threat, or the degree to which one feels susceptible to a severe threat (e.g. "I'm vulnerable to the deadly HIV"), is identified as important in the HBM and the EPPM. (b) Perceived efficacy, comprising self-efficacy (the degree to which one feels able to perform a recommended response to avert a health threat, e.g., "I am able to use condoms to prevent AIDS") and response efficacy (the degree to which one believes a recommended response effectively deters a health threat, e.g., "Using condoms prevents AIDS"), is a critical variable found in the HBM (i.e., perceived benefits is analogous to response efficacy), Social Learning Theory, the EPPM, and the Applied Behavioral Analysis approach (i.e., skills training is analogous to self-efficacy). (c) Barriers, or the perceived psychological, physical, or financial costs of performing a recommended response (e.g., "Condoms cost too much, reduce sensation, and are difficult to obtain"), are an important variable in the HBM and the Applied Behavioral Analysis approach.

These three variables appear to universally affect health behaviors, most often through (interpersonal or mass) communication, regardless of cultural background. For example, it appears that people make no effort to protect themselves against disease unless they perceive they are at risk for negative consequences. Similarly, it appears that people do not adopt healthy behaviors unless they believe them to be effective and unless they believe they are adequately able to perform them. Finally, barriers or costs to healthy actions seem to decrease the likelihood that people will adopt health promoting or disease preventing actions. These three variables appear to operate across all cultures—although certain modifying variables, discussed in the next section, may influence and interact with these variables in terms of their effect on health-related behaviors. Thus, taken together, the most motivating health communications are those that induce strong perceptions of threat and efficacy, and remove psychological and structural barriers.

Separate from the universal variables but equally important to health communication work is Prochaska's (1979) Stages of Change model. It is believed that members of diverse cultures are just as likely as members of Western cultures to fall into one of these four stages of readiness. It is critical to assess which stage one's target audience is in, with respect to an ideal health behavior, before a communication campaign is commenced. Campaign strategies should differ according to one's stage of readiness.

Culturally Specific Variables Influencing Health-Related Behaviors

Two key variables appear to modify or work with threat, efficacy, and barriers in influencing motivation for members of non-Western cultures: fatalism and family values. Additionally, the 11 cultural variables outlined in the section on understanding are also likely to affect motivation (e.g., communication patterns, mind-body link, physician expectations).

Fatalism. Fatalism may be defined as a perceived lack of control over one's environment, health, and day-to-day activities (Casey, 1994). African, Hispanic, and Asian cultures all have strong fatalistic outlooks on life. When one has a fatalistic perspective, he or she may not be concerned with health issues because "when it's my time to go, it's my time to go." For example, in many cultures, disease and health are matters controlled by God. For Mexican Americans, "health is a gift from God, and ill health, including accidents, may be due to a punishment from God or the saints. The suffering incurred is part of God's plan and should not be interfered with" (Klessig, 1992, p. 321). Similarly, for some Filipinos, "illness may be attributed to a punishment from God, and thus it would not be appropriate to interfere" (Klessig, 1992, p. 320). Likewise, many people "believe that we get pretty much what we deserve" (Anderson, 1983, p. 12).

Health promotion and disease prevention activities are seen as "planning ahead," which is a distinctly Western and not Eastern value (Lipson & Meleis, 1983, p. 55). Specifically:

Planning may be seen as defying God's will and capable of bringing on the Evil Eye or some other misfortune. Medical or any preparation for birth or death is diametrically opposed to Middle Eastern values. These events should be left in God's hands until the moment when they occur. To "interfere" is to outguess God, an act that could bring disaster to a family.... [R]esistance to birth control is related to a preference for spontaneity, trust in God's guidance and suspicion that family planning potentially challenges God's will. (Lipson & Meleis, 1983, p. 55)

Fatalism may be especially pronounced for less empowered people. For example, many women in developing countries feel powerless to enact changes in their own and their children's lives due to strong patriarchal societal norms. For example, this feeling of powerlessness or "lack of self-confidence has also been called 'silence,' extreme in self-denial and dependence on external authority for direction. ... Silence keeps women from seeking help for themselves and their children—whether it is prenatal care, education, or fair wages" (McGuire & Popkin, 1990, p. 13). In India, Griffiths (1988) "found that mothers felt powerless to undertake independent action. As a result, fathers and grandmothers of at-risk children are educated" (McGuire & Popkin, 1990, p. 14). Several programs have focused on empowerment and building self-confidence in women to diminish fatalistic attitudes toward their own and their children's health (e.g., Griffiths, 1988; McGuire & Popkin, 1990). Fatalism is an important variable to consider in health communication campaigns because people who believe they have no control over their health will have no motivation to engage in health promotion or disease prevention activities.

Family values. As noted in an earlier section, the family plays a large role in whether people practice health promotion and disease prevention activities in most non-Western cultures. Conflict with Western medical values and practices becomes particularly strong in matters of treatment decisions, informed consent, and advising the patient of bad news. For most non-Westerners, these issues are the family's concern, not the patient's. The real struggle appears to be between collectivist versus individualist orientations.

Western ethnomedical systems hold an individualist orientation and view patients as being autonomous decision makers. Patients have the moral and legal right to know everything about their health status. For example,

in the North American culture where the values of individualism, autonomy, and self-reliance are important, providing the "naked" truth about illness is seen as a way of giving patients hope. Disclosing all the facts gives patients a sense of control over their illness and allows them to help decide their fate. Furthermore, total possession of such information is a legal right. (Beyene, 1992, p. 330)

In contrast, the family holds all decision-making powers in most of the non-Western world. After family consultations, male heads of household make both treatment decisions (such as whether antibiotics will be taken or whether surgery will occur) and preventive health decisions (such as whether children will be immunized or whether birth control is allowed). Within this decision-making structure, diagnoses are expected to be communicated to the family and not to the patient. For example, "in traditional societies like Ethiopia, where the family's importance dominates over individual members, any information, including diagnostic facts, belongs to the family. The family then uses the information at its discretion for the benefit of the patient" (Beyene, 1992, p. 330). The same holds true in China, where decisions about which practitioners to see, when to go, and whether to comply or to change practitioners are typically made within the context of the family or social network. . . . The family, not the practitioner or the patient, is seen as most responsible for the sick person and decisions about treatment. (Muller & Desmond, 1992, p. 326)

In these cultures, sick people are to be protected (like children) and cannot be expected to make decisions nor should they hear bad news (Muller & Desmond, 1992). Females in particular are viewed as fragile and unable to handle bad news (Beyene, 1992). Thus the family and especially the male head of household expects to be consulted throughout the treatment process. Individual decisions made by women can be overturned if the men in the family disagree. For example, in Iran, a female "patient's autonomy may not be honored if her decision is not in agreement with her husband's or father's" (Klessig, 1992, p. 318). Even though male heads of household are expected to make final decisions, older women (such as one's mother or wife) can strongly influence their decisions (Klessig, 1992).

In a case where Western physicians tried to act in accord with their individualist values (where it is considered unethical to give medical information to somebody other than the patient), the "differing values resulted in a breakdown in communication between the house staff and family and a growing sense of mutual distrust and frustration" (Muller & Desmond, 1992, p. 325). "For the physicians, it was immoral not to deal directly with the patient when she was still able to make decisions for herself. For the [Chinese family], it was immoral not to deal with the family" (Muller & Desmond, 1992, p. 325). Overall, the importance of the family for all health-related decisions must be explicitly considered when crafting health promotion and disease prevention messages.

Summary. It is believed that fatalism and family values interact with threat, efficacy, and barriers in terms of their influence on motivation. Although the universal variables appear to operate in predictable manners across cultures, fatalism and family values may enhance or interfere with their normally predictable effects.

AN INTERCULTURAL HEALTH COMMUNICATION MODEL OF UNDERSTANDING AND MOTIVATION

When developing a health communication strategy, there are four issues to consider. First, health professionals must identify a health threat and specific recommended response to avert the threat. Second, an audience analysis must be conducted. In the audience analysis, practitioners must discern the audience's or patient's (a) perceptions of disease causation and perceived proper treatment, (b) perceived suscep-tibility to the threat and perceived severity of the threat, (c) perceived effectiveness of the recommended response and perceived ability to adequately perform the recommended response (i.e., efficacy), and (d) perceived barriers to performing the recommended response. A survey of salient beliefs should indicate whether definitions for verbal and nonverbal messages differ between the target audience and the health professional. An audience analysis will lead to better understanding of the patient's view on the practitioner's part. Similar definitions for verbal and nonverbal messages ensure better communication, which presumably leads to better health. For example, if a patient believes his or her perceived health problem is being addressed in an appropriate manner, compliance with medical regimens or recommended responses advocated by public health campaigns becomes more probable.

Third, the stage an audience is in with respect to a certain health issue should be determined. As Prochaska (1979) suggests, audiences will be in one of the precontemplation, contemplation, action, or maintenance stages. To determine which stage an audience is in, practitioners need to ascertain what current behaviors or thoughts are in relation to the health issue, and then analyze the degree to which current behaviors stray from the ideal behaviors.

Fourth, message strategies should be developed within the audience's worldview using their frame of reference—as discovered in the audi-ence analysis. To develop effective health promotion and disease pre-vention messages, the audience's salient beliefs should be analyzed according to (a) beliefs to reinforce, (b) beliefs to change, and (c) beliefs to introduce. For example, if an audience believed that AIDS was a white man's disease known as the "American Invention to Discourage Sex" (as is the case in South Africa) and that condoms effectively averted infection from a white man or woman, then the practitioner would want to (a) reinforce the belief that condoms are effective in preventing HIV transmission, (b) change the belief that AIDS is a white man's disease and not prevalent in Africa, and (c) introduce the belief that HIV can be transmitted between blacks too. Additional beliefs to introduce might include facts about the transmission of HIV.

It is easier to introduce beliefs that fit within an audience's frame of reference than it is to change their beliefs. For instance, if an audience believed that a certain disease was caused by the evil eye and was cured best by a sorcerer, practitioners would not necessarily have to convince the audience that the evil eye does not cause disease X; rather, practitioners merely have to convince audiences that there is an additional cause of the disease (i.e., there are two possible causes for the disease instead of one).

Furthermore, different message strategies are needed for the different stages of change an audience is in (Prochaska, 1979). Audiences in the precontemplation stage need knowledge and awareness campaigns. Audiences at the contemplation stage need motivational campaigns to induce behavior change. Audiences at the action and maintenance stages also need motivation campaigns as well as campaigns that focus on skills and resources. Stage-appropriate messages should be developed for maximum health communication success.

As the brief review of theories suggests, the important universal variables to consider in message construction are threat, efficacy, and barriers. These theoretical models suggest that, regardless of the communication channel or social context, health communications must first make people feel susceptible to a severe threat. Without a strong perception of threat, people are not motivated to protect themselves against diseases. Next, people must believe the recommended response is effective in averting the health threat and believe that they are able to perform the recommended response. Finally, barriers to the performance of the recommended response must be low. Thus the most effective and motivating health communications are those that induce strong perceptions of threat and efficacy, and remove psychological and structural barriers.

Figure 9.2 shows a modified version of the Extended Parallel Process Model that incorporates these universal variables as well as the cultural variables of fatalism and family values. As outlined previously, the EPPM argues that people respond to health threats in one of two ways. When people feel susceptible to a severe threat, *and* believe they are able to effectively prevent/avert it, then they are motivated to *control the danger* by accepting the message's recommendations to make behavioral or belief changes. In contrast, when people feel susceptible to a severe threat, *but* believe the recommended response does not work or that they are unable to effectively perform the response, then they are motivated to *control their fear* by defensively avoiding, denying, or reacting against the threat. In terms of perceived barriers, people would expect to engage in danger control actions when perceived barriers were low and fear control actions when perceived barriers were high. Thus, when perceived barriers get too high, people begin to perceive that they cannot perform the recommended responses to avert the health threat because the barriers are too large. The cultural variables of fatalism and family values influence how one perceives threats, efficacy, and barriers. Thus one's worldview (composed of certain fatalism and family values beliefs as well as other cultural beliefs) is the base from which one perceives threats and recommended responses. For example, if an

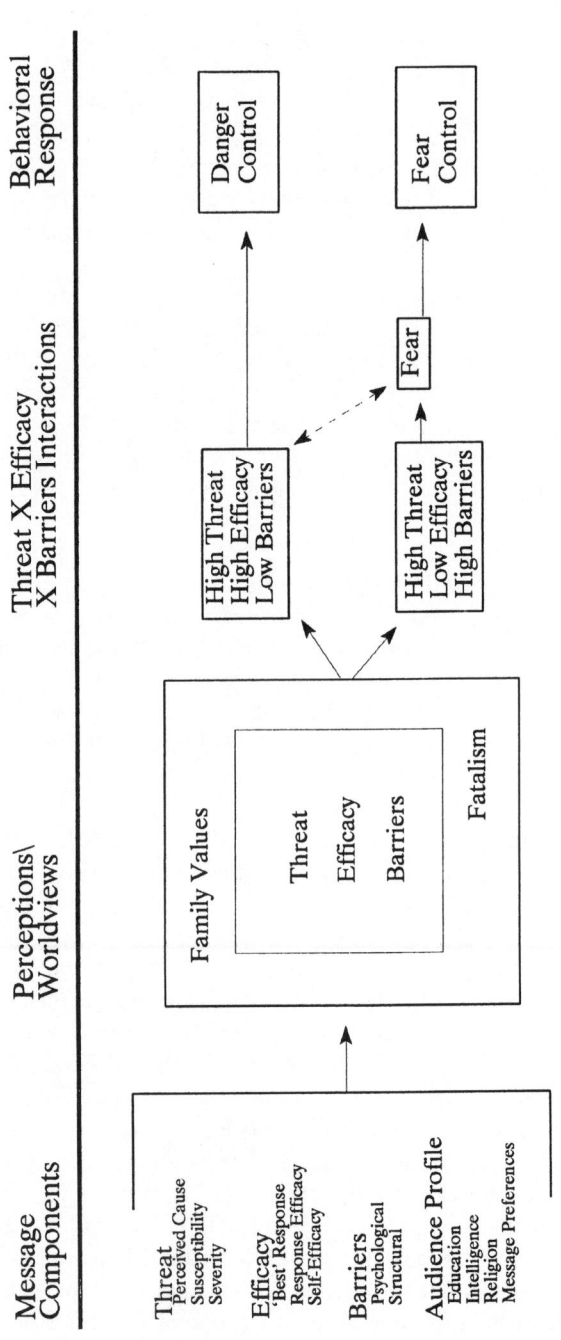

Figure 9.2 A Modified Version of the Extended Parallel Process Model

individual felt highly fatalistic and believed that his or her family should be in charge of any medical decisions, then he or she would have low efficacy and high perceived barriers with regard to any independent health-related decisions, regardless of the level of perceived threat. Thus fatalism and family values tend to amplify perceived barriers and minimize perceived efficacy. If this analysis holds true, then the combination of low perceived efficacy and high perceived barriers would indicate that any perceptions of threat would result in fear control actions because individuals would feel helpless to enact individual health promotive or disease preventive activities (i.e., a high-threat, low-efficacy, high-barriers condition).

To effectively motivate health promotion behaviors, communication strategies should emphasize low barriers, high efficacy, and moderate to high levels of threat. It is imperative that any threat message be sufficiently outweighed by a high-efficacy and low-barriers message. Only when people feel able to perform a recommended response (high perceived efficacy) with a minimum of effort (low perceived barriers) will perceptions of threat motivate them to protect themselves against health threats.

In sum, message strategies must be framed with verbal and nonverbal messages the patient or audience can understand. At the same time, salient beliefs must be targeted for either change, reinforcement, or introduction, to promote strong-efficacy, low-barriers, and moderate-to high-threat beliefs. Information gathered in the audience analysis can be used to craft culturally appropriate messages that are both motivating and clearly understandable. If health communications succeed in inducing high levels of perceived threat, self-efficacy, and response efficacy, and low levels of perceived barriers, then individuals will engage in health promotion and disease prevention activities (i.e., danger control actions). Great care must be taken to avoid unanticipated harmful outcomes by making sure perceived efficacy is high enough, and perceived barriers are low enough, to balance perceived threat.

CONCLUSION

The goal of most health communication specialists is to improve the health status of individuals, groups, and society through effective communication strategies. The literature outlined in this chapter suggests two key issues that merit attention by intercultural health communication experts. First, as the cultural distance increases between healers and patients or practitioners and audiences, communication becomes more difficult (due to different definitions for verbal and nonverbal messages) and understanding is decreased. When people do not share similar definitions for verbal or nonverbal messages, then miscommunication, misunderstanding, and poorer health are unfortunate and likely outcomes. Second, individuals must be motivated to engage in health promotion and disease prevention activities in culturally appropriate ways. Practical guidelines and a theoretical model are offered here to help practitioners with this task.

Great healers are also great communicators. They understand not only their patients' words but also the thoughts and feelings behind those words. As Rolling Thunder, a Native American medicine man, once said, "When a doctor 'sees the sickness and not the man . . . it certainly isn't healing' " (Boyd, 1989, p. 125). Great healers also know how to motivate patients. They frame messages in a way that achieves acceptance and adherence. Much work remains to be done in the area of culture, communication, and health. Those who study intercultural health communication will find a fascinating world of miracles and magic, science and mystery.

10

Intercultural Small Groups
An Effective Decision-Making Theory

JOHN G. OETZEL • Citrus College, Glendora, California

Decision-making effectiveness is an important aspect of task-oriented groups. In this context, decision-making effectiveness is viewed as an evaluation of the output (i.e., the decision) of a group of individuals (Hirokawa & Salazar, 1991). In essence, decision-making effectiveness is determined by focusing on whether a group has made a "good" or a "bad" decision. To understand effectiveness, the influence of various communication processes on decision quality have been examined. It is through communication that the functional requisites that allow groups to make effective decisions are satisfied (Hirokawa, 1988). Specific processes deemed important include task analysis, establishing criteria, evaluation of alternatives, decision-making rules, amount of contribution by the members, and conflict. It is necessary to determine the conditions under which these processes do (and do not) contribute to effective decision making. For example, in the United States, conflict has been found to be important for decision making because it assists the group in being thorough in the analysis of the problem and thus helps the group make more effective decisions (Dace, 1990; Pood, 1980; Putnam, 1986). Conflict also can have detrimental effects because of improper management of conflict resulting in strained personal relationships and a lack of commitment (Deutsch, 1969; Putnam, 1986). The key to whether conflict is productive or constructive for group decision-making effectiveness depends on how the conflict is managed.

Decision making has been shown to be a culturally grounded concept. Stewart (1985) argues:

AUTHOR'S NOTE: The author wants to thank Stella Ting-Toomey and William Gudykunst for their tremendous help and constructive comments on earlier drafts of this chapter.

247

Decision-making is defined as a process for representing experience and integrating the competencies of the individual to control-govern-guide his or her actions in performance. The salient characteristic of decision-making is that it bridges the gap between the cognitive processes and action. Because decision-making lacks content, its form acquires much of its character from the realities of the culture: patterns of thinking, values, and norms. (pp. 208-209)

Because individual decision making is shaped and given meaning by culture, the way decisions are negotiated in a group must be studied in a cultural context. For example, to understand how a Japanese person communicates about and makes decisions (individually and within a group), understanding Japanese cultural values and patterns of thought is necessary.

A number of researchers have examined the role of culture and its effect on decision making (Kume, 1985; Stewart, 1985). While these approaches have yielded important insights concerning different cultural perspectives on decision making, systematic theoretical study of decision-making effectiveness in intercultural small groups is needed. Because of growing cultural diversity in the United States and frequent interaction between members of different countries, it is likely that members from different cultures are placed in the same daily work groups. During interaction, conflict is likely to arise as members adjust to each other's decision-making styles and communication patterns. It is important to explore the processes that occur in intercultural small groups to help facilitate effective interaction and thus effective decision making.

Therefore, the purpose of this chapter is to explain how decision-making effectiveness is affected by small groups composed of members from different cultures. Specifically, the role of culture on group decision-making effectiveness in task-oriented groups is examined. The relationship between culture and decision-making effectiveness will be explored in two main sections. In the first section, vigilant interaction theory (which explains decision-making effectiveness) will be described. Then, using the cultural variability dimension of individualism-collectivism, it will be shown that vigilant interaction theory only applies to individualistic cultures. Consequently, decision-making effectiveness will be conceptualized to apply to individualistic and collectivistic cultures. Finally, new criteria will be added to vigilant interaction theory to meet this conceptualization. In the second section, theoretical assumptions and propositions will be offered.

EFFECTIVE DECISION MAKING: THEORETICAL DEVELOPMENT

The perspective presented is guided by the systems perspective (Monge, 1977). The systems perspective provides a set of metatheoretical assumptions that can be used to develop a content-specific theory. Monge (1977) argues that the system perspective has advantages over other perspectives in that it can incorporate important aspects of other positions. For example, the systems perspective can make linear predictions (i.e., culture will influence communication style) that are made from a covering-law perspective (Berger, 1977). In addition, this perspective focuses on the dynamic interaction of a system and how the system functions and survives within a specific environment. This provides a plausible metaphor for the nature of a task-oriented small group.

The decision-making group can be thought of as a system (Homans, 1950) with inputs, processes (i.e., throughput), and outputs. The input of the group is the individuals who compose the group. Individuals bring to the group various characteristics such as cultural/ethnic background, attitudes, values, beliefs, and abilities. The process of a group is the interaction and communication that occur between the individuals. This includes role formation, information processing, and conflict. The output of a group is the decision. The decision can be evaluated in terms of its effectiveness and also in terms of satisfaction for the individuals. Thus a task-oriented group is a system of individuals who come together to produce an output. For intercultural small groups, culture is one of the key inputs or explanatory variables, communication is the mediating, process variable, and the decision (evaluated in terms of effectiveness) is the output variable.

Vigilant Interaction Theory

One theory that explains decision-making effectiveness is Hirokawa and Rost's (1992) vigilant interaction theory, which is based on the systems perspective. The primary theoretical assumption of vigilant interaction theory is that the quality of interaction between group members mediates the input of the group members and directly influences the effectiveness of the group in making decisions. Specifically, Hirokawa and Rost (1992) argue that the way members talk about the problems and consequences associated with a decision affects how they think about problems and consequences, which, in turn, determines the effectiveness of final decisions.

Vigilant interaction theory assumes that the group's final decision is the result of prior subdecisions made during the group's interaction. These subdecisions include the following: (a) Is there something about the current state of affairs that requires improvement or change? (b) What does the group want to achieve or accomplish in deciding what to do about the problem? (c) What are the available choices? (d) What are the positive and negative consequences of those choices? Hirokawa and

Rost (1992) argue that "by conceptualizing the group decision-making process as a series of interrelated subdecisions leading to a final overall decision, vigilant interaction theory is able to specify the factors that contribute to high- or low-quality group decisions" (p. 270). They note that the group's decision is largely influenced by the three facets of critical thinking (i.e., vigilance) used by the group to reach a collective final decision. These facets provide the foundation for the propositions of the theory and include (a) the analysis of the problematic situation, (b) the establishment of goals and criteria, and (c) the evaluation of positive and negative qualities of available choices.

The first facet is the analysis of a problematic situation. Vigilant interaction theory posits that the quality of a group's decision will be influenced by the quality of the group's understanding of the problem. Errors made in the analysis of the problem will carry over to other stages of the decision-making process. For example, if a group misidentifies the problem, the solution offered is unlikely to apply directly. The second facet is the establishment of goals and objectives. Vigilant interaction theory also proposes that the quality of the objectives offered by the group will influence the quality of the decision. If a group is able to establish objectives that will remedy the problematic situation, it is likely that a quality solution will result. Finally, the third facet for influencing decision quality is the evaluation of the positive and negative qualities of the alternatives. Groups that recognize the consequences associated with the alternatives will be more likely to choose the highest quality choice. For example, if the group has two alternatives that meet the objectives, the group will need to be able to determine which choice has greater benefits and/or less costs associated with it.

Thus, these facets serve as functional requisites for the group. That is, groups that meet these critical goals are likely to make a quality decision. Vigilant interaction theory has received a great deal of support from historical case studies (i.e., Janis, 1982), laboratory research (i.e., Hirokawa, 1985, 1988), and field research (i.e., Hirokawa & Rost, 1992).

Cultural Sensitivity of Vigilant Interaction Theory

While vigilant interaction theory is useful in explaining effective group decision making in monocultural groups in the United States, the degree to which the theory is sensitive to the cultural background of the members has not been addressed. The theory has been validated only in monocultural groups in the United States and thus may need to be revised to explain effectiveness in intercultural small groups. To address this issue, a way of discussing the differences between cultures is needed.

To explain how cultures differ, a number of researchers have attempted to identify variables on which cultures can be similar or different (i.e., dimensions of cultural variability). The primary dimension used by researchers to discuss cultural variance is individualism-collectivism (Triandis, 1990). Parsons (1951) was the first to isolate this dimension and called it self-orientation/collective-orientation. Support for this dimension comes from Hofstede (1980, 1983), who analyzed organizational behaviors of people from 53 different countries/regions and empirically validated that individualism-collectivism is one of four primary dimensions that link behavior to cultural life. Empirical evidence has been provided showing that individualism-collectivism is the primary dimension that differentiates clusters of cultures (Gudykunst & Nishida, 1986b; Hui & Triandis, 1986). Hui and Triandis (1986) conclude that individualism-collectivism can be used as a powerful theoretical construct to explain interactional differences.

Individualism-collectivism refers to "a cluster of attitudes, beliefs, and behaviors toward a wide variety of people" (Hui & Triandis, 1986, p. 240). In individualistic cultures (such as the United States), most people focus on personal goals that overlap slightly with collective goals (immediate family, work, and so on). When personal and collective goals conflict, members of individualistic cultures will chose to pursue personal goals at the expense of collective goals. On the other hand, members of collectivistic cultures (such as Japan) consider it socially desirable to place group goals over individual goals. Collectivists draw from the "we" identity, while individualists draw on the "I" identity (Ting-Toomey, 1988).

Triandis (1990) notes that social behavior reflects the goal differences of individualists and collectivists. For example, during conflict, collectivists will be nonconfrontational to protect other members of the collective. In contrast, individualists will be more direct and assertive to achieve their personal goal. In general, collectivists share resources with ingroup members, feel interdependent with ingroup members, and feel involved in the lives of ingroup members (Triandis, 1989). On the other hand, individualists have a high concern for equity and their social relations are temporary and voluntary (Triandis, 1989).

It is important to note that there is a sharper difference in behavior toward members of ingroups and outgroups in collectivistic cultures than in individualistic cultures (Triandis, Bontempo, Villareal, Asai, & Lucca, 1988). An ingroup is a group whose goals, norms, and values shape the behavior of its members (i.e., family or social club), while an outgroup is a group with dissimilar attributes from those of the ingroup or a group that opposes the ingroup (Triandis, 1990). Collectivists who cooperate and are friendly with ingroup members tend to be competitive and even sometimes rude to outgroup members. In contrast, individualists do not make great changes in behavior when interacting with outgroup members unless the outgroup members are from different cultural groups. These differences in behavior are due to the way that the ingroup is defined. Individualists have many ingroups and often have difficulty in defining the boundaries between ingroup and outgroup. Individualists easily meet outsiders and form new groups. Collectivists have clear ingroup/outgroup boundaries, few ingroups, and difficulty interacting outside the ingroup. In addition, it is important to note that the definition of ingroup for collectivists depends upon the situation. While family often is the main ingroup, fellow villagers, coworkers, or even the country as a whole (i.e., interacting with a fellow countryperson while an exchange student in the United States) can become relevant ingroups (Triandis, Bontempo, et al., 1988).

While individualism-collectivism has been used widely to explain cultural differences in behavior, it has been argued that there are problems with using this dimension to explain behavior at the individual level (Kashima, 1989). First, Kashima argues that it is impossible to test causal explanations of behavior based on cultural-level explanations. Second, Kashima also notes that specific samples do not correspond with cultural-level scores of individualism and collectivism. Thus, a method to study individualism-collectivism on the individual level is needed.

One way to accomplish this is to use Markus and Kitayama's (1991) distinction between independent and interdependent self construals. The independent construal of self involves the view that an individual is a unique entity with a unique repertoire of feelings, thoughts, and so forth. Geertz (1975) points out that this person is

> a bounded, unique, more or less integrated motivational and cognitive universe, a dynamic center of awareness, emotion, judgment, and action organized into a distinctive whole and set contrastively both against other such wholes and against a social and natural background. (p. 48)

People who hold this view believe in "saying what you mean," striving for goals, being responsive to the environment, and expressing themselves. In addition, they may value individualism, achievement, self-direction, competition, and hedonism.

In contrast, the interdependent construal of self involves the feelings of being connected to those around you (Markus & Kitayama, 1991). Markus and Kitayama (1991) note that "people are motivated to find a way to fit in with relevant others, to fulfill and create obligation, and in general to become part of various interpersonal relationships" (p. 227). The self in relation to other guides the behavior in social situations. People who have an interdependent self construal want to fit in with others, act appropriately, promote other's goals, and be indirect. In addition, they value conformity, security, equality, cooperation, and tradition.

Gudykunst, Matsumoto, Ting-Toomey, Nishida, Heyman, and Kim (1994) argue that the independent self construal is predominantly associated with people from individualistic cultures and that the interdependent self construal is predominantly associated with people from collectivistic cultures. In addition, they argue that everybody uses both construals and that the self construal perceived to be the most salient will depend on the situation and with whom people are interacting. Thus, for example, a person from the United States could use an interdependent self construal and a person from Japan could use an independent self construal in a particular situation. Thus this would explain why people from collectivistic cultures can sometimes communicate in a competitive manner with people from outgroups.

In sum, individualists have an individual goal orientation that manifests itself in competitive behaviors, while collectivists have a collective goal orientation that manifests itself in cooperative behaviors. The differences in behavior between individualism (or independent self construals) and collectivism (or interdependent self construals) have important implications for group decision making. In its current form, vigilant interaction theory is limited to individualists. The theory focuses only on task outcomes and not on relational concerns. Individualists are highly concerned with task outcomes because quality task outcomes are associated with personal gain. In contrast, collectivists are concerned primarily with relational outcomes because the way the group interacts takes precedence over the work accomplished. This distinction will be further illustrated in the following section.

Cultural Differences in Decision-Making Preferences

Nadler, Keeshan-Nadler, and Broome (1985) note that individual decision making reflects a cultural mind-set because during decision making individuals make choices among alternatives that often are determined by cultural values. During interaction, participants must anticipate others' decision-making styles to predict the effect of various message strategies. What works in one's own culture may prove to be ineffective in intercultural settings. Therefore a number of researchers have examined cross-cultural decision-making styles in hopes of bridging these differences.

Stewart (1985) proposes a model of cross-cultural decision making based on three structural components: the decision maker, prediction system, and decision criterion. Stewart divides each of these into subcomponents and treats each as a phase in the process of decision making. The phases are as follows: decision maker, attributing decision making, prediction system, experience for decision maker, representing experience, using represented experience, strategy making, reaching conclusions, criterion, legitimating, and implementing. From these patterns, Stewart makes predictions about the differences between a decision maker using linear logic (such as in the United States) and a decision maker using spiral logic (such as in Japan). These differences are reflective of the difference in low-context communication and high-context communication, which predominate in individualistic and collectivistic cultures, respectively. Ting-Toomey (1985) notes that people from individualistic cultures tend to use direct and straight-line logic, while people from collectivistic cultures use spiral logic.

Kume (1985) studied the managerial attitudes toward decision making in North America and Japan by employing a model based on Stewart's (1985) structural components. Kume expanded the three components and categorized decision making into six communication functions to describe cultural differences: (a) locus of decision, (b) initiation and coordination, (c) temporal orientation, (d) mode of reaching decision, (e) decision criterion, and (f) communication style. Kume found that North Americans prefer an individual locus of decision making, top-down initiation of information, planning ahead and quick decision making, majority rule for decision making, practical criteria, and a direct confrontational communication style. On the other hand, Japanese managers prefer a group-oriented locus of decision making, cooperation in initiating information, present orientation and gradual decisions, consensus rule for decision making, holistic criteria, and an affective communication style.

With these differences in mind, the role of culture in how vigilant interaction theory defines effectiveness can be ascertained. Hirokawa and Salazar (1991) point out that decision-making effectiveness has been operationalized in a number of different ways by small group researchers. These ways include the following:

(1) correctness—the extent to which the decision is free from error, (2) quality—the extent to which the decision conforms to established standards, (3) utility—the ratio of benefits and costs associated with a decision, (4) acceptability—the degree of agreement that a decision elicits from group members, (5) process—the extent to which the group follows acceptable

procedures in arriving at a decision, (6) appropriateness—the extent to which a decision conforms to group goals, task requirements, and informational resources. (pp. 3-4)

Most of the past research has operationalized decision-making effectiveness in terms of criteria of utility, quality, and correctness because of the high concern with the "bottom line" in the United States (Dace, 1990; Hirokawa, 1985, 1988; Kirchmeyer & Cohen, 1992).[1] In fact, Hirokawa and Salazar (1991) argue for evaluating effectiveness solely in terms of the quality of decision. While the focus on the quality of the decision is attractive and applicable to individualistic cultures, its role for collectivistic cultures needs to be explored. Members of collectivistic cultures emphasize not only the quality of the decision but also the appropriateness, process, and acceptability of a decision.[2] The functional requisites of vigilant interaction theory can be used to determine the quality of a decision, but there must be other criteria if the theory is to be applicable to intercultural small groups that include collectivists.

The other criteria center on the appropriateness of the processes used by the group. Based on the differences in decision-making preferences presented by Stewart (1985) and Kume (1985), three criteria for evaluating the appropriateness of group decision making can be advocated: (a) consensus decision making, (b) commitment of members (in terms of supporting the final decision and feelings of belonging to the group), and (c) equal contribution by members. These criteria are signs of participatory decision making. In collectivistic cultures (such as Japan), members of the group contribute to the final decision and must reach agreement before a final decision is made (March, 1992). In addition, collectivists are expected to put aside personal preferences and be committed to the group (i.e., group harmony; March, 1992). If these procedures are followed, the group makes an effective decision. These criteria of appropriateness are not only applicable to collectivistic cultures, they have implications for quality decision making. Hirokawa (1980) found that groups that reach consensus make better decisions than groups who use majority or compromise decision rules. Kirchmeyer and Cohen (1992) found that commitment to the group (in terms of supporting the final decision and feelings of belonging to the group) increased the level of contribution for minorities and thus affected the quality of the decision for the group.

To summarize, groups composed of individualists will emphasize task goals over relational goals. To make a quality decision, individualists tend to be vigilant during interaction. Consensus decision making, equal contribution, and commitment assist in reaching quality decisions, but are not necessary. Groups composed of individualists are successful if they make a quality decision regardless of whether the members reached consensus, had equal contribution, or were committed. On the other hand, groups composed of collectivists will emphasize relational goals over task goals. Consensus decision making, equal contribution, and commitment are necessary features for a group to be regarded as successful. If these features are found in a group, then the group is effective.

Intercultural Small Groups

The preceding has focused on cross-cultural differences in decision making in small groups. When members of different cultures interact in small groups, intercultural small groups are formed. Cultural diversity in small groups can increase the creative potential (the ability to develop unique choices for solving a decision) of the group if all of the members of the group contribute to the decision (Kirchmeyer & Cohen, 1992; Shaw, 1981). The activation of personal and social identities will influence the equality of contribution and thus the effectiveness of the group.

Many scholars have noted that there are two important identities that influence communication with others: personal identity and social identity (Cupach & Imahori, 1993; Gudykunst, 1993; Turner, 1987a). Turner (1987a) explains that social identity is based on "ingroup-outgroup categorizations based on similarities and differences between people who define themselves as a member of certain social groups and not of others (i.e., 'American,' 'female,' 'black,' 'student,' 'working class')," while personal identity is based on "differences between oneself as a unique individual and other ingroup (or outgroup) members that define oneself as a specific individual person (i.e., in terms of one's personality)" (p. 45). Gudykunst (1993) argues that personal identity is the major generative mechanism for interpersonal behavior, while social identity is the major generative mechanism for intergroup behavior. Gudykunst and Kim (1992) point out that both personal and social identities operate in all situations because all interactions involve both interpersonal and intergroup behavior.

Gudykunst (1993) argues that successful intercultural communication depends on the ability of individuals to be mindful, as opposed to mindless, in their interaction. One important condition that leads to mindlessness is the use of categories. Categorization is often based on physical characteristics (i.e., race, gender) and cultural characteristics (i.e, ethnicity). To be mindful, an individual needs to be open to new information, be able to create new categories, and have awareness of other perspectives (Langer, 1989). Stated another way, successful intercultural communication depends on the ability of individuals to emphasize personal identities during intercultural encounters. Thus individuals in intercultural small groups need to emphasize personal identities rather than social identities for the group to be effective.

Support for this notion comes from status characteristics theory, which is a theory within the expectation states theoretical research program that explains individual differences in behavior in task-oriented small groups (Berger, Cohen, & Zelditch, 1973; Berger, Conner, & Fisek, 1974; Berger, Wagner, & Zelditch, 1985). The theory posits that individual differences are determined by specific status and external status characteristics. Specific status characteristics are the result of group interaction. Individuals are given status based on the quality of the arguments they present (Garlick & Mongeau, 1993). External status characteristics include such things as age, physical attractiveness, occupational status, and ethnicity. The general argument of the theory is that individual members who perceive that they have a higher external status than other members will participate more in the group discussion. In addition, other members who perceive the higher external status cues will allow the higher status individual to make most of the contributions and that individual will be perceived to be the most influential. Maass and Clark (1984) review studies that have examined minority influence. They note that a person who has a minority status (i.e., different ethnicity or culture than the majority of the group members) is considered to have low external status and thus has less influence than those individuals who have majority status.

From the identity perspective, this low external status comes from an activation of social identity. When social identities are activated, the implicit attitude in the group is that "we are superior to those people because of our ethnicity." The activation of social identity inhibits equal participation and thus makes the group ineffective. Instead, if individuals activate personal identities, equal participation is facilitated and groups are likely to be effective. When personal identities are activated, the implicit attitude in this group is "each individual has important contributions to make."

The differences in goal orientation for individualists and collectivists and the impact of identities on contribution in small groups clearly show the need for this conceptualization of group decision-making effectiveness. There are cross-cultural differences between individualists and collectivists. When groups are formed with both individualists and collectivists, multiple concerns should be considered. In addition, the conceptualization of group decision-making effectiveness to include both quality and appropriateness dimensions is consistent with the dimensions of intercultural communication competence. In recent years, scholars in various fields have been studying interaction between members of different cultures to help better understand what makes a communicator competent in intercultural settings. In general, scholars have agreed that there should be a dimension of effectiveness (or quality) that judges the ability to achieve one's goals and a dimension of appropriateness that refers to the suitability of a person's communication (Koester, Wiseman, & Sanders, 1993). In a small group, effectiveness (or quality) refers to the ability of a group to make a "good" decision. Although the nomenclature in this chapter is not consistent with that of the competence literature (competence = effectiveness + appropriateness, while in this chapter effectiveness = quality + appropriateness), the dimensions imply the same principles. Thus, the conceptualization is necessary to be thorough and accurate in the evaluation of intercultural decision-making groups.

Finally, one last discrepancy must be made before proceeding. Earlier it was noted that collectivists behave differently toward ingroup and outgroup members. Some may argue that because an intercultural small group is an outgroup situation and collectivists are likely to become more competitive in outgroup situations, why does group decision-making effectiveness need to be reconceptualized? First of all, when people interact with other cultures, they are likely to use their own culture as a reference point. That is, if people from Japan are told that they will be working in a small group, they will use their own expectations of how a group is supposed to interact to guide their behavior. Second, Triandis, Bontempo, and his colleagues (1988) point out that the notion of an ingroup depends on the situation and that one of these situations is the workplace. In a task-oriented small group, individualists and collectivists work together toward a common task-oriented goal. For collectivists, this will likely result in a less pronounced difference in communication style with ingroup and outgroup members because the small group may be defined as an ingroup. For example, a collectivist is less likely to be dominating with an individualist in a small group because the decision holds mutual benefits (i.e., satisfaction with a good decision, praise from superior, promotion, and so forth). From the collectivistic viewpoint, to be dominating toward a group member would be inappropriate because the member would not feel part of the group and might not contribute. This would likely result in a poor decision. These reasons, coupled with the fact that the criteria of appropriateness should help individualists as well, provide a strong rationale for the conceptualization of group decision-making effectiveness.

Because of the differences in decision-making preferences, there is increased potential for conflict in intercultural small groups. Any time a group of people from different backgrounds get together to solve a problem, there will be disagreements about the best way to make a decision, about the decision, and about the people. Thus, conflict is an important consideration for problem-solving groups.

Conflict and Conflict Styles

Conflict traditionally is conceptualized as a disagreement between individuals in task-oriented small groups (i.e., Dace, 1990). From an individualistic viewpoint, conflict is one of the interaction processes that help a group to be vigilant in the evaluation of the problem and developing of solutions. Conflict is viewed as a way for assisting group members to critically evaluate ideas (Janis, 1982). In essence, conflict allows the group to be more vigilant during interaction. However, small group researchers have noted that the conflict must be about the content or task issues (substantive conflict) facing the group, not about relational or socioemotional issues (affective conflict). Because decision making requires the presentation and testing of ideas, substantive conflict is viewed as having a beneficial impact on decision quality (Wilson & Hanna, 1990). Wilson and Hanna (1990) argue that groups who can maximize ideational conflict without adversely affecting roles and relationships will reach high-quality decisions. On the other hand, affective conflict is considered to be disruptive to decision making (Falk, 1982). This is because affective conflict takes away from the effort toward the task at hand and the members become more concerned with relationships rather than the group decision.

The idea that substantive conflict is beneficial has been supported only in U.S. contexts. The difference in values and social behavior between individualists and collectivists reveals a limitation in the research relating conflict to decision-making effectiveness—it assumes that the individuals in the group can separate the content and relational issues. Individualists tend to separate the issues. However, collectivists tend not to separate the person from the conflict because face or relational issues are always involved in conflicts (Ting-Toomey, 1988). Thus type of conflict alone cannot be used to predict decision-making effectiveness in intercultural small groups.

The key to making effective decisions when conflict arises in intercultural small groups is the style of handling conflict. Previous studies note there are three distinct ways conflict can be managed in small groups: avoiding, cooperating, or competing (Putnam, 1986). These studies focus primarily on the function or effects of conflict styles on the quality of decision making. An avoiding style of conflict is not effective in individualistic small groups because it leads to the phenomenon of "groupthink" (Janis, 1982). This is because avoidance of conflict helps to make the group overly cohesive and the group does not critically evaluate alternative decisions. Cooperative styles result when group members put group goals above personal goals. Quality decisions result from coping effectively with differences in opinions and ideas through cooperation (Putnam, 1986). With competitive styles, group members are suspicious of each other and blame others when problems arise. A competitive climate is seen as a hindrance to a quality decision (Putnam, 1986).

Three different researchers offer empirical support for the relationship between conflict styles and group effectiveness. First, Deutsch (1969) reviewed various outcomes of competitive and cooperative conflict. He posited that a competitive style only seeks to defeat the other member(s) so as to win the conflict and preserve individual power. This results in a suspicious, hostile attitude among members and communication becomes impoverished. In contrast, a cooperative style is beneficial because it aids in honest communication, encourages recognition of the legitimacy of other member's opinions and ideas, and leads to trusting, friendly attitudes. This notion was also supported by Pood (1980), whose research examined groups that used regulated versus unregulated responses. Not surprising, Pood found that groups who use regulated (cooperative) responses arrived at higher quality decisions than groups who used unregulated (competitive) responses. Finally, Dace (1990) examined the use of distributive and integrative strategies in decision-making groups. Distributive strategies are competitive in that concessions are sought from the other person(s). Integrative strategies recognize another's ideas, but maintain a neutral evaluation and do not seek concessions. Thus, they are consistent with a cooperative style. Dace found that groups who employed integrative strategies were more likely to make the correct decision on a task than were groups who used distributive strategies.

The styles of handling conflict are applicable to both individualistic and collectivistic cultures. It is considered appropriate to cooperate with other group members, and cooperation will help a group reach a quality decision. However, while vigilant interaction theory explains the criteria for a quality decision, it does not have the capacity (by design) to explain why conflict strategies are chosen. It is important to understand the motivation for choosing conflict strategies as the strategies affect the effectiveness of the group.

Ting-Toomey's (1985, 1988) face-negotiation theory argues that cultural differences in approaches to conflict can be explained by face needs and individualism-collectivism. The theory states that "conflict is a face-negotiation process in which the 'faces' or the situated identities of the conflict parties are being threatened and called into question" (Ting-Toomey, 1988, p. 214). Ting-Toomey (1988) explains that cultural variability will affect the face needs and subsequent strategies during conflict. Specifically, Ting-Toomey posits that members of individualistic cultures have a greater degree of self-face maintenance needs (protect own face) and thus employ more direct face-negotiation strategies and dominating or competitive conflict strategies. On the other hand, members of collectivistic cultures have a greater degree of mutual-face or other-face maintenance needs and thus employ more indirect face-negotiation strategies and avoidance or obliging conflict strategies.

In a test of face-negotiation theory, Ting-Toomey et al. (1991) found support for the propositions of face-negotiation theory. They determined that self-face maintenance is associated with dominating conflict strategies, other-face maintenance is associated with avoiding, compromising, and obliging conflict strategies, and mutual-face maintenance is associated with an integrative conflict style.

These ideas can be used at the individual level by examining the independent and interdependent construals of self (Markus & Kitayama, 1991). An individual with an independent construal of self (which predominates in individualistic cultures) is concerned with achieving goals and expressing him- or herself. Thus, a person with an independent construal of self is likely to use dominating conflict strategies. On the other hand, an individual with an interdependent construal of self (which predominates in collectivistic cultures) is concerned with the self in relation to others and thus will likely employ avoiding, compromising, and obliging strategies.

Knowing tendencies for an individual's behavior is important because these behaviors collectively affect the group's decision-making processes and thus affect the effectiveness of a group. For example, if a group consists of four individuals who have independent construals of self, it can then be surmised that this group will be marked by a high level of competition and dominating strategies. This group will likely be vigilant but may not use appropriate communication styles (everything else being equal). On the other hand, if the group consists of four individuals who have interdependent construals of self, it can then be surmised that the group will be marked by a high level of cooperation and avoiding, compromising, and obliging styles. This group will likely use appropriate communication styles but may not be vigilant (everything else being equal). Thus, the collective tendencies of the individuals in the group are of great concern for group decision-making effectiveness.

AN EFFECTIVE DECISION-MAKING THEORY OF INTERCULTURAL SMALL GROUPS

Using the explanatory framework established in this chapter, assumptions and propositions for an effective decision-making theory of intercultural small groups will be proffered. The theory focuses on the influence of culture on group processes and subsequently the impact of group processes on decision-making outcomes.

Assumptions

The assumptions about intercultural small group decision making derived from the explanatory framework are as follows:

1. Every decision has input, process, and output variables.
2. Every decision-making group can be composed of heterogeneous or homogeneous members.
3. Diverse backgrounds (based on cultural values) will result in different decision-making preferences by individuals in a small group.
4. Diverse backgrounds will result in potential conflicts between individuals in a small group.
5. Diverse backgrounds will result in different conflict strategies by individuals in a small group.
6. Quality decision making is influenced by appropriate interaction between group members.
7. Appropriate interaction is dependent on the activation of personal identities in individual members.
8. Quality decision making is influenced by creativity resulting from diversity.
9. Quality decision making for diverse groups is based on the ability of group members to manage conflict and differences in decision-making styles to allow creativity to enhance the decision.

These assumptions will hold in the following conditions: (a) task-oriented groups, (b) working on a complex task, and (c) sharing a common language with all members having a minimal degree of linguistic competence. These assumptions are based on task-oriented groups as social groups will not focus exclusively on decision making. The task needs to be complex (a task that has multiple solutions, high information requirement, and high evaluation demands is considered complex; Hirokawa, 1990) because simple tasks will not promote very much conflict and are better handled by individuals. Finally, a common language with a level of linguistic competence is necessary because the focus of the theory is on culturally diverse people working together in a group. For group members to feel comfortable with participating and to be able to understand one another, they must have a common language.

Theoretical Propositions

Based on the assumptions discussed in the previous section and the explanatory framework set up in the first section, 14 propositions about the collective behavior of the members of an intercultural group in being effective will be proffered. The propositions are in two categories. First, propositions 1 to 7 examine the effect of input on process. Specifically, the influence of culture on various group processes is discussed. Group processes need to be understood so as to explain effective outcomes because these processes should occur in groups in which members are not mindful of their communication. Second, propositions 8 to 14 examine the influence of group communication processes on decision outcomes. These propositions explain that, when individuals are aware, they can alter their communication to improve the effectiveness of the group. These propositions are the primary focus of this theory.

Individuals who have an independent self construal value achievement, competition, and striving for goals (Markus & Kitayama, 1991). During a small group interaction, these individuals will primarily be concerned with making a quality decision. Making a quality decision is reflective of personal goal achievement (i.e., "I look good if my group is good"). These individuals do not have a high concern for relationships among members because the relationships are secondary to achievement. On the other hand, individuals who have an interdependent self construal value connectedness, cooperation, and promoting others' concerns (Markus & Kitayama, 1991). During a small group interaction, these individuals will primarily be concerned with achieving harmony in the group. Harmony is a relational concern for group members. These individuals do not exclude task concerns, but the task is secondary to relationships. Thus, the first proposition is posited as follows:

Proposition 1: Homogeneous groups composed of members who activate independent construals of self will emphasize task outcomes over relational outcomes in the group; homogeneous groups composed of members who activate interdependent construals of self will emphasize relational outcomes over task outcomes in the group.

The level of contribution by members of a group is influenced by the status of the members (Berger et al., 1985). Status characteristics theory explains that groups composed of members with different external status are likely to have members contributing different amounts. Higher status individuals are likely to contribute more to the discussion than lower status individuals. One important determinant of external status is culture. If a group is composed of individuals from different cultures, it is likely that the members will contribute different amounts. In contrast, a group composed of members from the same culture is more likely to have equal levels of contribution by the members (all things being equal). Thus, the second proposition is proffered as follows:

Proposition 2: Homogeneous groups are more likely to have equal contributions by the members than heterogeneous groups.

Groups composed of individuals with interdependent self construals are likely to reach agreement on decisions affecting the groups. Individuals with interdependent self construals are highly concerned with maintaining harmony in the group, and consensus decision making is indicative of harmony. For example, Japanese groups (in which the interdependent self construal predominates) prefer consensus on decisions. On the other hand, groups composed of individuals with independent self construals are not concerned with reaching consensus. They are likely to use a majority rule because they are concerned with quick decisions and achievement. For example, U.S. American groups (where the independent self construal predominates) prefer majority rule. In addition, heterogeneous groups are not likely to reach consensus because disagreement may be common, and if there are individuals with independent self construals, they are not likely to go along with the majority to maintain harmony. Thus, the third proposition is offered:

Proposition 3: Homogeneous groups composed of members who activate interdependent construals of self are more likely to reach consensus decisions than homogeneous groups composed of members who activate independent construals of self and heterogeneous groups.

Kirchmeyer and Cohen (1992) found that the minorities in multicultural groups did not feel as committed to the group as nonminorities. Minorities felt that they did not belong and were not a part of the group. This supports the notion that heterogeneous groups are likely to have members who are not committed to the groups. In contrast, individuals of homogeneous groups are likely to be committed to the group. This is because individuals are able to identify and relate to other group members. There is a commonality that leads to a feeling of belonging. The fourth proposition is as follows:

> *Proposition 4:* Homogeneous groups are more likely to have higher levels of commitment to the group and the decision of the group than heterogeneous groups.

Conflict is present in most groups, but it is especially prevalent in groups composed of members with different experiences, values, and expectations. Groups with similar experiences are likely to have less instances of conflict because the individuals will agree on certain aspects. For example, a homogeneous group may have different ideas but will have similar ways to approach decision making. In contrast, a heterogeneous group will have different ways to approach decision making and different ideas. In addition, conflict is likely to occur in groups composed of individuals with independent self construals. These individuals value competition and individual goals and will engage in conflict to reach their goals. In contrast, groups composed of members with interdependent self construals will likely avoid conflict. This is because these individuals view themselves as connected to others and therefore do not like to engage in conflict. Thus, the fifth proposition is offered:

> *Proposition 5:* Homogeneous groups composed of members who activate interdependent construals of self are less likely to have conflict than homogeneous groups composed of members who activate independent construals of self and heterogeneous groups.

Individuals with an interdependent self construal value cooperation (Markus & Kitayama, 1991). When a conflict arises in a group interaction, these individuals will try to manage the conflict without competition. In contrast, individuals with an independent self construal value competition (Markus & Kitayama, 1991). When a conflict arises in a group interaction, these individuals will try to gain concessions from others to "win" the conflict. In addition, heterogeneous groups will likely have competition because individuals with independent construals of self will introduce competition in the group. The sixth proposition is proffered as follows:

> *Proposition 6:* Homogeneous groups composed of individuals with interdependent construals of self are more likely to manage conflict coopera-

tively than homogeneous groups composed of individuals with independent construals of self and heterogeneous groups.

Individuals who hold the independent construal of self view themselves as a unique entity with unique goals and feelings. They believe that expressing themselves and striving for goals is necessary and desirable (Markus & Kitayama, 1991). Thus a group of individuals predominantly with independent construals of self collectively are likely to be more confrontational and assertive in stating opinions and advocating positions. On the other hand, individuals who hold the interdependent construal of self view themselves as connected to others and are motivated to fit in with others. They believe in acting appropriately and promoting others (Markus & Kitayama, 1991). Thus, a group of individuals predominantly with interdependent construals of self collectively are likely to be more indirect and smoothing in stating opinions and advocating positions. The seventh proposition is offered as follows:

Proposition 7: Groups in which a majority of individuals activate an independent construal of self will predominantly employ dominating conflict strategies; groups where a majority of individuals activate an interdependent construal of self will predominantly employ avoiding, compromising, and/or obliging conflict strategies.

Groups that use a cooperative style of managing conflict have been shown to make higher quality decisions than groups that use either a competitive or an avoiding style (Dace, 1990). This is because groups who cooperate are able to compile a wide information base, critically evaluate ideas, and have creative solutions. Groups that compete have members who feel defensive, do not contribute, and/or try to defeat other members. Groups that avoid conflict fall into a pattern of "groupthink" and do not evaluate decisions. In addition, it is considered appropriate for individuals to put the group's goals ahead of personal goals. If this happens, a cooperative style will result. Because it results in quality and appropriateness, a cooperative style will be the most effective approach. The eighth proposition is as follows:

Proposition 8: Groups that manage conflict with a cooperative style (i.e., integrative or compromising strategies) will make more effective decisions than groups that manage conflict with an avoiding style (i.e., avoiding or obliging strategies) or a competing style (i.e., dominating strategies).

Status characteristics theory shows that groups composed of culturally diverse members have an unequal level of participation. Unequal participation will hurt the group for two reasons. First, it does not enable the group to use all of the available resources (i.e., different ideas), which will lower the quality of the decision. Second, unequal participation leads to lower levels of appropriateness. The reason for the unequal participation is the activation of social identities by individual group members. The activation of personal identities allows for the diverse resources to be used as this facilitates equal participation. Thus, the ninth proposition is proffered:

> *Proposition 9:* Groups in which members activate their personal identities will make more effective decisions than groups in which members activate their social identities.

The benefit of having diversity in a group is that many ideas can be discussed to enhance the quality of group decision making. Diversity will help the group be more thorough during interaction. However, the only way that diversity can affect decision-making quality is if ideas are contributed to the group. Thus, an intercultural small group that has equal contribution among its members will be more likely to make a quality decision than a group that has only one member (usually the member from the culture in which the small group convenes) discussing ideas. In addition, this is an effective decision because it is appropriate to have contribution from all of the members. The tenth proposition is as follows:

> *Proposition 10:* Groups that have equal levels of contribution by the members about the decision will make more effective decisions than groups that have unequal contributions by the members.

Kirchmeyer and Cohen (1992) found that the contribution of minorities in multicultural small groups was lower than that of nonminorities. This can be explained by the fact that minorities did not feel committed to the group and the decision that was made by the group and thus did not feel like they belonged. This may be a similar occurrence in intercultural small groups. If members of the small group feel that they do not belong, they are likely to avoid conflict and not contribute to the discussion. The lack of commitment will hurt the group because contribution will not be equal. Also, standards of appropriateness dictate that members should be committed to the group (i.e., the group before the individual). Thus, effective decisions result from members being committed to the group and the decision made by the group. The 11th and 12th propositions are posited as follows:

> *Proposition 11:* Groups in which all members are committed to the group will make more effective decisions than groups in which one or more members are not committed to the group.
>
> *Proposition 12:* Groups in which all members are committed to the decision of the group will make more effective decisions than groups in which one or more members are not committed to the decision of the group.

Hirokawa (1980) found groups that reach consensus make better decisions than groups that make decisions from majority or compromise rules. This is because a consensus decision results from all members considering the decision and evaluating the consequences. With majority or compromise rules, the alternatives, more often than not, are not critically evaluated. Members use a majority or compromise rule to avoid a conflict and save time, which hurts the quality of the decision. In addition, it is appropriate for all members to agree on a decision. Being a part of a group means that each member should have an opportunity to influence the final outcome. Thus, both quality and appropriate criteria are met, resulting in an effective decision. The 13th proposition is proffered as follows:

> *Proposition 13:* Groups that employ consensus decision rules will make more effective decisions than groups that employ majority or compromise decision rules.

Hirokawa and Rost's (1992) functional requisites are used to predict decision quality in homogeneous small groups. They should also be able to predict decision quality in diverse groups. Any group that understands the nature of the problem, establishes "good" criteria, develops a wide range of alternatives, and notes the positive and negative ramifications of the alternatives has met the functional requisites and should make a high-quality decision. However, this does not predict whether or not a group will reach the quality decision by the appropriate means. It is possible for one individual to meet the criteria by him- or herself. This would be inappropriate because all members should participate. Still, inappropriate groups can make quality, if not effective, decisions. Thus, the fourteenth proposition is as follows:

> *Proposition 14:* Groups that meet the functional requisites will make higher quality decisions than groups that do not meet the functional requisites.

IMPLICATIONS AND CONCLUSIONS

This theory of effective decision making has strong implications for the study of intercultural and small group communication at the theoretical and practical levels. First, the theoretical contributions will be discussed. Second, future research directions will be noted. Finally, the practical applications will be proffered.

At the theoretical level, the theory makes three important contributions. First, by conceptualizing decision-making effectiveness into quality and appropriate criteria, the theory is culturally sensitive. This is a necessary step to studying and understanding intercultural or multicultural small groups. It is unrealistic and unfair to measure decision making from an individualistic culture viewpoint only. Second, in the extant literature, there are numerous studies examining intercultural communication at the dyadic level. Small group interaction is very different and this theory begins to focus on how three or more people negotiate decision making in this setting. Third, the theory focuses on both interpersonal and intergroup behaviors. Gudykunst (1993) argues that a complete theory is able to explain behavior at both levels. At the interpersonal level (guided by personal identity), the theory explains the communication behaviors that individuals need to perform in a group situation to make effective decisions. At the intergroup level (guided by social identity), the theory explains that the use of social identities is ineffective for group decision making.

While being complete in the sense of explaining behavior at multiple levels, this most certainly is not a finished theory. There is a great deal of research to be accomplished. First of all, the propositions need to be empirically tested. This research can and should be done with multiple methods. Most cross-cultural research employs surveys because of convenience. This leads to interesting and important findings that should be supported with actual interactions. While it is difficult to acquire a sample large enough (at least 120 participants for 30 groups) to test these hypotheses, the long-range benefits would far outweigh the short-term costs. In addition to these methodological concerns, there are other research issues of concern. Specifically, future research needs to pay attention to (a) other group processes such as coalition formation, gender issues, and status, and determine their impact on decision-making effectiveness, (b) the basic ways that intercultural members negotiate decision-making procedures (i.e., the way that "appropriate" methods are negotiated), (c) conflict patterns that constitute decision-making effectiveness, (d) the importance of contextual features (such as common language, historical relations, and the country in which the group convenes) on decision-making effectiveness, and (e) how quality and appropriate criteria affect satisfaction for group members and whether this has an effect on decision-making effectiveness.

At the practical level, the theory has strong implications for managers and facilitators of small groups. The theory shows the essential communication functions needed to make an effective decision. The theory can be used to train individuals to become better participants and leaders in a small group. Most important, considering the multicultural workplace in the United States alone, the theory explains that diverse people approach decision-making groups differently and that adjustments are necessary to make the most effective decisions.

Decision-making effectiveness is viewed as a multidimensional construct consisting of both quality and appropriate dimensions for intercultural small groups. Conflict style is seen as an important contributor to effectiveness particularly in light of the fact that intercultural small groups will consist of very diverse people. It is hoped the theory lays the groundwork for integrating the efforts of researchers studying small group communication, intercultural negotiation, and decision making to combine and contribute to the understanding of group decision-making effectiveness.

NOTES

1. From this point, the criteria of correctness, utility, and quality will be collectively referred to as "quality." These criteria are similar in that they are evaluative measures of the decision. The specific criterion chosen to evaluate the decision will depend on the nature of the task.

2. From this point, the criteria of process, acceptability, and appropriateness will be collectively referred to as "appropriate." These criteria are similar in that they are evaluative measures of the process a group uses to reach a decision.

11

From "Context" to "Contexts" in Intercultural Communication Research

TAMAR KATRIEL • *University of Haifa, Israel*

SPEAKING OF CONTEXT

The centrality of the notion of context in the study of communicative phenomena is widely recognized in a variety of communication and intercultural communication research traditions. Goodwin and Duranti's (1992) book on the exploration of the ways in which the notion of context has been conceptualized and used in discourse-centered research states: "The notion of context stands at the cutting edge of much contemporary research into the relationship between language, culture and social organization, as well as into the study of how language is structured in the way that it is" (p. 32). The notion of context has also been discussed extensively in related fields such as folklore scholarship, under the heading of the text/context controversy (e.g., Ben-Amos, 1993; Young, 1985). While ethnographically oriented studies have pushed toward a greater recognition of the situated nature of talk, and contextual features are more frequently evoked in particular analyses, in intercultural communication research the notion of context has not been the object of much theoretical discussion. Such a move is warranted both to clarify and to enrich scholarly discussion concerning intercultural communication events.

Since Malinowski's (1935/1965) early distinction between "context of situation" and "context of culture," both dimensions of context—the unique physical and psychological environment of a speech situation, and the cultural understandings and expectations that go into its production—have been incorporated into studies of intercultural communication. Two strands can be discerned in the research in this area in recent years: culturally oriented researchers who focus mainly on the "context of culture" dimension, and sociolinguistically oriented researchers (especially those inspired by Gumperz's work) whose main concern is with the interactional construction of the situational context. Both research directions are valuable, yet only partly satisfying. This chapter will first present a discussion on the contribution made by each, and then propose an additional focus on an interim level of analysis—one that links the situational and cultural dimensions of context—the institutional context that frames intercultural encounters.

In attempting to account for instances of miscommunication in intercultural encounters, many researchers tend to develop accounts of divergent cultural codes, values, and meanings whose clashes produce misunderstandings and infelicitous outcomes. These accounts, while anchored in actual instances of talk, tend to focus on a general level of cultural interpretation without attending to the specific characteristics of the speech situation itself. While this level of analysis is clearly indispensable, studies of this type are illuminating yet they only provide partial understanding. Two examples of such studies are Johnstone's (1986) analysis of a journalistic interview conducted by Oriana Falacci with the Ayatollah Khomeini and Carbaugh's (1993) analysis of the Phil Donahue talk show in Russia. They both present interesting cultural analyses of the intercultural occasions they have isolated for study, but neither of these studies specifies the cultural codings given by participants to the particular situational contexts in which the intercultural encounter occurs: the distinctive context of the journalistic interview, and the particular context of a media event known to American audiences as a talk show. While a great deal was learned about cultural differences between Falacci's and Khomeini's understandings of the role and shape of language in persuasive discourse, one is left to wonder how each of them viewed the interview itself as a speech situation. In the case of *The Donahue Show* in Russia, the media context is almost obliterated in the discussion of the differences between particular forms and uses of talk within American and Soviet cultures. The Russian participants explicitly mention their lack of familiarity with media appearances in accounting for the way they responded to *The Donahue Show*. In the words of a Russian interviewee: "This is new to them. They've never been on television and this is the reason why they can't immediately talk to you as they do in America" (Carbaugh, 1993, pp. 186-187). This situational constraint is not incorporated into the analysis of this mass-mediated intercultural exchange. Similarly, the specific nature of *The Donahue Show* as a media performance, not just as an instance of American talk, is not brought into account.

Furthermore, understood as clashes of culturally coded rules of speaking, these intercultural encounters are also removed from the field of power relations. In both examples, the power matrix in which participants operated as part of each particular guest-host/interviewer-interviewee configuration is left submerged, and therefore does not play a role in the analysis. This point is obvious in the case of the Falacci-Khomeini encounter, which took place in the midst of the Iranian hostage crisis and was an intrinsic part of the political-cultural struggle between the West and the Islamic East. But it is also relevant to *The Donahue Show* in the Russia example. The very possibility of this media operation signaled the cultural traffic between the West and postglasnost Russia, which had opened itself to the West's economic and cultural imperialism as well as to its touristic gaze. Viewed in this light, at least some of the intercultural discourses discussed in terms of clashes of codes between Donahue and his Russian audience may also be viewed as acts of resistance on the interviewees' part, not only inability but perhaps also refusal to play the American media game.

Other studies of intercultural communication encounters, notably those by Gumperz (1982, 1992a, 1992b) and associates, have addressed the situational context of intercultural encounters more fully, incorporating available ethnographic knowledge of cultural meanings and values into the analysis of specific instances of talk. At the same time, issues of power have remained in the background. This becomes significant if we consider that these studies have been mostly conducted in institutional contexts and focused on gatekeeping interview situations involving minority applicants. However, these studies have contributed significantly to the ongoing analytic efforts engaged in by a variety of scholars to clarify the role of context in communicative conduct.

Goodwin and Duranti (1992) propose a systematic overview of the ways in which the notion of context has been treated in a variety of research programs, and they suggest some helpful guidelines for its conceptualization: First, it involves a fundamental juxtaposition of two entities—a focal event and a field of action in which it is embedded—which stand in a figure-ground relationship to each other: The line between the context and the behavior to which it is context is not always easy to determine. Drawing such a boundary, they argue (following Bateson), must clearly take into account "the perspective of the participants whose behavior is being analyzed" (Goodwin & Duranti, 1992, p. 4). Second, it is not easy to determine the relevant context from an analyst's standpoint. Again, such determination must take into account what participants treat as relevant context, which is, in turn, shaped by the ways they define the social activity in which they are engaged.

Third, given the dynamic nature of human interaction, what is defined as "relevant context" changes with the flow of talk. Thus: "In so far as participants' articulation of their environment is shaped by the activities of the moment, the context that is relevant to what they are doing changes radically when they move from one activity to another" (Goodwin & Duranti, 1992, p. 5).

Gumperz's (1982, 1992a) notion of "contextualization cues" speaks to the way in which talk itself both invokes context and serves as context for other talk, thus providing a resource for the regulation and negotiation of the flow of spoken interaction. According to Gumperz, contextualization operates in such a way as to affect the manner in which participants categorize the interactional activities they enact and the interactive etiquette they employ. This, in turn, affects the interpretation of the utterance level, signaling cues by which the illocutionary force of a stretch of talk (e.g., a question or request) is identified.

The extensive research Gumperz and associates have conducted on the dynamics of intercultural encounters has greatly illuminated understanding of the ways in which context is constructed, negotiated, and sustained both in and through talk. The cultural specificity of contextualization cues is argued to account for the divergent inferences participants in intercultural exchanges make in ways that often confirm negative stereotypes. Thus, in a study of selection interviews conducted in the British Midlands involving nonnative, English-speaking interviewees from South Asia, Gumperz uses the notion of "minorization" as proposed by Py and Jeanneret (1989), which refers to context-bound, interactive processes through which certain individuals are stereotyped as members of stigmatized minorities. Gumperz accounts for the problematics of intercultural interview situations in terms of the particular complexity and difficulty involved in interpreting communicative intentions across cultural borders:

> I will argue that when bilinguals must face such unaccustomed communicative complexities, they tend to fall back on rhetorical strategies acquired in their own native-language environment, mapping these onto their English speech in dealing with what, for them, are novel circumstances. Native English-speaking participants in turn, who find their communicative expectations violated and have difficulties in following the non-native speaker's arguments, react with interpretations characteristic of minorization situations. (Gumperz, 1992b, p. 304).

Because whatever happens in the course of the interaction itself affects its outcomes—and can work either to reinforce or to change stereotypes—the dynamic and complex role of contextualization processes is important.

Context, then, is not reducible to such broad categories as setting, behavioral and linguistic environment, and such features as background knowledge, including knowledge of discursive rules.

Murray and Sondhi (1987) further elaborate on the notion of context as it relates to intercultural communication research, arguing for a serious consideration of the question of power in intercultural encounters. Focusing on contemporary British society as a case in point, they distinguish different dimensions of context that inform intercultural encounters and that should be taken into account in studying the conditions and constraints that shape them. One dimension Murray and Sondhi (1987) propose relates to the broader structural issues involved, that is, to the "socio-political factors (both historical and contemporary) which create social distance in cross-cultural interactions, especially in institutional situations" (p. 20). The second dimension pertains to the cultural assumptions defining "the rules of the game" that are operative in the social institutions in which intercultural encounters take place, and in which the white person is typically the gatekeeper and the black person is typically the powerless client. Third, there is the biographical dimension, which relates to individuals' attitudes toward cultural others—from racism at one end to true acceptance at the other—attitudes that they have formed based on their previous exposure to encounters of a similar kind. A further dynamic element is introduced into their discussion through the role they assign to the immediate social and political context of cross-cultural encounters, such as fluctuations in levels of unemployment or ethnic riots, which may affect individuals' levels of tolerance (or intolerance) toward the foreigners in their midst. However, this treatment of context does not address the textual component of the intercultural encounter, the ways in which context is indexed and negotiated in participants' actual talk. This dimension, as noted earlier, is investigated in insightful ways by discourse-oriented approaches to the study of situated talk, which define the notion of context not only as socially constituted but also as interactively sustained.

Following will be an argument for a research agenda that will move away from the tendency to view the context of intercultural communication encounters in generic terms or to privilege one class of contexts, such as the institutional context of gatekeeping interviews. To illustrate the variability of the phenomena that ought to concern intercultural communication scholars, some observations are proposed concerning a very different context in which intercultural communication encounters routinely occur—the context of tourism. This is an attempt to further problematize, refine, and perhaps extend our theoretical discussion and empirical investigation of these matters.

FROM CONTEXT TO CONTEXTS

The opening lines of Knapp and Knapp-Potthoff's (1987) discussion of conceptual issues in the analysis of intercultural communication seem to be typical of the way in which this general topic tends to be introduced in both spoken and written presentations. They are quoted at some length as a convenient anchor for this discussion:

> The growth in foreign travel for business, study and pleasure, the migration of people seeking work in other countries, the continuous flow of refugees fleeing persecution or war and the expansion of international trade have naturally all led to a concomitant increase in contacts across national and ethnic borders. In recent years, there has been a growing awareness that these contacts may be negatively affected by severe communication problems which cannot be reduced to a lack of knowledge of the pronunciation, grammar and the lexicon of the languages involved, although such problems certainly also exist. As, for example, ethnographic studies in urban communication demonstrate, problems in situations of contact between members of immigrated minorities and those of the majority population within the host society are often made even worse when the immigrants acquire a nativelike fluency in the majority language, which is not paralleled by a shared knowledge of the ways of thinking, acting and speaking which enter into and are usually taken for granted in interaction. (Knapp & Knapp-Potthoff, 1987, p. 1)

First, the rationale given for studying intercultural communication rests significantly with the prevalence of intercultural encounters in contemporary life, including foreign travel, migrations of various kinds, and international trade. Also, these intercultural encounters are defined in generic terms as "contacts across ethnic and national borders." Again, although students of intercultural communication are cognizant of the wide variety of contexts in which encounters between members of different ethnic or cultural groups occur, there may be a tendency to think about the context of intercultural encounters in rather monolithic terms—with immigrant/host gatekeeping encounters serving as prototypical examples. This tendency to privilege gatekeeping encounters is understandable, as it responds to the pressing need to better understand and, it is hoped, contribute to the alleviation of hardships attending immigration. At the same time, an insistence on consideration of a range of intercultural communication contexts is likely to invite a broader perspective on the social-structural as well as on the cultural dimensions of such encounters. Social relations of power, as well as cultural assumptions about the world and about the conduct of talk, are not held constant across the very different contexts of tourism, immigration, and international trade. Therefore it is proposed that—for analytical, if not practical, purposes—each institutional context of intercultural communication deserves close scrutiny in its own right. An attempt will be made to exemplify the kinds of considerations that would go into such an analysis with reference to the context of international tourism, which has been given only scant attention in the intercultural communication literature. In this context, too, contacts across national and/or ethnic borders are a matter of routine. This chapter focuses on this contact as a context of intercultural communication because it can be contrasted with immigrant-minority/host-majority encounters in a fruitful way, inviting the reexamination and elaboration of assumptions that have characterized our efforts in the area of intercultural research.

TOURISTIC ENCOUNTERS AS INTERCULTURAL COMMUNICATION CONTEXTS

What would it mean to study touristic encounters as intercultural communication contexts? First, in the language of Goodwin and Duranti, the touristic encounter itself (e.g., a bargaining exchange in the Old City of Jerusalem marketplace) will be viewed as our "focal event." Then the "field of action in which it is embedded" will be explored. This, as they have cogently argued, is not a simple matter; it involves taking into account the participants' perspectives, particularly their own evolving definitions of what the relevant context is in given situations and the metacommunicative devices they employ in the interactional negotiation of context. Just as the studies of intercultural encounters in institutional settings have been grounded in an understanding of the role of formal gatekeeping situations in institutional life, the study of intercultural encounters in touristic settings must be grounded in an understanding of the nature of tourism as a socially grounded, contemporary recreational practice. The impressive expansion of tourism as a worldwide industry in the second half of our century has not escaped the notice of social scientists; indeed, in recent years, increasing research attention has been devoted to the study of the touristic experience by anthropologists and interpretive sociologists (e.g., Cohen, 1979; Fine & Speer, 1985; MacCannell, 1989; Smith, 1989). Even though little of this literature is specifically concerned with the encounter level of analysis, it nevertheless serves as a helpful starting point for delineating the "cultural field" in which touristic encounters are embedded. A broad consideration of the touristic experience is particularly necessary if we accept the anthropological perspective on the touristic quest as a contemporary form of "secular pilgrimage" practiced by the citizens of modernity. Such a view implies that the touristic voyage involves a departure from our everyday life and the tourist-pilgrim's immersion in a qualitatively different order of experience, whose distinctive contours need to be explored. The rest of this section will be devoted to the outline of such an exploration. To render it directly relevant to a general concern with intercultural communication encounters, comparisons will be made between touristic encounters and the intercultural gatekeeping encounters mentioned earlier.

Clearly, while both touristic and gatekeeping encounters can be seen as examples of "intercultural communication contexts," they differ from each other in many important ways. The most obvious way relates to the broader structural issues associated with power relations. Many researchers who have studied immigrant groups in Western societies (including some of those cited in previous sections) point out that their position vis-à-vis the host majority is marked by social disadvantage and powerlessness. Arguing against attempts to frame intercultural encounters in the urban West as politically neutral, Murray and Sondhi have phrased this in no uncertain terms: "This is the socio-political context in which cross-cultural encounters take place: one in which there is no possibility of an equal exchange between black and white" (Murray & Sondhi, 1987, p. 23). In most contacts between immigrants and majority members, the immigrants have to operate within an alien culture and respond appropriately to the expectations of the host society's various "gatekeepers," whether finding employment, obtaining help from social agencies, or negotiating their children's educational options. As Murray and Sondhi point out, this state of affairs, whereby the host culture is taken to be the cultural "given" to which newcomers must accommodate, is reflected in the way that "miscommunication" in intercultural encounters is interpreted—as a "problem" to be located in the immigrant community rather than in the host society or, indeed, in the interaction of the two societies. Another feature of immigrant-host encounters is the fact that they are inescapable, repetitive, and, at times, critical moments in immigrants' strivings to make a life for themselves and their families in the new society. It is here that repeated instances of "miscommunication" become cumulatively significant in producing attitudes of defensiveness and resentment among minority members and in reinforcing negative attitudes held toward them by some majority members, especially those who fall under Murray and Sondhi's categories of "racist" and "racially prejudiced" (whose numbers are multiplied in times of sociopolitical and economic stress).

Even though touristic encounters have not been the topic of much intercultural research, some students of language and social life have considered examples of intercultural contact involving tourists and members of the host culture as a way of demonstrating the cultural coding of participants' behavioral idioms in such encounters. For example, in considering the language of bargaining in situations involving Arab traders and Jewish tourists in the Old City of Jerusalem marketplace, Caplan (1980) and Spolsky and Cooper (1991) have addressed the frequent occurrence of "miscommunication" in such encounters, delineating the cultural assumptions that underlie and give shape to the activity of bargaining in tourist settings from the standpoint of both tourist and local trader. They remark:

> Bargaining is a complex business, and each culture has its own rules. The wise buyer appreciates the flexibility in the situation, and takes advantage of it. . . . But the absence of common rules, and, even worse, the conflict between systems, can lead to serious discomfort. . . . The European tradition views the market-place as a battlefield, with the seller praising his wares and the buyer attempting to show that they are not worth the price. . . . The Oriental style, Caplan suggests, is quite different; bargaining is seen as an enjoyable pastime, one in which both sides can take pleasure. As it is a social relationship, the shopkeeper feels most comfortable with the customers he knows. Regular customers need not bargain. (Spolsky & Cooper, 1991, p. 111)

Another example of "misunderstanding" in tourists' encounters with members of the host culture (Anglo-Americans touring Native American terrain in this case) appears in Basso's (1979) book, *Portraits of the "Whiteman."* One of these portraits—as depicted in the jocular exchanges the Western Apaches enact among themselves—is that of the tourist gushing over the beauty of the landscape. The playful imitation of the Anglo-American tourist improvisationally enacted in English by a young man, as he was trying to dissuade another man from leaving a drinking party, runs as follows: "Don't go away yet, my Indian friend. You going to miss sunset. Sure pretty good. You see it? Look at sun, look at clouds, look at stars. You see it? Just like postcard. You see it? Good wind. Nice and cool. You feel it? You sure lucky live over here. Sure beautiful country" (Basso, 1979, p. 87). Basso remarks that, in the Western Apaches' views, the white man's inclination to discourse at length on the patently obvious is most clearly signaled in tourists' excited gushings, adding:

> Unfortunately, when these spasms of enthusiasm are directed at Apaches, they may take offense, for what is implied, they claim, is that they have been judged insensitive to the beauty of their own homeland . . . and need to be *told* that it is a region of unsurpassing natural splendor. Gratuitous instruction of this kind is totally uncalled for, and Apaches regard it as yet another form of Anglo-American condescension. (pp. 87-88)

280 INTERCULTURAL COMMUNICATION CONTEXTS

In both these examples, tourists and their hosts have different conceptions of the kinds of activities they engage in, and have difficulty interpreting each other's interactional moves. Their exchanges are therefore (potentially) marked and shaped by cultural divergences in communicative styles and by differences in the interpretation of the meanings of interactional signals such as the sequential positioning of a bargaining move (e.g., in asking for the price before or after signaling a commitment to buy) or the intensity of affective displays (e.g., in showing appreciation). These examples demonstrate that the discussion of communicative style must be anchored in an exploration of specific types of contexts and activities—in this case, the concrete contexts of intercultural exchanges between tourists and locals. The minimal discussion of such examples found in the literature tends to be cast in terms of communicative failure (miscommunication) and is grounded in a lack of shared knowledge. Issues of power are not considered, nor is any discussion devoted to the particular nature of the touristic experience that frames encounters of the kind discussed by the above authors. Therefore a better understanding of the phenomenological dimensions of touristic encounters as intercultural communication settings, and of the expectations and power relations they entail, can further enrich our discussion of what it means to communicate across cultural borders.

Notably, as part of an international "tourism industry," touristic encounters, no less than immigrant-host encounters, are grounded in the material base of economic exchange. For the traveler moving from one tourist destination to another, encounters with members of the host society are framed as part of a voluntary, recreational engagement in a touristic experience. This touristic experience is in great measure contained within deliberately designed sites and attractions. It is also punctuated by face-to-face encounters, most of them of the service-encounter variety. However fleeting and essentially instrumental these encounters generally are, they nevertheless contain seeds of a promise for genuine (if fleeting) human contact between tourists and members of the host culture, the interpersonal arena where the preset text of touristic exchanges can be—potentially—interrupted, subverted, renegotiated. They are the most immediate means of responding to the ever-present urge to penetrate beyond touristic facades, to participate in those behind-the-scenes moments not designed for tourists, and look behind the "staged authenticity" of touristic displays (MacCannell, 1989). It is not surprising therefore that travel anecdotes are often centered on these moments.

Members of the host culture have a completely different agenda. They may vary considerably in the way they conceive of their participation in touristic exchanges. Some may seek employment in the tourism industry or informal encounters with tourists out of a desire to experience unmediated contact with cultural outsiders, joining the tourist's playground even while staying at home. Others, on the other hand, like some of the Arab merchants mentioned by Spolsky and Cooper (1991), may experience their contacts with cultural outsiders as an unwelcome necessity and an interactional burden.

Although in touristic encounters it is the tourist who is out of his or her "cultural waters," so to speak, this outsider position is not accompanied by an a priori condition of helplessness and disadvantage, as is often the case with immigrants. Indeed, tourists' positioning as client-consumers in a system of market exchange puts them in an advantageous position. Even while routinely engaging in various economic and social transactions with local residents, they are seldom expected to accommodate to the societies they visit, beyond such token gestures as the wearing of appropriate apparel in holy places, and the like. It is, indeed, mainly members of the host societies who are expected to accommodate themselves to the tourists' presence in a variety of ways, including the cultivation of some degree of bicultural competence and the courting of touristic tastes in the production of "tourist arts" (Graburn, 1976). The kind of intercultural accommodation often required of members of host cultures is not only a question of interactional competence but also a matter of goodwill. The more the presence of tourists is perceived as a foreign invasion tolerated out of economic necessity, the more is the reserve, or even resentment, of local people likely to be felt and expressed in a variety of subtle ways. The Western Apaches' ingroup joking about tourists, as discussed earlier, is a mild expression of this kind of ambivalence, and similar examples are found in repertoires of "touristic folklore" in other places as well.

The bridging of cultural gaps in touristic encounters is thus highly limited. Indeed, touristic exchanges stand out among intercultural communication encounters in that they essentially celebrate—rather than try to overcome and pacify—the experience of cultural difference. The whole point of tourism—at least, cultural tourism—is that it provides a socially approved context for recapturing a sense of authenticity through the concrete experience of the "otherness" of the Other. Some of the phenomenological dimensions of touristic encounters can be gleaned from a consideration of the stories people tell about them. Touristic folklore and personal experience narratives about foreign traveling reflect this cultural accent on the experience of "othering" in touristic encounters. Thus, as noted, many of the narratives people tell about their touristic endeavors involve memorable encounters with members of the host culture, often ones that serve either to justify or to transform the tourist's prior expectations and stereotypes of the host culture. Stories of bargaining exchanges in native stores are told and retold with much gusto, whether they are tales of triumph (in those cases in which the tourist managed not to be fooled) or tales of woe about paying an inordinately high price for a purchase. These tales both give expression to and re-create the sense of intercultural distance that is at the heart of the touristic quest. They become a narrative locus for the sense-making processes in and through which the meaning of cultural difference and the possibility of intercultural contact are imaginatively explored. They often involve the dramatization of trust and mistrust (rather than understanding and misunderstanding, which is the central concern of most sociolinguistic studies of intercultural communication) and frame the touristic encounter as a competitive game in which each party tries to outdo the other, as contrasted with selection interviews, which are conducted within a largely cooperative frame that participants may or may not be able to sustain.

Clearly, the successful or unsuccessful outcomes of bargaining encounters in a touristic setting carry little import compared with the personal weight that attends gatekeeping encounters involving immigrants and hosts. However anxious tourists may be in making a purchase, the game metaphor still applies to their transactions in local marketplaces, even when they approach bargaining transactions in a combative spirit, as Spolsky and Cooper (1991) suggest is the case for Israeli Jewish tourists in the East Jerusalem market. For members of the host culture, who depend on the successful outcomes of their transactions with tourists for their living, the battlefield metaphor may be more applicable, yet no particular bargaining exchange carries the kind of weight that selection interviews do. Particular touristic encounters—despite the intensity of the tourists' souvenir hunt or the traders' impassioned bargaining moves—are essentially fleeting, interchangeable, and not very consequential occasions compared with the gatekeeping encounters mentioned earlier. These encounters are essentially conducted within the ludic frame of tourism.

Therefore even a preliminary attempt to delineate the experiential dimensions that give shape and meaning to touristic encounters, whether from the standpoint of tourists or from the perspective of their hosts, brings out their complexity and distinctiveness as types of intercultural communication contexts in contemporary societies. Our understanding of the field of action in which touristic encounters are embedded must be grounded in an understanding of tourism as a cultural practice and the situational occasions it gives rise to.

CONCLUDING REMARKS

This chapter has taken context-sensitive studies of intercultural encounters as its starting point and has attempted to argue for an integration of prevalent approaches and a move from the notion of context to a recognition of contexts in intercultural communication research. An attempt has been made to show that such a move involves serious attention to a middle-range level of context, which relates to culturally defined categories of interactional situations and the practices associated with them as well as to the meanings they hold for differently positioned participants in those encounters. It has been suggested that people view touristic encounters as one type of such a situational category, to be fruitfully contrasted with the gatekeeping encounters that have been studied by discourse analysts in insightful ways.

Locating our concern at this middle-range level allows researchers to give proper consideration to the cultural construction of social situations and practices such as those associated with immigration or tourism. At the same time, it invites people to attend to the interactional framing and negotiation of these practices in the give-and-take of everyday life. In this view, intercultural communication contexts are not only arenas where preexisting cultural patterns of communication are brought into contact but are also uniquely defined products of socially patterned and historically grounded forms of intercultural exchange. In other words, intercultural bargaining occasions in the Old City of Jerusalem market are not only intercultural encounters between Arabs and Jews but also touristic encounters between guests and hosts. They draw their meanings, forms, and interactional constraints as much from the world of tourism (as locally interpreted) as from the cultural worlds they bring into contact. How local worlds of tourism are interactionally created and negotiated in given situations is a neglected area of empirical research well worth exploring both in its own right, as a major contemporary context of intercultural contact, and as a way of expanding our view of the interactional features to be reckoned with in attending to intercultural encounters. As noted earlier, touristic encounters foreground rather than efface cultural difference, underlining the negotiation of interactional trust and degree of playfulness in encounters where tourists and hosts come together face-to-face.

Gatekeeping and touristic encounters are clearly not the only contemporary "middle-range" context categories in which intercultural communication routinely occurs. Notably, recent developments in electronic communication have created new opportunities for intercultural exchanges, such as the Internet Relay Chat electronic network (IRC), which provides a global arena for real-time, electronically mediated interactions that cut across cultural borders on a global scale. Of interest, the few studies that have explored this form of electronic communication so far have focused on precisely the level of analysis that has been argued for in this chapter—attempting to characterize the distinctive features of IRC as a newly emerging context for the discursive production of "virtual communities" (Danet, Ruedenberg, & Rosenbaum-Tamari, 1994; Rheingold, 1993). However, IRC exchanges are considered neither by practitioners of this communication form nor by students of it as intercultural communication contexts. They are seen as part of a transcultural world, where cultural differences grounded in participants' real lives are neither celebrated nor surmounted—they are simply transcended. Future research will need to address the question of whether and how cultural differences in communication, which have been identified in other contexts, are at all relevant to electronic communication, or to identify the kind of interactional work that is done in transcending them, such as through various forms of inattention and accommodation.

International trade, diplomacy, and scholarly exchanges are other examples of middle-range intercultural encounter categories that come to mind. Each has its own distinctive characteristic and texture. Each deserves to be studied in its own right, drawing on whatever is known about cultural communication forms in the relevant cultures, on the one hand, and on interpretation of the specifics of given intercultural situations, on the other. It is suggested that a conceptual move from a focus on cultural context writ large to the various institutional contexts in which culture plays itself out is a first step to this end.

References

Abe, H., & Wiseman, R. (1983). A cross-cultural confirmation of the dimensions of intercultural effectiveness. *Intercultural Journal of Intercultural Relations, 7,* 53-67.

Abe, J., & Zane, N. (1990). Psychological maladjustment among Asian and white American college students: Controlling for confounds. *Journal of Counseling Psychology, 37*(4), 437-444.

Abelson, R. (1976). Script processing in attitude formation and decision making. In J. Carroll & J. Payne (Eds.), *Cognition and social behavior* (pp. 33-45). Hillsdale, NJ: Lawrence Erlbaum.

Adler, P. S. (1975). The transitional experience: An alternative view of culture shock. *Journal of Humanistic Psychology, 15,* 13-23.

Adler, P. S. (1976). Beyond cultural identity: Reflections on cultural and multicultural man. In L. Samovar & R. Porter (Eds.), *Intercultural communication: A reader* (2nd ed., pp. 362-378). Belmont, CA: Wadsworth.

Adorno, T. W., Frenkel-Brunswick, E., Levinson, D. J., & Sanford, R. N. (Eds.). (1982). *The authoritarian personality* (abridged ed.). New York: Norton. (Original work published 1950)

Albrecht, T. L. (1994). Epilogue: Social support and community: A historical account of the rescue networks in Denmark. In B. R. Burleson, T. L. Albrecht, & I. G. Sarason (Eds.), *Communication of social support* (pp. 267-280). Thousand Oaks, CA: Sage.

Allport, G. (1950, November). Prejudice: A problem in psychological and social causation. *Journal of Social Issues (Supplemental Series), 4,* 4-26.

Allport, G. (1979). *The nature of prejudice.* Reading, MA: Addison-Wesley. (Original work published 1954)

Althusser, L. (1971). *Lenin philosophy and other essays* (B. Brewster, Trans.). London: NLB.

Anderson, J. N. (1983). Health and illness in Filipino immigrants. *Western Journal of Medicine, 139,* 7-15.

Andrews, F., & Whithey, S. (1976). *Social indicators of well-being: America's perception of life quality.* New York: Plenum.

Appiah, A. (1990). *Racism* and *racisms.* In D. T. Goldberg (Ed.), *Anatomy of racism* (pp. 3-17). Minneapolis: University of Minnesota Press.

Argyle, M. (1987). *The psychology of happiness.* London: Methuen.

Argyle, M. (1991). *Cooperation.* London: Routledge.

Argyle, M., & Martin, M. (1991). The psychological causes of happiness. In F. Strack, M. Argyle, & N. Schwarz (Eds.), *Subjective well-being: An interdisciplinary perspective* (pp. 77-100). Oxford: Pergamon.

Arkin, R. (1981). Self-presentation styles. In J. Tedeschi (Ed.), *Impression management and social psychological research* (pp. 311-333). New York: Academic Press.

Armes, K., & Ward, C. (1989). Cross-cultural transitions and sojourner adjustment in Singapore. *Journal of Social Psychology, 129*(2), 273-275.

Arnberg, L. (1987). *Raising children bilingually: The preschool years.* Clevedon, UK: Multilingual Matters.

Asante, M. K. (1987). *The Afrocentric idea.* Philadelphia: Temple University Press.

Austin, C. (1983). *Cross-cultural reentry: An annotated bibliography.* Abilene, TX: Abilene Christian University Press.

Bakan, D. (1966). *The duality of human existence: An essay on psychology and religion.* Chicago: Rand McNally.

Baker, J. M. (1989). *Privacy regulation mechanisms in Japan and the United States.* Unpublished master's thesis, Arizona State University, Tempe.

Baldwin, J. R. (1994a). *European Americans' perception of "race" and racist communication: An interpretive (and critical) study.* Unpublished doctoral dissertation, Arizona State University, Tempe.

Baldwin, J. R. (1994b, November). *Putting sociology into interethnic communication studies.* Paper presented at the annual convention of the Speech Communication Association, New Orleans, LA.

Baldwin, J. R., & Hecht, M. L. (1993, November). *"Different is better": Conceptualizing and measuring tolerance for human diversity.* Paper presented at the annual convention of the Speech Communication Association, Miami, FL.

Ball, P., Giles, H., Byrne, J. L., & Berechree, P. (1984). Situational constraints on the evaluative significance of speech accommodation: Some Australian data. *International Journal of the Sociology of Language, 46,* 115-129.

Ball-Rokeach, S. (1973). From pervasive ambiguity to definition of the situation. *Sociometry, 36,* 378-389.

Bandura, A. (1977). Self-efficacy: Toward a unifying theory of behavioral change. *Psychological Review, 84,* 191-215.

Bandura, A. (1989). Perceived self-efficacy in the exercise of control over AIDS infection. In V. M. Mays, G. W. Albee, & S. F. Schneider (Eds.), *Primary prevention of AIDS: Psychological approaches* (pp. 128-141). Newbury Park, CA: Sage.

Bandura, A. (1990). Selective activation and disengagement of moral control. *Journal of Social Issues, 46,* 27-46.

Banks, S., Gao, G., & Baker, J. (1991). Intercultural encounters and miscommunication. In N. Coupland, H. Giles, & J. Wiemann (Eds.), *"Miscommunication" and problematic talk* (pp. 103-120). Newbury Park, CA: Sage.

Banton, M. (1986). Epistemological assumptions in the study of racial differentiation. In J. Rex & D. Mason (Eds.), *Theories of race and ethnic relations* (pp. 42-63). Cambridge: Cambridge University Press.

Banton, M. (1987). *Racial theories.* Cambridge: Cambridge University Press.

Bargh, J. (1989). Conditional automaticity. In J. Uleman & J. Bargh (Eds.), *Unintended thought* (pp. 3-51). New York: Guilford.

Barker, J. C. (1992). Cultural diversity: Changing the context of medical practice. *Western Journal of Medicine, 157,* 248-254.

Barker, M. (1990). Biology and the new racism. In D. T. Goldberg (Ed.), *Anatomy of racism* (pp. 18-37). Minneapolis: University of Minnesota Press.

Barker, M., & Beezer, A. (Eds.). (1992). *Reading into cultural studies.* London: Routledge.

Barnlund, D. C. (1994). Communication in a global village. In L. A. Samovar & R. E. Porter (Eds.), *Intercultural communication: A reader* (7th ed., pp. 26-36). Belmont, CA: Wadsworth.

Bar-Tal, D. (1990). Causes and consequences of delegitimization: Models of conflict and ethnocentrism. *Journal of Social Issues, 46,* 65-81.

Basso, K. (1970). To give up on words. *Southern Journal of Anthropology, 26,* 213-230.

Basso, K. (1979). *Portraits of "the whiteman": Linguistic play and cultural symbols among the Western Apache.* Cambridge: Cambridge University Press.

Bavelas, J., Black, A., Chovil, N., & Mullett, J. (1990). *Equivocal communication.* Newbury Park, CA: Sage.

Baxter, L. A. (1988). A dialectical perspective on communication strategies in relationship development. In S. Duck (Ed.), *Handbook of personal relationships* (pp. 257-273). London: Wiley.

Baxter, L. A. (1990). Dialectical contradictions in relationship development. *Journal of Social and Personal Relationships, 7,* 69-88.

Becker, C. S. (1992). *Living and relating: An introduction to phenomenology.* Newbury Park, CA: Sage.

Becker, E. (1971). *The birth and death of meaning.* New York: Harper & Row.

Bell, R. (1987). Social involvement. In J. McCroskey & J. Daly (Eds.), *Personality and interpersonal communication* (pp. 195-242). Newbury Park, CA: Sage.

Bellah, R., Madsen, R., Sullivan, W., Swidler, A., & Tipton, S. (1985). *Habits of the heart.* Berkeley: University of California Press.

Bem, S. L. (1974). The measurement of psychological androgeny. *Journal of Consulting and Clinical Psychology, 42,* 155-162.

Ben-Amos, D. (1993). Context in context. *Western Folklore, 52,* 209-226.

Bennett, M. J. (1986a). A developmental approach to training for intercultural sensitivity. *International Journal of Intercultural Relations, 10,* 179-196.

Bennett, M. J. (1986b). Towards ethnorelativism: A developmental model of intercultural sensitivity. In M. P. Paige (Ed.), *Cross-cultural orientation: New conceptualizations and applications* (pp. 26-69). Lanham, MD: University Press of America.

Berger, C. R. (1977). The covering law perspective as a theoretical basis for the study of human communication. *Communication Quarterly, 25,* 7-18.

Berger, C. R. (1979). Beyond initial interactions. In H. Giles & R. St. Clair (Eds.), *Language and asocial psychology* (pp. 122-144). Oxford: Blackwell.

Berger, C. R., & Bradac, J. (1982). *Language and social knowledge.* London: Edward Arnold.

Berger, C. R., & Calabrese, R. (1975). Some explorations in initial interactions and beyond: Toward a developmental theory of interpersonal communication. *Human Communication Research, 1,* 99-112.

Berger, C. R., & Gudykunst, W. B. (1991). Uncertainty and communication. In B. Dervin & M. Voigt (Eds.), *Progress in communication sciences* (Vol. 10, pp. 21-66). Norwood, NJ: Ablex.

Berger, J., Cohen, B. P., & Zelditch, M. (1973). Status characteristics and social interaction. In R. Ofshe (Ed.), *Interpersonal behavior in small groups* (pp. 194-216). Englewood Cliffs, NJ: Prentice Hall.

Berger, J., Conner, T. L., & Fisek, M. H. (1974). *Expectation states theory: A theoretical research program.* Cambridge: MA: Winthrop.

Berger, J., Wagner, D. G., & Zelditch, M. (1985). Introduction: Expectation states theory: Review and assessment. In J. Berger & M. Zelditch (Eds.), *Status, rewards, and influence* (pp. 1-72). San Francisco: Jossey-Bass.

Bernieri, F. J., & Rosenthal, R. (1991). Interpersonal coordination: Behavior matching and interactional synchrony. In R. S. Feldman & B. Rimé (Eds.), *Fundamentals of nonverbal behavior* (pp. 401-432). Cambridge: Cambridge University Press.

Bernstein, R. J. (1976). *The restructuring of social and political theory.* Philadelphia: University of Pennsylvania Press.

Berry, J. W. (1980). Psychology of acculturation: Understanding individuals moving between cultures. In R. Brislin (Ed.), *Applied cross-cultural psychology* (pp. 232-253). Beverly Hills, CA: Sage.

Berry, J. W. (1990). Psychology of acculturation: Understanding individuals moving between cultures. In R. Brislin (Ed.), *Applied cross-cultural psychology* (pp. 232-253). Newbury Park, CA: Sage.

Berry, J. W., & Dasen, P. R. (1974). *Culture and cognition: Readings in cross-cultural psychology.* London: Methuen.

Berscheid, E. (1985). Interpersonal attraction. In G. Lindzey & E. Aronson (Eds.), *The handbook of social psychology* (3rd ed., Vol. 2, pp. 413-484). New York: Random House.

Berscheid, E., Graziano, W., Monson, T., & Dermer, M. (1976). Outcome dependency: Attention, attribution, and attraction. *Journal of Personality and Social Psychology, 34,* 978-989.

288 • INTERCULTURAL COMMUNICATION THEORY

Bertalanffy, L. (1956). *Robots, men, and minds.* New York: Braziller.

Beyene, Y. (1992). Medical disclosure and refugees: Telling bad news to Ethiopian patients. *Western Journal of Medicine, 157,* 328-332.

Bhawuk, D. P. S., & Brislin, R. W. (1992). The measurement of intercultural sensitivity using the concepts of individualism and collectivism. *International Journal of Intercultural Relations, 16,* 413-436.

Bierly, M. M. (1985). Prejudice toward contemporary outgroups as a generalized attitude. *Journal of Applied Social Psychology, 15,* 189-199.

Billig, M. (1976). *Social psychology and intergroup relations.* London: Academic Press.

Billig, M., Condor, S., Edwards, D., Gane, M., Middleton, D., & Radley, A. (1988). *Ideological dilemmas.* Newbury Park, CA: Sage.

Bilous, F. R., & Krauss, R. M. (1988). Dominance and accommodation in the conversational behaviors of same- and mixed-gender dyads. *Language and Communication, 8,* 183-194.

Black, J. (1990). The relationship of personal characteristics with the adjustment of Japanese expatriate managers. *Management International Review, 30*(2), 119-134.

Black, J. (1992). Coming home: The relationship of expatriate expectations with repatriation adjustment and job performance. *Human Relations, 45*(2), 177-192.

Black, J., Mendenhall, M., & Oddou, G. (1991). Toward a comprehensive model of international adjustment: An integration of multiple theoretical perspectives. *Academy of Management Review, 16*(2), 291-317.

Black, J., & Stephens, G. (1989). The influence of spouse on American expatriate adjustment and intent to stay in Pacific Rim overseas assignments. *Journal of Management, 15*(4), 529-544.

Blake, A. (1992). Tony Bennett and Janet Woolacott, *Bond and beyond.* In M. Barker & A. Beezer (Eds.), *Reading into cultural studies* (pp. 49-64). London: Routledge.

Blalock, H. M. (1969). *Theory construction.* Englewood Cliffs, NJ: Prentice Hall.

Blalock, H. M. (1982a). *Conceptualization and measurement in the social sciences.* Beverly Hills, CA: Sage.

Blalock, H. M. (1982b). *Race and ethnic relations.* Englewood Cliffs, NJ: Prentice Hall.

Blanchard, F., Lilly, T., & Vaughn, I. (1991). Reducing the expression of racial prejudice. *Psychological Science, 2,* 101-105.

Blau, P., & Schwartz, B. (1984). *Cross-cutting social circles.* New York: Academic Press.

Blum-Kulka, S. (1987). Indirectness and politeness in requests: Same or different? *Journal of Pragmatics, 11,* 131-146.

Blum-Kulka, S., Danet, B., & Gherson, R. (1985). The language of requesting in Israeli society. In J. Forgas (Ed.), *Language and social situation* (pp. 113-141). New York: Springer-Verlag.

Blum-Kulka, S., & House, J. (1989). Cross-cultural and situational variation in requesting behavior. In S. Blum-Kulka, J. House, & G. Kasper (Eds.), *Cross-cultural pragmatics: Requests and apologies* (pp. 123-154). Norwood, NJ: Ablex.

Bochner, S. (1983). Doctors, patients and their cultures. In D. Pendleton & J. Hasler (Eds.), *Doctor-patient communication* (pp. 127-138). London: Academic Press.

Bochner, S., Lin, A., & McLeod, B. (1980). Anticipated role conflict of returning overseas students. *Journal of Social Psychology, 110,* 265-272.

Bodenhausen, G. (1993). Emotions, arousal, and stereotypic judgments. In D. Mackie & D. Hamilton (Eds.), *Affect, cognition, and stereotyping* (pp. 13-37). San Diego, CA: Academic Press.

Bodenhausen, G., Gaelick, L., & Wyer, R. (1987). Affective and cognitive factors in intragroup and intergroup communication. In C. Hendrick (Ed.), *Group processes and intergroup relations* (pp. 137-166). Newbury Park, CA: Sage.

Boekestijn, C. (1988). Intercultural migration and the development of personal identity. *International Journal of Intercultural Relations, 12*(2), 83-105.

Boggs, G. L. (1990). Beyond Eurocentrism. *Monthly Review, 41*(9), 12-18.

Bostrom, R., & Donohew, L. (1992). The case for empiricism: Clarifying fundamental issues in communication theory. *Communication Monographs, 59,* 109-129.

Boulding, K. (1977). *The images: Knowledge in life and society*. Ann Arbor: University of Michigan Press. (Original work published 1956)

Bourhis, R. Y. (1979). Language in ethnic interaction: A social psychological approach. In H. Giles & B. St. Jacques (Eds.), *Language and ethnic relations* (pp. 117-141). Oxford: Pergamon.

Bourhis, R. Y. (1991). Organizational communication and accommodation: Toward some conceptual and empirical links. In H. Giles, N. Coupland, & J. Coupland (Eds.), *Contexts of accommodation: Developments in applied sociolinguistics* (pp. 270-303). New York: Cambridge University Press.

Bourhis, R. Y., Giles, H., & Rosenthal, D. (1981). Notes on the construction of a subjective vitality questionnaire for ethnolinguistic groups. *Journal of Multilingual and Multicultural Development, 2*, 144-155.

Bourhis, R. Y., & Sachdev, I. (1984). Vitality perceptions and language attitudes: Some Canadian data. *Journal of Language and Social Psychology, 3*, 97-126.

Bowser, B. P. (1992). African-American culture and AIDS prevention: From barrier to ally. *Western Journal of Medicine, 157*, 286-289.

Boyd, D. (1989). *Mystics, magicians, and medicine people: Tales of a wanderer*. New York: Paragon House.

Brabant, S., Palmer, C., & Gramling, R. (1990). Returning home: An empirical investigation of cross-cultural reentry. *International Journal of Intercultural Relations, 14*(4), 387-404.

Bradac, J. J., Mulac, A., & House, A. (1988). Lexical diversity and magnitude of convergent versus divergent style-shifting: Perceptual and evaluative consequences. *Language and Communication, 8*, 213-228.

Brandt, D. R. (1988). How service marketers can identify value-enhancing service elements. *Journal of Services Marketing, 2*(3), 35-41.

Brein, H., & David, K. (1971). Intercultural communication and the adjustment of the sojourner. *Psychological Bulletin, 76*(3), 215-230.

Breton, R. (1964). Institutional completeness of ethnic communities and the personal relations of immigrants. *American Journal of Sociology, 70*(2), 193-205.

Brewer, J., & Hunter, A. (1989). *Multimethod research: A synthesis of styles*. Newbury Park, CA: Sage.

Brewer, M. B. (1991). The social self. *Personality and Social Psychology Bulletin, 17*, 475-485.

Brickman, P., Coates, D., & Janoff-Bulman, R. (1978). Lottery winners and accident victims: Is happiness relative? *Journal of Personality and Social Psychology, 36*, 917-927.

Brislin, R. W. (1991). Prejudice in intercultural communication. In L. A. Samovar & R. E. Porter (Eds.), *Intercultural communication: A reader* (6th ed., pp. 366-369). Belmont, CA: Wadsworth.

Brod, M., & Heurtin-Roberts, S. (1992). Older Russian emigres and medical care. *Western Journal of Medicine, 157*, 333-336.

Broome, B. J. (1990). "Palevome": Foundations of struggle and conflict in Greek interpersonal communication. *Southern Communication Journal, 55*, 260-275.

Brown, P., Hinkel, S., Ely, P. G., Fox-Cardamone, L., Maras, P., & Taylor, L. A. (1992). Recognizing group diversity: Individualist-collectivist and autonomous-relational social orientations and their implications for intergroup processes. *British Journal of Social Psychology, 31*, 327-342.

Brown, P., & Levinson, S. (1978). Universals in language usage: Politeness phenomenon. In E. Goody (Ed.), *Questions and politeness: Strategies in social interaction* (pp. 56-289). Cambridge: Cambridge University Press.

Buck, R. (1984). *The communication of emotion*. New York: Guilford.

Budner, S. (1962). Intolerance of ambiguity as a personality variable. *Journal of Personality, 30*, 29-50.

Buller, D. B., & Burgoon, J. K. (1986). The effects of vocalics and nonverbal sensitivity on compliance: A replication and extension. *Human Communication Research, 4*, 126-144.

Burgess, M. (1978). The resurgence of ethnicity: Myth or reality? *Ethnic and Racial Studies,* *1*(3), 265-285.

Burgoon, J. K. (1978). A communication model of personal space violations: Explication and an initial test. *Human Communication Research, 4,* 129-142.

Burgoon, J. K. (1983). Nonverbal violation of expectations. In J. M. Wiemann & R. P. Harrison (Eds.), *Nonverbal interaction* (pp. 77-111). Beverly Hills, CA: Sage.

Burgoon, J. K. (1986, February). *Expectancy violations: Theory, research, and critique.* Paper presented at the annual meeting of the Western States Communication Association, Tucson, AZ.

Burgoon, J. K. (1992). Applying a comparative approach to nonverbal expectancy violations theory. In J. Blumler, K. E. Rosengren, & J. M. McLeod (Eds.), *Comparatively speaking* (pp. 53-69). Newbury Park, CA: Sage.

Burgoon, J. K. (1993). Interpersonal expectations, expectancy violations, and emotional communication. *Journal of Language and Social Psychology, 12,* 30-48.

Burgoon, J. K., & Aho, L. (1982). Three field experiments on the effects of violations of conversational distance. *Communication Monographs, 49,* 71-88.

Burgoon, J. K., Buller, D. B., Hale, J. L., & deTurck, M. A. (1984). Relational messages associated with nonverbal behaviors. *Human Communication Research, 10,* 351-378.

Burgoon, J. K., Buller, D. B., & Woodall, W. G. (1989). *Nonverbal communication: The unspoken dialogue.* New York: HarperCollins.

Burgoon, J. K., Coker, D. A., & Coker, R. A. (1986). Communicative effects of gaze behavior: A test of two contrasting explanations. *Human Communication Research, 12,* 495-524.

Burgoon, J. K., Dillman, L., & Stern, L. A. (1993). Adaptation in dyadic interaction: Defining and operationalizing patterns of reciprocity and compensation. *Communication Theory, 3,* 295-316.

Burgoon, J. K., & Hale, J. L. (1988). Nonverbal expectancy violations theory: Model elaboration and application to immediacy behaviors. *Communication Monographs, 55,* 58-79.

Burgoon, J. K., & Jones, S. B. (1976). Toward a theory of personal space expectations and their violations. *Human Communication Research, 2,* 131-146.

Burgoon, J. K., & Le Poire, B. A. (1993). Effects of communication expectancies, actual communication, and expectancy disconfirmation on evaluation of communicators and their communication behavior. *Human Communication Research, 20,* 67-96.

Burgoon, J. K., Le Poire, B. A., & Rosenthal, R. (in press). Effects of preinteraction expectancies and target communication on perceiver reciprocity and compensation in dyadic interaction. *Journal of Experimental Social Psychology.*

Burgoon, J. K., Manusov, V., Mineo, P., & Hale, J. L. (1985). Effects of eye gaze on hiring, credibility, attraction and relational message interpretation. *Journal of Nonverbal Behavior, 9,* 133-146.

Burgoon, J. K., & Newton, D. A. (1991). Applying a social meaning model to relational message interpretations of conversational involvement: Comparing observer and participant perspectives. *Southern Communication Journal, 56,* 96-113.

Burgoon, J. K., Newton, D. A., Walther, J. A., & Baesler, E. J. (1989). Nonverbal expectancy violations and conversational involvement. *Journal of Nonverbal Behavior, 12,* 97-120.

Burgoon, J. K., Olney, C. A., & Coker, R. (1988). The effects of communicator characteristics on patterns of reciprocity and compensation. *Journal of Nonverbal Behavior, 11,* 146-165.

Burgoon, J. K., Stacks, D. W., & Burch, S. A. (1982). The role of nonverbal violations of expectations in interpersonal influence. *Communication, 11,* 114-128.

Burgoon, J. K., Stacks, D. W., & Woodall, W. G. (1979). A communicative model of violations of distancing expectations. *Western Journal of Speech Communication, 43,* 153-167.

Burgoon, J. K., Stern, L. A., & Dillman, L. (in press). *Interpersonal adaptation: Dyadic interaction processes.* Cambridge: Cambridge University Press.

Burgoon, J. K., & Walther, J. B. (1990). Nonverbal expectancies and the evaluative consequences of violations. *Human Communication Research, 17,* 232-265.

Burgoon, J. K., Walther, J. B., & Baesler, E. J. (1992). Interpretations, evaluations, and consequences of interpersonal touch. *Human Communication Research, 19*, 237-263.

Burgoon, M. (1974). Toward a message-centered theory of persuasion: Three empirical investigations of language intensity. *Human Communication Research, 1*, 240-256.

Burgoon, M., Birk, T. S., & Hall, J. R. (1991). Compliance and satisfaction with physician-patient communication: An expectancy theory interpretation of gender differences. *Human Communication Research, 18*, 177-208.

Burgoon, M., & Hall, J. R. (1994). Myths as health belief systems: The language of salves, sorcery, and science. *Health Communication, 6*, 97-116.

Burns, D. (1985). *Intimate connections.* New York: Signet.

Burrel, G., & Morgan, G. (1979). *Sociological paradigms and organisational analysis.* London: Heinemann.

Byrd, M. L. (1991, November). *Research note on an exploratory investigation of the concept of tolerance toward cultural diversity.* Paper presented at the annual convention of the Speech Communication Association, Atlanta, GA.

Byrd, M. L. (1993). *The intracultural communication book.* New York: McGraw-Hill.

Byrne, D. (1971). *The attraction paradigm.* New York: Academic Press.

Cadotte, E. R., Woodruff, R. B., & Jenkins, R. L. (1987). Expectations and norms in models of consumer satisfaction. *Journal of Marketing Research, 24*, 305-314.

Cahn, D., & Hanford, J. (1984, Summer). Perspectives on human communication research: Behaviorism, phenomenology, and an integrated view. *Western Journal of Speech Communication, 48*, 277-292.

Calhoun, M. A. (1986). The Vietnamese woman: Health/illness attitudes and behaviors. In P. N. Stern (Ed.), *Women, health and culture* (pp. 61-72). New York: Hemisphere.

Campbell, A. (1981). *The sense of well-being in America.* New York: McGraw-Hill.

Campbell, A., Converse, P., & Rodgers, W. (1976). *The quality of American life.* New York: Sage.

Canary, D. J., & Hause, K. (1993). Is there any reason to research sex differences in communication? *Communication Quarterly, 41*, 129-144.

Caplan, G. (1980). *Arab and Jew in Jerusalem.* Cambridge, MA: Harvard University Press.

Cappella, J. N. (1987). Interpersonal communication: Definitions and fundamental questions. In C. R. Berger & S. H. Chaffee (Eds.), *Handbook of communication science* (pp. 184-238). Newbury Park, CA: Sage.

Carbaugh, D. (Ed.). (1990). *Cultural communication and intercultural contact.* Hillsdale, NJ: Lawrence Erlbaum.

Carbaugh, D. (1993). "Soul" and "self": Soviet and American cultures in conversation. *Quarterly Journal of Speech, 79*(2), 182-200.

Cargile, A. C., Giles, H., & Clément, R. (in press). The role of language in ethnic conflict. In J. Gittler (Ed.), *Conflict knowledge and conflict resolution.* Greenwich, CT: JAI Press.

Casey, M. K. (1994). *Fatalism and the modification of the extended parallel process model.* Unpublished manuscript.

CCCS (Centre for Contemporary Cultural Studies). (1982). *The Empire strikes back: Race and racism in 70s Britain.* London: Hutchinson.

Chaffee, S. H., & Berger, C. R. (1987). Levels of analysis: An introduction. In C. R. Berger & S. H. Chaffee (Eds.), *Handbook of communication science* (pp. 143-145). Newbury Park, CA: Sage.

Chamberlain, K. (1985). Value dimensions, cultural differences, and the prediction of perceived quality of life. *Social Indicators Research, 17*, 345-401.

Chang, H.-C., & Holt, G. R. (1991). The concept of *yuan* and Chinese interpersonal relationships. In S. Ting-Toomey & F. Korzenny (Eds.), *Cross-cultural interpersonal communication* (pp. 28-57). Newbury Park, CA: Sage.

Chin, S. (1992). This, that, and the other: Managing illness in a first generation Korean-American family. *Western Journal of Medicine, 157*, 305-309.

Chinese Culture Connection. (1987). Chinese values and the search for culture-free dimensions. *Journal of Cross-Cultural Psychology, 18*, 143-164.

Chu, L. L. (1988). Mass communication theory: A Chinese perspective. In W. Dissanayake (Ed.), *Communication theory: An Asian perspective* (pp. 126-138). Singapore: Asian Mass Communication and Information Centre.

Church, A. (1982). Sojourner adjustment. *Psychological Bulletin, 91*(3), 540-572.

Clark, H., & Marshall, C. (1981). Definite reference and mutual knowledge. In A. Joshi, B. Webber, & I. Sag (Eds.), *Elements of discourse understanding* (pp. 10-63). Cambridge: Cambridge University Press.

Clark, M. M. (1983). Cultural context of medical practice. *Western Journal of Medicine, 139*, 2-6.

Clarke, S., & Obler, J. (1976). Ethnic conflict, community-building, and the emergence of ethnic political traditions in the United States. In S. Clarke & J. Obler (Eds.), *Urban ethnic conflicts: A comparative perspective* (pp. 1-34). Chapel Hill: University of North Carolina Press.

Clément, R., & Noels, R. A. (1992). Towards a situated approach to ethnolinguistic identity: The effects of status on individual groups. *Journal of Language and Social Psychology, 11*, 203-232.

Clough, P. T. (1992). *The end(s) of ethnography: From realism to social criticism.* Newbury Park, CA: Sage.

Cohen, E. (1979). A phenomenology of tourist experiences. *Sociology, 13*(2), 179-200.

Collier, M. J. (1994). Cultural identity and intercultural communication. In L. A. Samovar & R. E. Porter (Eds.), *Intercultural communication: A reader* (7th ed., pp. 36-45). Belmont, CA: Wadsworth.

Collier, M. J., & Thomas, M. (1988). Cultural identity in inter-cultural communication: An interpretive perspective. In Y. Y. Kim & W. B. Gudykunst (Eds.), *International and intercultural communication annual: Vol. 12. Theories in intercultural communication* (pp. 94-120). Newbury Park, CA: Sage.

Collins, P. H. (1990). *Black feminist thought: Knowledge, consciousness, and the politics of empowerment.* Boston: HarperCollins Academic.

Cook, W. (1962). The systematic analysis of socially significant events: A strategy for social research. *Journal of Social Issues, 18*(2), 66-88.

Copeland, L., & Griggs, L. (1985). *Going international.* New York: Random House.

Corliss, R. (1994, March 21). Dashing Daniel. *Time,* pp. 66-69.

Cornell, S. (1988). *The return of the Natives: American Indian political resurgence.* New York: Oxford University Press.

Coté, R., & Clément, R. (1994). Language attitudes: An interactive situated approach. *Language and Communication, 14*, 237-252.

Coupland, N., Coupland, J., Giles, H., & Henwood, K. (1988). Accommodating the elderly: Invoking and extending a theory. *Language in Society, 17*, 1-41.

Coupland, N., & Giles, H. (1988). Introduction: The communicative contexts of accommodation. *Language and Communication, 8*, 175-182.

Coupland, N., Giles, H., & Wiemann, J. M. (Eds.). (1991). *Miscommunication and problematic talk.* Newbury Park, CA: Sage.

Craig, R. T. (1986). Goals in discourse. In D. G. Ellis & W. A. Donohue (Eds.), *Contemporary issues in language and discourse processes* (pp. 257-273). Hillsdale, NJ: Lawrence Erlbaum.

Creighton, M. R. (1990). Revisiting shame and guilt cultures. *Ethos, 18*, 279-307.

Cronen, V. E., Chen, V., & Pearce, W. B. (1988). Coordinated management of meaning: A critical theory. In Y. Y. Kim & W. B. Gudykunst (Eds.), *Theories in intercultural communication* (pp. 66-98). Newbury Park, CA: Sage.

Cronen, V. E., Pearce, B., & Tomm, K. (1985). A dialectical view of personal change. In K. Gergen & K. Davis (Eds.), *The social construction of the person* (pp. 203-224). New York: Springer-Verlag.

Crosby, F., Bromley, S., & Saxe, L. (1980). Recent unobtrusive studies of black and white discrimination and prejudice. *Psychological Bulletin, 87*, 546-563.

Cross, S. E., & Markus, H. R. (1991, July). *Cultural adaptation and the self: Self-construal, coping, and stress.* Paper presented at the Ninety-Ninth Annual Convention of the American Psychological Association, San Francisco.

Csikszentmihalyi, M. (1990). *Flow: The psychology of optimal experience.* New York: Harper & Row.

Cupach, W. R., & Imahori, T. T. (1993). Identity management theory: Communication competence in intercultural episodes and relationships. In R. L. Wiseman & J. Koester (Eds.), *Intercultural communication competence* (pp. 112-131). Newbury Park, CA: Sage.

Dace, K. (1990). *The conflict-group decision-making link: An exploratory study.* Unpublished doctoral dissertation, University of Iowa.

da Matta, R. (1979). *Carnavais, malandros e hérois: Para uma sociologia do dilema brasileiro* [*Carnavals*, hoodlums, and heroes: Toward a sociology of the Brazilian dilemma]. Rio de Janeiro: Zahar.

Dance, F., & Larson, C. (1976). *The functions of human communication: A theoretical approach.* New York: Holt, Rinehart & Winston.

Danet, B., Ruedenberg, L., & Rosenbaum-Tamari, Y. (1994). *"Smoking dope" at a virtual party: Language, play and performance on Internet Relay Chat.* Unpublished manuscript, Hebrew University, Jerusalem.

David, H. (1969). Involuntary international migration: Adaptation of refugees. In E. Brody (Ed.), *Behavior in new environments: Adaptation of migrant populations* (pp. 73-95). Beverly Hills, CA: Sage.

Davis, E., & Fine-Davis, M. (1991). Social indicators of living conditions in Ireland with European comparisons. *Social Indicators Research, 25*, 103-365.

Dawis, R., & Lofquist, L. (1984). *A psychological theory of work adjustment.* Minneapolis: University of Minnesota Press.

Deaux, K. (1991). Social identities. In R. Curtis (Ed.), *The relational self* (pp. 77-93). New York: Guilford.

DeCocq, G. (1976). European and North American self-help movements: Some contrasts. In A. Katz & E. Bender (Eds.), *The strength in us: Self-help groups in the modern world* (pp. 202-208). New York: New Viewpoint.

Demerath, L. (1993). Knowledge-based affect. *Social Psychology Quarterly, 56*, 136-147.

Denzin, N. K. (1978). *The research act: A theoretical introduction to sociological methods.* New York: McGraw-Hill.

Denzin, N. K. (1989). *Interpretive biography.* Newbury Park, CA: Sage.

Detweiler, R. A., Brislin, R. W., & McCormack, W. (1983). Situational analysis. In D. Landis & R. W. Brislin (Eds.), *Handbook of intercultural training* (Vol. 2, pp. 100-123). New York: Pergamon.

Deutsch, M. (1969). Conflicts: Productive and destructive. *Journal of Social Issues, 25*, 7-41.

Deutsch, M. (1973). *The resolution of conflict.* New Haven, CT: Yale University Press.

Deutsch, S., & Won, G. (1963). Some factors in the adjustment of foreign nationals in the United States. *Journal of Social Issues, 19*(3), 115-122.

Devine, P. (1989). Stereotypes and prejudice: Their automatic and controlled components. *Journal of Personality and Social Psychology, 56*, 5-18.

Diggs, N., & Murphy, B. (1991). Japanese adjustment to American communities: The case of the Japanese in the Dayton area. *International Journal of Intercultural Relations, 15*, 103-116.

Dijker, A. (1987). Emotional reactions to ethnic minorities. *European Journal of Social Psychology, 17*, 305-325.

Dinges, N. (1983). Intercultural competence. In D. Landis & R. Brislin (Eds.), *Handbook of intercultural training: Vol. 1. Issues in theory and design* (pp. 176-202). New York: Pergamon.

Doi, L. T. (1973). The Japanese patterns of communication and the concept of *amae*. *Quarterly Journal of Speech, 59*, 180-185.

Douglas, W. (1983). Self-monitoring. *Human Communication Research, 10*, 81-96.

Douglas, W. (1984). Initial interaction scripts. *Human Communication Research, 11*, 203-219.

Downey, H., Hellriegel, D., & Slocum, J. (1977). Individual characteristics as sources of perceived uncertainty variability. *Human Relations, 30*, 161-174.

Dubin, R. (1978). *Theory building* (rev. ed.). New York: Free Press.

Duck, S. W., & Sants, H. K. A. (1983). On the origin of the specious: Are personal relationships really interpersonal states? *Journal of Social and Clinical Psychology, 1*, 27-41.

Dunbar, E. (1992). Adjustment and satisfaction of expatriate U.S. personnel. *International Journal of Intercultural Relations, 16*, 1-16.

Duran, R. (1983). Communicative adaptability. *Communication Quarterly, 31*, 320-326.

Dyal, J., & Dyal, R. (1981). Acculturation, stress and coping. *International Journal of Intercultural Relations, 5*(4), 301-328.

Eagly, A. H. (1987). *Sex differences in social behavior: A social-role interpretation*. Hillsdale, NJ: Lawrence Erlbaum.

Eagly, A. H., & Chaiken, S. (1993). *The psychology of attitudes*. Fort Worth, TX: Harcourt Brace Jovanovich.

Easterlin, R. (1974). Does economic growth improve the human lot? Some empirical evidence. In P. David & M. Reder (Eds.), *Nations and households in economic growth* (pp. 89-126). New York: Academic Press.

Eaton, W., & Lasry, J. (1978). Mental health and occupational mobility in a group of immigrants. *Science and Medicine, 12*, 53-58.

Edwards, D., & Potter, J. (1992). *Discursive psychology*. London: Sage.

Ekman, P., & Friesen, W. V. (1969). The repertoire of nonverbal behavior: Categories, origins, usage, and coding. *Perceptual and Motor Skills, 24*, 711-724.

Elliott, G. (1979). Some effects of deception and level of self-monitoring on planning and reacting to a self-presentation. *Journal of Personality and Social Psychology, 37*, 1282-1292.

Emmons, R., & Diener, E. (1985). Factors predicting satisfaction judgments: A comparative examination. *Social Indicators Research, 16*, 157-167.

Epstein, S. (1976). Anxiety arousal and the self-concept. In I. Sarason & C. Spielberger (Eds.), *Stress and anxiety* (Vol. 3, pp. 185-224). New York: Wiley.

Essed, F. (1990). *Everyday racism: Reports from women of two cultures* (C. Jaffe, Trans.). Claremont, CA: Hunter House.

Essed, F. (1991). *Understanding everyday racism: An interdisciplinary theory*. Newbury Park, CA: Sage.

Ezorsky, G. (1991). *Racism and justice: The case for affirmative action*. Ithaca, NY: Cornell University Press.

Falk, G. (1982). An empirical study measuring conflict in problem-solving groups which are assigned different decision rules. *Human Relations, 35*, 1123-1138.

Fantini, A. (1985). *Language acquisition of a bilingual child: A sociolinguistic perspective (to age ten)*. Clevedon, UK: Multilingual Matters.

FBI: Racism cause of most hate crime. (1993, January 5). *Tempe Daily Tribune*, p. A3.

Fenigstein, A. (1984). Self-consciousness and the overperception of self as a target. *Journal of Personality and Social Psychology, 47*, 860-870.

Fielding, N., & Fielding, J. (1986). *Linking data*. Newbury Park, CA: Sage.

Fine, E., & Speer, J. (1985). Tour guide performances as sight sacralization. *Annals of Tourism Research, 12*, 73-95.

Fish, S. E. (1978). Normal circumstances, literal language, direct speech acts, the ordinary, the everyday, the obvious, what goes without saying, and other special cases. *Critical Inquiry, 4*, 625-644.

Fishbein, M., & Ajzen, I. (1975). *Belief, attitude, intention, and behavior: An introduction to theory and research*. Reading, MA: Addison-Wesley.

Fishman, J. A. (1971). *Sociolinguistics: A brief introduction.* Rowley, MA: Newbury House.

Fiske, A. P. (1991). *Structures of social life.* New York: Free Press.

Fitzgerald, F. T. (1988). Patients from other cultures: How they view you, themselves, and disease. *Consultant, 28,* 65-73.

Fitzpatrick, M. A., & Indvik, J. (1986). On alternative conceptions of relational communication. *Communication Quarterly, 34,* 19-23.

Ford, D., & Lerner, R. (1992). *Developmental systems theory: An integrative approach.* Newbury Park, CA: Sage.

Forgas, J. P., & Bond, M. H. (1985). Cultural influences on the perception of interaction episodes. *Personality and Social Psychology Bulletin, 11,* 75-88.

Foschi, M., & Hales, W. (1979). The theoretical role of cross-cultural comparisons in experimental social psychology. In L. Eckensberger, W. Lonner, & Y. Poortinga (Eds.), *Cross-cultural contributions to psychology* (pp. 244-254). Amsterdam: Swets & Zeitlinger.

Foster, G. M., & Anderson, B. G. (1978). *Medical anthropology.* New York: Wiley.

Fox, S., & Giles, H. (1993). Accommodating intergenerational contact: A critique and theoretical model. *Journal of Aging Studies, 7,* 423-451.

Franklin, R. S. (1991). *Shadows of race and class.* Minneapolis: University of Minnesota Press.

Frese, M., Stewart, J., & Hannover, B. (1987). Goal orientation and planfulness: Action styles as personality concepts. *Journal of Personality and Social Psychology, 52,* 1182-1194.

Frey, L. R., Botan, C. H., Friedman, P. G., & Kreps, G. L. (1991). *Investigating communication: An introduction to research methods.* Englewood Cliffs, NJ: Prentice Hall.

Furnham, A., & Bochner, S. (1986). *Culture shock: Psychological reactions to unfamiliar environments.* New York: Routledge.

Gallois, C., Barker, M., Jones, E., & Callan, V. J. (1992). Intercultural communication: Evaluations of lecturers and Australian and Chinese students. In S. Iwawaki, Y. Kashima, & K. Leung (Eds.), *Innovations in cross-cultural psychology* (pp. 86-102). Amsterdam: Swets & Zeitlinger.

Gallois, C., & Callan, V. J. (1988). Communication accommodation and the prototypical speaker: Predicting evaluations of status and solidarity. *Language and Communication* (Special issue: Communication Accommodation: Recent Developments), *8,* 271-283.

Gallois, C., & Callan, V. J. (1991). Interethnic accommodation: The role of norms. In H. Giles, J. Coupland, & N. Coupland (Eds.), *Contexts of accommodation: Developments in applied sociolinguistics* (pp. 245-269). Cambridge: Cambridge University Press.

Gallois, C., Franklyn-Stokes, A., Giles, H., & Coupland, N. (1988). Communication accommodation theory and intercultural encounters: Intergroup and interpersonal considerations. In Y. Y. Kim & W. B. Gudykunst (Eds.), *International and intercultural communication annual: Vol. 12. Theories in intercultural communication* (pp. 157-185). Newbury Park, CA: Sage.

Gao, G., & Gudykunst, W. B. (1990). Uncertainty, anxiety, and adaptation. *International Journal of Intercultural Relations, 14,* 301-317.

Garlick, R., & Mongeau, P. A. (1993). Argument quality and group member status as determinants of attitudinal minority influence. *Western Journal of Communication, 57,* 289-308.

Gates-Williams, J., Jackson, M. N., Jenkins-Monroe, V., & Williams, L. R. (1992). The business of preventing African-American infant mortality. *Western Journal of Medicine, 157,* 350-356.

Geertz, C. (1975). On the nature of anthropological understanding. *American Scientist, 63,* 47-53.

Gendlin, E. (1962). *Experiencing and the creation of meaning.* New York: Free Press.

Genesee, F., & Bourhis, R. Y. (1982). The social psychological significance of code switching in cross-cultural communication. *Journal of Language and Social Psychology, 1,* 1-27.

Genesee, F., & Bourhis, R. Y. (1988). Evaluative reactions to language choice strategies: The role of sociostructural factors. *Language and Communication, 8,* 229-250.

Genesee, F., & Holobow, N. E. (1989). Change and stability in intergroup perceptions. *Journal of Language and Social Psychology, 8,* 17-38.

Gerth, H. H., & Mills, C. W. (Eds.). (1946). *From Max Weber: Essays in sociology.* New York: Oxford University Press.

Geyer, F. (1980). *Alienation theories: A general systems approach.* New York: Pergamon.

Giles, H. (1973). Accent mobility: A model and some data. *Anthropological Linguistics, 15,* 87-105.

Giles, H. (1979). Ethnicity markers in speech. In K. R. Scherer & H. Giles (Eds.), *Social markers in speech* (pp. 251-290). Cambridge: Cambridge University Press.

Giles, H., Bourhis, R. Y., & Taylor, D. M. (1977a). Toward a theory of second language acquisition. *Journal of Multilingual and Multicultural Development, 3,* 17-40.

Giles, H., Bourhis, R. Y., & Taylor, D. M. (1977b). Towards a theory of language in ethnic group relations. In H. Giles & R. St. Clair (Eds.), *Language, ethnicity, and intergroup relations* (pp. 307-348). London: Academic Press.

Giles, H., & Byrne, J. (1982). An intergroup approach to second language acquisition. *Journal of Multilingual and Multicultural Development, 3,* 17-40.

Giles, H., & Coupland, N. (1991). *Language: Contexts and consequences.* Pacific Grove, CA: Brooks/Cole.

Giles, H., Coupland, J., & Coupland, N. (Eds.). (1991). *Contexts of accommodation: Developments in applied sociolinguistics.* Cambridge, UK: Cambridge University Press.

Giles, H., Coupland, N., Williams, A., & Leets, L. (1991). Integrating theory in the study of minority languages. In R. L. Cooper & B. Spolsky (Eds.), *The influence of language on culture and thought* (pp. 113-136). Berlin: Mouton de Gruyter.

Giles, H., & Evans, A. (1986). The power approach to intergroup hostility. *Journal of Conflict Resolution, 30,* 469-485.

Giles, H., & Johnson, P. (1986). Perceived threat, ethnic commitment, and interethnic language behavior. In Y. Y. Kim (Ed.), *Interethnic communication: Current research* (pp. 91-116). Newbury Park, CA: Sage.

Giles, H., & Johnson, P. (1987). Ethnolinguistic identity theory: A social psychological approach to language maintenance. *International Journal of the Sociology of Language, 68,* 66-99.

Giles, H., Leets, L., & Coupland, N. (1990). Minority language group status: A theoretical conspectus. *Journal of Multilingual and Multicultural Development, 11,* 1-19.

Giles, H., Mulac, A., Bradac, J. J., & Johnson, P. (1987). Speech accommodation theory: The next decade and beyond. In M. McLaughlin (Ed.), *Communication yearbook 10* (pp. 13-48). Newbury Park, CA: Sage.

Giles, H., & Smith, P. (1979). Accommodation theory. In H. Giles & R. St. Clair (Eds.), *Language and social psychology* (pp. 45-65). Oxford: Blackwell.

Giles, H., & Viladot, A. (1994). Ethnolinguistic differentiation in Catalonia. *Multilingua, 13,* 301-312.

Gilligan, C. (1982). *In a different voice: Psychological theory and women's development.* Cambridge, MA: Harvard University Press.

Gilligan, C. (1987). Moral orientation and moral development. In E. F. Kittay & D. T. Meyers (Eds.), *Women and moral theory* (pp. 19-33). Totowa, NJ: Rowman & Littlefield.

Gilman, S. C. (1990). "I'm down on whores": Race and gender in Victorian London. In D. T. Goldberg (Ed.), *Anatomy of racism* (pp. 146-170). Minneapolis: University of Minnesota Press.

Gilman, S. C., Justice, J., Saepharn, K., & Charles, G. (1992). Use of traditional and modern health services by Laotian refugees. *Western Journal of Medicine, 157,* 310-315.

Gilroy, P. (1990). One nation under a grove: The cultural politics of "race" and racism in Britain. In D. T. Goldberg (Ed.), *Anatomy of racism* (pp. 263-282). Minneapolis: University of Minnesota Press.

Glass, B. (1986). Geneticists embattled: Their stand against rampant eugenics and racism in America during the 1920s and 1930s. *Proceedings of the American Philosophical Society, 130,* 130-154.

Glatzer, W. (1991). Quality of life in advanced industrialized countries. In F. Strack, M. Argyle, & N. Schwarz (Eds.), *Subjective well-being: An interdisciplinary perspective* (pp. 261-279). Oxford: Pergamon.

Glazer, N., & Moynihan, D. (1975). *Ethnicity: Theory and experience.* Cambridge, MA: Harvard University Press.

Goffman, E. (1959). *The presentation of self in everyday life.* Garden City, NY: Anchor/Doubleday.

Gold, S. J. (1992). Mental health and illness in Vietnamese refugees. *Western Journal of Medicine, 157,* 290-294.

Goldberg, D. T. (1990). The social formation of racist discourse. In D. T. Goldberg (Ed.), *Anatomy of racism* (pp. 295-318). Minneapolis: University of Minnesota Press.

Goldberg, D. T. (1993). *Racist culture: Philosophy and the politics of meaning.* Oxford: Blackwell.

Golden, J. L., Berquist, G. F., & Coleman, W. E. (1989). *The rhetoric of Western thought* (4th ed.). Dubuque, IA: Kendell/Hunt.

Goodwin, C., & Duranti, A. (1992). Rethinking context: An introduction. In A. Duranti & C. Goodwin (Eds.), *Rethinking context: Language as an interactive phenomenon* (pp. 1-42). Cambridge: Cambridge University Press.

Gordon, M. (1973). Assimilation in America: Theory and reality. In P. Rose (Ed.), *The study of society* (pp. 350-365). New York: Random House.

Gordon, M. (1981). Models of pluralism: The new American dilemma. *Annals of the American Academy of Political and Social Science, 454,* 178-188.

Gould, S. J. (1981). *The mismeasure of man.* New York: Norton.

Graburn, N. (Ed.). (1976). *Ethnic and tourist arts: Cultural expressions from the fourth world.* Berkeley: University of California Press.

Graeff, J. A., Elder, J. P., & Booth, E. M. (1993). *Communication for health and behavior change: A developing country perspective.* San Francisco: Jossey-Bass.

Gramsci, A. (1983). *The modern prince & other writings* (L. Marks, Trans.). New York: International Publishers. (Original work published 1957)

Grant, P. R. (1993). Ethnocentrism in response to a threat to social identity. *Journal of Social Behavior and Personality, 8,* 143-154.

Graumann, C. F. (in press). Commonality, mutuality, reciprocity: A conceptual introduction. In I. Markovà, C. F. Graumann, & K. Foppa (Eds.), *Mutualities in dialogue.* Cambridge: Cambridge University Press.

Greene, J. O., & Lindsey, A. E. (1989). Encoding processes in the production of multiple-goal messages. *Human Communication Research, 16,* 120-140.

Grice, H. P. (1975). Logic and conversation. In P. Cole & J. Morgan (Eds.), *Syntax and semantics 3: Speech acts* (pp. 107-142). New York: Academic Press.

Griffiths, M. (1988, April). *Maternal self-confidence and child well-being.* Paper presented at the annual meeting of the Society for Applied Anthropology, Tampa, FL.

Grossberg, L., Nelson, C., & Treichler, P. A. (Eds.). (1992). *Cultural studies.* New York: Routledge.

Grove, C., & Torbiörn, I. (1985). A new conceptualization of intercultural adjustment and the goals of training. *International Journal of Intercultural Relations, 9,* 205-233.

Gudykunst, W. B. (1984). Toward a typology of stranger-host relationships. *International Journal of Intercultural Relations, 7,* 401-413.

Gudykunst, W. B. (1985a). A model of uncertainty reduction in intercultural encounters. *Journal of Language and Social Psychology, 4,* 79-98.

Gudykunst, W. B. (1985b). Normative power and conflict potential in intergroup relations. In W. B. Gudykunst, L. Stewart, & S. Ting-Toomey (Eds.), *Communication, culture, and organizational processes* (pp. 155-176). Beverly Hills, CA: Sage.

Gudykunst, W. B. (1985c). The influence of cultural similarity, type of relationship, and self-monitoring on uncertainty reduction processes. *Communication Monographs, 52,* 203-217.

Gudykunst, W. B. (1986). Toward a theory of intergroup communication. In W. B. Gudykunst (Ed.), *Intergroup communication* (pp. 152-167). Baltimore, MD: Edward Arnold.

Gudykunst, W. B. (1988). Uncertainty and anxiety: An extension of uncertainty reduction theory to intergroup communication. In Y. Kim & W. Gudykunst (Eds.), *Theories in intercultural communication* (pp. 123-156). Newbury Park, CA: Sage.

Gudykunst, W. B. (1989a). Cultural variability in ethnolinguistic identity. In S. Ting-Toomey & F. Korzenny (Eds.), *Language, communication and culture* (pp. 222-241). Newbury Park, CA: Sage.

Gudykunst, W. B. (1989b). Culture and the development of interpersonal relationships. In J. Anderson (Ed.), *Communication yearbook 12* (pp. 315-354). Newbury Park, CA: Sage.

Gudykunst, W. B. (1990). Diplomacy: A special case of intergroup communication. In F. Korzenny & S. Ting-Toomey (Eds.), *Communicating for peace* (pp. 19-39). Newbury Park, CA: Sage.

Gudykunst, W. B. (1991). *Bridging differences: Effective intergroup communication.* Newbury Park, CA: Sage.

Gudykunst, W. B. (1993). Toward a theory of effective interpersonal and intergroup communication: An anxiety/uncertainty management (AUM) perspective. In R. L. Wiseman & J. Koester (Eds.), *Intercultural communication competence* (pp. 33-71). Newbury Park, CA: Sage.

Gudykunst, W. B. (1994). *Bridging differences: Effective intergroup communication* (2nd ed.). Thousand Oaks, CA: Sage.

Gudykunst, W. B., Chua, E., & Gray, A. (1987). Cultural dissimilarities and uncertainty reduction processes. In M. McLaughlin (Ed.), *Communication yearbook 10* (pp. 456-469). Newbury Park, CA: Sage.

Gudykunst, W. B., Gao, G., Nishida, T., Nadamitsu, Y., & Sakai, J. (1992). Self-monitoring in Japan and the United States. In S. Iwawaki, Y. Kashima, & K. Leung (Eds.), *Innovations in cross-cultural psychology* (pp. 185-198). Amsterdam: Swets & Zeitlinger.

Gudykunst, W. B., Gao, G., Schmidt, K., Nishida, T., Bond, M. H., Leung, K., Wang, G., & Barraclough, R. (1992). The influence of individualism-collectivism, self-monitoring, and predicted outcome values on communication in ingroup and outgroup relationships. *Journal of Cross-Cultural Psychology, 23*, 196-213.

Gudykunst, W. B., & Hammer, M. R. (1988a). The influence of social identity and intimacy of interethnic relationships on uncertainty reduction processes. *Human Communication Research, 14*, 569-601.

Gudykunst, W. B., & Hammer, M. R. (1988b). Strangers and hosts. In Y. Kim & W. Gudykunst (Eds.), *Cross-cultural adaptation* (pp. 106-139). Newbury Park, CA: Sage.

Gudykunst, W. B., & Kim, Y. Y. (1992). *Communicating with strangers* (2nd ed.). New York: McGraw-Hill.

Gudykunst, W. B., Matsumoto, Y., Ting-Toomey, S., Nishida, T., Kim, K. S., & Heyman, S. (1994, July). *Measuring self construals across cultures.* Paper presented at the International Communication Association Convention, Sydney.

Gudykunst, W. B., & Nishida, T. (1984). Individual and cultural influences on uncertainty reduction. *Communication Monographs, 51*, 23-36.

Gudykunst, W. B., & Nishida, T. (1986a). Attributional confidence in low- and high-context cultures. *Human Communication Research, 12*, 525-549.

Gudykunst, W. B., & Nishida, T. (1986b). The influence of cultural variability on perceptions of communication behavior associated with relationship terms. *Human Communication Research, 13*, 147-166.

Gudykunst, W. B., & Nishida, T. (1989). Theoretical perspectives for studying intercultural communication. In M. K. Asante & W. B. Gudykunst (Eds.), *Handbook of international and intercultural communication* (pp. 17-46). Newbury Park, CA: Sage.

Gudykunst, W. B., & Nishida, T. (1994). *Bridging Japanese/North American differences.* Thousand Oaks, CA: Sage.

Gudykunst, W. B., Nishida, T., & Chua, E. (1987). Perceptions of social penetration in Japanese-North American dyads. *International Journal of Intercultural Relations, 11*, 171-189.

Gudykunst, W. B., & Shapiro, R. (in press). Communication in everyday interpersonal and intergroup encounters. *International Journal of Intercultural Relations.*

Gudykunst, W. B., & Ting-Toomey, S., with Chua, E. (1988). *Culture and interpersonal communication.* Newbury Park, CA: Sage.

Gudykunst, W. B., Ting-Toomey, S., Sudweeks, S., & Stewart, L. P. (1995). *Building bridges.* Boston: Houghton Mifflin.

Gudykunst, W. B., Yoon, Y. C., & Nishida, T. (1987). The influence of individualism-collectivism on perceptions of communication in ingroup and outgroup relationships. *Communication Monographs, 54,* 295-306.

Guillaumin, C. (1980). The idea of race and its elevation to autonomous, scientific, and legal status. In UNESCO (Ed.), *Sociological theories: Race and colonialism* (pp. 305-345). Paris: UNESCO.

Gullahorn, J. T., & Gullahorn, J. E. (1963). An extension of the U-curve hypothesis. *Journal of Social Issues, 19*(3), 33-47.

Gumperz, J. J. (1982). *Discourse strategies.* Cambridge: Cambridge University Press.

Gumperz, J. (1992a). Contextualization and understanding. In A. Duranti & C. Goodwin (Eds.), *Rethinking context: Language as an interactive phenomenon* (pp. 229-252). Cambridge: Cambridge University Press.

Gumperz, J. (1992b). Interviewing in intercultural situations. In P. Drew & J. Heritage (Eds.), *Talk at work: Interaction in institutional settings* (pp. 302-327). Cambridge: Cambridge University Press.

Haberly, D. T. (1983). *Three sad races: Racial identity and national consciousness in Brazilian literature.* London: Cambridge.

Haffner, L. (1992). Translation is not enough: Interpreting in a medical setting. *Western Journal of Medicine, 157,* 255-260.

Hale, J. L., & Burgoon, J. K. (1984). Models of reactions to changes in nonverbal immediacy. *Journal of Nonverbal Behavior, 8,* 287-314.

Hall, B. J. (1992). Theories of culture and communication. *Communication Theory, 2,* 50-70.

Hall, E. T. (1959). *The silent language.* New York: Doubleday.

Hall, E. T. (1966). *The hidden dimension* (2nd ed.). Garden City, NY: Anchor/Doubleday.

Hall, E. T. (1976). *Beyond culture.* Garden City, NY: Anchor.

Hall, S. (1982). Race, articulation and societies structured in dominance. In UNESCO (Ed.), *Sociological theories: Race and colonialism* (pp. 305-345). Paris: UNESCO.

Hall, S. (1985). Signification, representation, ideology: Althusser and the post-structuralist debates. *Critical Studies in Mass Communication, 2,* 91-114.

Hall, S. (1986). Gramsci's relevance for the study of race and ethnicity. *Journal of Communication Inquiry, 10*(2), 5-27.

Hall, S. (1992). Cultural studies and its theoretical legacies. In L. Grossberg, C. Nelson, & P. Treichler (Eds.), *Cultural studies* (pp. 277-294). New York: Routledge.

Hallinan, M. T., & Smith, S. (1985). The effects of classroom racial composition on students' interracial friendliness. *Social Psychology Quarterly, 48,* 3-16.

Hallinan, M. T., & Teixeira, R. A. (1987). Opportunities and constraints: Black-white differences in the formation of interracial friendships. *Child Development, 58,* 1358-1371.

Hallinan, M. T., & Williams, R. A. (1987). The stability of students' interracial friendships. *American Sociological Review, 52,* 653-664.

Hallinan, M. T., & Williams, R. A. (1989). Interracial friendship choices in secondary schools. *American Sociological Review, 54,* 67-78.

Hamaguchi, E. (1985). A contextual model of the Japanese: Toward a methodological innovation in Japan studies. *Journal of Japanese Studies, 11,* 289-321.

Hamill, J. (1990). *Ethno-logic: The anthropology of human reasoning.* Urbana: University of Illinois Press.

300 • INTERCULTURAL COMMUNICATION THEORY

Hamilton, D., Sherman, S., & Ruvolo, C. (1990). Stereotyped-based expectancies. *Journal of Social Issues, 46*(2), 35-60.

Hammer, M. (1987). Behavioral dimensions of intercultural effectiveness: A replication and extension. *International Journal of Intercultural Relations, 11*, 65-88.

Hammer, M. R. (1989). Intercultural communication competence. In M. Asante & W. Gudykunst (Eds.), *Handbook of international and intercultural communication* (2nd ed., pp. 247-260). Newbury Park, CA: Sage.

Hammer, M. R., Gudykunst, W. B., & Wiseman, R. L. (1978). Dimensions of intercultural effectiveness: An exploratory study. *International Journal of Intercultural Relations, 2*, 382-392.

Hammer, M. R., Wiseman, R. L., Rasmussen, J., & Bruschke, J. (1992, November). *A comprehensive test of uncertainty/anxiety reduction theory: The intercultural adaptation context.* Paper presented at the Speech Communication Association Convention, Chicago.

Hammersley, M. (1992). *What's wrong with ethnography? Methodological explorations.* London: Routledge.

Harris, P. R., & Moran, R. T. (1987). *Managing cultural differences: High-performance strategies for today's global managers.* Houston: Gulf.

Harwood, J., & Giles, H. (1993). Creating intergenerational distance: Language, communication, and middle age. *Language Sciences, 15*, 15-38.

Harwood, J., Giles, H., & Bourhis, R. Y. (in press). The genesis of vitality theory: Historical patterns and discoursal dimensions. *International Journal of Sociology of Language, 108.*

Harwood, J., Giles, H., Fox, S., Ryan, E. B., & Williams, A. (1993). Patronizing young and elderly adults: Response strategies in a community setting. *Journal of Applied Communication Research, 21*, 211-226.

Hasenbalg, C. A. (1982). O negro na publicidade [Blacks in advertisements]. In L. Gonzalez & C. Hasenbalg, *Lugar de negro* [The place of blacks] (pp. 103-114). Rio de Janeiro: Marco Zero Limitada.

Hawes, F., & Kealey, D. (1981). An empirical study of Canadian technical assistance. *International Journal of Intercultural Relations, 5*, 239-258.

Hayduk, L. A. (1978). Personal space: An evaluative and orienting overview. *Psychological Bulletin, 85*, 117-134.

Headey, B., Holström, E., & Wearing, A. (1984a). Well-being and ill-being: Different dimensions? *Social Indicators Research, 14*, 115-139.

Headey, B., Holström, E., & Wearing, A. (1984b). The impact of life events and changes in domain satisfaction on well-being. *Social Indicators Research, 15*, 203-227.

Headey, B., & Wearing, A. (1991). Subjective well-being: A stocks and flows framework. In F. Strack, M. Argyle, & N. Schwarz (Eds.), *Subjective well-being: An interdisciplinary perspective* (pp. 49-76). Oxford: Pergamon.

Hecht, M. L. (1984). Satisfying communication and relationship labels: Intimacy and length of relationship as perceptual frames of naturalistic conversations. *Western Journal of Speech Communication, 48*, 201-216.

Hecht, M. L. (1993). 2002—A research odyssey: Toward the development of a communication theory of identity. *Communication Monographs, 60*, 76-82.

Hecht, M. L., Collier, M. J., & Ribeau, S. (1993). *African American communication: Ethnic identity and cultural interpretations.* Newbury Park, CA: Sage.

Hecht, M. L., Ribeau, S., & Alberts, J. A. (1989). An Afro-American perspective on interethnic communication. *Communication Monographs, 56*, 385-410.

Hecht, M. L., Ribeau, S., & Sedano, M. V. (1990). A Mexican American perspective on interethnic communication. *International Journal of Intercultural Relations, 14*, 31-55.

Heinemann, W., Pellander, F., Vogelbusch, A., & Wojtek, B. (1981). Meeting a deviant person: Subjective norms and affective reactions. *European Journal of Social Psychology, 11*, 1-25.

Helman, C. G. (1990). *Culture, health, and illness* (2nd ed.). London: Wright.

Herman, S., & Schield, E. (1961). The stranger group in cross-cultural interaction. *Sociometry, 24*, 165-176.

Hewes, D. E., & Planalp, S. (1987). The individual's place in communication science. In C. R. Berger & S. H. Chaffee (Eds.), *Handbook of communication science* (pp. 146-183). Newbury Park, CA: Sage.

Hewstone, M., & Brown, R. (1986). Contact is not enough: An intergroup perspective on the "contact hypothesis." In M. Hewstone & R. Brown (Eds.), *Contact and conflict in intergroup encounters* (pp. 1-44). Oxford: Blackwell.

Hildebrandt, N., & Giles, H. (1983). The Japanese as subordinate group: Ethnolinguistic identity theory in a foreign language context. *Anthropological Linguistics, 25*, 436-466.

Hilton, J. L., Klein, J. G., & von Hippel, W. (1991). *Attention allocation and impression formation*. Manuscript submitted for publication.

Hinkel, S., & Brown, R. J. (1990). Intergroup comparisons and social identity: Some links and lacunae. In D. Abrams & M. A. Hogg (Eds.), *Social identity theory: Constructive and critical advances* (pp. 48-70). New York: Springer-Verlag.

Hinkel, S., Taylor, L. A., Fox-Cardamone, L., & Crook, K. F. (1989). Intergroup identification and intergroup differentiation: A multicomponent approach. *British Journal of Social Psychology, 28*, 305-317.

Hirokawa, R. Y. (1980). A comparative analysis of communication patterns within effective and ineffective decision-making groups. *Communication Monographs, 47*, 312-321.

Hirokawa, R. Y. (1985). Discussion procedures and decision-making performance: A test of a functional perspective. *Human Communication Research, 12*, 203-224.

Hirokawa, R. Y. (1988). Group communication and decision-making performance: A continued test of the functional perspective. *Human Communication Research, 14*, 487-515.

Hirokawa, R. Y. (1990). The role of communication in effective group decision-making: A task contingency perspective. *Small Group Behavior, 21*, 190-204.

Hirokawa, R. Y., & Rost, K. M. (1992). Effective group decision-making in organizations: Field test of the vigilant interaction theory. *Management Communication Quarterly, 5*, 267-288.

Hirokawa, R. Y., & Salazar, A. J. (1991, November). *The necessity of chimera hunting: Why group communication scholars should maintain a "bottom-line" focus in group decision-making research*. Paper presented at the annual meeting of the Speech Communication Association, Atlanta, GA.

Ho, D. Y. F. (1993). Relational orientation in Asian social psychology. In U. Kim & J. W. Berry (Eds.), *Indigenous psychologies: Research and experience in cultural context* (pp. 240-259). Newbury Park, CA: Sage.

Hoetink, H. (1974). National identity and the social norm image. In W. Bell & W. E. Freeman (Eds.), *Ethnicity and nation-building: Comparative, international, and historical perspectives* (pp. 29-44). Beverly Hills, CA: Sage.

Hofstede, G. (1979). Value systems in forty countries. In L. Eckensberger, W. Lonner, & Y. Poortinga (Eds.), *Cross-cultural contributions to psychology* (pp. 389-407). Lisse, The Netherlands: Swets & Zeitlinger.

Hofstede, G. (1980). *Culture's consequences: International differences in work-related values*. Beverly Hills, CA: Sage.

Hofstede, G. (1983). National cultures in four dimensions: A research-based theory of cultural differences among nations. *International Studies of Management and Organizations, 13*, 46-74.

Hofstede, G. (1991). *Cultures and organizations*. London: McGraw-Hill.

Hofstede, G., & Bond, M. H. (1984). Hofstede's culture dimensions. *Journal of Cross-Cultural Psychology, 15*, 417-433.

Hogg, M. A., & Abrams, D. (1993). Towards a single-process uncertainty-reduction model of social motivation in groups. In M. A. Hogg & D. Abrams (Eds.), *Group motivation: Social psychological perspectives* (pp. 173-190). New York: Harvester-Wheatsheaf.

Holmes, J., & Rempel, J. (1989). Trust in close relationships. In C. Hendrick (Ed.), *Close relationships* (pp. 187-220). Newbury Park, CA: Sage.

Holmes, T., & Rahe, R. (1967). The Social Readjustment Rating Scale. *Journal of Psychometric Research, 11*, 213-218.

Holtgraves, T., & Yang, J. N. (1990). Politeness as universal: Cross-cultural perceptions of request strategies and inferences based on their use. *Journal of Personality and Social Psychology, 59*, 719-729.

Holtgraves, T., & Yang, J. N. (1992). Interpersonal underpinnings of request strategies: General principles and differences due to culture and gender. *Journal of Personality and Social Psychology, 62*, 246-256.

Homans, G. C. (1950). *The human group.* New York: Harcourt Brace.

hooks, b. (1990). *Yearning: Race, gender, and cultural politics.* Boston: South End.

Horton, D., & Wohl, R. (1979). Mass communication and para-social interaction. In G. Gumpert & R. Cathcart (Eds.), *Inter/Media: Interpersonal communication in a media world* (pp. 32-55). New York: Oxford University Press.

Houston, J. (1981, May). *Beyond Manzanar: A personal view on the Asian-American womanhood.* Audio-recording of a lecture delivered at Governors State University, University Park, IL.

Howett, D. (Ed.), Billig, M., Cramer, D., Edwards, D., Kniveton, B., Potter, J., & Radley, A. (1989). *Social psychology: Conflicts and continuities.* Philadelphia: Open University Press.

Hoyle, R. H., & Lennox, R. D. (1991). Latent structure of self-monitoring. *Multivariate Behavioral Research, 26*, 511-540.

Hui, C. H., & Triandis, H. C. (1986). Individualism-collectivism: A study of cross-cultural researchers. *Journal of Cross-Cultural Psychology, 17*, 225-248.

Hurh, W., & Kim, K. (1988). *Uprooting and adjustment: A sociological study of Korean immigrants' mental health.* Final report submitted to National Institute of Mental Health, U.S. Department of Health and Human Services (Grant No. 1 R01 MH40312-01/5 MH40312-02), Washington, DC.

Hutchinson, E. O. (1991, November 4). Fighting the wrong enemy. *Nation*, pp. 554-555.

Hymes, D. (1972). Models of the interaction of language and social life. In J. J. Gumperz & D. Hymes (Eds.), *Directions in sociolinguistics: The ethnography of communication* (pp. 35-71). New York: Holt, Rinehart & Winston.

Ickes, W. (1984). Composition in black and white. *Journal of Personality and Social Psychology, 47*, 330-341.

Imahori, T., & Lanigan, M. (1989). Relational model of intercultural communication competence. *International Journal of Intercultural Relations, 13*(3), 269-286.

Indvik, J., & Fitzpatrick, M. A. (1986). Perceptions of inclusion, affiliation, and control in five interpersonal relationships. *Communication Quarterly, 34*, 1-13.

Inglis, M., & Gudykunst, W. (1982). Institutional completeness and communication. *International Journal of Intercultural Relations, 6*, 251-272.

Irvine, S., & Carroll, W. (1980). Testing and assessment across cultures: Issues in methodology and theory. In H. Triandis (Ed.), *Handbook of cross-cultural psychology, II* (pp. 181-244). Boston: Allyn & Bacon.

Irwin, P., Allen, G., Kramer, S., & Danoff, B. (1982). Quality of life after radiation therapy: A study of 309 cancer patients. *Social Indicators Research, 10*, 187-210.

Islam, M. R., & Hewstone, M. (1993). Dimensions of contact as predictors of intergroup anxiety, perceived out-group variability, and outgroup attitudes. *Personality and Social Psychology Bulletin, 19*, 700-710.

Ito, Y. (1989a). A non-Western view of the paradigm dialogues. In B. Dervin, L. Grossberg, B. J. O'Keefe, & E. Wartella (Eds.), *Rethinking communication* (pp. 173-177). Newbury Park, CA: Sage.

Ito, Y. (1989b, May). *Socio-cultural backgrounds of Japanese interpersonal communication style.* Paper presented at the annual meeting of the International Communication Association, San Francisco.

Jackman, M. R., & Crane, M. (1986). "Some of my best friends are black": Interracial friendships and whites' racial attitudes. *Public Opinion Quarterly, 50*, 459-486.

Jackson, J. (1966). A conceptual and measurement model for norms and roles. *Pacific Sociological Review, 9*, 35-47.

Janis, I. L. (1958). *Psychological stress.* New York: Wiley.

Janis, I. L. (1967). Effects of fear arousal on attitude change: Recent developments in theory and experimental research. In L. Berkowitz (Ed.), *Advances in experimental social psychology* (Vol. 3, pp. 166-225). New York: Academic Press.

Janis, I. L. (1971). *Stress and frustration.* New York: Harcourt Brace Jovanovich.

Janis, I. L. (1982). *Victims of groupthink: A psychological study of foreign-policy decisions and fiascoes* (2nd ed.). Boston: Houghton.

Janis, I. L. (1985). Stress inoculation in health care. In A. Monat & R. Lazarus (Eds.), *Stress and coping* (pp. 330-355). New York: Columbia University Press.

Janz, N., & Becker, M. (1984). The health belief model: A decade later. *Health Education Quarterly, 11*, 1-47.

Johnson, F. (1985). The Western concept of self. In A. Marsella, G. De Vos, & F. L. K. Hsu (Eds.), *Culture and self* (pp. 91-138). London: Tavistock.

Johnston, L., & Hewstone, M. (1990). Intergroup contact. In D. Abrams & M. Hogg (Eds.), *Social identity theory* (pp. 185-210). New York: Springer-Verlag.

Johnstone, B. (1986). Arguments with Khumeini: Rhetorical situation and persuasive style in cross-cultural perspective. *Text, 6*, 171-187.

Jones, E. (1994). *Communication in an academic context: The effects of status, ethnicity, and sex.* Unpublished doctoral dissertation, University of Queensland, St. Lucia, Australia.

Jones, E., Gallois, C., Barker, M., & Callan, V. J. (1994a). Communication between Australian and Chinese students and academic staff. In A. Bouvy, F. J. R. Van de Vijver, P. Boski, & P. Schmitz (Eds.), *Journeys into cross-cultural psychology* (pp. 184-196). Amsterdam: Swets & Zeitlinger.

Jones, E., Gallois, C., Barker, M., & Callan, V. J. (1994b). Evaluations of interactions between students and academic staff: Influence of communication accommodation, ethnic group, and status. *Journal of Language and Social Psychology, 13*, 158-191.

Kagitcibasi, C. (1987). Individual and group loyalties: Are they possible? In C. Kagitcibasi (Ed.), *Growth and progress in cross-cultural psychology* (pp. 94-103). Lisse, the Netherlands: Swets & Zeitlinger.

Kashima, Y. (1989). Conceptions of person: Implications in individualism/collectivism research. In C. Kagitcibasi (Ed.), *Growth and progress in cross-cultural psychology* (pp. 104-112). Amsterdam: Swets & Zeitlinger.

Katriel, T. (1986). *Talking straight: Dugri speech in Israeli Sabra culture.* Cambridge: Cambridge University Press.

Keene, D. (1994). *On familiar terms: A journey across cultures.* New York: Kodansha International.

Keesing, R. (1974). Theories of culture. *Annual Review of Anthropology, 3*, 73-97.

Kellermann, K. (1993). Extrapolating beyond: Processes of uncertainty reduction. In S. Deetz (Ed.), *Communication yearbook 16* (pp. 503-514). Newbury Park, CA: Sage.

Kellner, D. (1989). *Critical theory, Marxism and modernity.* Baltimore, MD: John Hopkins University.

Kelly, C. (1993). Group identification, intergroup perceptions and collective action. In S. Wolfgang & M. Hewstone (Eds.), *European review of social psychology* (Vol. 4, pp. 59-84). Chichester, UK: Wiley.

Kim, J. (1980). Explaining acculturation in a communication framework: An empirical test. *Communication Monograph, 47*(3), 155-179.

Kim, M. S. (1993). Culture-based interactive constraints in explaining intercultural strategic competence. In R. L. Wiseman & J. Koester (Eds.), *Intercultural communication competence* (pp. 132-150). Newbury Park, CA: Sage.

Kim, M. S. (1994). Cross-cultural comparisons of the perceived importance of interactive constraints. *Human Communication Research, 21*(1), 128-151.

Kim, M. S., Sharkey, W. F., & Singelis, T. M. (1994). The relationship between individual's self-construals and perceived importance of interactive constraints. *International Journal of Intercultural Relations, 18,* 1-24.

Kim, M. S., & Wilson, S. R. (1994). A cross-cultural comparison of implicit theories of requesting. *Communication Monographs, 61*(3), 210-235.

Kim, U., Triandis, H., Kagitcibasi, C., & Yoon, G. (Eds.). (1994). *Individualism and collectivism: Theoretical and methodological issues.* Newbury Park, CA: Sage.

Kim, Y. (1976). *Communication patterns of foreign immigrants in the process of acculturation: A survey among the Korean population in Chicago.* Unpublished doctoral dissertation, Northwestern University, Evanston, IL.

Kim, Y. (1977a). Communication patterns of foreign immigrants in the process of acculturation. *Human Communication Research, 4*(1), 66-77.

Kim, Y. (1977b). Inter-ethnic and intra-ethnic communication: A study of Korean immigrants in Chicago. *International and Intercultural Communication Annual, 4,* 53-68.

Kim, Y. (1978a). A communication approach to acculturation processes: Korean immigrants in Chicago. *International Journal of Intercultural Relations, 2*(2), 197-224.

Kim, Y. (1978b, November). *Acculturation and patterns of interpersonal communication relationships: A study of Japanese, Mexican, and Korean communities in the Chicago area.* Paper presented at the Speech Communication Association Conference, Minneapolis, MN.

Kim, Y. (1979). Toward an interactive theory of communication-acculturation. In B. Ruben (Ed.), *Communication yearbook 3* (pp. 435-453). New Brunswick, NJ: Transaction.

Kim, Y. (1980). *Research project report on Indochinese refugees in Illinois: Vol. 1. Introduction, summary and recommendations. Vol. 2. Methods and procedures. Vol. 3. Population characteristics and service needs. Vol. 4. Psychological, social and cultural adjustment of Indochinese refugees. Vol. 5. Survey of agencies serving Indochinese refugees* (Based on a grant from the Department of Health, Education and Welfare Region V, pp. 95-549). Chicago: Travelers Aid Society.

Kim, Y. (1986a). Understanding the social context of intergroup communication: A personal network approach. In W. Gudykunst (Ed.), *Intergroup communication* (pp. 86-95). London: Edward Arnold.

Kim, Y. (Ed.). (1986b). *Interethnic communication: Current research.* Newbury Park, CA: Sage.

Kim, Y. (1987). Facilitating immigrant adaptation: The role of communication and interpersonal ties. In T. Albrecht & M. Adelman (Eds.), *Communicating social support: Process in context* (pp. 192-211). Newbury Park, CA: Sage.

Kim, Y. (1988a). *Communication and cross-cultural adaptation: An integrative theory.* Clevedon, UK: Multilingual Matters.

Kim, Y. (1988b). On theorizing intercultural communication. In Y. Kim & W. Gudykunst (Eds.), *Theories in intercultural communication* (pp. 11-21). Newbury Park, CA: Sage.

Kim, Y. (1989). Personal, social, and economic adaptation: The case of 1975-1979 arrivals in Illinois. In D. Haines (Ed.), *Refugees as immigrants: Survey research on Cambodians, Laotians, and Vietnamese in America* (pp. 86-104). Totowa, NJ: Rowman & Littlefield.

Kim, Y. (1990). Communication and adaptation of Asian Pacific refugees in the United States. *Journal of Pacific Rim Communication, 1,* 191-207.

Kim, Y. (1991). Intercultural communication competence. In S. Ting-Toomey & F. Korzenny (Eds.), *Cross-cultural interpersonal communication* (pp. 259-275). Newbury Park, CA: Sage.

Kim, Y. (1993, May). *Synchrony and intercultural communication competence.* Paper presented at the annual meeting of the International Communication Association, Chicago.

Kim, Y. (1994). Intercultural personhood: An integration of Eastern and Western perspectives. In L. A. Samovar & R. E. Porter (Eds.), *Intercultural communication: A reader* (6th ed., pp. 415-425). Belmont, CA: Wadsworth.

Kim, Y. (in press-a). *Becoming intercultural: An integrative theory of cross-cultural adaptation.* Thousand Oaks, CA: Sage.

Kim, Y. (in press-b). Identity development: From cultural to intercultural. In H. Mokros (Ed.), *Information and behavior: Vol. 6. Interaction and identity*. New Brunswick, NJ: Transaction.

Kim, Y., & Gudykunst, W. (Eds.). (1988). *Cross-cultural adaptation: Current theory and research*. Newbury Park, CA: Sage.

Kim, Y., Lujan, P., Shaver, L., & Boyle, A. (1991, November). *"I can walk both ways": Subjective experiences of ethnic identity among American Indians in Oklahoma*. Paper presented at the annual convention of the Speech Communication, Atlanta, GA.

Kim, Y., & Paulk, S. (1994a). Intercultural challenges and personal adjustments: A qualitative analysis of the experiences of American and Japanese coworkers. In R. Wiseman & R. Shuter (Eds.), *International and intercultural communication annual: Vol. 18. Communication in multinational organization* (pp. 117-140). Thousand Oaks, CA: Sage.

Kim, Y., & Paulk, S. (1994b, November). *Intercultural communication in a multinational organization: A replication study*. Paper presented at the annual convention of the Speech Communication Association, New Orleans, LA.

Kim, Y., & Ruben, B. (1988). Intercultural transformation: A systems theory. In Y. Kim & W. Gudykunst (Eds.), *Theories in intercultural communication* (pp. 299-321). Newbury Park, CA: Sage.

King, C. E. (1991, February). *Educating a diverse workforce: Moving from melting pot to stir fry*. Paper presented at the annual convention of the Western Speech Communication Association, Boise, ID.

Kino, F. (1973). Aliens' paranoid reaction. In C. Zwingmann & M. Pfister-Ammende (Eds.), *Uprooting and after* (pp. 60-66). New York: Springer-Verlag.

Kirchmeyer, C., & Cohen, A. (1992). Multicultural groups: Their performance and reactions with constructive conflict. *Group and Organization Management, 17*, 153-170.

Kirk, J., & Miller, M. (1986). *Reliability and validity in qualitative research*. Newbury Park, CA: Sage.

Klessig, J. (1992). The effect of values and culture on life support decisions. *Western Journal of Medicine, 157*, 316-322.

Kline, S. L. (1984). *Social cognitive determinants of face support in persuasive messages*. Unpublished doctoral dissertation, University of Illinois, Champaign-Urbana.

Kluckhohn, F., & Strodtbeck, F. (1961). *Variations in value orientations*. Evanston, IL: Row, Peterson.

Knapp, K., & Knapp-Potthoff, A. (1987). Instead of an introduction: Conceptual issues in analyzing intercultural communication. In K. Knapp, W. Enninger, & A. Knapp-Potthoff (Eds.), *Analyzing intercultural communication* (pp. 1-13). Berlin: Mouton de Gruyter.

Koester, J., Wiseman, R. L., & Sanders, J. A. (1993). Multiple perspectives of intercultural communication competence. In R. L. Wiseman & J. Koester (Eds.), *Intercultural communication competence* (pp. 3-15). Newbury Park, CA: Sage.

Kraemer, R., & Olshtain, E. (1989). Perceived ethnolinguistic vitality and language attitudes: The Israeli setting. *Journal of Multilingual and Multicultural Development, 10*, 197-212.

Krau, E. (1991). *The contradictory immigrant problem: A sociopsychological analysis*. New York: Peter Lang.

Krauss, R., & Fussell, S. (1991). Constructing shared communicative environments. In L. Resnick, J. Levine, & S. Behrend (Eds.), *Perspectives on socially shared cognitions* (pp. 172-200). Washington, DC: American Psychological Association.

Kruglanski, A. (1989). *Lay epistemics and human knowledge*. New York: Plenum.

Kume, T. (1985). Managerial attitudes toward decision-making: North American and Japan. In W. Gudykunst, L. Stewart, & S. Ting-Toomey (Eds.), *Communication, culture, and organizational processes* (pp. 231-251). Beverly Hills, CA: Sage.

Labov, W. (1966). *The stratification of English in New York City*. Washington, DC: Center for Applied Linguistics.

Lacan, J. (1977). *Écrits: A selection* (A. Sheridan, Trans.). New York: Norton.

Laderman, C. (1991). Malay medicine, Malay person. *Medical Anthropology, 13*, 83-97.

Lakoff, R. (1977). What you can do with words: Politeness, pragmatics and performatives. In A. Rogers, B. Wall, & J. Murphy (Eds.), *Proceedings of the Texas conference on performatives, presuppositions and implicatures* (pp. 79-105). Arlington, VA: Center for Applied Linguistics.

Lal, B. B. (1986). The Chicago School of American sociology, symbolic interactionism, and race relations theory. In J. Rex & D. Mason (Eds.), *Theories of race and ethnic relations* (pp. 280-298). Cambridge: Cambridge University Press.

Lance, C., & Sloan, C. (1993). Relationships between overall and life facet satisfaction: A multitrait-multimethod (MTMM) study. *Social Indicators Research, 30*, 1-15.

Langer, E. J. (1978). Rethinking the role of thought in social interaction. In J. J. Harvey, W. Ickes, & R. F. Kidd (Eds.), *New directions in attribution research* (Vol. 2, pp. 36-58). Hillsdale, NJ: Lawrence Erlbaum.

Langer, E. J. (1989). *Mindfulness*. Reading, MA: Addison-Wesley.

Langer, E. J., & Imber, L. (1980). Role of mindlessness in the perception of deviance. *Journal of Personality and Social Psychology, 39*, 360-367.

Lazarus, R. (1966). *Psychological stress and the coping process*. St. Louis, MO: McGraw-Hill.

Lazarus, R. (1991). *Emotion and adaptation*. New York: Oxford University Press.

Leary, M., Kowalski, R., & Bergen, D. (1988). Interpersonal information acquisition and confidence in first encounters. *Personality and Social Psychology Bulletin, 14*, 68-77.

Lee, H. O., & Boster, F. (1991). Social information for uncertainty-reduction during initial interaction. In S. Ting-Toomey & F. Korzenny (Eds.), *Cross-cultural interpersonal communication* (pp. 189-212). Newbury Park, CA: Sage.

Leech, G. N. (1983). *Principles of pragmatics*. New York: Longman.

Leeds-Hurwitz, W. (1990). Notes in the history of intercultural communication: The Foreign Service Institute and the mandate for intercultural training. *Quarterly Journal of Speech, 76*, 262-281.

Leelakulthanit, O., & Day, R. (1993). Cross-cultural comparisons of quality of life of Thais and Americans. *Social Indicators Research, 30*, 49-70.

Leets, L., & Giles, H. (in press). Intergroup cognitions and communication climates: New directions of minority language maintenance. In W. K. Fase, K. Jaspaert, & S. Kroon (Eds.), *Maintenance and loss of minority languages: A cross-cultural perspective*. Amsterdam: Swets & Zeitlinger.

Lennox, R., & Wolfe, R. (1984). Revision of the self-monitoring scale. *Journal of Personality and Social Psychology, 46*, 1349-1364.

Le Poire, B. A., & Burgoon, J. K. (1995). *Usefulness of the "orientation response" for theories of nonverbal involvement violations: The orienting versus arousal debate*. Manuscript submitted for publication.

Le Poire, B. A., & Burgoon, J. K. (1994). Two contrasting explanations of involvement violations: Expectancy violations theory versus discrepancy arousal theory. *Human Communication Research, 20*, 560-591.

Leslie, M. (1992). Representations of blacks on prime time television in Brazil. *Howard Journal of Communications, 4*, 1-9.

Leung, K. (1989). Cross-cultural differences: Individual-level vs. culture-level analysis. *International Journal of Psychology, 24*, 703-719.

Leung, K., & Bond, M. H. (1989). On the empirical identification of dimensions for cross-cultural comparison. *Journal of Cross-Cultural Psychology, 20*, 133-151.

Leung, K., Bond, M. H., Carment, D. W., Kirshnan, L., & Liebrand, W. B. G. (1990). Effects of cultural femininity on preference for methods of conflict processing: A cross-cultural study. *Journal of Experimental Social Psychology, 26*, 373-388.

Leventhal, H. (1970). Findings and theory in the study of fear communications. In L. Berkowitz (Ed.), *Advances in experimental social psychology* (Vol. 5, pp. 119-186). New York: Academic Press.

Levine, D. (1979). Simmel at a distance: On the history and systematics of the sociology of the stranger. In W. Shack & E. Skinner (Eds.), *Strangers in African societies* (pp. 21-36). Berkeley: University of California Press.

Levine, R. M. (1984). Elite intervention in urban popular culture in modern Brazil. *Luso-Brazilian Review, 21*(2), 9-22.

Levinson, D. J. (1982a). The study of anti-Semitic ideology. In T. W. Adorno, E. Frenkel-Brunswick, D. J. Levinson, & R. N. Sanford (Eds.), *The authoritarian personality* (abridged ed., pp. 57-101). New York: Norton.

Levinson, D. J. (1982b). The study of ethnocentric ideology. In T. W. Adorno, E. Frenkel-Brunswick, D. J. Levinson, & R. N. Sanford (Eds.), *The authoritarian personality* (abridged ed., pp. 102-150). New York: Norton.

Lévi-Strauss, C. (1963). *Structural anthropology* (C. Jacobson & B. Grundfest Schoepf, Trans.). New York: Basic Books.

Levy, J. E., Neutra, R., & Parker, D. (1987). *Hand trembling, frenzy witchcraft, and moth madness: A study of Navajo seizure disorders.* Tucson: University of Arizona Press.

Lewinsjohn, P., Redner, J., & Seeley, J. (1991). The relationship between life satisfaction and psychosocial variables: New perspectives. In F. Strack, M. Argyle, & N. Schwarz (Eds.), *Subjective well-being: An interdisciplinary perspective* (pp. 141-172). Oxford: Pergamon.

Lieberson, S. (1985). *Making it count: The improvement of social research and theory.* Berkeley: University of California Press.

Lifton, R. (1993). *The protean self: Human resilience in an age of fragmentation.* New York: Basic Books.

Lin, T. (1983). Psychiatry and Chinese culture. *Western Journal of Medicine, 139*, 58-63.

Lincoln, Y. S., & Guba, E. G. (1985). *Naturalistic inquiry.* Beverly Hills, CA: Sage.

Linville, P., Fischer, G., & Salovey, P. (1989). Perceived distribution of the characteristics of ingroup and outgroup members. *Journal of Personality and Social Psychology, 57*, 165-188.

Lipson, J. G., & Meleis, A. I. (1983). Issues in health care of Middle Eastern patients. *Western Journal of Medicine, 139*, 50-57.

Lipson, J. G., & Omidian, P. A. (1992). Health issues of Afghan refugees in California. *Western Journal of Medicine, 139*, 271-275.

Littlejohn, S. W. (1983). *Theories of human communication* (2nd ed.). Belmont, CA: Wadsworth.

Lobdell, C. L. (1990, June). *Expectations of family and friends of sojourners during the reentry adjustment process.* Paper presented at the annual meeting of the International Communication Association, Dublin, Ireland.

Lock, M. (1983). Japanese responses to social change: Making the strange familiar. *Western Journal of Medicine, 139*, 25-30.

Lutzker, D. (1960). Internationalism as a predictor of cooperative behavior. *Journal of Conflict Resolution, 4*, 426-430.

Lysgaard, S. (1955). Adjustment in a foreign society: Norwegian Fulbright grantees visiting the United States. *International Social Science Bulletin, 7*(2), 131-148.

Ma, R. (1990). An exploratory study of discontented responses in American and Chinese relationships. *Southern Communication Journal, 55*, 305-318.

Maass, A., & Clark, R. D. (1984). Hidden impact of minorities: Fifteen years of minority influence research. *Psychological Bulletin, 95*, 428-450.

MacCannell, D. (1989). *The tourist: A new theory of the leisure class.* New York: Schocken.

Malinowski, B. (1965). *The language of magic and gardening: Coral gardens and their magic* (Vol. 2). Bloomington: Indiana University Press. (Original work published 1935)

Maltz, D. N., & Borker, R. A. (1982). A cultural approach to male-female miscommunication. In J. J. Gumperz (Ed.), *Language and social identity* (pp. 196-216). Cambridge: Cambridge University Press.

Manusov, V., & Hegde, R. (1993). Communicative outcomes of stereotype-based expectancies: An observational study of cross-cultural dyads. *Communication Quarterly, 41*, 338-354.

March, R. M. (1992). *Working for a Japanese company: Insights into the multicultural workplace.* Tokyo: Kodansha International.

Marcuse, H. (1974). Marxism and feminism. *Women's Studies, 2*, 279-288.
Markus, H. R., & Kitayama, S. (1991). Culture and the self: Implications for cognition, emotion, and motivation. *Psychological Review, 98*, 224-253.
Marmot, M., & Syme, S. (1976). Acculturation and coronary heart disease in Japanese-Americans. *American Journal of Epidemiology, 104*(3), 225-247.
Marsella, A., DeVoss, G., & Hsu, F. L. K. (1985). *Culture and the self.* London: Tavistock.
Martínez-Echazábel, L. (1988). Positivismo y racismo en el ensayo hispanoamericano [Positivism and racism in the Latin American essay]. *Cuadernos Americanos* (No. 9, Nueva época), pp. 121-129.
Mason, D. (1986). Introduction: Controversies and continuities in race and ethnic relations theory. In J. Rex & D. Mason (Eds.), *Theories of race and ethnic relations* (pp. 1-19). Cambridge: Cambridge University Press.
Mastekaasa, A. (1984). Multiplicative and additive models of job and life satisfaction. *Social Indicators Research, 14*, 141-163.
Matsumoto, D. (1993). Ethnic differences in affect intensity, emotion judgements, display rule attitudes, and self-reported emotional expression in an American sample. *Motivation and Emotion, 17*, 107-123.
Matsumoto, D., & Ekman, P. (1989). American-Japanese cultural differences in intensity ratings of facial expressions of emotion. *Motivation and Emotion, 13*, 143-157.
May, R. (1977). *The meaning of anxiety.* New York: Ronald.
McCarthy, B., & Duck, W. S. (1976). Friendships' duration and responses to attitudinal agreement-disagreement. *British Journal of Social and Clinical Psychology, 15*, 377-386.
McConahay, J. B. (1986). Modern racism, ambivalence, and the modern racism scale. In J. S. Dovidio & S. L. Gaertner (Eds.), *Prejudice, discrimination and racism* (pp. 91-125). Orlando, FL: Academic Press.
McCroskey, J. C. (1984). The communication apprehension perspective. In J. A. Daly & J. C. McCroskey (Eds.), *Avoiding communication* (pp. 13-38). Beverly Hills, CA: Sage.
McGuire, J., & Popkin, B. (1990). *Helping women improve nutrition in the developing world: Beating the zero sum game* (World Bank technical paper No. 114). Washington, DC: World Bank.
McKerrow, R. E. (1989). Critical rhetoric: Theory and praxis. *Communication Monographs, 56*, 91-111.
McKerrow, R. E. (1991). Critical rhetoric in a postmodern world. *Quarterly Journal of Speech, 77*, 75-78.
McKirnan, D. J., & Hamayan, E. V. (1984). Speech norms and perceptions of ethnolinguistic group differences: Towards a conceptual and research framework. *European Journal of Social Psychology, 14*, 151-168.
McLeod, J. M., & Blumler, J. G. (1987). The macrosocial level of communication science. In C. R. Berger & S. H. Chaffee (Eds.), *Handbook of communication science* (pp. 271-322). Newbury Park, CA: Sage.
McPherson, K. (1983). Opinion-related information seeking. *Personality and Social Psychology Bulletin, 9*, 116-124.
Mead, G. H. (1934). *Mind, self, and society.* Chicago: University of Chicago Press.
Mead, M. (1964). *Continuities in cultural evolution.* New Haven, CT: Yale University Press.
Meira-Penna, J. O. de. (1980). *O Brasil na Idade da Razão* [Brazil in the Age of Reason]. Rio de Janeiro: Forense-Universitária.
Mendenhall, M., & Oddou, G. (1985). The dimensions of expatriate acculturation: A review. *Academy of Management Review, 10*(1), 39-47.
Meredith, B. S. (1994). *Code choice in intercultural conversations: Speech accommodation theory and pragmatics.* Submitted for publication.
Menard, S. (1991). *Longitudinal research.* Newbury Park, CA: Sage.
Merton, R. K. (1957). *Social theory and social structure.* New York: Free Press.
Michalos, A. (1980). Satisfaction and happiness. *Social Indicators Research, 8*, 385-422.

Michalos, A. (1985). Multiple discrepancies theory (MDT). *Social Indicators Research, 16*, 347-413.

Michalos, A. (1991). *Global report on student well-being: Vol. 1. Life satisfaction and happiness.* New York: Springer-Verlag.

Middleton, D., & Edwards, D. (1990). *Collective remembering.* London: Sage.

Milbrath, L., & Sahr, R. (1975). Perceptions of environmental quality. *Social Indicators Research, 1,* 397-438.

Miles, R. (1989). *Racism.* London: Routledge.

Miller, G. R., & Steinberg, M. (1975). *Between people.* Chicago: SRA.

Miller, J. G. (1984). Culture and the development of everyday social explanation. *Journal of Personality and Social Psychology, 46,* 961-978.

Miller, J. G. (1988). Bridging the content-structure dichotomy: Culture and the self. In M. M. Bond (Ed.), *The cross-cultural challenge to social psychology* (pp. 266-281). Newbury Park, CA: Sage.

Miranda, M., & Castro, F. (1977). Culture distance and success in psychotherapy with Spanish speaking clients. In J. Martinez Jr. (Ed.), *Chicano psychology* (pp. 249-262). New York: Academic Press.

Mirandé, A. (1985). *The Chicano experience: An alternative perspective.* Notre Dame, IN: University of Notre Dame Press.

Mitchell, F. M. (1983). Popular medical concepts in Jamaica and their impact on drug use. *Western Journal of Medicine, 139,* 37-43.

Mitchell, M. (1984). Race, legitimacy and the state in Brazil. *Afrodiáspora, 4,* 109-124.

Mizutani, O. (1981). *Japanese: The spoken language in Japanese life.* Tokyo: Japan Times.

Mo, B. (1992). Modesty, sexuality, and breast health in Chinese-American women. *Western Journal of Medicine, 157,* 260-264.

Monge, P. R. (1977). The systems perspective as a theoretical basis for the study of human communication. *Communication Quarterly, 25,* 19-29.

Montgomery, B. M. (1986). A commentary on Indvik and Fitzpatrick's study of relationship defining communication. *Communication Quarterly, 34,* 14-18.

Morris, D. (1971). *Intimate behavior.* New York: Random House.

Muecke, M. A. (1983). In search of healers: Southeast Asian refugees in the American health care system. *Western Journal of Medicine, 139,* 31-36.

Mulac, A., Studley, L. B., Wiemann, J. M., & Bradac, J. J. (1987). Male/female gaze in same-sex and mixed-sex dyads: Gender-linked differences and mutual influence. *Human Communication Research, 13,* 323-343.

Muller, J. H., & Desmond, B. (1992). Ethical dilemmas in a cross-cultural context: A Chinese example. *Western Journal of Medicine, 157,* 323-327.

Murray, A., & Sondhi, R. (1987). Socio-political influences on cross-cultural encounters: Notes towards a framework for the analysis of context. In K. Knapp, W. Enninger, & A. Knapp-Potthoff (Eds.), *Analyzing intercultural communication* (pp. 17-33). Berlin: Mouton de Gruyter.

Nadler, L. B., Keeshan-Nadler, M., & Broome, B. J. (1985). Culture and the management of conflict situations. In W. Gudykunst, L. Stewart, & S. Ting-Toomey (Eds.), *Communication, culture, and organizational processes* (pp. 87-113). Beverly Hills, CA: Sage.

Nagata, K. (1969). *A statistical approach to the study of acculturation of an ethnic group based on communication oriented variables: The case of Japanese Americans in Chicago.* Unpublished doctoral dissertation, University of Illinois, Urbana-Champaign.

Naiman, N., Frohlich, M., Stern, H., & Todesco, A. (1978). *The good language learner.* Toronto: Ontario Institute for Studies in Education.

Nakagawa, M. (1993, March 19). Community leaders, police talk, hate crimes. *Asian Week,* p. 12.

Nakayama, T. K. (in press). Show/down time: "Race," gender, sexuality, and popular culture. *Critical Studies in Mass Communication.*

310 • *INTERCULTURAL COMMUNICATION THEORY*

Nascimento, A. do. (1978). *O genocídio do negro brasileiro: Processo de um racismo mascarado* [The genocide of the black Brazilian: The process of a disguised racism]. Rio de Janeiro: Paz e Terra.

Natale, M. (1975). Convergence of mean vocal intensity in dyadic communications as a function of social desirability. *Journal of Personality and Social Psychology, 32,* 790-804.

Newtson, D. (1973). Attribution and the unit of perception of ongoing behavior. *Journal of Personality and Social Psychology, 28,* 28-38.

Niedzielski, N., & Giles, H. (in press). Linguistic accommodation: Essay #41. In H. Goebl, P. H. Nelde, Z. Stary, & W. Wolck (Eds.), *Contact linguistics: An international handbook of contemporary research.* Berlin: de Gruyter.

Niles, T. A., & Baldwin, J. R. (1994, November). *African- and European Americans' views of "race" and "racism": A comparative analysis.* Poster session presented at the annual meeting of the Speech Communication Association, New Orleans, LA.

Oberg, K. (1960). Cultural shock: Adjustment to new cultural environments. *Practical Anthropology, 7,* 177-182.

Okabe, R. (1983). Cultural assumptions of East and West: Japan and the United States. In W. Gudykunst (Ed.), *Intercultural communication theory* (pp. 21-44). Beverly Hills, CA: Sage.

O'Keefe, D., & Sypher, H. (1981). Cognitive complexity measures and the relationship of cognitive complexity to communication. *Human Communication Research, 8,* 72-92.

Oliver, R. L. (1980). A cognitive model of the antecedents and consequences of satisfaction decisions. *Journal of Marketing Research, 27,* 460-469.

Omi, M., & Winant, H. (1986). *Racial formation in the United States: From the 1960s to the 1980s* (rev ed.). New York: Routledge.

Opotow, S. (1990). Moral exclusion and injustice: An introduction. *Journal of Social Issues, 46,* 1-20.

Ortiz, R. (1985). *Cultura brasileira e identidade nacional* [Brazilian culture and national identity]. São Paulo: Brasiliense.

Ostroot, N., Shin, D., & Snyder, W. (1982). Quality of life perceptions in two cultures. *Social Indicators Research, 11,* 113-138.

Outlaw, L. (1990). Towards a critical theory of "race." In D. T. Goldberg (Ed.), *Anatomy of racism* (pp. 58-82). Minneapolis: University of Minnesota Press.

Pacheco, E. (1976). *Colonização e racismo: Relações raciais em uma zona de colonização européia* [Colonization and racism: Racial relations in a zone of European colonization]. São Cristóvão Rio, RJ: Artenova.

Paim, P. (1988). O racismo disfarçado e o despertar da consciência negra no Brasil [Disguised racism and the awakening of the black consciousness in Brazil]. In *Dia internacional para a Eliminação da Discriminação Racial* (pp. 5-37). Brasília: Centro de Documentação e Informação, Coordenação de Publicações.

Pang, K. Y. (1989). The practice of traditional Korean medicine in Washington, D.C. *Social Science and Medicine, 28,* 875-884.

Parillo, V. N. (1980). *Strangers to these shores: Race and ethnic relations in the United States.* Boston: Houghton Mifflin.

Parker, B., & McEvoy, G. (1993). Initial examination of a model of intercultural adjustment. *International Journal of Intercultural Relations, 17,* 355-379.

Parks, M., & Adelman, M. (1983). Communication networks and the development of romantic relationships. *Human Communication Research, 10,* 55-80.

Parsons, T. (1951). *The social system.* Glencoe, IL: Free Press.

Pearce, W. B., & Cronen, V. (1980). *Communication, action, and meaning.* New York: Praeger.

Pelto, P. (1968, April). The difference between "tight" and "loose" societies. *Transaction,* pp. 37-40.

Pennebraker, J. (1989). Stream of consciousness and stress. In J. Uleman & J. Bargh (Eds.), *Unintended thought* (pp. 327-350). New York: Guilford.

Pettigrew, T. (1988). Integration and pluralism. In P. Katz & D. Taylor (Eds.), *Eliminating racism* (pp. 19-30). New York: Plenum.

Phinney, J., & Rosenthal, D. (1992). Ethnic identity in adolescence: Process, context, and outcome. In G. Adams, T. Gullota, & R. Montemayer (Eds.), *Adolescent identity formation* (pp. 145-172). Newbury Park, CA: Sage.

Piaget, J. (1963). *The origins of intelligence in children.* New York: Norton.

Pilisuk, M. (1963). Anxiety, self acceptance and open-mindedness. *Journal of Clinical Psychology, 19,* 386-391.

Planalp, S. (1985). Relational schemata: A test of alternative forms of relational knowledge as guides to communication. *Human Communication Research, 12,* 3-29.

Planalp, S., Rutherford, D., & Honeycutt, J. (1988). Events that increase uncertainty in personal relationships II. *Human Communication Research, 14,* 516-547.

Platt, J., & Weber, H. (1984). Speech convergence miscarried: An investigation into inappropriate accommodation strategies. *International Journal of the Sociology of Language, 46,* 131-146.

Polkinghorne, D. (1983). *Methodology for the human sciences: Systems of inquiry.* Albany: State University of New York Press.

Poloma, M., & Pendleton, B. (1990). Religious domains and general well-being. *Social Indicators Research, 22,* 255-276.

Pood, E. A. (1980). Functions of communication: An experimental study in group conflict situations. *Small Group Behavior, 11,* 76-87.

Prochaska, J. (1979). *Systems of psychotherapy: A transtheoretical analysis.* Belmont, CA: Dorsey.

Putnam, L. L. (1986). Conflict in group decision-making. In R. Y. Hirokawa & M. S. Poole (Eds.), *Communication and group decision-making* (pp. 175-196). Newbury Park, CA: Sage.

Py, B., & Jeanneret, R. (Eds.). (1989). *Minorisation Linguistique et Interaction.* Geneva: Droz.

Ramakrishna, J., & Weiss, M. G. (1992). Health, illness, and immigration: East Indians in the United States. *Western Journal of Medicine, 157,* 265-270.

Rasinski, D. (1993). Cross-cultural concerns and communication in health care. In B. C. Thornton & G. L. Kreps (Eds.), *Perspectives on health communication* (pp. 165-177). Prospect Heights, IL: Waveland.

Ray, J. J., & Lovejoy, F. H. (1986). The generality of racial prejudice. *Journal of Social Psychology, 126,* 563-564.

Reischauer, E. (1977). *The Japanese.* Cambridge, MA: Harvard University Press.

Rex, J. (1980). The theory of race relations: A Weberian approach. In UNESCO (Ed.), *Sociological theories: Race and colonialism* (pp. 117-140). Paris: UNESCO.

Rex, J. (1986). The role of class analysis in the study of race relations: A Weberian perspective. In J. Rex & D. Mason (Eds.), *Theories of race and ethnic relations* (pp. 64-83). Cambridge: Cambridge University Press.

Reynolds, P. (1971). *A primer in theory construction.* Indianapolis: Bobbs-Merrill.

Reynolds, V., Falger, V., & Vine, I. (Eds.). (1987). *The sociobiology of ethnocentrism: Evolutionary dimensions of xenophobia, discrimination and nationalism.* London: Croom Helm.

Rheingold, H. (1993). *Virtual communities: Homesteading on the Electronic Frontier.* Reading, MA: Addison-Wesley.

Ridgeway, C. L. (1981). Nonconformity, competence, and influence in groups: A test of two theories. *American Sociological Review, 46,* 333-347.

Ridgeway, C. L., & Berger, J. (1986). Expectations, legitimation, and dominance behavior in task groups. *American Sociological Review, 51,* 603-617.

Ridgeway, C. L., & Jacobson, C. K. (1977). Sources of status and influence in all female and mixed sex groups. *Sociological Quarterly, 18,* 413-425.

Riedl, R. (1984). The consequences of causal thinking. In P. Watzlawick (Ed.), *The invented reality: How do we know what we believe we know? (Contributions to constructivism)* (pp. 69-94). New York: Norton.

Riezler, K. (1960). The social psychology of fear. In M. Stein, A. Vidich, & D. White (Eds.), *Identity and anxiety* (pp. 144-156). Glencoe, IL: Free Press.

Rogers, E. (1979). Mass media and interpersonal communication. In G. Gumpert & R. Cathcart (Eds.), *Inter/Media: Interpersonal communication in a media world* (pp. 192-213). New York: Oxford University Press.

Rogers, J., & Ward, C. (1993). Expectation-experience discrepancies and psychological adjustment during cross-cultural reentry. *International Journal of Intercultural Relations, 17*(2), 185-196.

Rogers, R. W. (1975). A Protection Motivation Theory of fear appeals and attitude change. *Journal of Psychology, 91*, 93-114.

Rogers, R. W. (1983). Cognitive and physiological processes in fear appeals and attitude change: A revised theory of protection motivation. In J. Cacioppo & R. E. Petty (Eds.), *Social psychophysiology* (pp. 153-176). New York: Guilford.

Rokeach, M. (1960). *The open and closed mind: Investigations into the nature of belief systems and personality systems.* New York: Basic Books.

Roosens, E. (1989). *Creating ethnicity: The process of ethnogenesis.* Newbury Park, CA: Sage.

Root, M. (1993). Within, between, and beyond race. In M. Root (Ed.), *Racially mixed people in America* (pp. 3-11). Newbury Park, CA: Sage.

Rosenstock, I. M. (1974). The health belief model and preventive health behavior. *Health Education Monographs, 2*, 354-386.

Ross, M. H. (1991). The role of evolution in ethnocentric conflict and its management. *Journal of Social Issues, 47*, 167-185.

Ross, S., & Shortreed, I. M. (1990). Japanese foreigner talk: Convergence or divergence? *Journal of Asian Pacific Communication, 1*, 134-145.

Ruben, B. (1980, March). *Culture shock: The skull and the lady—Reflections on cultural adjustment and stress.* Paper presented at the annual conference of the Society for International Education, Training, and Research, Mt. Pocono, PA.

Ruben, B., & Kealey, D. (1979). Behavioral assessment of communication competency and the prediction of cross-cultural adaptation. *International Journal of Intercultural Relations, 3*, 15-47.

Ruben, B., & Kim, J. (1975). *General systems theory and human communication.* Rochelle Park, NJ: Hayden.

Ruesch, J., & Bateson, G. (1968). *Communication: The social matrix of psychiatry.* New York: Norton. (Original work published 1951)

Ryan, E. B., Giles, H., & Sebastian, R. J. (1982). An integrative perspective for the study of attitudes toward language variation. In E. B. Ryan & H. Giles (Eds.), *Attitudes toward language variation: Social and applied contexts* (pp. 1-19). London: Edward Arnold.

Rychlak, J. (1965). The similarity, compatibility, or incompatibility of needs in interpersonal selection. *Journal of Personality and Social Psychology, 2*, 334-340.

Sachdev, I., Bourhis, R., Phang, S., & D'Eye, J. (1987). Language attitudes and vitality perceptions: Intergenerational effects among Chinese Canadian communities. *Journal of Language and Social Psychology, 6*, 287-307.

Salzman, K., & Hunter, J. E. (1983). *The voicer/nonvoicer distinction: A dimension in the experience of conscious thought.* Unpublished manuscript.

Sampson, E. (1993). *Celebrating the other.* Boulder, CO: Westview.

Sarbaugh, L. E. (1979). *Intercultural communication.* Rochelle Park, NJ: Hayden.

Schank, R. C., & Abelson, R. P. (1977). *Scripts, plans, goals, and understanding.* Hillsdale, NJ: Lawrence Erlbaum.

Scheff, T. (1990). *Microsociology: Discourse, emotion, and social structure.* Chicago: University of Chicago Press.

Schneiderman, L. (1960). Repression, anxiety and the self. In M. Stein, A. Vidich, & D. White (Eds.), *Identity and anxiety* (pp. 157-165). Glencoe, IL: Free Press.

Schram, J., & Lauver, P. (1988). Alienation in international students. *Journal of College Student Development, 29*, 146-150.

Schramm, W. (1979). Channels and audiences. In G. Gumpert & R. Cathcart (Eds.), *Inter/ Media: Interpersonal communication in a media world* (pp. 160-174). New York: Oxford University Press.

Schuman, H., & Presser, S. (1981). *Questions and answers in attitude surveys: Experiments on question form, wording and context.* New York: Academic Press.

Schwartz, S. H. (1990). Individualism-collectivism: Critique and proposed refinements. *Journal of Cross-Cultural Psychology, 21,* 139-157.

Schwartz, S. H., & Bilsky, W. (1990). Toward a theory of the universal content and structure of values. *Journal of Personality and Social Psychology, 53,* 550-562.

Schwarz, N., & Strack, F. (1991). Evaluating one's life: A judgment model of subjective well-being. In F. Strack, M. Argyle, & N. Schwarz (Eds.), *Subjective well-being: An interdisciplinary perspective* (pp. 27-48). Oxford: Pergamon.

Schwichtenberg, C. (1989). Feminist cultural studies. *Critical Studies in Mass Communication, 6,* 202-208.

Scollon, R., & Scollon, S. (1981). *Narrative, literacy and face in interethnic communication.* Norwood, NJ: Ablex.

Searle, W., & Ward, C. (1990). The prediction of psychological and sociocultural adjustment during cross-cultural transitions. *International Journal of Intercultural Relations, 14,* 449-464.

Sears, D. O. (1988). Symbolic racism. In P. A. Katz & D. A. Taylor (Eds.), *Eliminating racism: Profiles in controversy* (pp. 53-84). New York: Plenum.

Selznick, P. (1992). *The moral commonwealth.* Berkeley: University of California Press.

Sewell, W., & Davidsen, O. (1956). The adjustment of Scandinavian students. *Journal of Social Issues, 12*(1), 9-19.

Shah, H. (1991). Communication and cross-cultural adaptation patterns among Asian Indians. *International Journal of Intercultural Relations, 15*(3), 311-321.

Shaw, M. E. (1981). *Group dynamics: The psychology of small group behavior.* New York: McGraw-Hill.

Sheldon, A. (1990). Pickle fights: Gendered talk in preschool disputes. *Discourse Processes, 13,* 5-31.

Sherif, M. (1966). *Group conflict and co-operation: Their social psychology.* London: Routledge & Kegan Paul.

Shibutani, T., & Kwan, K. (1965). *Ethnic stratification: A comparative approach.* New York: Macmillan.

Shockey, L. (1984). All in a flap: Long-term accommodation in phonology. *International Journal of the Sociology of Language, 46,* 87-96.

Simard, L., Taylor, D., & Giles, H. (1976). Attributional processes and interpersonal accommodation in a bilingual setting. *Language and Speech, 19,* 374-387.

Simmel, G. (1950). The stranger. In K. Wolff (Ed. and Trans.), *The sociology of Georg Simmel* (pp. 402-408). New York: Free Press. (Original work published 1908)

Singelis, T. M. (1994). Bridging the gap between culture and communication. In F. Van de Vijuer, P. Schmitz, & P. Boski (Eds.), *Selected papers from the 12th International Conference of the Association for Cross-Cultural Psychology* (pp. 278-293). Lisse, the Netherlands: Swets & Zeitlinger.

Singer, M. R. (1987). *Intercultural communication: A perceptual approach.* Englewood Cliffs, NJ: Prentice Hall.

Sirgy, M. J. (1984). A social cognition model of consumer satisfaction/dissatisfaction. *Psychology and Marketing, 1*(2), 27-44.

Slavin, M., & Kriegman, D. (1992). *The adaptive design of the human psyche.* New York: Guilford.

Smiley, M. (1992). *Moral responsibility and the boundaries of community.* Chicago: University of Chicago Press.

Smith, P. B., & Bond, M. H. (1993). *Social psychology across cultures.* New York: Harvester.

Smith, V. (Ed.). (1989). *Hosts and guests: The anthropology of tourism.* Philadelphia: University of Pennsylvania Press.

Smock, C. (1955). The influence of psychological stress on the intolerance of ambiguity. *Journal of Abnormal and Social Psychology, 50,* 177-182.

Snow, L. F. (1983). Traditional health beliefs and practices among lower class black Americans. *Western Journal of Medicine, 139,* 16-24.

Snyder, M. (1974). Self-monitoring of expressive behavior. *Journal of Personality and Social Psychology, 30,* 526-537.

Snyder, M., & Monson, T. (1975). Persons, situations, and the control of social behavior. *Journal of Personality and Social Psychology, 32,* 637-644.

Solomos, J. (1986). Varieties of Marxist conceptions of "race," class and the state: A critical analysis. In J. Rex & D. Mason (Eds.), *Theories of race and ethnic relations* (pp. 84-109). Cambridge: Cambridge University Press.

Spicer, E. (1968). Acculturation. In D. Sills (Ed.), *International encyclopedia of the social sciences* (pp. 21-27). New York: Macmillan.

Spitzberg, B. H., & Cupach, W. R. (1984). *Interpersonal communication competence.* Beverly Hills, CA: Sage.

Spolsky, B., & Cooper, R. (1991). *The languages of Jerusalem.* Oxford: Oxford University Press.

Spradley, J., & Phillips, M. (1972). Culture and stress: A quantitative analysis. *American Anthropologist, 74,* 518-529.

Stacks, D. W., & Burgoon, J. K. (1981). The role of nonverbal behaviors as distractors in resistance to persuasion in interpersonal contexts. *Central States Speech Journal, 32,* 61-73.

Staines, G. L., & Libby, P. L. (1986). Men and women in role relationships. In R. D. Asmore & F. K. Del Boca (Eds.), *The social psychology of male-female relations* (pp. 211-258). New York: Academic Press.

Staub, E. (1989). *The roots of evil.* New York: Cambridge University Press.

Staub, E. (1990). Moral exclusion, personal goal theory, and extreme destructiveness. *Journal of Social Issues, 46,* 47-64.

Steele, S. (1990). *The content of our character: A new vision of race in America.* New York: St. Martin's.

Stening, B., & Hammer, M. (1992). Cultural baggage and the adaptation of expatriate American and Japanese managers. *Management International Review, 32,* 77-89.

Stepan, N. L. (1991). *"The hour of eugenics": Race, gender, and nation in Latin America.* Ithaca, NY: Cornell University Press.

Stephan, W. (1985). Intergroup relations. In G. Lindzey & E. Aronson (Eds.), *The handbook of social psychology* (3rd ed., Vol. 2, pp. 599-658). Reading, MA: Addison-Wesley.

Stephan, W. G., & Stephan, C. (1985). Intergroup anxiety. *Journal of Social Issues, 41,* 157-166.

Stephan, W. G., & Stephan, C. (1989). Antecedent to intergroup anxiety in Asian-Americans and Hispanic-Americans. *International Journal of Intercultural Relations, 13,* 203-219.

Stephan, W. G., & Stephan, C. (1992). Reducing intercultural anxiety through intercultural contact. *International Journal of Intercultural Relations, 16,* 89-106.

Stern, P. N. (1986). A comparison of culturally approved behaviors and beliefs between Filipina immigrant women, U.S.-born dominant culture women, and Western female nurses of the San Francisco bay area: Religiosity of health care. In P. N. Stern (Ed.), *Women, health, and culture* (pp. 123-133). New York: Hemisphere.

Stern, P. N., Tilden, V. P., & Maxwell, E. K. (1986). Culturally induced stress during childbearing: The Filipino-American experience. In P. N. Stern (Ed.), *Women, health, and culture* (pp. 105-121). New York: Hemisphere.

Stewart, E. C. (1985). Culture and decision-making. In W. Gudykunst, L. Stewart, & S. Ting-Toomey (Eds.), *Communication, culture, and organizational processes* (pp. 177-211). Beverly Hills, CA: Sage.

Stewart, K., & Wheeless, V. (1981). The psychometric properties of the Bem Sex-Role Inventory: Questions concerning reliability and validity. *Communication Quarterly, 29,* 173-186.

Strauss, A., & Corbin, J. (1990). *Basics of qualitative research: Grounded theory procedures and techniques.* Newbury Park, CA: Sage.

Street, R. L., Brady, R. N., & Putman, W. B. (1983). The influence of speech rate stereotypes and role similarity on listeners' evaluations of speakers. *Journal of Language and Social Psychology, 2,* 37-56.

Street, R. L., & Cappella, J. N. (1985). Sequence and pattern in communicative behavior: A model and commentary. In R. L. Street & J. N. Cappella (Eds.), *Sequence and pattern in communicative behavior* (pp. 243-276). Baltimore, MD: Edward Arnold.

Stroup, A. P. (1993, November). *Cross-cultural communication strategies of Navajo and non-Navajo health care workers on the Navajo reservation.* Paper presented at the annual meeting of the Speech Communication Association, Miami, FL.

Subervi-Velez, F. (1986). The mass media and ethnic assimilation and pluralism. *Communication Research, 13*(1), 71-96.

Sunnafrank, M. (1983). Attitude similarity and interpersonal attraction in communication processes. *Communication Monographs, 50,* 273-284.

Sunnafrank, M. (1986). Predicted outcome value during initial interactions. *Human Communication Research, 13,* 3-33.

Sunnafrank, M., & Miller, G. (1981). The role of initial conversation in determining attraction to similar and dissimilar strangers. *Human Communication Research, 8,* 16-25.

Sutherland, A. (1992). Gypsies and health care. *Western Journal of Medicine, 157,* 276-280.

Suzuki, T. (1975). *Tozasareta Gengo: Nihongo no Sekai.* Tokyo: Iwanami Shoten.

Swan, J. E., & Trawick, I. F. (1981). Disconfirmation of expectations and satisfaction with a retail service. *Journal of Retailing, 57,* 49-67.

Szalay, L., & Inn, A. (1987). Cross-cultural adaptation and diversity: Hispanic Americans. In Y. Kim & W. Gudykunst (Eds.), *Cross-cultural adaptation: Current approaches* (pp. 212-232). Newbury Park, CA: Sage.

Szapocznik, J., Scopetta, M., Kurtines, W., & Aranalde, M. (1978). Theory and measurement of acculturation. *Interamerican Journal of Psychology, 12,* 118-130.

Taft, R. (1977). Coping with unfamiliar cultures. In N. Warren (Ed.), *Studies in cross-cultural psychology* (Vol. 1, pp. 121-153). London: Academic Press.

Taft, R. (1988). The psychological adaptation of Soviet immigrants in Australia. In Y. Kim & W. Gudykunst (Eds.), *Cross-cultural adaptation: Current approaches* (pp. 150-167). Newbury Park, CA: Sage.

Tajfel, H. (1978a). Interindividual and intergroup behavior. In H. Tajfel (Ed.), *Differentiation between social groups* (pp. 27-60). London: Academic Press.

Tajfel, H. (1978b). Social categorization, social identity, and social comparisons. In H. Tajfel (Ed.), *Differentiation between groups* (pp. 61-76). London: Academic Press.

Tajfel, H. (1981). *Human categories and social groups.* Cambridge, UK: Cambridge University Press.

Tajfel, H. (Ed.). (1982). *Social identity and intergroup relations.* Cambridge, UK: Cambridge University Press.

Tajfel, H., & Turner, J. C. (1978). An integrative theory of intergroup conflict. In W. Austin & S. Worchel (Eds.), *The social psychology of intergroup relations* (pp. 33-47). Monterey, CA: Brooks/Cole.

Tajfel, H., & Turner, J. C. (1986). The social identity theory of intergroup relations. In S. Worchel & W. Austin (Eds.), *Psychology of intergroup relations* (2nd ed., pp. 7-17). Chicago: Nelson-Hall.

Tamam, E. (1993, December). *The influence of ambiguity tolerance, open-mindedness, and empathy on sojourners' psychological adaptation and perceived intercultural communication effectiveness.* Unpublished doctoral dissertation, University of Oklahoma, Norman.

Tanaka, T., Takai, J., Kohyama, T., & Fujihara, T. (1994). Adjustment patterns of international students in Japan. *International Journal of Intercultural Relations, 18*(1), 55-76.

Taylor, C. (1992). The politics of recognition. In A. Gutmann (Ed.), *Multiculturalism and "the politics of recognition"* (pp. 25-74). Princeton, NJ: Princeton University Press.

Taylor, S. E., & Crocker, J. (1981). Schematic bases of social information processing. In E. T. Higgins, C. P. Herman, & M. P. Zanna (Eds.), *Social cognition: The Ontario symposium* (Vol. 1, pp. 89-134). Hillsdale, NJ: Lawrence Erlbaum.

Thayer, L. (1975). Knowledge, order, and communication. In B. Ruben & J. Kim (Eds.), *General systems theory and human communication* (pp. 237-245). Rochelle Park, NJ: Hayden.

Thibaut, J., & Kelley, H. H. (1959). *The social psychology of groups.* New York: Wiley.

Thomas, J. (1983). Cross-cultural pragmatic failure. *Applied Linguistics, 4,* 91-112.

Ting-Toomey, S. (1985). Toward a theory of conflict and culture. In W. Gudykunst, L. Stewart, & S. Ting-Toomey (Eds.), *Communication, culture, and organizational processes* (pp. 71-85). Beverly Hills, CA: Sage.

Ting-Toomey, S. (1988). Intercultural conflict styles: A face-negotiation theory. In Y. Y. Kim & W. B. Gudykunst (Eds.), *Theories in intercultural communication* (pp. 213-238). Newbury Park, CA: Sage.

Ting-Toomey, S. (1989a). Culture and interpersonal relationship development. In J. Anderson (Ed.), *Communication yearbook 12* (pp. 371-382). Newbury Park, CA: Sage.

Ting-Toomey, S. (1989b). Identity and interpersonal bonding. In M. K. Asante & W. B. Gudykunst (Eds.), *Handbook of international and intercultural communication* (pp. 163-185). Newbury Park, CA: Sage.

Ting-Toomey, S. (1993). Communicative resourcefulness: An identity negotiation perspective. In R. L. Wiseman & J. Koester (Eds.), *Intercultural communication competence* (pp. 72-111). Newbury Park, CA: Sage.

Ting-Toomey, S., Gao, G., Trubisky, P., Yang, Z., Kim, H. S., Lin, S., & Nishida, T. (1991). Culture, face maintenance, and styles of handling interpersonal conflict: A study in five cultures. *International Journal of Conflict Management, 2,* 275-296.

Torbiörn, I. (1982). *Living abroad.* New York: Wiley.

Triandis, H. C. (1988). Collectivism vs. individualism. In G. Verma & C. Bagley (Eds.), *Cross-cultural studies of personality, attitudes, and cognition* (pp. 60-95). London: Macmillan.

Triandis, H. C. (1989). The self and social behavior in differing cultural contexts. *Psychological Review, 96,* 506-520.

Triandis, H. C. (1990). Cross-cultural studies of individualism and collectivism. In J. Berman (Ed.), *Nebraska Symposium on Motivation, 1989* (pp. 41-133). Lincoln: University of Nebraska Press.

Triandis, H. C. (1993). Collectivism and individualism as cultural syndromes. *Cross-Cultural Research, 27,* 155-180.

Triandis, H. C. (1994). *Culture and social behavior.* New York: McGraw-Hill.

Triandis, H. C. (in press). *Individualism and collectivism.* Boulder, CO: Westview.

Triandis, H. C., Bontempo, R., Villareal, M. J., Asai, M., & Lucca, N. (1988). Individualism and collectivism: Cross-cultural perspectives on self-ingroup relationships. *Journal of Personality and Social Psychology, 54,* 323-338.

Triandis, H. C., Brislin, R., & Hui, C. H. (1988). Cross-cultural training across the individualism-collectivism divide. *International Journal of Intercultural Relations, 12,* 269-289.

Triandis, H. C., Hui, C. H., Albert, R. D., Leung, S.-M., Lisansky, J., Diaz-Loving, R., Plascencia, L., Marín, G., Betancourt, H., & Loyola-Cintron, L. (1984). Individual models of social behavior. *Journal of Personality and Social Psychology, 46,* 1389-1404.

Triandis, H. C., Leung, K., Villareal, M., & Clack, F. (1985). Allocentric versus idiocentric tendencies. *Journal of Research in Personality, 19,* 395-415.

Triandis, H. C., McCusker, C., & Hui, C. H. (1990). Multimethod probes of individualism and collectivism. *Journal of Personality and Social Psychology, 59,* 1006-1020.

Trudgill, P. (1986). *Dialects in contact.* Oxford: Blackwell.

Tse, D. K., & Wilton, P. C. (1988). Models of consumer satisfaction formation: An extension. *Journal of Marketing Research, 25*, 204-212.

Tuan, Y.-F. (1979). *Landscapes of fear.* New York: Pantheon.

Tucker, M., Raik, H., Rossiter, D., & Uhmes, S. L. (1973). *Improving cross-cultural training and measurement of cross-cultural learning* (ACTION contract PC-72-42043). Denver, CO: CRE.

Tucker, R. C. (Ed.). (1978). *The Marx-Engels reader* (2nd ed.). New York: Norton.

Tung, R. (1982). Selection and training procedures of U.S., European, and Japanese multinationals. *California Management Review, 25*(1), 57-71.

Turner, G. (1990). *British cultural studies: An introduction.* Boston: Unwin Hyman.

Turner, J. C. (Ed.). (1987a). *Rediscovering the social group: A self-categorization theory.* Oxford: Blackwell.

Turner, J. C. (1987b). Towards a cognitive redefinition of the social group. In H. Tajfel (Ed.), *Social identity and intergroup interactions* (pp. 15-40). Cambridge: Cambridge University Press.

Turner, J. H. (1988). *A theory of social interaction.* Palo Alto, CA: Stanford University Press.

Turner, R. H. (1987). Articulating self and social structure. In K. Yardley & T. Honess (Eds.), *Self and society* (pp. 119-132). Chichester, UK: Wiley.

van den Berghe, P. L. (1986). Ethnicity and the sociology debate. In J. Rex & D. Mason (Eds.), *Theories of race and ethnic relations* (pp. 246-263). Cambridge: Cambridge University Press.

van Dijk, T. A. (1984). *Prejudice in discourse.* Amsterdam: Benjamins.

van Dijk, T. A. (1987). *Communicating racism: Ethnic prejudice in thought and talk.* Newbury Park, CA: Sage.

Van Lear, C. A. (1991). Testing a cyclical model of communicative openness in relationship development. *Communication Monographs, 58*, 337-361.

Veenhoven, R. (1991). Questions on happiness: Classical topics, modern answers, blind spots. In F. Strack, M. Argyle, & N. Schwarz (Eds.), *Subjective well-being: An interdisciplinary perspective* (pp. 7-26). Oxford: Pergamon.

Vermunt, R., Spaans, E., & Zorge, F. (1989). Satisfaction, happiness and well-being of Dutch students. *Social Indicators Research, 21*, 1-33.

Walker, D. (1993, May). *The role of the mass media in the adaptation of Haitian immigrants in Miami.* Unpublished doctoral dissertation, Indiana University, Indianapolis.

Wallace, M. (1992). Negative images: Towards a black feminist cultural criticism. In L. Grossberg, C. Nelson, & P. Treichler (Eds.), *Cultural studies* (pp. 654-671). New York: Routledge.

Walsh, J. E. (1973). *Intercultural education in the community of man.* Honolulu: University of Hawaii Press.

Walter-Busch, E. (1983). Subjective and objective indicators of regional quality of life in Switzerland. *Social Indicators Research, 12*, 337-391.

Ward, C., & Kennedy, A. (1993). Where's the "culture" in cross-cultural transition? Comparative studies of sojourner adjustment. *Journal of Cross-Cultural Psychology, 24*(2), 221-249.

Ward, C., & Searle, W. (1991). The impact of value discrepancies and cultural identity on psychological and sociocultural adjustment of foreigners. *International Journal of Intercultural Relations, 15*, 209-225.

Warner, M. (1991). Introduction: Fear of a queer planet. *Social Text, 29*, 3-17.

Warner, M. (1992, June). From queer to eternity. *Voice Literary Supplement,* pp. 18-19.

Watzlawick, P. (1984a). Effect or cause? In P. Watzlawick (Ed.), *The invented reality: How do we know what we believe we know? (Contributions to constructivism)* (pp. 63-68). New York: Norton.

Watzlawick, P. (1984b). Self-fulfilling prophecies. In P. Watzlawick (Ed.), *The invented reality: How do we know what we believe we know? (Contributions to constructivism)* (pp. 95-116). New York: Norton.

318 • INTERCULTURAL COMMUNICATION THEORY

Watzlawick, P., Beavin, J., & Jackson, D. (1967). *Pragmatics of human communication.* New York: Norton.
Weinreich, P. (1986). The operationalisation of identity theory in racial and ethnic relations. In J. Rex & D. Mason (Eds.), *Theories of race and ethnic relations* (pp. 299-320). Cambridge: Cambridge University Press.
Weller, S., & Romney, A. (1988). *Systematic data collection.* Newbury Park, CA: Sage.
West, C. (1982). *Prophesy deliverance! An Afro-American revolutionary Christianity.* Philadelphia: Westminster.
White, C. H. (1989). *Effects of expectancy violations on uncertainty in interpersonal interactions.* Unpublished thesis, Texas Tech University.
White, R. (1976). Strategies of adaptation: An attempt at systematic description. In R. Moos (Ed.), *Human adaptation: Coping with life crises* (pp. 17-32). Lexington, MA: D. C. Heath.
Whitley, B. E. (1988). Masculinity, femininity, and self-esteem: A multitrait-multimethod analysis. *Sex Roles, 18,* 319-341.
Wiesel, E. (1992, December 22). Cry against injustice in Yugoslavia. *USA Today,* p. 9A.
Wilder, D. (1993). The role of anxiety in facilitating stereotypic judgment of outgroup behavior. In D. Mackie & D. Hamilton (Eds.), *Affect, cognition, and stereotyping* (pp. 87-109). New York: Academic Press.
Wilder, D., & Allen, V. (1978). Group membership and preference for information about others. *Personality and Social Psychology Bulletin, 4,* 106-110.
Wilder, D., & Shapiro, P. (1989). Effects of anxiety on impression formation in a group context. *Journal of Experimental Social Psychology, 25,* 481-499.
Wilensky, R. (1983). *Planning and understanding: A computational approach to human reasoning.* Reading, MA: Addison-Wesley.
Willemyns, M., Pittam, J., & Gallois, C. (1993). The Subjective Ethnolinguistic Vitality Questionnaire: A confirmatory factor analysis. *Journal of Multilingual and Multicultural Development, 14,* 481-497.
Williams, A., Giles, H., Coupland, N., Dalby, M., & Manasse, H. (1990). The communicative contexts of elderly social support and health: A theoretical model. *Health Communication, 2,* 123-143.
Williams, R. (1980). *Problems in materialism and culture.* London: Verso.
Williams, R., & Westmeyer, J. (1986). Psychiatric problems among adolescent Southeast Asian refugees: A descriptive study. *Pacific/Asian American Mental Health Research Center Newsletter, 4*(3-4), 22-24.
Wilson, G. L., & Hanna, M. S. (1990). *Groups in context: Leadership and participation in small groups.* New York: McGraw-Hill.
Wilson, J. Q. (1993). *The moral sense.* New York: Free Press.
Wilson, S. R., & Putnam, L. L. (1990). Interaction goals in negotiation. In J. A. Anderson (Ed.), *Communication yearbook 13* (pp. 374-427). Newbury Park, CA: Sage.
Wilson, W. J. (1978). *The declining significance of race: Blacks and changing American institutions.* Chicago: University of Chicago Press.
Wiseman, R. L., & Abe, H. (1986). Cognitive complexity and intercultural effectiveness. In M. McLaughlin (Ed.), *Communication yearbook 9* (pp. 611-622). Newbury Park, CA: Sage.
Wiseman, R. L., & Koester, J. (Eds.). (1993). *Intercultural communication competence.* Newbury Park, CA: Sage.
Witkin, H., & Berry, J. (1975). Psychological differentiation in cross-cultural perspective. *Journal of Cross-Cultural Psychology, 6,* 4-87.
Witte, K. (1991). The role of culture in health and disease. In L. A. Samovar & R. E. Porter (Eds.), *Intercultural communication: A reader* (6th ed., pp. 199-207). Belmont, CA: Wadsworth.
Witte, K. (1992a). Putting the fear back into fear appeals: Reconciling the literature. *Communication Monographs, 59,* 329-349.
Witte, K. (1992b). The role of threat and efficacy in AIDS prevention. *International Quarterly of Community Health Education, 12,* 225-249.

Witte, K. (1993). A theory of cognition and negative affect: Extending Gudykunst and Hammer's theory of uncertainty and anxiety. *International Journal of Intercultural Relations, 17*, 197-216.

Wolfe, R., Lennox, R., & Cutler, B. (1986). Getting along and getting ahead. *Journal of Personality and Social Psychology, 50*, 356-361.

Wolfgang, A. (Ed.). (1975). *Education of immigrant students: Issues and answers.* Toronto: Ontario Institute for Studies in Education.

Wolpe, H. (1986). Class concepts, class struggle, and racism. In J. Rex & D. Mason (Eds.), *Theories of race and ethnic relations* (pp. 110-130). Cambridge: Cambridge University Press.

Wood, L., & Johnson, J. (1989). Life satisfaction among the rural elderly: What do the numbers mean? *Social Indicators Research, 21*, 379-408.

Woodall, W. G., & Burgoon, J. K. (1981). The effects of nonverbal synchrony on message comprehension and persuasiveness. *Journal of Nonverbal Behavior, 5*, 207-223.

Word, C., Zanna, M., & Cooper, J. (1974). The nonverbal mediation of self-fulfilling prophecies. *Journal of Experimental Social Psychology, 10*, 109-120.

Wright, G., & Phillips, L. (1980). Cultural variation in probabilistic thinking. *International Journal of Personality, 15*, 239-257.

Yaeger-Dror, M. (1994). Linguistic analysis of dialect "correction" and its interaction with cognitive salience. *Language Variation and Change, 5*, 189-224.

Yang, K. S. (1981). Social orientation and individual modernity among Chinese students in Taiwan. *Journal of Social Psychology, 113*, 159-170.

Yang, K. S., & Ho, D. Y. F. (1988). The role of yuan in Chinese social life: A conceptual and empirical analysis. In A. C. Paranjpe, D. Y. F. Ho, & R. W. Rieber (Eds.), *Asian contributions to psychology* (pp. 263-281). New York: Praeger.

Yang, S. (1988, June). *The role of mass media in immigrants' political socialization: A study of Korean immigrants in Northern California.* Unpublished doctoral dissertation, Stanford University, Stanford, CA.

Yin, R. (1984). *Case study research: Design and methods.* Beverly Hills, CA: Sage.

Ying, Y., & Liese, L. (1990). Initial adaptation of Taiwan foreign students to the United States: The impact of prearrival variables. *American Journal of Community Psychology, 18*(6), 825-846.

Ying, Y., & Liese, L. (1991). Emotional well-being of Taiwan students in the U.S.: An examination of pre- to post-arrival differential. *International Journal of Intercultural Relations, 15*, 345-366.

Young, K. (1985). The notion of context. *Western Folklore, 44*, 115-122.

Yousef, F. S. (1976). Some intricate and diverse dimensions in intercultural communication. In L. A. Samovar & R. E. Porter (Eds.), *Intercultural communication: A reader* (2nd ed., pp. 230-235). Belmont, CA: Wadsworth.

Ytsma, J., Viladot, A., & Giles, H. (1994). Subjective ethnolinguistic vitality and ethnic identity: Some Catalan and Frisian data. *International Journal of the Sociology of Language, 108*, 63-78.

Yum, J. (1988). The impact of Confucianism on interpersonal relationships and communication patterns in East Asia. *Communication Monographs, 55*, 374-388.

Zaharna, R. (1989). Self-shock: The double-binding challenges of identity. *International Journal of Intercultural Relations, 13*(4), 501-525.

Zajonc, R. (1952). Aggressive attitude of the "stranger" as a function of conformity pressures. *Human Relations, 5*, 205-216.

Zatz, M. S. (1987). The changing forms of racial/ethnic biases in sentencing. *Journal of Research in Crime and Delinquency, 24*, 69-92.

Zenner, W. (1987). Common ethnicity and separate identities: Interaction between Jewish immigrant groups. In Y. Kim & W. Gudykunst (Eds.), *Cross-cultural adaptation: Current approaches* (pp. 267-285). Newbury Park, CA: Sage.

Zerubavel, E. (1991). *The fine line: Making distinctions in everyday life.* New York: Basic Books.

Index

About the Contributors

JEFFREY C. ADY received his doctorate in communication from the University of Kansas in 1992 and is Assistant Professor in the Department of Communication at the University of Hawaii at Manoa. He teaches courses in intercultural and organizational communication. He has published in the *International and Intercultural Communication Annual, World Communication*, and in several journals overseas. He is a member of the International Communication Association, the Speech Communication Association, the Communication Association of Japan, and the Japan-America Society. His research interests include intercultural conflict, cross-cultural conflict in organizations, and sojourner adjustment processes.

JOHN R. BALDWIN earned his doctorate from Arizona State University and is Assistant Professor of Communication at Illinois State University. His research interests include communication in intimate intercultural relationships and the social construction and communication of racism in the United States and Latin America. He was coauthor with Michael Hecht and Sidney Ribeau of a chapter in the seventh edition of Samovar and Porter's *Intercultural Communication: A Reader*. An underlying purpose of his research is to bring various communication and multidisciplinary perspectives together to inform each other on various issues.

JUDEE K. BURGOON is Professor of Communication and Director of Graduate Studies at the University of Arizona, where she also is a member of the Arizona Executive Program and Executive Development faculties in the College of Business and Public Administration. The author of over 140 books, articles, chapters, and reviews in communication and psychology, her book credits include *The Unspoken Dialogue, Nonverbal Communication, Mexican Americans and the Mass Media, The World of the Working Journalist, Small Group Communication*, and (forthcoming from Cambridge University Press) *Interpersonal Adaptation*. She is a past editor of *Communication Monographs* and has served on the editorial boards of communication and psychology journals (e.g., *Human Communication Research, Quarterly Journal of Speech, Journal of Social and Personal Relationships, Journal of Nonverbal Behavior*). Her current research centers on interpersonal deception, dyadic interaction and conflict patterns, and relational communication.

AARON C. CARGILE is a doctoral candidate in the Department of Communication at the University of California, Santa Barbara. His research has appeared in *Language and Communication* and *Perspectives for the Social Disciplines*. His current research focuses on language attitudes, interpersonal relationships, and intercultural training.

CYNTHIA GALLOIS received her doctorate in social psychology and communication from the University of Florida. She is now a Reader in Psychology at the University of Queensland in Brisbane. Her research interests center on intercultural and intergroup (ethnicity, gender, sexual orientation) communication, especially in organizational and health contexts. She has published widely in these areas, including two recent books (with Keithia Wilson, *Assertion and Its Social Context*, 1993, and with Deborah Terry and Malcolm McCamish, *The Theory of Reasoned Action: Its Application to AIDS-Preventive Behaviour*, 1993) and has edited two recent special issues of the *Journal of Language and Social Psychology* ("Emotion, Culture, and Power," 1993, and with Jeffery Pittam, "Approaches to the Analysis of Real Language Texts," in press).

HOWARD GILES is Professor and Chair of Communication at the University of California, Santa Barbara, where he holds affiliated positions in the Departments of Psychology and Linguistics. He was founding editor of the *Journal of Language and Social Psychology* and founding coeditor of the *Journal of Asian Pacific Communication*. He is currently completing his term as editor of *Human Communication Research*. He has long-standing projects under way in language effects, intercultural accommodation, and bilingualism. Currently, his main research activity is in intergenerational communication phenomena and processes from an intercultural perspective and across the Pacific Rim.

WILLIAM B. GUDYKUNST is Professor of Speech Communication at California State University, Fullerton. His work focuses on developing a theory of interpersonal and intergroup effectiveness that can be applied to improving the quality of communication. He is the author of *Bridging Differences* (Sage, 1994) and coauthor of *Culture and Interpersonal*

Communication (with Stella Ting-Toomey, 1988), *Communicating with Strangers* (with Young Yun Kim, 1992), *Bridging Japanese/North American Differences* (with Tsukasa Nishida, 1994), and *Building Bridges* (with Stella Ting-Toomey, Sandra Sudweeks, and Lea Stewart, 1995).

MICHAEL L. HECHT earned his doctorate from the University of Illinois and is Professor of Communication at Arizona State University. He is the author of a number of books and articles in the area of interethnic communication, including the text *African American Communication* (with Mary Jane Collier and Sidney A. Ribeau, 1993). His research interests also include intercultural health campaigns and interpersonal communication competence.

ELIZABETH JONES received her doctorate from the University of Queensland in 1994. At present, she lectures in organizational psychology at Griffith University in Brisbane. Her research interests relate to the communication of power and status. In addition, she is interested in the analysis of verbal and nonverbal behavior in conversational interaction, where she has developed innovative methods for exploring accommodation processes; some of this work appears in the *Journal of Language and Social Psychology* (special issue on language and power, in press). Her publications include articles in the *Journal of Language and Social Psychology*.

TAMAR KATRIEL is Associate Professor in the Department of Communication and School of Education, University of Haifa, Israel. Her research areas are the ethnography of communication and discourse studies. She is the author of *Talking Straight: "Dugri" Speech in Israeli Sabra Culture* (Cambridge University Press, 1986) and *Communal Webs: Communication and Culture in Contemporary Israel* (1991) as well as many articles in a variety of communication, anthropology, and language journals.

MIN-SUN KIM earned her doctorate from Michigan State University and is currently Assistant Professor in the Department of Speech at the University of Hawaii at Manoa. Her research interests focus on intercultural conversational styles from a goals perspective. Her publications have appeared in *Human Communication Research, Communication Monographs*, the *International and Intercultural Communication Annual, Journal of Communication, The Howard Journal of Communication, Research on Language and Social Interaction, Journal of Asian*

Pacific Communication, among others. She is currently investigating cross-cultural conflict styles involving Korea, Japan, Hawaii, and the mainland.

YOUNG YUN KIM earned her doctorate from Northwestern University in 1976 and is Professor of Communication at the University of Oklahoma. She teaches courses and directs doctoral theses in the area of international, intercultural, and interethnic communication. Her research has been aimed at explaining the role of communication in cross-cultural adaptation of immigrants and sojourners as well as of native-born ethnic minorities. Currently, she is developing an interdisciplinary framework for understanding the communication between individuals of different ethnic identities. Her work has been published in *Communication Yearbook, Human Communication Research, International Journal of Intercultural Relations*, and *International and Intercultural Communication Annual*. Her recent books are *Interethnic Communication* (Sage, 1986), *Communication and Cross-Cultural Adaptation* (Multilingual Matters, 1988), *Theories in Intercultural Communication* (with W. Gudykunst, 1988), and *Communicating with Strangers* (with W. Gudykunst, 1984, 1992). She currently serves on the editorial boards for *Communication Research, Human Communication Research*, and *International Journal of Intercultural Relations*.

KELLY MORRISON earned her masters' degree at Michigan State University in 1994 and is currently a doctoral candidate in the Department of Communication at Michigan State University. Her research interests include applying persuasive theory to health issues, message production, and deception. Currently she is examining methods of persuading significant others to take protective action against rape. Her research has been published in journals such as *Health Communication* and the *Journal of Applied Communication*.

JOHN G. OETZEL is a doctoral candidate in the Communication Studies Department at the University of Iowa and an Instructor of Speech at Citrus College in Glendora, California. His research interests include communication in diverse groups and organizations and training and education about cultural diversity. His writings have appeared in *The Speech Communication Teacher*.

HIROSHI OTA is a doctoral student at the University of California, Santa Barbara. His research areas are intergenerational communication as related to intergroup communication, intercultural adaptation, and communicative competence. He has a special interest in communication in Japan and the United States from an intergroup as well as intercultural perspective. Recently, he has been involved in an international project on aging and communication.

TASHA VAN HORN is a master's candidate in the Speech Communication Department at California State University, Fullerton. Her interests include pedagogical issues, ethics in communication, and intercultural communication. She has served as editorial assistant for Volumes 17 and 18 of the *International and Intercultural Communication Annual*, titled, respectively, "Intercultural Communication Competence" and "Communicating in the Multinational Organization."

RICHARD L. WISEMAN is Professor of Speech Communication at California State University, Fullerton. His research interests include intercultural communication competence, interpersonal persuasion, and teaching effectiveness. He coedited *Intercultural Communication Competence* (with Jolene Koester, 1993) and *Communicating in the Multinational Organization* (with Robert Shuter, 1994). His published work has appeared in *Communication Yearbook, Communication Monographs, Journal of Business Communication, Research in Higher Education*, and the *International Journal of Intercultural Relations*. He has served as Chairperson to the Intercultural Communication Divisions of the Speech Communication Association and the Western States Communication Association.

KIM WITTE earned her doctorate from the University of California at Irvine and is currently Assistant Professor at Michigan State University. Her current research examines how members of diverse cultures respond to health risk messages. Additional areas of research include the study of fear appeals, the use of Chaos Theory in health communication, and the development of culturally appropriate public health campaigns. She is Vice-Chair of the Health Communication Commission of the Speech Communication Association and serves on the Michigan Department of Public Health's Radon Awareness and HIV Prevention Planning Committees. Her work has appeared in *Communication Monographs*, the *International Quarterly of Community Health Education, Communication Yearbook*, and elsewhere. She has received several "Top Paper" awards for her research at both national and international conferences.